Additional Mathematics - I

Fourth Edition

Dr. Pandurangappa C.
Professor & Head
Department of Mathematics
University B.D.T. College of Engineering
(*A Constituent College of Visvesvaraya Technological University*)
Davangere - 577 004
Karnataka.

Dr. Ejanul Haque.
Lecturer in Mathematics
RMIT University
Melbourne VIC 3001
Australia.

SANGUINE

Sanguine Technical Publishers
Bangalore
2019

978-9383506-66-8

Additional Mathematics - I, *4th Edition*
Dr. Pandurangappa. C & Dr. Ejanul Haque.

Direct inquiries: E-mail info@sanguineindia.com. Visit our website at www.sanguineindia.com

Published by ***Lal Prasad*** for ***Sanguine.***
Cover Design: ***Lakshmi M Prasad.*** NIFT, Kannur.
Printed in India.

Preface

This is a textbook for the Bridge Course for Additional Mathematics–I for the Engineering Students through Lateral Entry of a typical Indian University, introduced from the year 2018–2019. This book contains five chapters: Complex Trignometry, Differential Calculus, Integral Calculus, Vector Differentiation and Differential Equations.

Each chapter contains several solved problems to elucidate the concepts. Some of these examples have appeared in the various University examinations. The problems are solved in simple steps as can be understood by students. Assignment problems with answers appear at the end of each topic. Both theory and problems have been explained using necessary diagrams.

Each topic is presented with care and it is hoped that the book will meet the requirements of the students and the teachers.

Suggestions for further improvement of the book are welcome.

We are indebted to my professors, colleagues and students, who have directly or indirectly contributed to this work. I express my thanks with gratitude to Dr. Venugopal K. R, VC, Bangalore University, Dr. T. Basavaraju, Dr. Shivaprasad B Dandagi, Dr. K.S. Sreedhara, UBDTCE, Dr. Lakshmi Narayanachari. K, Dr. R. Arun Kumar, SVIT, Dr. M. Sankar, Presidency University, Dr. D.V. Chandrashekar, VKIT, Dr. Hariprasad RRCE, Dr. C. Vinay, JSSATE, Dr. G.S. Prasad, RRCE, Dr. M. Suresha, VIT, Dr. Siddalinga Prasad, SIT, Mr. Krishna, Sri K. G. Jagadeesh, Dr. K. M. Niranjan, Dr. Ravichandra Nayakar, Dr. Mahesh, Smt. Mamatha, UBDTCE for their advice and help while preparing this book.

I also express my sincere thanks to my wife Dr. Bharathi. K and my children Rithvik. P.R and Manasa. P.R for their continuous support and encouragement.

We express our sincere thanks to Sanguine Technical Publishers, Bangalore for publishing the book in such an excellent form, and Interline Publishing, Bangalore for online publication of this book.

We also express our sincere thanks to Mr. Sathish S for keen interesting in typesetting the book.

September 2019 **AUTHORS**

Foreword

It gives me great pleasure in writing a foreword to this book on Engineering Mathematics by Dr. Pandurangappa C. I know the author for over two decades as my student and has earned a good reputation as a teacher.

The results and properties on specific topics have been stated in the form of theorems and followed by the proofs. This really helps the students to understand the meaning of the results and properties. A large number of solved examples on each topic are also given. In each exercise, a large number of graded problems are given for rigorous practice.

In addition, this book also contains the required preliminaries that the students have studied earlier. This helps the students to brush up the requisite preliminaries and glance through the current topics for the examination purposes.

I am confident that the above book will be of great help to the teachers also in selecting the graded problems from worked out examples and exercises for effective teaching.

Dr. M. Venkatachalappa

Professor (Retired),
Department of Mathematics,
Bangalore University,
Bangalore.

Contents

Prelimenaries – Short Notes

Theory of indices

i. $a^m.a^n = a^{m+n}$

ii. $\frac{a^m}{a^n} = a^{m-n}$

iii. $(a^m)^n = a^{mn}$

iv. $(ab)^m = a^m b^m$

v. $\left(\frac{a}{b}\right)^m = \frac{a^m}{b^m}$

vi. $a^{-m} = \frac{1}{a^m}$

vii. $a^0 = 1[a \neq \infty]$

viii. $\sqrt[n]{a} = a^{\frac{1}{n}}$

ix. If $a^m = a^n$ and $a \neq 1$, then $m = n$

Logarithms

If $a^m = x$, then m is called the logarithm of x base a, i.e., if $a^m = x \Rightarrow m = \log_a x$ or

i. $\log_a (mn) = \log_a m + \log_a n$

ii. $\log_a \left(\frac{m}{n}\right) = \log_a m - \log_a n$

iii. $\log_a (m)^n = n \log_a m$

iv. $\log_b a = (\log_e a) / (\log_e b)$

v. $\log_a a = 1$

vi. $\log_a 1 = 0$

vii. $\log_e 0 = -\infty$

Progressions

Arithmetic progression (AP)

A sequence in which the difference between any two consecutive terms is always constant is called an Arithmetic Progression (AP).

i.e., $a,\ a+d,\ a+2d,\ a+3d,\ldots$ is an AP.

$$t_n = n^{\text{th}} \text{ term} = a + (n-1)\,d$$

$$s_n = \text{sum of } n \text{ terms} = \frac{n}{2}\{2a + (n-1)\,d\}$$

Geometric progression (GP)

A sequence in which the ratio of any two consecutive terms is always constant is called a Geometric Progression (GP).

i.e., $a,\ ar,\ ar^2,\ ar^3,\ldots$ is a GP

$$t_n = n^{\text{th}} \text{ term} = ar^{n-1}$$

$$s_n = \text{sum of n terms} = \frac{a\,(1-r^n)}{1-r}$$

Mathematical induction

Using mathematical induction we can prove certain results valid for positive integral values of n. This process consists of three parts namely;

(i) To prove the result is true for $n = 1$

(ii) Assume the result is true for $n = k$

(iii) To prove the result is true for $n = k + 1$

Hence, we can say that the result is true for all the integral values of n.

Permutations and combinations

Arrangement of n different things taken r at a time is called the number of Permutations. It is denoted and defined by

$$^{n}p_r = n\,(n-1)\,(n-2)\cdots(n-r+1) = \frac{n\,!}{(n-r)\,!}$$

Selection of n different things taken r at a time is called number of combinations. It is denoted and defined by

$$^{n}c_r = \frac{n\,!}{r\,!\,(n-r)\,!}$$

Binomial theorem

$$(a+b)^n = a^n + {}^nc_1\, a^{n-1}b + {}^nc_2 a^{n-2}b^2 + {}^nc_3 a^{n-3}b^3 + \cdots + b^n$$

Partial fractions

Conversion of a single proper fraction into sum of two or more proper fractions is called Partial Fraction.

Let $f(x)$ and $g(x)$ be two polynomials of some degree, then the fraction $f(x)/g(x)$ is called rational fraction.

If the degree of $f(x)$ is less than the degree of $g(x)$, then the rational fraction $f(x)/g(x)$ is called proper fraction, otherwise it is improper fraction.

Example

(i) $\dfrac{x+3}{3x^2+2x+1}$ proper fraction.

(ii) $\dfrac{x^2+2x+1}{(x-1)\,(x+2)}$ improper fraction.

(iii) $\dfrac{x^3+3x+5}{x^2+x+1}$ improper fraction.

Rules of making the partial fractions

(i) To each non-repeated linear factors in the denominator i.e.,

$$\frac{f(x)}{(a_1x+b_1)\,(a_2x+b_2)\cdots(a_nx+b_n)} = \frac{A_1}{a_1x+b_1} + \frac{A_2}{a_2x+b_2} + \cdots + \frac{A_n}{a_nx+b_n}$$

(ii) To each repeated linear factors in the denominator, i.e.,

$$\frac{f(x)}{(ax+b)^n} = \frac{A_1}{ax+b} + \frac{A_2}{(ax+b)^2} + \cdots + \frac{A_n}{(ax+b)^n}$$

(iii) To each non-repeated quadratic factors in the denominator i.e.,

$$\frac{f(x)}{\left(a_1x^2+b_1x+c_1\right)\left(a_2x^2+b_2x+c_2\right)\cdots\left(a_nx^2+b_nx+c_n\right)}$$
$$=\frac{A_1x+B_1}{a_1x^2+b_1x+c_1}+\frac{A_2x+B_2}{a_2x^2+b_2x+c_2}+\cdots+\frac{A_nx+B_n}{a_nx^2+b_nx+c_n}$$

(iv) To each repeated quadratic factors in the denominator i.e.,

$$\frac{f(x)}{(ax^2+bx+c)^n}=\frac{A_1x+B_1}{ax^2+bx+c}+\frac{A_2x+B_2}{(ax^2+bx+c)^2}+\cdots+\frac{A_nx+B_n}{(ax^2+bx+c)^n}$$

where $A_1,\ A_2,\ \ldots A_n$ and $B_1,\ B_2, \ldots B_n$ are constants to be determined.

Illustrations

1. $\dfrac{2x+1}{(x+1)\,(x+2)}=\dfrac{A}{x+1}+\dfrac{B}{x+2}$
2. $\dfrac{x+1}{(x+3)^2\,(2x+1)}=\dfrac{A}{x+3}+\dfrac{B}{(x+3)^2}+\dfrac{C}{2x+1}$
3. $\dfrac{1}{(x-1)\,\left(x^2+2x+3\right)}=\dfrac{A}{x-1}+\dfrac{Bx+C}{x^2+2x+3}$
4. $\dfrac{1}{\left(x^2+1\right)\,\left(x^2+2x+5\right)^2}=\dfrac{Ax+B}{x^2+1}+\dfrac{Cx+D}{x^2+2x+5}+\dfrac{Ex+F}{\left(x^2+2x+5\right)^2}$

Partial fraction can be applied only for the proper fractions. If the fraction is improper fraction we divide and rewrite using the known concept as shown here

$$\frac{f(x)}{g(x)}=\text{Quotient}+\frac{\text{Remainder}}{\text{Divisor}}=Q(x)+\frac{F(x)}{g(x)}$$

where $F(x)/g(x)$ is proper fraction.

Trigonometry

Consider the right-angled triangle ABC of which $A\hat{C}B=\theta$. The side AB is called the opposite side, BC is the adjacent side and AC is the hypotenuse side

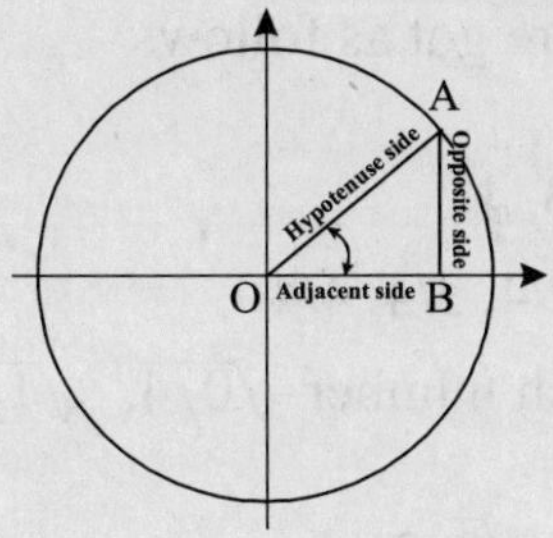

All the six trigonometric ratios are defined as follows

$$\sin\theta = \frac{AB}{OA} \qquad \cos\theta = \frac{OB}{OA}$$

$$\tan\theta = \frac{AB}{OB} \qquad \sec\theta = \frac{OA}{OB}$$

$$\cos ec\ \theta = \frac{OA}{AB} \qquad \cot\theta = \frac{OB}{AB}$$

Reciprocal relations

1. $\sin\theta = \dfrac{1}{\text{cosec}\ \theta}$ 2. $\cos\theta = \dfrac{1}{\sec\theta}$ 3. $\tan\theta = \dfrac{1}{\cot\theta}$

4. $\tan\theta = \dfrac{\sin\theta}{\cos\theta}$ 5. $\cot\theta = \dfrac{\cos\theta}{\sin\theta}$

Identities

4. $\sin^2\theta + \cos^2\theta = 1$
5. $1 + \tan^2\theta = \sec^2\theta$
6. $1 + \cot^2\theta = \text{cosec}^2\theta$

Trigonometric ratios of standard angles

θ	0°	30°	45°	60°	90°
$\sin\theta$	0	$\frac{1}{2}$	$\frac{1}{\sqrt{2}}$	$\frac{\sqrt{3}}{2}$	1
$\cos\theta$	1	$\frac{\sqrt{3}}{2}$	$\frac{1}{\sqrt{2}}$	$\frac{1}{2}$	0
$\tan\theta$	0	$\frac{1}{\sqrt{3}}$	1	$\sqrt{3}$	∞

Note: The values of sine ratio are got as follows

(i) Write the numbers 0, 1, 2, 3, 4

(ii) Divide each by 4 0/4, 1/4, 2/4, 3/4, 4/4

(iii) Take the square root for each number $\sqrt{0/4}$, $\sqrt{1/4}$, $\sqrt{2/4}$, $\sqrt{3/4}$, $\sqrt{4/4}$

Final values are $0,\ 1/2, 1/\sqrt{2},\ \sqrt{3}/2,\ 1$

Write these numbers for sine ratio of the angles 0°, 30°, 45°, 60° and 90° respectively. Reverse them for cosine ratio and get the value of other ratios by using the following formulae.

$$\tan\theta = \frac{\sin\theta}{\cos\theta} \qquad \cot\theta = \frac{\cos\theta}{\sin\theta}$$

$$\sec\theta = \frac{1}{\cos\theta} \qquad \operatorname{cosec}\theta = \frac{1}{\sin\theta}$$

Allied angles

Signs of trignometrical ratios

A – S – T – C rule

A = All positive in I^{st} quadrant

S = sin and its reciprocal cosec are positive in IInd quadrant

T = tan and its reciprocal cot are positive in IIIrd quadrant

C = cos and its reciprocal sec are positive in IVth quadrant

Angles like $\frac{n\pi}{2} \pm \theta$ are all called allied angles to θ where n is any positive integer.

Example $90-\theta,\ \ 90+\theta,\ \ 180-\theta,\ \ 270+\theta$ etc

Trigonometric ratios of allied angles

Case (i): For $90 \pm \theta,\ \ 270 \pm \theta$

$$\begin{array}{lll} \sin \to \cos & \tan \to \cot & \sec \to \operatorname{cosec} \\ \cos \to \sin & \cot \to \tan & \operatorname{cosec} \to \sec \end{array}$$

Case (ii): For $0 \pm \theta$, $180 \pm \theta$, $360 \pm \theta$

sin → sin	tan → tan	sec → sec
cos → cos	cot → cot	cosec → cosec

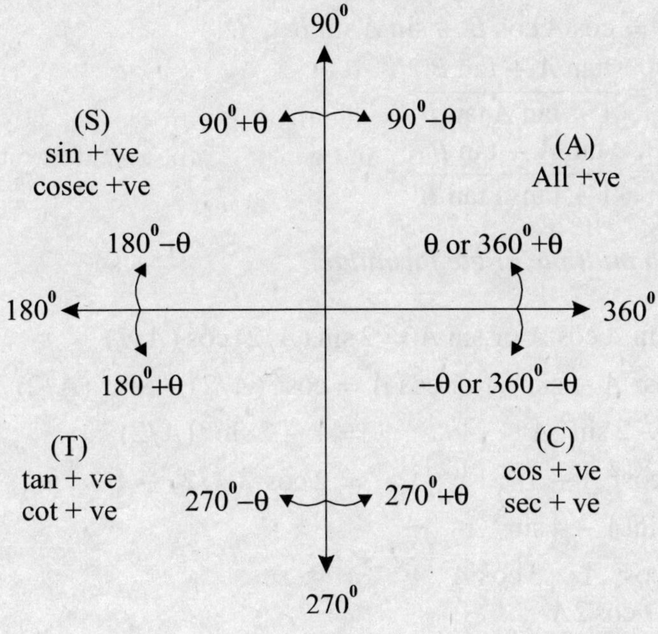

Illustrations

(i) $\sin(90 - \theta)$

According to case (i) sin → cos and $90 - \theta$ is in I[st] quadrant, in I[st] quadrant sin is positive. $\sin(90 - \theta) = \cos\theta$

(ii) $\tan(180 - \theta)$

Using case (ii) tan → tan and $180 - \theta$ is in IInd quadrant, in the IInd quadrant tan is negative. $\tan(180 - \theta) = -\tan\theta$

(iii) $\cos(-\theta) = \cos\theta$

(iv) $\cos(90 + \theta) = -\sin\theta$

(v) $\cot(270 + \theta) = -\tan\theta$

Compound angle formulae

1. $\sin(A+B) = \sin A \cos B + \cos A \sin B$

   $\sin(A-B) = \sin A \cos B - \cos A \sin B$
2. $\cos(A+B) = \cos A \cos B - \sin A \sin B$

   $\cos(A-B) = \cos A \cos B + \sin A \sin B$
3. $\tan(A+B) = \dfrac{\tan A + \tan B}{1 - \tan A \tan B}$

   $\tan(A-B) = \dfrac{\tan A - \tan B}{1 + \tan A \tan B}$

Multiple and sub multiple angle formulae

4. $\sin 2A = 2\sin A \cos A$ or $\sin A = 2\sin(A/2)\cos(A/2)$
5. $\cos 2A = \cos^2 A - \sin^2 A$ or $\cos A = \cos^2(A/2) - \sin^2(A/2)$

   $= 1 - 2\sin^2 A \qquad = 1 - 2\sin^2(A/2)$

   $= 2\cos^2 A - 1 \qquad = 2\cos^2(A/2) - 1$
6. $\sin 3A = 3\sin A - 4\sin^3 A$
7. $\cos 3A = 4\cos^3 A - 3\cos A$
8. $\sin^2 A = \dfrac{1 - \cos 2A}{2}$
9. $\cos^2 A = \dfrac{1 + \cos 2A}{2}$
10. $\sin^3 A = \frac{1}{4}[3\sin A - \sin 3A]$
11. $\cos^3 A = \frac{1}{4}[3\cos A + \cos 3A]$

Transformation formulae
Conversion from product into sum or difference

12. $\sin A \cos B = \frac{1}{2}[\sin(A+B) + \sin(A-B)]$
13. $\cos A \sin B = \frac{1}{2}[\sin(A+B) - \sin(A-B)]$
14. $\cos A \cos B = \frac{1}{2}[\cos(A+B) + \cos(A-B)]$
15. $\sin A \sin B = \frac{1}{2}[\cos(A-B) - \cos(A+B)]$

Conversion from sum or difference into product

16. $\sin C + \sin D = 2\sin\left(\frac{C+D}{2}\right).\cos\left(\frac{C-D}{2}\right)$

17. $\sin C - \sin D = 2\cos\left(\frac{C+D}{2}\right).\sin\left(\frac{C-D}{2}\right)$

18. $\cos C + \cos D = 2\cos\left(\frac{C+D}{2}\right).\cos\left(\frac{C-D}{2}\right)$

19. $\cos C - \cos D = -2\sin\left(\frac{C+D}{2}\right).\sin\left(\frac{C-D}{2}\right)$

Relation between the sides and angles of a triangle

The sine rule

20. $\frac{a}{\sin A} = \frac{b}{\sin B} = \frac{c}{\sin C} = 2R$

The cosine rule

21. $a^2 = b^2+c^2-2bc\cos A$, $b^2 = a^2+c^2-2ac\cos B$, and $c^2 = a^2+b^2-2ab\cos C$

Hyperbolic functions

22. $\sinh x = \frac{e^x - e^{-x}}{2}$

23. $\cosh x = \frac{e^x + e^{-x}}{2}$

24. $\tanh x = \frac{\sinh x}{\cosh x}$

25. $\coth x = \frac{\cosh x}{\sinh x}$

26. $\text{sech}\, x = \frac{1}{\cosh x}$

27. $\text{cosech}\, x = \frac{1}{\sinh x}$

28. $\cosh^2 x - \sinh^2 x = 1$
29. $1 - \tanh^2 x = \text{sech}^2 x$
30. $\coth^2 x - 1 = \text{cosech}^2 x$
31. $\cosh^2 x + \sinh^2 x = \cosh 2x$
32. $\sinh 2x = 2 \sinh x . \cosh x$

Analytical geometry of two dimensions

Let $A = (x_1, y_1)$ and $B\ (x_2, y_2)$ be any two points

Distance formula

$$AB = \sqrt{(x_2 - x_1)^2 + (y_2 - y_1)^2}$$

Section formula

Co-ordinates of the point P which divides the line joining AB internally in the ratio $m : n$ is

$$P = \left(\frac{mx_2 + nx_1}{m + n}, \frac{my_2 + ny_1}{m + n} \right)$$

Midpoint formula

$$P = \left(\frac{x_1 + x_2}{2}, \frac{y_1 + y_2}{2} \right)$$

Straight lines
Slope

(i) If a straight line makes an angle θ with the positive direction of the x-axis, then the slope $= \tan \theta$

(ii) If a straight line passing through the points $(x_1,\ y_1)$ & $(x_2,\ y_2)$, then slope $= \frac{y_2 - y_1}{x_2 - x_1}$

(iii) If $y = f(x)$ be the equation of the curve, then $\frac{dy}{dx} = f'(x)$ represents the slope of the tangent to the curve.

(iv) If $ax + by + c = 0$ be the equation of a straight line, then the slope $= -\ (a/b)$

Different forms of equations of straight line

1. The equation of a straight line whose slope is 'm' and y intercept is 'c' is given by $y = mx + c$.
2. The equation of a straight line passing through the point (x_1, y_1) and the slope m is given by $y - y_1 = m\,(x - x_1)$.
3. The equation of a straight line passing through two points (x_1, y_1) and (x_2, y_2) is given by $y - y_1 = \frac{y_2 - y_1}{x_2 - x_1}\,(x - x_1)$.
4. The equation of a straight line whose x-intercept if 'a' and y-intercept is b is given by $\frac{x}{a} + \frac{y}{b} = 1$
5. $x = 0$ and $y = 0$ respectively represent the equations of y-axis and x-axis.
6. $x = a$ and $y = b$ respectively represent the equations of a line parallel to y-axis and a line parallel to x- axis.

Angle between two lines

Angle θ between two lines having slopes $m_1$and m_2 is given by $\tan\theta = \frac{m_1 - m_2}{1 + m_1 m_2}$

Note

(i) If $m_1 = m_2$, then two lines are parallel

(ii) If $m_1 \cdot m_2 = -1$, then two lines are perpendicular

Length of the perpendicular

Length of the perpendicular from the point (x_1, y_1) to the line $ax + by + c = 0$ is $\frac{|ax_1 + by_1 + c|}{\sqrt{a^2 + b^2}}$

Circles

(i) The equation of the circle with centre is at the origin and radius r is $x^2 + y^2 = r^2$.

(ii) General equation of the circle is $x^2 + y^2 + 2gx + 2fy + c = 0$ whose centre is $(-g, -f)$ and Radius is $\sqrt{g^2 + f^2 - c}$

Conics

Parabola

(i) $y^2 = 4ax$

Parametric equations: $x = at^2$, $y = 2at$

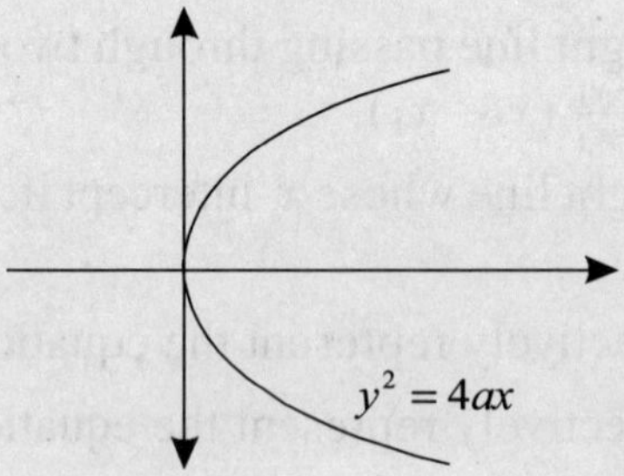

(ii) $y^2 = -4ax$

Parametric equations: $x = -at^2$, $y = 2at$

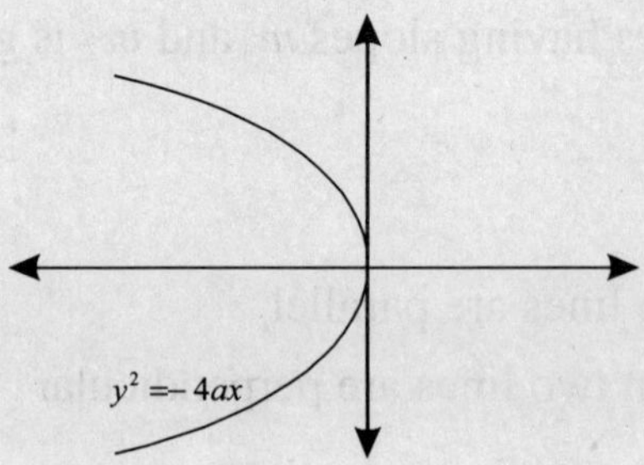

(iii) $x^2 = 4ay$

Parametric equations: $y = at^2$, $x = 2at$

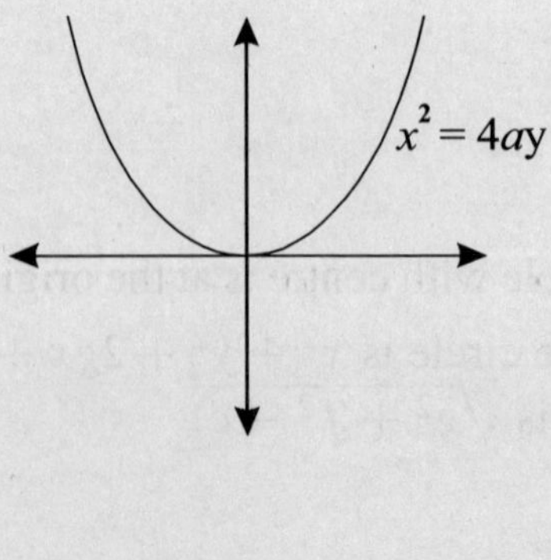

(iv) $x^2 = -4ay$

Parametric equations: $y = -at^2,\ x = 2at$

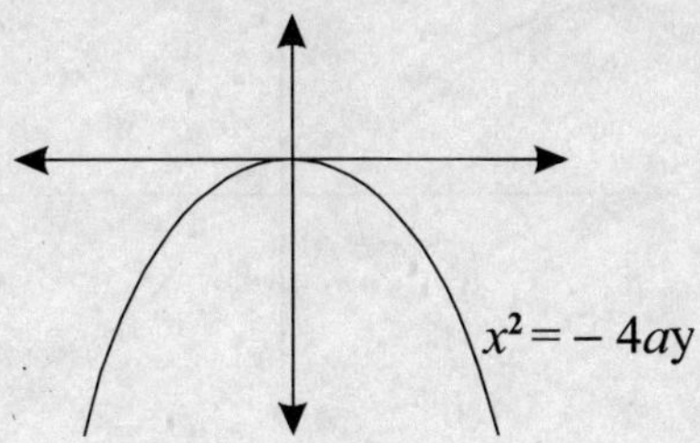

(v) $(y-k)^2 = 4a\,(x-h)$

Parametric equations: $x = at^2 + h,\ y = 2at + k$

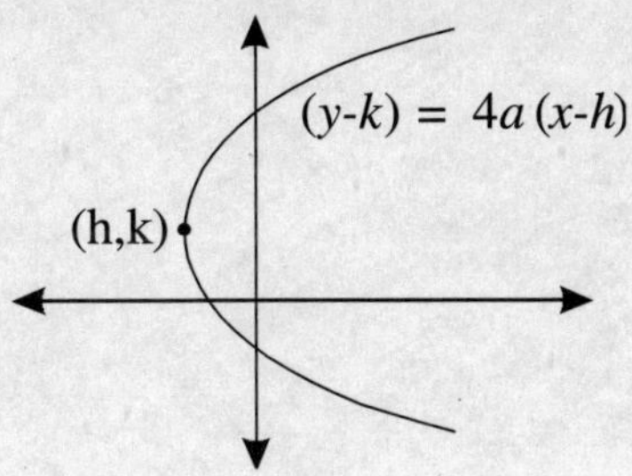

Ellipse

$$\frac{x^2}{a^2} + \frac{y^2}{b^2} = 1$$

Parametric equations: $x = a\cos t,\ y = b\sin t$

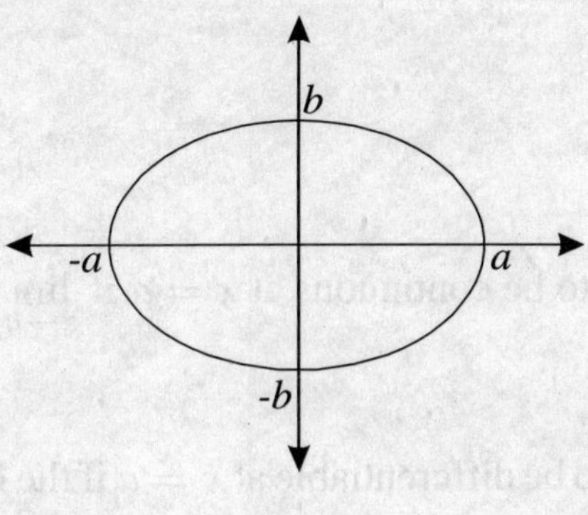

3. Hyperbola: $\frac{x^2}{a^2} - \frac{y^2}{b^2} = 1$

Parametric equations: $x = a \sec t,\ y = b \tan t$

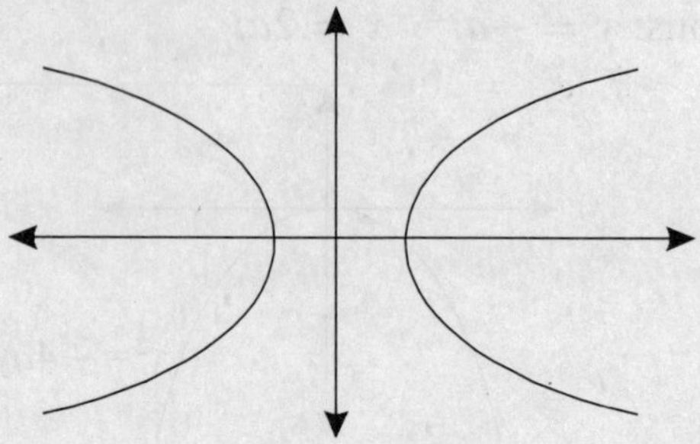

Calculus

Limits

1. $\lim\limits_{x \to a} \frac{x^n - a^n}{x - a} = na^{n-1}$
2. $\lim\limits_{x \to 0} \frac{\sin x}{x} = 1$
3. $\lim\limits_{x \to 0} \frac{\tan x}{x} = 1$
4. $\lim\limits_{x \to 0} (1 + x)^{\frac{1}{x}} = e$
5. $\lim\limits_{x \to \infty} \left(1 + \frac{1}{x}\right)^x = e$
6. $\lim\limits_{x \to \infty} \left(1 + \frac{a}{x}\right)^x = e^a$
7. $\lim\limits_{x \to \infty} x^{\frac{1}{x}} = 1$
8. $\lim\limits_{x \to 0} \frac{a^x - 1}{x} = \log_e a$

Differentiation

Continuity

A function $f(x)$ is said to be continuous at $x = a$ if $\lim\limits_{x \to a} f(x) = f(a)$ exists.

Differentiability

A function $f(x)$ is said to be differentiable at $x = a$ if the limit $\lim\limits_{x \to a} \frac{f(x) - f(a)}{x - a} = f'(a)$ exists

In general

$$f'(x) = \lim_{\delta x \to 0} \frac{f(x+\delta x) - f(x)}{\delta x}$$

List of derivatives of some standard functions

1. $\frac{d}{dx}(c) = 0$
2. $\frac{d}{dx}\left(x^n\right) = nx^{n-1}$
3. $\frac{d}{dx}\left(e^x\right) = e^x$
4. $\frac{d}{dx}(\log x) = \frac{1}{x}$
5. $\frac{d}{dx}\left(a^x\right) = a^x \log a$
6. $\frac{d}{dx}(\sin x) = \cos x$
7. $\frac{d}{dx}(\cos x) = -\sin x$
8. $\frac{d}{dx}(\tan x) = \sec^2 x$
9. $\frac{d}{dx}(\cot x) = -\text{cosec}^2 x$
10. $\frac{d}{dx}(\sec x) = \sec x \tan x$
11. $\frac{d}{dx}(\text{cosec}x) = -\text{cosec}x \cot x$
12. $\frac{d}{dx}\left(\sin^{-1} x\right) = \frac{1}{\sqrt{1-x^2}}$
13. $\frac{d}{dx}\left(\cos^{-1} x\right) = -\frac{1}{\sqrt{1-x^2}}$
14. $\frac{d}{dx}\left(\tan^{-1} x\right) = \frac{1}{1+x^2}$
15. $\frac{d}{dx}\left(\cot^{-1} x\right) = -\frac{1}{1+x^2}$
16. $\frac{d}{dx}\left(\sec^{-1} x\right) = \frac{1}{x\sqrt{x^2-1}}$
17. $\frac{d}{dx}\left(\text{cosec}^{-1} x\right) = -\frac{1}{x\sqrt{x^2-1}}$
18. $\frac{d}{dx}(\sinh x) = \cosh x$
19. $\frac{d}{dx}(\cosh x) = \sinh x$
20. $\frac{d}{dx}(\tanh x) = \text{sech}^2 x$
21. $\frac{d}{dx}(\coth x) = -\text{cosech}^2 x$
22. $\frac{d}{dx}(\text{sech}x) = -\text{sech}x \tanh x$
23. $\frac{d}{dx}(\text{cosech}x) = -\text{cosech}x \coth x$
24. $\frac{d}{dx}\left(\sin^{-1} x\right) = \frac{1}{\sqrt{x^2+1}}$
25. $\frac{d}{dx}\left(\cosh^{-1} x\right) = \frac{1}{\sqrt{x^2-1}}$
26. $\frac{d}{dx}\left(\tanh^{-1} x\right) = \frac{1}{1-x^2}$
27. $\frac{d}{dx}\left(\coth^{-1} x\right) = \frac{1}{1-x^2}$
28. $\frac{d}{dx}\left(\text{sech}^{-1} x\right) = -\frac{1}{x\sqrt{1-x^2}}$
29. $\frac{d}{dx}\left(\text{cosech}^{-1} x\right) = -\frac{1}{x\sqrt{1+x^2}}$

Rules of differentiation

If u and v are any two functions of x and a and b are constants, then

1. $\frac{d}{dx}(au \pm bv) = a\frac{du}{dx} \pm b\frac{dv}{dx}$
2. $\frac{d}{dx}(uv) = u\frac{dv}{dx} + v\frac{du}{dx}$ (Product rule)
3. $\frac{d}{dx}\left(\frac{u}{v}\right) = \frac{v\frac{du}{dx} - u\frac{dv}{dx}}{v^2}$ (Quotient rule)

Illustrations

(i) If $y = e^x + \sin x - x^2$ then

$$\begin{aligned}\frac{dy}{dx} &= \frac{d}{dx}\left(e^x + \sin x - x^2\right)\\ &= \frac{d}{dx}\left(e^x\right) + \frac{d}{dx}(\sin x) - \frac{d}{dx}\left(x^2\right)\\ &= e^x + \cos x - 2x\end{aligned}$$

(ii) If $y = x^2 \log x$ then

$$\begin{aligned}\frac{dy}{dx} &= \frac{d}{dx}(x^2 \log x)\\ &= x^2\frac{d}{dx}(\log x) + \log x\frac{d}{dx}\left(x^2\right)\\ &= x^2\frac{1}{x} + \log x\,(2x)\\ &= x + 2x\log x\end{aligned}$$

(iii) If $y = \frac{2^x}{\tan x}$ then

$$\begin{aligned}\frac{dy}{dx} &= \frac{\tan x\frac{d}{dx}(2^x) - 2^x\frac{d}{dx}(\tan x)}{(\tan x)^2}\\ &= \frac{\tan x\,(2^x \log 2) - 2^x \sec^2 x}{\tan^2 x}\\ &= \frac{2^x \log 2 \tan x - 2^x \sec^2 x}{\tan^2 x}\end{aligned}$$

Differentiation of composite functions
Chain rule

(i) If y is a function of u and u is a function of x i.e., $y = f(u)$ and $u = g(x)$ then differentiation of y with respect to x is given by

$$\frac{dy}{dx} = \frac{dy}{du} \cdot \frac{du}{dx}$$

(ii) If $y = f(u)$, $u = g(v)$ and $v = h(x)$ then

$$\frac{dy}{dx} = \frac{dy}{du} \cdot \frac{du}{dv} \cdot \frac{dv}{dx}$$

Illustrations

(i) If $y = \sin(e^x)$

Let $u = e^x$ then

$$y = \sin u \quad \text{and} \quad u = e^x$$

$$\Rightarrow \frac{dy}{du} = \cos u = \cos\left(e^x\right) \quad \text{and} \quad \frac{du}{dx} = e^x$$

$$\therefore \frac{dy}{dx} = \frac{dy}{du} . \frac{du}{dx} = \cos\left(e^x\right) . e^x = e^x \cos\left(e^x\right)$$

OR

$$y = \sin e^x$$

$$\Rightarrow \frac{dy}{dx} = \cos\left(e^x\right) . \frac{d}{dx}\left(e^x\right) = \cos\left(e^x\right) . e^x = e^x \cos\left(e^x\right)$$

(iii) $y = \tan^3(\log x)$

$$\frac{dy}{dx} = 3\tan^2(\log x)\,\frac{d}{dx}\,(\tan(\log x))$$

$$= 3\tan^2(\log x).\sec^2(\log x)\,\frac{d}{dx}\,(\log x)$$

$$= 3\tan^2(\log x).\sec^2(\log x)\,\frac{1}{x}$$

$$\frac{dy}{dx} = \frac{3}{x}\tan^2(\log x)\sec^2(\log x)$$

Differentiation of implicit functions

If y is expressed in terms of a function of x then y is called explicit function of x otherwise y is implicit function of x.

The process of finding the derivatives of such functions is called implicit differentiation. In implicit differentiation, note the following

(i) $\left.\begin{aligned}\frac{d}{dx}(x) &= 1\\ \frac{d}{dx}(y) &= \frac{dy}{dx}\end{aligned}\right\}$ (ii) $\left.\begin{aligned}\frac{d}{dx}\left(x^4\right) &= 4x^3\\ \frac{d}{dx}\left(y^4\right) &= 4y^3\frac{dy}{dx}\end{aligned}\right\}$ (iii) $\left.\begin{aligned}\frac{d}{dx}\left(e^x\right) &= e^x\\ \frac{d}{dx}\left(e^y\right) &= e^y\frac{dy}{dx}\end{aligned}\right\}$

Illustrations

(i) $\frac{d}{dx}\left(x^2y\right) = x^2\frac{dy}{dx} + 2x.y$

(ii) $\frac{d}{dx}\left(\frac{\sin y}{x}\right) = \frac{x\cos y\frac{dy}{dx} - 1.y}{x^2}$

(iii) If $x^2 + y^2 + x + y - 1 = 0$ find $\frac{dy}{dx}$

Differentiating with respect to x, we get

$$2x + 2y\frac{dy}{dx} + 1 + \frac{dy}{dx} = 0$$

$$(2x+1) + (2y+1)\frac{dy}{dx} = 0$$

$$\frac{dy}{dx} = -\frac{(2x+1)}{(2y+1)}$$

Differentiation of parametric functions

If x and y are the functions of the parameter t i.e., $x = x(t)$ *and* $y = y(t)$, then differentiation of y with respect to x is given by

$$\frac{dy}{dx} = \frac{dy/dt}{dx/dt}$$

Illustration

(i) $x = 2at \qquad y = at^2$

$$\frac{dx}{dt} = 2a \qquad \frac{dy}{dt} = 2at$$

$$\therefore \frac{dy}{dx} = \frac{dy/dt}{dx/dt} = \frac{2at}{2a} = t$$

Integration

List of integrals of some standard functions

1. $\int x^n dx = \frac{x^{n+1}}{n+1}, \; n \neq -1$
2. $\int \frac{1}{x} dx = \log x, \; x \neq 0$
3. $\int e^x dx = e^x$
4. $\int a^x dx = \frac{a^x}{\log a}, \; a \neq 1$
5. $\int \sin x dx = -\cos x$
6. $\int cosx dx = \sin x$
7. $\int \tan x dx = \log(\sec x)$
8. $\int \cot x dx = \log(\sin x)$
9. $\int \sec x dx = \log(\sec x + \tan x)$
10. $\int \operatorname{cosec} x dx = \log(\operatorname{cosec} x - \cot x)$
11. $\int \sec^2 x dx = \tan x$
12. $\int \operatorname{cosec}^2 x dx = -\cot x$
13. $\int \operatorname{cosec} x \cot x dx = -\operatorname{cosec} x$
14. $\int \sec x \tan x dx = \sec x$
15. $\int \sinh x dx = \cosh x$
16. $\int \cosh x dx = \sinh x$
17. $\int \tanh x dx = \log \cosh x$
18. $\int \coth x dx = \log \sinh x$
19. $\int \operatorname{sech} a \tanh x dx = -\operatorname{sech} x$
20. $\int \operatorname{sech}^2 x dx = \tanh x$
21. $\int \operatorname{cosech} x \coth x dx = -\operatorname{cosech} x$
22. $\int \operatorname{cosech}^2 dx = -\coth x$
23. $\int \frac{1}{x^2-a^2} dx = \frac{1}{2a} \log\left(\frac{x-a}{x+a}\right), \; a > x > 0$
24. $\int \frac{1}{x^2+a^2} dx = \frac{1}{a} \tan^{-1}\left(\frac{x}{a}\right)$
25. $\int \frac{1}{a^2-x^2} dx = \frac{1}{2a} \log\left(\frac{a+x}{a-x}\right), \; a > x > 0$
26. $\int \frac{1}{\sqrt{a^2-x^2}} dx = \sin^{-1}\left(\frac{x}{a}\right)$

27. $\int \frac{1}{\sqrt{x^2+a^2}} dx = \sinh^{-1}\left(\frac{x}{a}\right) = \log\left(\frac{x+\sqrt{x^2+a^2}}{a}\right)$

28. $\int \frac{1}{\sqrt{x^2-a^2}} dx = \cosh^{-1}\left(\frac{x}{a}\right) = \log\left(\frac{x+\sqrt{x^2-a^2}}{a}\right)$

29. $\int \sqrt{a^2 - x^2} dx = \frac{x}{2}\sqrt{a^2 - x^2} + \frac{a^2}{2}\sin^{-1}\left(\frac{x}{a}\right)$

30. $\int \sqrt{x^2 + a^2} dx = \frac{x}{2}\sqrt{x^2 + a^2} + \frac{a^2}{2}\log\frac{x+\sqrt{x^2+a^2}}{a} = \frac{x}{2}\sqrt{x^2 + a^2} + \frac{a^2}{2}\sinh^{-1}\frac{x}{a}$

31. $\int \sqrt{x^2 - a^2} dx = \frac{x}{2}\sqrt{x^2 - a^2} - \frac{a^2}{2}\log\frac{x+\sqrt{x^2-a^2}}{a} = \frac{x}{2}\sqrt{x^2 - a^2} - \frac{a^2}{2}\cosh^{-1}\frac{x}{a}$

32. $\int \frac{1}{x\sqrt{x^2-a^2}} dx = \frac{1}{a}\sec^{-1}\left(\frac{x}{a}\right)$

33. $\int \frac{1}{x\sqrt{x^2+a^2}} dx = -\frac{1}{a}\sinh^{-1}\left(\frac{a}{x}\right)$

34. $\int e^{ax}\sin(bx + c)\, dx = \frac{e^{ax}}{a^2+b^2}(a\sin(bx + c) - b\cos(bx + c))$

35. $\int e^{ax}\cos(bx + c)\, dx = \frac{e^{ax}}{a^2+b^2}(a\cos(bx + c) + b\sin(bx + c))$

Methods of integration

Integration by substitution

(i) $\int [f(x)]^n f'(x)dx$

put $f(x) = t \Rightarrow f'(x)dx = dt$

$$\therefore \int [f(x)]^n f'(x)dx = \int t^n dt = \frac{t^{n+1}}{n+1} + c$$

$$= \frac{[f(x)]^{n+1}}{n+1} + c$$

Similarly if we take the above substitution for the following integrals, we get

(ii) $\int \frac{f'(x)}{f(x)} dx = \int \frac{1}{t} dt = \log t + c = \log[f(x)] + c$

(iii) $\int \frac{f'(x)}{\sqrt{f(x)}} dx = \int \frac{1}{\sqrt{t}} dt = 2\sqrt{t} + c = 2\sqrt{f(x)} + c$

(iv) $\int e^{f(x)} f'(x)dx = \int e^t dt = e^t + c = e^{f(x)} + c$

(v) $\int \sin[f(x)]f'(x)dx = \int \sin t\, dt = \cos t + c = \cos[f(x)] + c$

(vi) If $\int f'(x)dx = f(x) + c$ then, $\int f'(ax + b)\, dx = \frac{f(ax+b)}{a} + c$

Illustrations

1. $\int \left(x^2+x+5\right)^{10}(2x+1)\,dx$ put $x^2+x+5=t$, $(2x+1)dx=dt$

$$\int \left(x^2+x+5\right)^{10}(2x+1)\,dx = \int t^{10}dt = \frac{t^{11}}{11}+c$$

$$= \frac{1}{11}\left(x^2+x+5\right)^{11}+c$$

2. $\int \frac{x+1}{x^2+2x+3}dx$ put $x^2+2x+3=t$, $(2x+2)\,dx=dt \Rightarrow 2(x+1)\,dx=dt \Rightarrow$ $(x+1)\,dx=\frac{dt}{2}$

$$\int \frac{x+1}{x^2+2x+3}dx = \int \frac{dt/2}{t} = \frac{1}{2}\log t + c$$

$$= \frac{1}{2}\log\left(x^2+2x+3\right)+c$$

3. $\int e^x \sin(e^x)\,dx$ put $e^x=t \Rightarrow e^x dx = dt$

$$\int e^x \sin\left(e^x\right)dx = \int \sin t\,dt = \cos t + c = \cos\left(e^x\right)+c$$

4. $\int \cos(2x+3)\,dx = -\frac{\sin(2x+3)}{2}+c$
5. $\int e^{4x-1}dx = \frac{e^{4x-1}}{4}+c$

Integration by parts

$$\int uv\,dx = u\left(\int v\,dx\right) - \int \frac{du}{dx}\left(\int v\,dx\right)dx$$

Illustrations

1.
$$\int xe^x dx = x\int e^x dx - \int \frac{d}{dx}(x)\left[\int e^x dx\right]dx$$

$$= xe^x - \int 1.e^x dx$$

$$= xe^x - e^x + c$$

2.
$$\int x\log x dx = \int \log x . x dx$$
$$= \log x.\frac{x^2}{2} - \int \frac{1}{x}.\frac{x^2}{2}dx$$
$$= \frac{x^2}{2}\log x - \frac{1}{2}\int x dx$$
$$= \frac{x^2}{2}\log x - \frac{x^2}{4} + c$$

Bernoulli's rule (Generalized rule)

If the I[st] function is a polynomial function and Integration of the second function is known, then this rule can be used.

$\int uv dx = uv_1 - u'v_2 + u''v_3 - u'''v_4 + \cdots$, where $u', u'', u''' \ldots$ indicates the derivatives and $v_1, v_2, v_3 \ldots$ indicates the integrals.

Illustrations

1.
$$\int x^2 \sin x dx = x^2(-\cos x) - 2x(-\sin x) + (2)(\cos x)$$
$$= -x^2\cos x + 2x\sin x + 2\cos x$$

2.
$$\int (2x^2+3)e^{2x}dx = (2x^2+3)\left(\frac{e^{2x}}{2}\right) - (4x)\left(\frac{e^{2x}}{2^2}\right) + (4)\left(\frac{e^{2x}}{2^3}\right)$$
$$= \frac{1}{2}(2x^2+3)e^{2x} - xe^{2x} + \frac{1}{2}e^{2x}$$

Integration by partial fractions

If the integral is of the form $\int \frac{f(x)}{g(x)}dx$, then apply partial fractions to $\frac{f(x)}{g(x)}$. After resolving into partial fractions we have to integrate term by term.

Illustrations

1.
$$\int \frac{x+1}{(x-1)(x+2)}dx = \int \left(\frac{(2/3)}{x-1} + \frac{(1/3)}{x+2}\right)dx \quad \text{by partial fractions}$$
$$= \frac{2}{3}\log(x-1) + \frac{1}{3}\log(x+2) + c$$

2. $$\int \frac{1}{x^2 - 5x + 6} dx = \int \frac{1}{(x-2)(x-3)} dx$$
$$= \int \left(\frac{1}{x-3} - \frac{1}{x-2} \right) dx \quad \text{by partial fractions}$$
$$= \log(x-3) - \log(x-2) + c$$

Integrals of the forms

(i) $\int \frac{1}{ax^2+bx+c} dx$ (ii) $\int \frac{1}{\sqrt{ax^2+bx+c}} dx$ (iii) $\int \sqrt{ax^2+bx+c}\,dx$

by completing the square we can express $ax^2 + bx + c$ as $(a_1 x \pm b_1)^2 \pm c_1$ then integrate by using the formulae (23) to (31).

Illustrations

1. $$\int \frac{1}{x^2 + 2x + 5} dx$$

$$\text{let } x^2 + 2x + 5 = x^2 + 2.x.1 + 1^2 - 1^2 + 5$$
$$= (x+1)^2 + 4$$
$$\therefore \int \frac{1}{x^2 + 2x + 5} dx = \int \frac{1}{(x+1)^2 + 4} dx$$
$$= \frac{1}{2} \tan^{-1} \left(\frac{x+1}{4} \right) + c$$

2. $$\int \frac{1}{\sqrt{4x^2 + 4x + 3}} dx$$

$$\text{let } 4x^2 + 4x + 3 = (2x)^2 + 4x + 3$$
$$= (2x)^2 + 2.(2x).1 + 1^2 - 1^2 + 3$$
$$= (2x+1)^2 + 2$$
$$\therefore \int \frac{1}{\sqrt{4x^2 + 4x + 3}} dx = \int \frac{1}{\sqrt{(2x+1)^2 + 2}} dx$$
$$= \frac{\sinh^{-1}\left(\frac{2x+1}{\sqrt{2}} \right)}{2} + c$$

3. $\int \sqrt{x^2+4x+13}dx$

$$\text{let } x^2+4x+13 = x^2+2.x.2+2^2-2^2+13$$
$$= (x+2)^2+9$$
$$\int \sqrt{x^2+4x+13}dx = \int \sqrt{(x+2)+9}dx$$
$$= \left(\frac{x+2}{2}\right)\sqrt{(x+2)^2+9}+\frac{9}{2}\sinh^{-1}\left(\frac{x+2}{3}\right)+c$$

Integrals of the forms

(i) $\int \frac{px+q}{ax^2+bx+c}dx$ (ii) $\int \frac{px+q}{\sqrt{ax^2+bx+c}}dx$

if the integrals can not be integrated by substitution method, then we take

$$px+q = A\frac{d}{dx}\left(ax^2+bx+c\right)+B = A\,(2ax+b)+B$$

by equating the coefficients of x and constant term, we can find A and B

(i) $\therefore \int \frac{px+q}{ax^2+bx+c}dx = \int \frac{A\frac{d}{dx}\left(ax^2+bx+c\right)+B}{ax^2+bx+c}dx$

$$= A\int \frac{2ax+b}{ax^2+bx+c}dx + B\int \frac{1}{ax^2+bx+c}dx$$
$$= A\log\left(ax^2+bx+c\right)+B\int \frac{1}{ax^2+bx+c}dx$$

The second integral can be evaluated by completing the square.

Similarly the integral (ii) can be evaluated by taking the above substitution.

Illustrations

1. $\int \frac{4x+2}{x^2+4x+13}dx$

Let

$$4x+2 = A\frac{d}{dx}\left(x^2+4x+13\right)+B$$

$$4x + 2 = 2Ax + 4A + B$$

$$\Rightarrow 4 = 2A \quad \text{and} \quad 4A + B = 2$$

$$\Rightarrow A = 2 \qquad 8 + B = 2$$

$$B = -6$$

$$\therefore\ 4x + 2 = 2\,(2x + 4) - 6$$

$$\therefore \int \frac{4x+2}{x^2+4x+13}dx = \int \frac{2\,(2x+4)}{x^2+4x+13}dx + \int \frac{-6}{x^2+4x+13}dx$$

$$= 2\log\left(x^2+4x+13\right) - 6\int \frac{1}{(x+2)^2+9}dx$$

$$= 2\log\left(x^2+4x+13\right) - 6.\frac{1}{3}\tan^{-1}\left(\frac{x+2}{3}\right) + c$$

$$= 2\log\left(x^2+4x+13\right) - 2\tan^{-1}\left(\frac{x+2}{3}\right) + c$$

2. $\displaystyle\int \frac{4x+2}{\sqrt{x^2+4x+13}}dx$

We know from the illustration 1 that $4x + 2 = 2\,(2x + 4) - 6$

$$\therefore \int \frac{4x+2}{\sqrt{x^2+4x+13}}dx = \int \frac{2\,(2x+4)}{\sqrt{x^2+4x+13}}dx - 6\int \frac{1}{\sqrt{x^2+4x+13}}dx$$

$$= 2\int \frac{dt}{\sqrt{t}} - 6\int \frac{1}{\sqrt{(x+2)^2+9}}dx$$

$$= 2\left(2\sqrt{t}\right) - 6\sinh^{-1}\left(\frac{x+2}{3}\right) + c$$

$$= 4\sqrt{x^2+4x+13} - 6\sinh^{-1}\left(\frac{x+2}{3}\right) + c$$

Integrals of the forms

(i) $\displaystyle\int \frac{1}{a+b\cos x}dx$ (ii) $\displaystyle\int \frac{1}{a+b\sin x}dx$ (iii) $\displaystyle\int \frac{1}{a+b\cos x + c\sin x}dx$

In all these cases make the substitution

$$\tan\left(\frac{x}{2}\right) = t \quad \text{then} \quad dx = \frac{2dt}{1+t^2}$$

$$\sin x = \frac{2t}{1+t^2} \quad \text{and,} \quad \cos x = \frac{1-t^2}{1+t^2}$$

Substituting these values in the given integrals, they reduce to the form $\int \frac{1}{a_1t^2+b_1t+c_1}dt$, which can be evaluated by completing the square.

Definite integrals

If $\int f(x)dx = F(x)$ then

$$\int_a^b f(x)dx = F(x)]_a^b = F(b) - F(a)$$

Properties

1. $\int_a^b f(x)dx = \int_a^b f(y)\,dy$
2. $\int_a^b f(x)dx = -\int_b^a f(x)dx$
3. $\int_a^b f(x)dx = \int_a^c f(x)dx + \int_c^b f(x)dx, \; a < c < b$
4. $\int_0^a f(x)dx = \int_0^a f(a-x)\,dx$
5. $\int_{-a}^a f(x)dx = \begin{cases} 2\int_0^a f(x) & \text{if } f(x) \text{ is even} \\ 0 & \text{if } f(x) \text{ is odd} \end{cases}$

CHAPTER 1

Complex Trigonometry

1.1 Introduction

The real number system was known to mathematicians in the past that was used to solve algebraic equations. It therefore became necessary to extend the real number system to obtain necessary solutions to simple equations like $x^2+1=0$, which could not be solved in the domain of real number. The equation becomes solvable if we introduce new quantities- square roots of negative number. An Italian mathematician Cardano first introduced square roots of negative numbers in the 16th century. Two hundred years later Euler and John Bernoulli recognized the complex numbers and introduced the symbol i for $\sqrt{-1}$. Gauss and Hamilton gave a solid foundation for the theory of complex numbers in 19th century. The concept of complex numbers is a powerful and widely used tool in mathematics. It is necessary for engineering students to have some knowledge of complex numbers. Here in this chapter we discuss the basics of complex numbers and vector algebra.

Definition

Any number of the form $z = x+iy$, where and x and y are real numbers and $i = \sqrt{-1}$ is called complex number. The number x is called the real part of complex number denoted by $R(z)$ or $Re(z)$ and the number y is called imaginary part denoted by $I(z)$ or $Im(z)$.

The system of complex numbers is the set of ordered pairs (x, y) of real numbers and let c denote the set of all ordered pairs of real numbers.

Thus $c = \{(x, y) : x, y \in R\}$

Note that $i^2 = -1; i^3 = -i;\ i^4 = 1$ and $i^{4n} = 1$, where n is an integer.

1.2 Algebra of Complex Numbers

If $z_1 = x_1 + iy_1$ and $z_2 = x_2 + iy_2$, then

1. *Addition*

$$z_1 + z_2 = (x_1 + x_2) + i\,(y_1 + y_2)$$

2. *Subtraction*

$$z_1 - z_2 = (x_1 - x_2) + i\,(y_1 - y_2)\,.$$

3. *Multiplication*

$$z_1 \times z_2 = (x_1 + iy_1) \times (x_2 + iy_2) = (x_1x_2 - y_1y_2) + i\,(x_1y_2 + x_2y_1)$$

If k is a real number, then $kz_1 = k\,(x_1 + iy_1) = kx_1 + iky_1$

4. *Division*

$$\frac{z_1}{z_2} = \frac{x_1 + iy_1}{x_2 + iy_2} = \frac{x_1 + iy_1}{x_2 + iy_2} \times \frac{x_2 - iy_2}{x_2 - iy_2} = \frac{(x_1x_2 + y_1y_2)}{\left(x_2^2 + y_2^2\right)} + i\,\frac{(y_1x_2 - x_1y_2)}{\left(x_2^2 + y_2^2\right)}$$

1.2.1 Equality of Complex Numbers

Two complex numbers are said to be equal if and only if they are identical i.e., if their respective real and imaginary parts are equal.

Let $z_1 = x_1 + iy_1$ and $z_2 = x_2 + iy_2$

If $z_1 = z_2$, then we have

$$\begin{aligned}
& x_1 + iy_1 = x_2 + iy_2 \\
& \Rightarrow x_1 - x_2 = iy_2 - iy_1 \\
& \Rightarrow x_1 - x_2 = -i\,(y_1 - y_2) \\
& \Rightarrow (x_1 - x_2)^2 = (-i)^2\,(y_1 - y_2)^2 \\
& \Rightarrow (x_1 - x_2)^2 = -1\,(y_1 - y_2)^2 \\
& \Rightarrow (x_1 - x_2)^2 + (y_1 - y_2)^2 = 0
\end{aligned}$$

$$\Rightarrow (x_1 - x_2)^2 = 0 \text{ and } (y_1 - y_2)^2 = 0$$
$$\Rightarrow (x_1 - x_2) = 0 \text{ and } y_1 - y_2 = 0$$
$$\Rightarrow x_1 = x_2 \text{ and } y_1 = y_2$$

This shows that two complex numbers will be equal if and only if their real and imaginary parts are equal.

1.2.2 Conjugate of a Complex Number

If $z = x + iy$ is any complex number, then its conjugate or complex conjugate is denoted and is defined as

$$\bar{z} = x - iy$$

Properties

(i) If $z = x + iy$, then $\bar{z} = x - iy$

(ii) If $z = x - iy$, then $\bar{z} = x + iy$

(iii) $\overline{(\bar{z})} = z$

(iv) $z + \bar{z} = 2x = 2\text{Re}\,(z)$

(v) $z - \bar{z} = 2iy = i2\text{Im}\,(z)$

(vi) $z\bar{z} = x^2 + y^2$, real number

(vii) $\overline{z_1 + z_2} = \bar{z}_1 + \bar{z}_2$

(viii) $\overline{z_1 z_2} = \bar{z}_1\,\bar{z}_2$

(ix) $\overline{\left(\dfrac{z_1}{z_2}\right)} = \dfrac{\bar{z}_1}{\bar{z}_2}$

1.3 Geometrical Representation and Polar Form of a Complex Number

Let $P\,(x, y)$ be a point that represents the complex number $z = x + iy$ referred to rectangular axes *OX* and *OY*, usually *OX* is called the real axis and *OY* is called the imaginary axis. The plane is called Argand plane or complex plane or Gaussian plane.

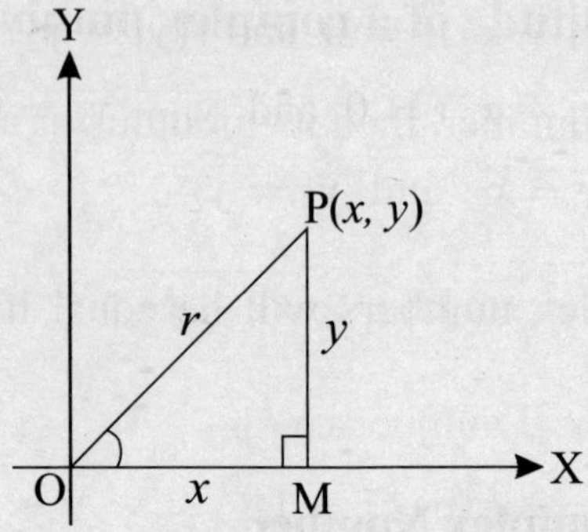

Figure 1.1

The point is called the image of the complex number z and z is said to be affix or complex co-ordinate of point P.

Let $OP = r$, $X\hat{O}P = \hat{\theta}$, then $OP^2 = OM^2 + PM^2$

$$\Rightarrow r^2 = x^2 + y^2 \Rightarrow r = \sqrt{x^2 + y^2}$$

Also

$$\cos\theta = \frac{OM}{OP} = \frac{x}{r} \Rightarrow x = r\cos\theta$$

and

$$\sin\theta = \frac{PM}{OP} = \frac{y}{r} \Rightarrow y = r\sin\theta$$

Therefore,

$$z = x + iy = r\,(\cos\theta + i\sin\theta)$$

The representation of complex number in the form $r\,(\cos\theta + i\sin\theta)$ is called the polar form and $z = x + iy$ is called the rectangular form or Cartesian form.

1.4 Modulus and amplitude of a complex number

If $z = x + iy$ is a complex number, then its modulus or absolute value is denoted by $|z|$ and is defined as

$$|z| = \sqrt{x^2 + y^2}$$

where $|z|$ is a non negative real number i.e., $|z| \geq 0$.

It can be proved that (i) $|\bar{z}| = |z|$ (ii) $z\bar{z} = |z|^2$

(iii) $|z_1 \cdot z_2| = |z_1|\ |z_2|$ (iv) $\left|\dfrac{z_1}{z_2}\right| = \dfrac{|z_1|}{|z_2|}$

The amplitude of the complex number is denoted by amp z or arg (z) and is defined as

$$\text{amp}\, z = \tan^{-1}\left(\frac{y}{x}\right)$$

We know that $\tan^{-1}\left(\dfrac{y}{x}\right)$ has many values. The smallest numerical value falling in the quadrant of the complex number is called the fundamental amplitude. The general value $2n\pi + \tan^{-1}\left(\dfrac{y}{x}\right)$ of the fundamental amplitude is called the general amplitude.

1.4.1 Method of calculating fundamental amplitude

Let $\alpha = \tan^{-1}\left|\dfrac{y}{x}\right|$

If z is in the first quadrant then amp $z = \alpha$

If z is in the second quadrant then amp $z = \pi - \alpha$

If z is in the third quadrant then amp $z = \pi + \alpha$

If z is in the fourth quadrant then amp $z = 2\pi - \alpha$

Illustrations

1. $z = \sqrt{3} + i$

$$\alpha = \tan^{-1}\left|\frac{1}{\sqrt{3}}\right| = \frac{\pi}{6}$$

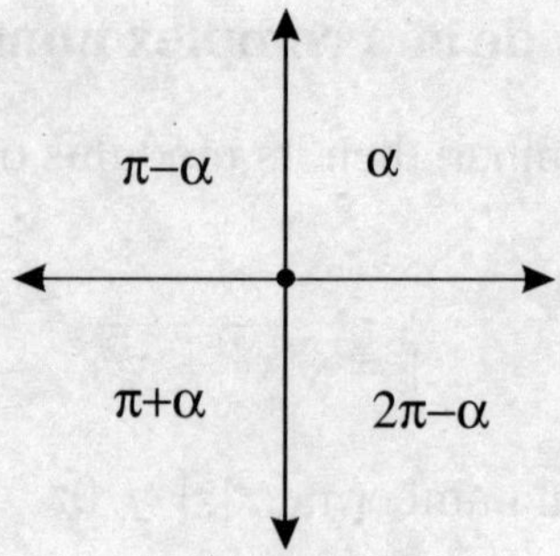

Figure 1.2

Since $z = \sqrt{3} + i = (\sqrt{3}, 1)$ is in first quadrant.

Therefore, $\text{amp}\, z = \alpha = \dfrac{\pi}{6}$

2. $z = -\sqrt{3} + i$

$$\alpha = \tan^{-1}\left|\frac{1}{-\sqrt{3}}\right| = \tan^{-1}\left(\frac{1}{\sqrt{3}}\right) = \frac{\pi}{6}$$

Since $z = -\sqrt{3} + i = (-\sqrt{3}, 1)$ is in second quadrant

Therefore, $\text{amp}\, z = \pi - \alpha = \pi - \dfrac{\pi}{6} = \dfrac{5\pi}{6}$

3. $z = -\sqrt{3} - i$

$$\alpha = \tan^{-1}\left|\frac{-1}{-\sqrt{3}}\right| = \tan^{-1}\left(\frac{1}{\sqrt{3}}\right) = \frac{\pi}{6}$$

Since $z = -\sqrt{3} - i = (-\sqrt{3}, -1)$ is the third quadrant

Therefore, $\text{amp}\, z = \pi + \alpha = \pi + \dfrac{\pi}{6} = \dfrac{7\pi}{6}$

4. $z = \sqrt{3} - i$

$$\alpha = \tan^{-1}\left|\frac{-1}{\sqrt{3}}\right| = \tan^{-1}\left(\frac{1}{\sqrt{3}}\right) = \frac{\pi}{6}$$

Since $z = \sqrt{3} - i = (\sqrt{3}, -1)$ is in fourth quadrant

Therefore, $\text{amp}\, z = 2\pi - \alpha = 2\pi - \dfrac{\pi}{6} = \dfrac{11\pi}{6}$

Properties

(i) $\text{amp}\,(z_1 \cdot z_2) = \text{amp}\, z_1 + \text{amp}\, z_2$

(ii) $\text{amp}\left(\dfrac{z_1}{z_2}\right) = \text{amp}\, z_1 - \text{amp}\, z_2$

(iii) $\text{amp}\, z^2 = 2\text{amp}\, z$

(iv) $\text{amp}\, z^n = n\text{amp}\, z$

1.4.2 Exponential Form

We have

$$\sin x = \frac{x}{1!} - \frac{x^3}{3!} + \frac{x^5}{5!} - + \cdots$$
$$\cos x = 1 - \frac{x^2}{2!} + \frac{x^4}{4!} - + \cdots$$
$$e^x = 1 + \frac{x}{1!} + \frac{x^2}{2!} + \frac{x^3}{3!} + \cdots$$

Therefore,

$$\begin{aligned} e^{ix} &= 1 + \frac{ix}{1!} + \frac{i^2x^2}{2!} + \frac{i^3x^3}{3!} + \frac{i^4x^4}{4!} + \cdots \\ &= \left(1 - \frac{x^2}{2!} + \frac{x^4}{4!} - + \cdots\right) + i\left(\frac{x}{1!} - \frac{x^3}{3!} + - \cdots\right) \\ &= \cos x + i \sin x, \quad \text{which is known as Euler's formula.} \end{aligned}$$

Now, $x + iy = r(\cos\theta + i\sin\theta) = re^{i\theta}$, which is known as exponential form of the complex number $x + iy$.

Worked Examples

1. *Express the following complex numbers in the form of* $x + iy$

(i) $\dfrac{(1+i)}{(1-i)}$ (ii) $\dfrac{(3+4i)}{(3-4i)}$ (iii) $\dfrac{1}{3+2i}$ (iv) $(2+3i) + \dfrac{1}{(1-i)}$

(v) $\dfrac{2-i\sqrt{3}}{1+i}$ (vi) $\dfrac{(3+i)(1-3i)}{2+i}$ (vii) $\dfrac{(1+i)(1+3i)}{1+5i}$

(viii) $\dfrac{1}{(2+i)^2}-\dfrac{1}{(2-i)^2}$ (ix) $\dfrac{5+5i}{3-4i}+\dfrac{20}{4+3i}$ (x) $\dfrac{3i^{30}-i^{19}}{2i-1}$

➡

(i) Let

$$z=\frac{1+i}{1-i}=\frac{1+i}{1-i}\times\frac{1+i}{1+i}=\frac{(1+i)^2}{1^2-i^2}$$
$$=\frac{1^2+i^2+2.1.i}{1-(-1)}=\frac{1-1+2i}{2}=i$$

(ii) Let

$$z=\frac{3+4i}{3-4i}=\frac{3+4i}{3-4i}\times\frac{3+4i}{3+4i}=\frac{(3+4i)^2}{9-16i^2}$$
$$=\frac{9+16i^2+24i}{25}=\frac{-7+24i}{25}=\frac{-7}{25}+\frac{24}{25}i$$

(iii) Let $z=\dfrac{1}{3+2i}=\dfrac{1}{3+2i}\times\dfrac{3-2i}{3-2i}=\dfrac{3-2i}{9-4i^2}=\dfrac{3-2i}{13}=\dfrac{3}{13}-\dfrac{2}{13}i$

(iv) Let

$$z=2+3i+\frac{1}{1-i}=2+3i+\frac{1}{1-i}\times\frac{1+i}{1+i}$$
$$=2+3i+\frac{1+i}{1^2-i^2}=2+3i+\frac{1+i}{1+1}$$
$$=2+3i+\frac{1}{2}+\frac{1}{2}i=\frac{5}{2}+\frac{7}{2}i$$

(v) Let

$$z=\frac{2-i\sqrt{3}}{1+i}=\frac{2-i\sqrt{3}}{1+i}\times\frac{1-i}{1-i}$$
$$=\frac{2-2i-i\sqrt{3}+i^2\sqrt{3}}{1^2-i^2}=\frac{2-\sqrt{3}-i(2+\sqrt{3})}{2}$$
$$=\frac{2-\sqrt{3}}{2}-\frac{2+\sqrt{3}}{2}i$$

(vi) Let

$$z = \frac{(3+i)(1-3i)}{2+i} = \frac{3-9i+i-3i^2}{2+i} = \frac{3-8i+3}{2+i}$$
$$= \frac{6-8i}{2+i} \times \frac{2-i}{2-i} = \frac{12-6i-16i+8i^2}{2^2-i^2} = \frac{12-22i-8}{4+1} = \frac{4}{5} - \frac{22}{5}i$$

(vii) Let

$$z = \frac{(1+i)(1+3i)}{1+5i} = \frac{1+3i+i+3i^2}{1+5i} = \frac{1-3+4i}{1+5i}$$
$$= \frac{-2+4i}{1+5i} \times \frac{1-5i}{1-5i} = \frac{-2+10i+4i-20i^2}{1-25i^2} = \frac{18+14i}{26} = \frac{9}{13} + \frac{7}{13}i$$

(viii) Let

$$z = \frac{1}{(2+i)^2} - \frac{1}{(2-i)^2} = \frac{(2-i)^2-(2+i)^2}{(2+i)^2(2-i)^2}$$
$$= \frac{-4(2)(i)}{[(2+i)(2-i)]^2} \qquad [\because\ (a-b)^2-(a+b)^2 = -4ab]$$
$$= \frac{-8i}{[4-i^2]^2} = \frac{-8i}{25} = \frac{-8}{25}i$$

(ix) Let

$$z = \frac{5+5i}{3-4i} + \frac{20}{4+3i} = \frac{5+5i}{3-4i} \times \frac{3+4i}{3+4i} + \frac{20}{4+3i} \times \frac{4-3i}{4-3i}$$
$$= \frac{15+15i+20i+20i^2}{9-16i^2} + \frac{80-60i}{16-9i^2} = \frac{-5+35i}{25} + \frac{80-60i}{25}$$
$$= \frac{-5+35i+80-60i}{25} = \frac{75-25i}{25} = 3-i$$

(x) Let

$$z = \frac{3i^{30}-i^{19}}{2i-1} = \frac{3\left(i^2\right)^{15} - \left(i^2\right)^9 i}{2i-1}$$

$$= \frac{3(-1)^{15} - (-1)^9 i}{2i - 1} = \frac{-3 + i}{2i - 1} \times \frac{2i + 1}{2i + 1}$$

$$= \frac{-6i + 2i^2 - 3 + i}{4i^2 - 1} = \frac{-5i - 5}{-5}$$

$$= i + 1$$

2. *If* $z_1 = 2 + i$, $z_2 = 3 - 2i$ *and* $z_3 = -\frac{1}{2} + \frac{\sqrt{3}}{2}i$, *evaluate the following*

(i) $|3z_1 - 4z_2|$ (ii) z_3^4 and (iii) $\left|\frac{2z_2 + z_1 - 5 - i}{2z_1 - z_2 + 3 - i}\right|$

➡

(i)

$$|3z_1 - 4z_2| = |3(2 + i) - 4(3 - 2i)| = |6 + 3i - 12 + 8i|$$

$$= |-6 + 11i| = \sqrt{(-6)^2 + 11^2} = \sqrt{157}$$

(ii)

$$z_3^4 = \left(-\frac{1}{2} + \frac{\sqrt{3}}{2}i\right)^4$$

$$= \left[\left(-\frac{1}{2} + \frac{\sqrt{3}}{2}i\right)^2\right]^2 = \left[\frac{1}{4} + \frac{3}{4}i^2 - 2 \cdot \frac{1}{2}\frac{\sqrt{3}}{2}i\right]^2$$

$$= \left[\frac{1}{4} - \frac{3}{4} - \frac{\sqrt{3}}{2}i\right]^2 = \left[-\frac{1}{2} - \frac{\sqrt{3}}{2}i\right]^2 = \left[-1\left(\frac{1}{2} + \frac{\sqrt{3}}{2}i\right)\right]^2$$

$$= \left(\frac{1}{2} + \frac{\sqrt{3}}{2}i\right)^2 = \frac{1}{4} + \frac{3}{4}i^2 + 2 \cdot \frac{1}{2} \cdot \frac{\sqrt{3}}{2}i$$

$$= \frac{1}{4} - \frac{3}{4} + \frac{\sqrt{3}}{2}i$$

$$= -\frac{1}{2} + \frac{\sqrt{3}}{2}i$$

(iii)

$$\left|\frac{2z_2 + z_1 - 5 - i}{2z_1 - z_2 + 3 - i}\right| = \left|\frac{2(3-2i) + (2+i) - 5 - i}{2(2+i) - (3-2i) + 3 - i}\right|$$

$$= \left|\frac{6 - 4i + 2 + i - 5 - i}{4 + 2i - 3 + 2i + 3 - i}\right|$$

$$= \left|\frac{3-4i}{4+3i}\right| = \frac{\sqrt{3^2 + (-4)^2}}{\sqrt{4^2 + 3^2}}$$

$$= \frac{\sqrt{25}}{\sqrt{25}} = 1$$

3. *Express the following in the form $a + ib$ and plot them on a complex plane (or organd plane)*
(i) $\dfrac{(2+i)^2}{1+i}$ (ii) $\dfrac{3+i}{(4-2i)(1+i)}$ (iii) $\dfrac{1}{(1-i)^2} - \dfrac{1}{(1+i)^2}$

➡

(i) Let

$$z = \frac{(2+i)^2}{1+i} = \frac{4 + i^2 + 4i}{1+i} = \frac{4 - 1 + 4i}{1+i}$$

$$= \frac{3+4i}{1+i} \times \frac{1-i}{1-i} = \frac{3 + 4i - 3i - 4i^2}{1^2 - i^2}$$

$$z = \frac{3 + i + 4}{1+1} = \frac{7}{2} + \frac{1}{2}i = \left(\frac{7}{2}, \frac{1}{2}\right) \text{ say}$$

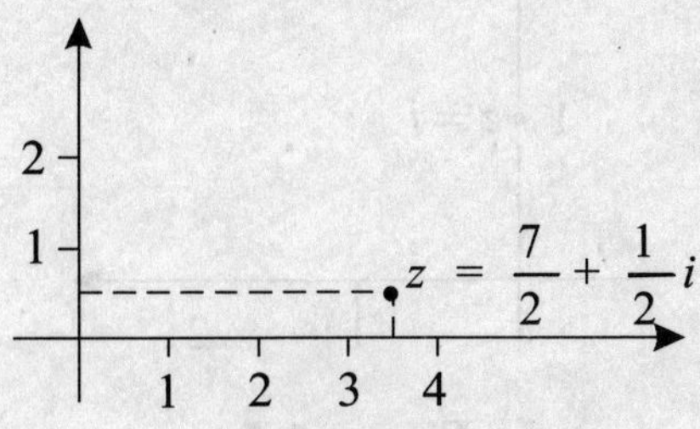

Figure 1.3

(ii) Let

$$z = \frac{3+i}{(4-2i)(1+i)} = \frac{3+i}{4-2i+4i-2i^2}$$

$$= \frac{3+i}{6+2i} = \frac{3+i}{2(3+i)}$$

$$z = \frac{1}{2} = \frac{1}{2} + 0.i = \left(\frac{1}{2}, 0\right) \text{ (say)}$$

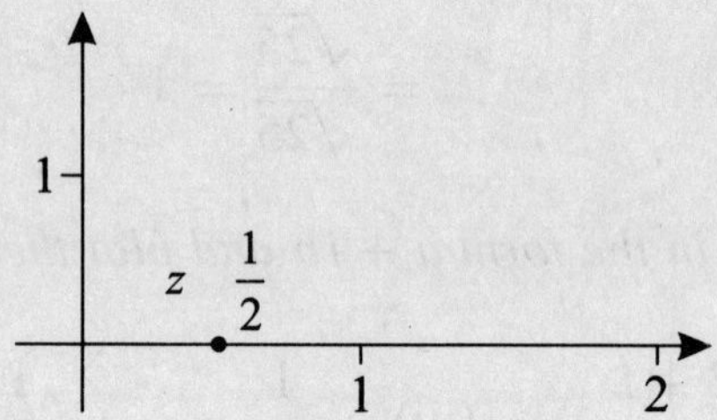

Figure 1.4

(iii) Let

$$z = \frac{1}{(1-i)^2} - \frac{1}{(1+i)^2} = \frac{1}{1^2+i^2-2i} - \frac{1}{1^2+i^2+2i}$$

$$= \frac{1}{-2i} - \frac{1}{2i} = -\frac{1}{2i} - \frac{1}{2i} = -\frac{1}{i}$$

$z = i = (0, 1)$ (say.)

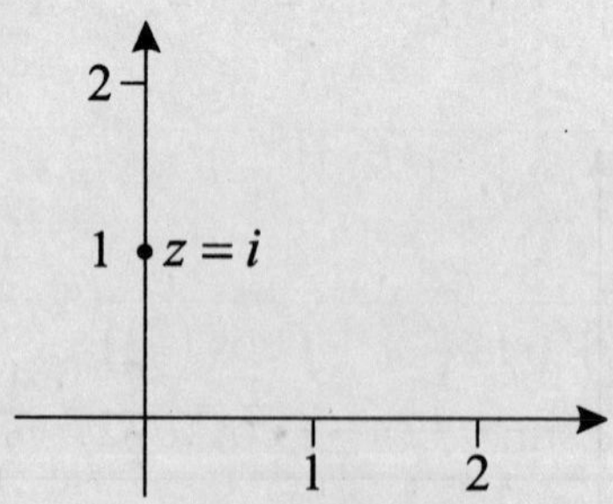

Figure 1.5

4. *Express the following in the form $a + ib$ and also find the conjugate*

(i) $\dfrac{3}{1+i} - \dfrac{1}{2-i} + \dfrac{1}{1-i}$ (ii) $\dfrac{1}{1-\cos\theta + 2i\sin\theta}$ (iii) $\dfrac{1}{1 - i\tan\alpha}$

(i) Let

$$z = \frac{3}{1+i} - \frac{1}{2-i} + \frac{1}{1-i} = \frac{3}{1+i} + \frac{1}{1-i} - \frac{1}{2-i}$$

$$= \frac{3(1-i) + (1+i)}{(1+i)(1-i)} - \frac{1}{2-i} = \frac{3 - 3i + 1 + i}{1 - i^2} - \frac{1}{2-i}$$

$$= \frac{4-2i}{1+1} - \frac{1}{2-i}$$

$$= 2 - i - \left(\frac{1}{2-i} \times \frac{2+i}{2+i}\right) = 2 - i - \left(\frac{2+i}{4-i^2}\right)$$

$$= 2 - i - \frac{(2+i)}{5} = \frac{10 - 5i - (2+i)}{5} = \frac{8-6i}{5}$$

$$z = \frac{8}{5} - \frac{6i}{5}$$

Therefore, $\bar{z} = \dfrac{8}{5} + \dfrac{6}{5}i$

(ii) Let

$$z = \frac{1}{1 - \cos\theta + i\sin\theta}$$

$$= \frac{1}{2\sin^2(\theta/2) + 2i\ \sin(\theta/2)\cos(\theta/2)}$$

$$= \frac{1}{2\sin(\theta/2)\ (\sin(\theta/2) + i\cos(\theta/2))}$$

$$= \frac{1}{2\sin\left(\frac{\theta}{2}\right)\ \left(\sin\left(\frac{\theta}{2}\right) + i\cos\left(\frac{\theta}{2}\right)\right)} \times \frac{\left(\sin\left(\frac{\theta}{2}\right) - i\cos\left(\frac{\theta}{2}\right)\right)}{\left(\sin\left(\frac{\theta}{2}\right) - i\cos\left(\frac{\theta}{2}\right)\right)}$$

$$= \frac{\sin(\theta/2) - i\cos(\theta/2)}{2\sin(\theta/2)\ \left[\sin^2(\theta/2) - i^2\cos^2(\theta/2)\right]}$$

$$= \frac{\sin(\theta/2) - i\cos(\theta/2)}{2\sin(\theta/2)\ \left(\sin^2(\theta/2) + \cos^2(\theta/2)\right)}$$

$$= \frac{\sin(\theta/2) - i\cos(\theta/2)}{2\sin(\theta/2)\ (1)}$$

$$= \frac{1}{2}\left(\frac{\sin(\theta/2)}{\sin(\theta/2)} - i\frac{\cos(\theta/2)}{\sin(\theta/2)}\right)$$

$$z = \frac{1}{2}\left(1 - i\cot\left(\frac{\theta}{2}\right)\right)$$

Therefore, $\bar{z} = \frac{1}{2}\left(1 + i\cot\left(\frac{\theta}{2}\right)\right)$

(iii) Let

$$z = \frac{1}{1 - i\tan\alpha} \times \frac{1 + i\tan\alpha}{1 + i\tan\alpha}$$

$$= \frac{1 + i\tan\alpha}{1 - i^2\tan^2\alpha} = \frac{1 + i\tan\alpha}{1 + \tan^2\alpha}$$

$$= \frac{1 + i\tan\alpha}{\sec^2\alpha} = \frac{1}{\sec^2\alpha} + \frac{\tan\alpha}{\sec^2\alpha}$$

$$= \cos^2\alpha + i\cos^2\alpha\tan\alpha$$

$$= \cos^2\alpha + i\cos\alpha\sin\alpha$$

Therefore, $\bar{z} = \cos^2\alpha - i\cos\alpha\sin\alpha$

5. *Find the real values of* θ *if* $\frac{1-i\sin\theta}{1+i\sin\theta}$ *is purely real.*

➡ Let

$$z = \frac{1 - i\sin\theta}{1 + i\sin\theta} \times \frac{1 - i\sin\theta}{1 - i\sin\theta} = \frac{(1 - i\sin\theta)^2}{1 - i^2\sin^2\theta}$$

$$= \frac{1 + i^2\sin^2\theta - 2i\sin\theta}{1 + \sin^2\theta} = \frac{1 - \sin^2\theta - 2i\sin\theta}{1 + \sin^2\theta}$$

$$= \frac{\cos^2\theta}{1 + \sin^2\theta} - i\frac{2\sin\theta}{1 + \sin^2\theta}$$

Since z is purely real $\Rightarrow \text{Im}(z) = 0$.

$$\text{i.e.,}\quad -\frac{2\sin\theta}{1+\sin^2\theta}=0$$

$$\sin\theta = 0 \Rightarrow \theta = n\pi \quad \text{where} \quad n = 0, 1, 2, \ldots$$

6. *Find z if* $(3x-2iy)(2+i)^2 = 10(1+i)$ *where* $z = x+iy$

➡ $(3x-2iy)(2+i)^2 = 10(1+i)$

$$(3x-2iy)\left(2^2+i^2+2.2.i\right) = 10(1+i)$$
$$(3x-2iy)(4-1+4i) = 10(1+i)$$
$$(3x-2iy)(3+4i) = 10(1+i)$$
$$9x-6iy+12ix-8i^2y = 10+10i$$
$$(9x+8y)+i(12x-6y) = 10+10i$$

Equating real and imaginary parts, we get

$$9x+8y = 10 \qquad (1)$$

and

$$12x-6y = 10 \qquad (2)$$

On solving equations (1) and (2) for x and y, we get

$$x = \frac{14}{15}, \qquad y = \frac{1}{5}$$

Therefore, $z = x+iy = \dfrac{14}{15}+\dfrac{i}{5} = \dfrac{14+3i}{15}$

7. *Find the modulus and amplitude of each of the following and express each in polar form.*

(i) $1-i$ (ii) $\sqrt{3}+i$ (iii) $1-i\sqrt{3}$

(iv) $-\sqrt{3}-i$ (v) $2i$ (vi) -8

➡ (i) Let $z = x+iy = 1-i \Rightarrow x = 1, y = -1$

$$\alpha = \tan^{-1}\left|\frac{y}{x}\right| = \tan^{-1}\left|\frac{-1}{1}\right| = \tan^{-1} 1 = \frac{\pi}{4}$$

Here $z = (x, y) = (1, -1)$ is in the 4th quadrant

Therefore, $\text{amp} z = 2\pi - \alpha = 2\pi - \frac{\pi}{4} = \frac{7\pi}{4} \Rightarrow\Rightarrow \theta = \frac{7\pi}{4}$

$$|z| = r = \sqrt{x^2 + y^2} = \sqrt{1^2 + (-1)^2} = \sqrt{2} = \text{modulus}$$

The polar form of the given complex number is

$$1 - i = r(\cos\theta + i\sin\theta) = \sqrt{2}\left(\cos\frac{7\pi}{4} + i\sin\frac{7\pi}{4}\right)$$

(ii) Let $z = x + iy = \sqrt{3} + i \Rightarrow x = \sqrt{3}, y = 1$

$$\alpha = \tan^{-1}\left|\frac{y}{x}\right| = \tan^{-1}\left(\frac{1}{\sqrt{3}}\right) = \frac{\pi}{6}$$

Here $z = (x, y) = (\sqrt{3}, 1)$ is in the first quadrant.

Therefore, $\text{amp } z = \alpha = \frac{\pi}{6} \Rightarrow \theta = \frac{\pi}{6}$

$$|z| = r = \sqrt{x^2 + y^2} = \sqrt{\left(\sqrt{3}\right)^2 + 1^2} = \sqrt{3+1} = \sqrt{4} = 2$$

The polar form of the given complex number is

$$\sqrt{3} + i = r(\cos\theta + i\sin\theta) = 2\left(\cos\frac{\pi}{6} + i\sin\frac{\pi}{6}\right)$$

(iii) Let $z = x + iy = 1 - i\sqrt{3} \Rightarrow x = 1, y = -\sqrt{3}$

$$\alpha = \tan^{-1}\left|\frac{y}{x}\right| = \tan^{-1}\left|\frac{-\sqrt{3}}{1}\right| = \tan^{-1}(\sqrt{3}) = \frac{\pi}{3}$$

Here, $z = (x, y) = (1, -\sqrt{3})$ is in fourth quadrant.

Therefore, $\text{amp } z = 2\pi - \alpha = 2\pi - \frac{\pi}{3} = \frac{5\pi}{3} \Rightarrow \theta = 5\pi/3$

$$|z| = r = \sqrt{x^2 + y^2} = \sqrt{1^2 + (-\sqrt{3})^2} = \sqrt{1+3} = 2$$

The polar form of the given complex number is

$$1 - i\sqrt{3} = r\,(\cos\theta + i\sin\theta)$$

$$\Rightarrow 1 - i\sqrt{3} = 2\left(\cos\frac{5\pi}{3} + i\sin\frac{5\pi}{3}\right)$$

(iv) Let $z = x + iy = -\sqrt{3} - i \Rightarrow x = -\sqrt{3} y = -1$

$$\alpha = \tan^{-1}\left|\frac{y}{x}\right| = \tan^{-1}\left|\frac{-1}{-\sqrt{3}}\right| = \tan^{-1}\left(\frac{1}{\sqrt{3}}\right) = \frac{\pi}{6}$$

Here $z = (x, y) = (-\sqrt{3}, -1)$ is in the 3rd quadrant.

Therefore, amp $z = \alpha + \pi = \dfrac{\pi}{6} + \pi = \dfrac{7\pi}{6} \Rightarrow \theta = \dfrac{7\pi}{6}$

$$|z| = r = \sqrt{x^2 + y^2} = \sqrt{3 + 1} = 2$$

The polar form of the given complex number is

$$-\sqrt{3} - i = r\,(\cos\theta + i\sin\theta)$$

$$\Rightarrow -\sqrt{3} - i = 2\left[\cos\frac{7\pi}{6} + i\sin\frac{7\pi}{6}\right]$$

(v) Let $z = x + iy = 2i \Rightarrow x = 0 \;\; y = 2$

$$\alpha = \tan^{-1}\left|\frac{y}{x}\right| = \tan^{-1}\left|\frac{2}{0}\right| = \tan^{-1}|\infty| = \frac{\pi}{2}$$

Here $z = (x, y) = (0, 2)$ is in the 1st quadrant

Therefore, amp $z = \theta = \alpha = \dfrac{\pi}{2}$

$$|z| = r = \sqrt{x^2 + y^2} = \sqrt{0 + 4} = 2$$

Therefore, the polar form of given complex number is

$$2i = r\,(\cos\theta + i\sin\theta) = 2\left[\cos\frac{\pi}{2} + i\sin\frac{\pi}{2}\right]$$

(vi) Let $z = x + iy = -8 \Rightarrow x = -8 \;\; y = 0$

$$\alpha = \tan^{-1}\left|\frac{y}{x}\right| = \tan^{-1}\left|\frac{0}{-8}\right| = \tan^{-1}(0) = 0$$

Here $z = (x, y) = (-8, 0)$ is in the 2nd quadrant
Therefore, amp $z = \theta = \pi - \alpha = \pi - 0 = \pi$

$$|z| = r = \sqrt{x^2 + y^2} = \sqrt{64 + 0} = 8$$

Therefore, polar form of the given complex number

$$-8 = r(\cos\theta + i\sin\theta) = 8\,[\cos\pi + i\sin\pi]$$

8. *Find the modulus and amplitude of the complex number* $\dfrac{(3-\sqrt{2}i)^2}{1+2i}$

➡ Let

$$z = \frac{\left(3-\sqrt{2}i\right)^2}{1+2i} = \frac{9+2i^2-6\sqrt{2}i}{1+2i} = \frac{9-2-6\sqrt{2}i}{1+2i} \times \frac{1-2i}{1-2i}$$

$$= \frac{\left(7-6\sqrt{2}i\right)(1-2i)}{1-2^2i^2} = \frac{7-14i-6\sqrt{2}i+12\sqrt{2}i^2}{1+4}$$

$$= \frac{7-i\left(14+6\sqrt{2}\right)-12\sqrt{2}}{5} = \frac{\left(7-12\sqrt{2}\right)-i\left(14+6\sqrt{2}\right)}{5}$$

$$z = \left(\frac{7-12\sqrt{2}}{5}\right) - i\left(\frac{14+6\sqrt{2}}{5}\right) = \left[-\frac{12\sqrt{2}-7}{5}, -\frac{14+6\sqrt{2}}{5}\right]$$

Therefore,

$$|z| = \sqrt{\left(\frac{7-12\sqrt{2}}{5}\right)^2 + \left(\frac{14+6\sqrt{2}}{5}\right)^2}$$

$$= \sqrt{\frac{49+288-2\times 7\times 12\sqrt{2}}{25} + \frac{196+72+168\sqrt{2}}{25}}$$

$$= \sqrt{\frac{337 - 168\sqrt{2} + 268 + 168\sqrt{2}}{25}}$$

$$= \sqrt{\frac{605}{25}} = \sqrt{\frac{121}{5}} = \frac{11}{\sqrt{5}}$$

$$\alpha = \tan^{-1}\left(\frac{-\left(\frac{14+6\sqrt{2}}{5}\right)}{\left(\frac{7-12\sqrt{2}}{5}\right)}\right)$$

$$= \tan^{-1}\left(\frac{14 + 6\sqrt{2}}{12\sqrt{2} - 7}\right)$$

Here $z = \left[-\frac{12\sqrt{2} - 7}{5}, -\frac{14 + 6\sqrt{2}}{5}\right]$ is in 3rd quadrant.

Therefore, amp $z = \pi + \alpha = \pi + \tan^{-1}\left(\frac{14 + 6\sqrt{2}}{12\sqrt{2} - 7}\right)$

9. *Find modulus and amplitude of* $\frac{(1+i)^2}{3+i}$

➡ Let

$$z = \frac{(1+i)^2}{3+i} = \frac{1 + i^2 + 2i}{3+i} = \frac{1 - 1 + 2i}{3+i}$$

$$= \frac{2i}{3+i} \times \frac{3-i}{3-i} = \frac{6i - 2i^2}{9 - i^2} = \frac{6i + 2}{10}$$

$$z = \frac{1}{5} + \frac{3}{5}i = \left(\frac{1}{5}, \frac{3}{5}\right)$$

Therefore,

$$|z| = \sqrt{\left(\frac{1}{5}\right)^2 + \left(\frac{3}{5}\right)^2} = \sqrt{\frac{1}{25} + \frac{9}{25}} = \sqrt{\frac{10}{25}} = \sqrt{\frac{2}{5}}$$

and $\alpha = \tan^{-1}\left(\frac{3/5}{1/5}\right) = \tan^{-1}(3)$

Here $z = \left(\frac{1}{5}, \frac{3}{5}\right)$ is in 1st quadrant.

Therefore, amp $z = \alpha = \tan^{-1} 3$

10. *Find the modulus and amplitude of* $\dfrac{(2-3i)(2+i)^2}{1+i}$

➡ Let

$$z = \frac{(2-3i)\,(2+i)^2}{1+i}$$
$$= \frac{(2-3i)\left(4+i^2+4i\right)}{1+i} = \frac{(2-3i)\,(4-1+4i)}{4i}$$
$$= \frac{(2-3i)\,(3+4i)}{1+i} = \frac{6+8i-9i-12i^2}{1+i}$$
$$= \frac{18-i}{1+i} \times \frac{1-i}{1-i} = \frac{18-18i-i+i^2}{1^2-i^2} = \frac{17-19i}{2}$$
$$z = \frac{17}{2} - \frac{19}{2}i$$

Therefore,

$$|z| = \sqrt{\left(\frac{17}{2}\right)^2 + \left(-\frac{19}{2}\right)^2} = \sqrt{\frac{325}{2}}$$

and

$$\text{amp } z = \tan^{-1}\left(\frac{-19/2}{17/2}\right) = \tan^{-1}\left(-\frac{19}{17}\right)$$

11. *Find the modulus and principal argument of* $\dfrac{1+2i}{1-3i}$

➡ Let

$$z = \frac{1+2i}{1-3i} = \frac{1+2i}{1-3i} \times \frac{1+3i}{1+3i} = \frac{1+3i+2i+6i^2}{1-9i^2}$$
$$z = \frac{-5+5i}{10} = -\frac{1}{2} + \frac{1}{2}i = \left(-\frac{1}{2}, \frac{1}{2}\right)$$

$$|z| = \sqrt{\left(\frac{-1}{2}\right)^2 + \left(\frac{1}{2}\right)^2} = \sqrt{\frac{1}{4} + \frac{1}{4}} = \sqrt{\frac{1}{2}} = \frac{1}{\sqrt{2}}$$

$$\alpha = \tan^{-1}\left|\frac{1/2}{-1/2}\right| = \tan^{-1}(1) = \frac{\pi}{4}$$

Here $z = -\frac{1}{2} + \frac{1}{2}i = \left(-\frac{1}{2}, \frac{1}{2}\right)$ is in 2nd quadrant

Therefore, amp $z = \pi - \alpha = \pi - \frac{\pi}{4} = \frac{3\pi}{4}$.

12. *Find the Modulus and amplitude of* $\frac{4+2i}{2-3i}$

➡ Let

$$z = \frac{4+2i}{2-3i} = \frac{4+2i}{2-3i} \times \frac{2+3i}{2+3i} = \frac{8+12i+4i+6i^2}{4-9i^2}$$

$$= \frac{2+16i}{13} = \frac{2}{13} + \frac{16}{13}i = \left(\frac{2}{13}, \frac{16}{13}\right)$$

$$|z| = \sqrt{\left(\frac{2}{13}\right)^2 \left(\frac{16}{13}\right)^2} = \sqrt{\frac{4}{169} + \frac{256}{169}} = \sqrt{\frac{260}{169}} = \sqrt{\frac{20}{13}}$$

$$\alpha = \tan^{-1}\left|\frac{16/13}{2/13}\right| = \tan^{-1} 8$$

Here $z = \left(\frac{2}{13}, \frac{16}{13}\right)$ is in first quadrant.

Therefore amp $z = \alpha = \tan^{-1} 8$.

13. *Put the complex number* $\left(\frac{2+i}{3-i}\right)^2$ *into polar form.*

➡ Let

$$z = \left(\frac{2+i}{3-i}\right)^2 = \frac{2^2+4i+i^2}{3^2-6i+i^2} = \frac{4+4i-1}{9-6i-1}$$

$$= \frac{3+4i}{8-6i} \times \frac{8+6i}{8+6i}$$

$$= \frac{24 + 18i + 32i + 24i^2}{64 - 36i^2} = \frac{24 + 50i - 24}{64 + 36}$$

$$= \frac{50i}{100} = \frac{i}{2} = \left(0, \frac{1}{2}\right)$$

$$r = \sqrt{0^2 + \left(\frac{1}{2}\right)^2} = \sqrt{\frac{1}{4}} = \frac{1}{2}$$

$$\alpha = \tan^{-1}\left|\frac{1/2}{0}\right| = \tan^{-1}\infty = \frac{\pi}{2}$$

Here $z = \left(0, \frac{1}{2}\right)$ is in 1st quadrant.

Therefore $\theta = \alpha = \frac{\pi}{2}$.

Hence, polar form of given complex number is

$$z = r(\cos\theta + i\sin\theta)$$

$$= \frac{1}{2}\left[\cos\frac{\pi}{2} + i\sin\frac{\pi}{2}\right]$$

14. *Express the following in polar form and hence find their modulus and amplitude.*

(i) $\sqrt{3} + i$ (ii) $1 + i$ (iii) $1 - i\sqrt{3}$

➡ (i) Let $z = \sqrt{3} + i = 2\left[\frac{\sqrt{3}}{2} + \frac{1}{2}i\right]$

$$z = 2\left[\cos\left(\frac{\pi}{6}\right) + i\sin\left(\frac{\pi}{6}\right)\right] \text{ is in polar form.}$$

Therefore, modulus $= r = 2$ and amplitude $= \theta = \frac{\pi}{6}$

(ii) Let $z = 1 + i = \sqrt{2}\left[\frac{1}{\sqrt{2}} + \frac{1}{\sqrt{2}}i\right]$

$$z = \sqrt{2}\left[\cos\left(\frac{\pi}{4}\right) + i\sin\left(\frac{\pi}{4}\right)\right] \text{ is in polar form.}$$

Therefore, modulus $= r = \sqrt{2}$ and amplitude $= \theta = \frac{\pi}{4}$

(iii) Let

$$z = 1 - \sqrt{3}i = 2\left[\frac{1}{2} - \frac{\sqrt{3}}{2}i\right]$$
$$= 2\left[\cos\left(\frac{\pi}{3}\right) - i\sin\left(\frac{\pi}{3}\right)\right]$$
$$= 2\left[\cos\left(2\pi - \frac{\pi}{3}\right) + i\sin\left(2\pi - \frac{\pi}{3}\right)\right]$$
$$z = 2\left[\cos\frac{5\pi}{3} + i\sin\frac{5\pi}{3}\right] \text{ is in polar form,}$$

therefore, modulus $= r = 2$ and amplitude $= \theta = \dfrac{5\pi}{3}$

15. *Find the modulus and amplitude of each of the following complex numbers.*

(i) $1 - \cos\alpha + i\sin\alpha$ (ii) $1 + \cos\alpha + i\sin\alpha$

(iii) $\dfrac{1}{1 - \cos\alpha + i\sin\alpha}$ (iv) $\dfrac{1}{\sin a - i\cos a}$

(v) $\dfrac{1}{1 + i\cot\alpha}$ (vi) $\dfrac{1 + \cos\alpha + i\sin\alpha}{1 - \cos\alpha + i\sin\alpha}$

➡ (i) Let

$$z = 1 - \cos\alpha + i\sin\alpha$$
$$= 2\sin^2\left(\frac{\alpha}{2}\right) + i2\sin\left(\frac{\alpha}{2}\right)\cos\left(\frac{\alpha}{2}\right)$$
$$= 2\sin\left(\frac{\alpha}{2}\right)\left[\sin\left(\frac{\alpha}{2}\right) + i\cos\left(\frac{\alpha}{2}\right)\right]$$
$$\therefore\ z = 2\sin\left(\frac{\alpha}{2}\right)\left[\cos\left(\frac{\pi}{2} - \frac{\alpha}{2}\right) + i\sin\left(\frac{\pi}{2} - \frac{\alpha}{2}\right)\right]$$

Since cos and sin are positive in the first quadrant
Therefore, $|z| = 2\sin\left(\dfrac{\alpha}{2}\right)$ and amp $z = \dfrac{\pi}{2} - \dfrac{\alpha}{2}$

Remark: Polar form of a complex number is

$$z = r(\cos\theta + i\sin\theta) \Rightarrow |z| = r \text{ and amp } z = \theta$$

(ii) Let

$$z = 1 + \cos\alpha + i\sin\alpha$$
$$= 2\cos^2\left(\frac{\alpha}{2}\right) + i2\sin\left(\frac{\alpha}{2}\right)\cdot\cos\left(\frac{\alpha}{2}\right)$$
$$z = 2\cos\left(\frac{\alpha}{2}\right)\left(\cos\left(\frac{\alpha}{2}\right) + i\sin\left(\frac{\alpha}{2}\right)\right)$$

Therefore, $|z| = 2\cos\left(\frac{\alpha}{2}\right)$ and amp $z = \frac{\alpha}{2}$

(iii) Let

$$z = \frac{1}{1 - \cos\alpha + i\sin\alpha}$$
$$= \frac{1}{2\sin^2\left(\frac{\alpha}{2}\right) + i2\sin\left(\frac{\alpha}{2}\right)\cos\left(\frac{\alpha}{2}\right)}$$
$$= \frac{1}{2\sin\left(\frac{\alpha}{2}\right)\left(\sin\left(\frac{\alpha}{2}\right) + i\cos\left(\frac{\alpha}{2}\right)\right)} \times \frac{\sin\left(\frac{\alpha}{2}\right) - i\cos\left(\frac{\alpha}{2}\right)}{\sin\left(\frac{\alpha}{2}\right) - i\cos\left(\frac{\alpha}{2}\right)}$$
$$= \frac{\sin\left(\frac{\alpha}{2}\right) - i\cos\left(\frac{\alpha}{2}\right)}{2\sin\left(\frac{\alpha}{2}\right)\left(\sin^2\left(\frac{\alpha}{2}\right) - i^2\cos^2\left(\frac{\alpha}{2}\right)\right)}$$
$$= \frac{\sin\left(\frac{\alpha}{2}\right) - i\cos\left(\frac{\alpha}{2}\right)}{2\sin\left(\frac{\alpha}{2}\right)\left(\sin^2\left(\frac{\alpha}{2}\right) + \cos^2\left(\frac{\alpha}{2}\right)\right)}$$
$$= \frac{\sin\left(\frac{\alpha}{2}\right) - i\cos\left(\frac{\alpha}{2}\right)}{2\sin\left(\frac{\alpha}{2}\right)(1)}$$
$$= \frac{1}{2}\cos ec\left(\frac{\alpha}{2}\right)\left(\sin\left(\frac{\alpha}{2}\right) - i\cos\left(\frac{\alpha}{2}\right)\right)$$
$$z = \frac{1}{2}\cos ec\left(\frac{\alpha}{2}\right)\left[\cos\left(\frac{3\pi}{2} + \frac{\alpha}{2}\right) + i\sin\left(\frac{3\pi}{2} + \frac{\alpha}{2}\right)\right]$$

Since cos is positive and sin is negative in the 4th quadrant,

$|z| = \frac{1}{2}\text{cosec}\left(\frac{\alpha}{2}\right)$ and amp $z = \frac{3\pi}{2} + \frac{\alpha}{2}$

(iv) Let

$$z = \frac{1}{\sin a - i\cos a} \times \frac{\sin a + i\cos a}{\sin a + i\cos a} = \frac{\sin a + i\cos a}{\sin^2 a - i^2\cos^2 a}$$

$$= \frac{\sin a + i\cos a}{\sin^2 a + \cos^2 a} = \sin a + i\cos a$$

$$z = \cos\left(\frac{\pi}{2} - a\right) + i\sin\left(\frac{\pi}{2} - a\right)$$

Since cos and sin are positive in the first quadrant,

$$|z| = 1 \text{ and amp } z = \frac{\pi}{2} - a$$

(v) Let

$$z = \frac{1}{1 + i\cot\alpha} \times \frac{1 - i\cot\alpha}{1 - i\cot\alpha}$$

$$= \frac{1 - i\cot\alpha}{1^2 - i^2\cot^2\alpha} = \frac{1 - i\cot\alpha}{1 + \cot^2\alpha}$$

$$= \frac{1 - i\cot\alpha}{\cos ec^2\alpha} = \sin^2\alpha\left(1 - i\frac{\cos\alpha}{\sin\alpha}\right)$$

$$= \sin\alpha\,(\sin\alpha - i\cos\alpha)$$

$$z = \sin\alpha\left[\cos\left(\frac{3\pi}{2} + \alpha\right) + i\sin\left(\frac{3\pi}{2} + \alpha\right)\right]$$

Since cos is positive and sin is negative in the fourth quadrant

$$|z| = \sin\alpha \text{ and amp } z = \frac{3\pi}{2} + \alpha$$

(vi) Let

$$z = \frac{1 + \cos\alpha + i\sin\alpha}{1 - \cos\alpha + i\sin\alpha}$$

$$= \frac{2\cos^2\left(\frac{\alpha}{2}\right) + i2\sin\left(\frac{\alpha}{2}\right)\cos\left(\frac{\alpha}{2}\right)}{2\sin^2\left(\frac{\alpha}{2}\right) + i2\sin\left(\frac{\alpha}{2}\right)\cos\left(\frac{\alpha}{2}\right)}$$

$$= \frac{2\cos\left(\frac{\alpha}{2}\right)\left(\cos\left(\frac{\alpha}{2}\right) + i\sin\left(\frac{\alpha}{2}\right)\right)}{2\sin\left(\frac{\alpha}{2}\right)\left(\sin\left(\frac{\alpha}{2}\right) + i\cos\left(\frac{\alpha}{2}\right)\right)} \times \frac{\sin\left(\frac{\alpha}{2}\right) - i\cos\left(\frac{\alpha}{2}\right)}{\sin\left(\frac{\alpha}{2}\right) - i\cos\left(\frac{\alpha}{2}\right)}$$

$$= \frac{\cot\frac{\alpha}{2}\left[\sin\frac{\alpha}{2}\cos\frac{\alpha}{2} + i\sin^2\frac{\alpha}{2} - i\cos^2\frac{\alpha}{2} - i^2\sin\frac{\alpha}{2}\cos\frac{\alpha}{2}\right]}{\sin^2\frac{\alpha}{2} - i^2\cos^2\frac{\alpha}{2}}$$

$$= \frac{\cot\left(\frac{\alpha}{2}\right)\left[2\sin\left(\frac{\alpha}{2}\right)\cos\left(\frac{\alpha}{2}\right) + i\left(\sin^2\left(\frac{\alpha}{2}\right) - \cos^2\left(\frac{\alpha}{2}\right)\right)\right]}{\sin^2\left(\frac{\alpha}{2}\right) + \cos^2\left(\frac{\alpha}{2}\right)}$$

$$= \cot\left(\frac{\alpha}{2}\right)\left(\sin\alpha - i\left(\cos^2\left(\frac{\alpha}{2}\right) - \sin^2\left(\frac{\alpha}{2}\right)\right)\right)$$

$$= \cot\left(\frac{\alpha}{2}\right)(\sin\alpha - i\cos\alpha)$$

$$z = \cot\left(\frac{\alpha}{2}\right)\left(\cos\left(\frac{3\pi}{2} + \alpha\right) + i\sin\left(\frac{3\pi}{2} + \alpha\right)\right)$$

Since cos is positive and sin is negative in the 4th quadrant

$$|z| = \cot\left(\frac{\alpha}{2}\right) \text{ and amp } z = \frac{3\pi}{2} + \alpha$$

16. *Express the following in exponential form*

(i) $-1 + i$ (ii) $\frac{1 - i}{1 + i}$ (iii) $-\frac{\sqrt{3}}{2} - \frac{1}{2}i$ (iv) $\frac{(1 + i)(1 + 2i)}{1 + 3i}$

➡ (i) Let $z = -1 + i$

$$r = \sqrt{(-1)^2 + 1^2} = \sqrt{2}$$

$$\alpha = \tan^{-1}\left|\frac{1}{-1}\right| = \tan^{-1} 1 = \frac{\pi}{4}$$

Here $z = -1 + i = (-1, 1)$ is in the second quadrant.

Therefore, $\theta = \text{amp } z = \pi - \alpha = \pi - \frac{\pi}{4} = \frac{3\pi}{4}$

Hence, exponential form of a given complex number is

$$z = re^{i\theta} = \sqrt{2}e^{\frac{\pi}{4}i}$$

(ii) Let $z = \frac{1 - i}{1 + i} \times \frac{1 - i}{1 - i} = \frac{(1 - i)^2}{1^2 - i^2} = \frac{1^2 + i^2 - 2i}{2} = \frac{1 - 1 - 2i}{2} = -i$

$$r = |z| = \sqrt{0^2 + (-1)^2} = 1$$

$$\alpha = \tan^{-1}\left|\frac{-1}{0}\right| = \tan^{-1}(\infty) = \frac{\pi}{2}$$

Here $z = -i = (0, -1)$ is on negative y-axis

Therefore, $\theta = \text{amp } z = \pi + \frac{\pi}{2} = \frac{3\pi}{2}$

Hence, exponential form of a given complex number is

$$z = re^{i\theta} = 1 \cdot e^{i\frac{3\pi}{2}} = e^{\frac{3\pi}{2}i}$$

(iii) Let $z = -\frac{\sqrt{3}}{2} - \frac{1}{2}i$

$$r = |z| = \sqrt{\frac{3}{4} + \frac{1}{4}} = 1$$

$$\alpha = \tan^{-1}\left|\frac{-(1/2)}{-\left(\sqrt{3}/2\right)}\right| = \tan^{-1}\left(\frac{1}{\sqrt{3}}\right) = \frac{\pi}{6}$$

Here, $z = -\frac{\sqrt{3}}{2} - \frac{1}{2}\, i$ is in the third quadrant

Therefore, $\theta = \text{amp } z = \pi + \alpha = \pi + \frac{\pi}{6} = \frac{13\pi}{6}$

Hence, exponential form of a given complex number is

$$z = re^{i\theta} = 1 \cdot e^{i\frac{13\pi}{6}} = e^{\frac{13\pi}{6}i}$$

(iv) Let

$$z = \frac{(1+i)\,(1+2i)}{1+3i} = \frac{1+i+2i+2i^2}{1+3i} = \frac{1+3i-2}{1+3i}$$

$$= \frac{-1+3i}{1+3i} \times \frac{1-3i}{1-3i} = \frac{-1+3i+3i-9i^2}{1-9i^2} = \frac{6i+8}{10}$$

$$z = \frac{4}{5} + \frac{3}{5}i$$

$$r = \sqrt{\frac{16}{25} + \frac{9}{25}} = 1$$

$$\alpha = \tan^{-1}\left|\frac{3/5}{4/5}\right| = \tan^{-1}\left(\frac{3}{4}\right)$$

$$\theta = \alpha = \tan^{-1}\left(\frac{3}{4}\right)$$

Hence, exponential form of a given complex number is

$$z = re^{i\theta} = 1.e^{i\tan^{-1}\left(\frac{3}{4}\right)} = e^{i\tan^{-1}\left(\frac{3}{4}\right)}$$

17. *Prove that* $\dfrac{1+\cos\theta + i\sin\theta}{1-\cos\theta - i\sin\theta} = i\cot\left(\dfrac{\theta}{2}\right)$

➡

$$\begin{aligned}\frac{1+\cos\theta + i\sin\theta}{1-\cos\theta - i\ \sin\theta} &= \frac{2\cos^2\left(\frac{\theta}{2}\right) + i2\sin\left(\frac{\theta}{2}\right)\cos\left(\frac{\theta}{2}\right)}{2\sin^2\left(\frac{\theta}{2}\right) - i2\sin\left(\frac{\theta}{2}\right)\cos\left(\frac{\theta}{2}\right)} \\ &= \frac{2\cos^2\left(\frac{\theta}{2}\right) + 2i\sin\left(\frac{\theta}{2}\right)\cos\left(\frac{\theta}{2}\right)}{2\left(-i^2\right)\sin^2\left(\frac{\theta}{2}\right) - 2i\sin\left(\frac{\theta}{2}\right)\cos\left(\frac{\theta}{2}\right)} \\ &= \frac{2\cos\left(\frac{\theta}{2}\right)\left(\cos\left(\frac{\theta}{2}\right) + i\sin\left(\frac{\theta}{2}\right)\right)}{-2i\sin\left(\frac{\theta}{2}\right)\left(\cos\left(\frac{\theta}{2}\right) + i\sin\left(\frac{\theta}{2}\right)\right)} \\ &= -\frac{1}{i}\cot\left(\frac{\theta}{2}\right) = i\cot\left(\frac{\theta}{2}\right)\end{aligned}$$

Therefore, $\dfrac{1+\cos\theta + i\sin\theta}{1-\cos\theta - i\sin\theta} = i\cot\left(\dfrac{\theta}{2}\right)$.

18. *Express the following in the form of* $x + iy$

(i) $\log i$ (ii) $\log(\log i)$

➡ (i) Since $i = \cos\dfrac{\pi}{2} + i\sin\dfrac{\pi}{2} = e^{i\frac{\pi}{2}}$

Therefore, $\log i = \log e^{i\frac{\pi}{2}} = i\frac{\pi}{2}\log_e e$

$$\log i = i\frac{\pi}{2} \tag{1}$$

(ii) From equation (1), we have

$$\log i = i\frac{\pi}{2}$$

Therefore, $\log(\log i) = \log\left(i\frac{\pi}{2}\right) = \log i + \log\frac{\pi}{2} = i\frac{\pi}{2} + \log\frac{\pi}{2}$

$$\log(\log i) = \log\frac{\pi}{2} + i\frac{\pi}{2}$$

19. If z_1 and z_2 are two complex numbers, then show that $|z_1 + z_2|^2 + |z_1 - z_2|^2 = 2\{|z_1|^2 + |z_2|^2\}$
➡ Let $z_1 = x_1 + iy_1$ and $z_2 = x_2 + iy_2$

$$\Rightarrow |z_1| = \sqrt{x_1^2 + y_1^2} \quad \text{and} \quad |z_2| = \sqrt{x_2^2 + y_2^2}$$

$$z_1 + z_2 = x_1 + x_2 + i(y_1 + y_2)$$

$$|z_1 + z_2| = \sqrt{(x_1 + x_2)^2 + (y_1 + y_2)^2}$$

$$|z_1 + z_2|^2 = (x_1 + x_2)^2 + (y_1 + y_2)^2$$

$$= x_1^2 + x_2^2 + 2x_1x_2 + y_1^2 + y_2^2 + 2y_2y_2$$

$$= x_1^2 + y_1^2 + x_2^2 + y_2^2 + 2x_1x_2 + 2y_1y_2$$

$$|z_1 + z_2|^2 = |z_1|^2 + |z_2|^2 + 2x_1x_2 + 2y_1y_2 \tag{1}$$

and $\quad z_1 - z_2 = x_1 - x_2 + i(y_1 - y_2)$

$$|z_1 - z_2|^2 = (x_1 - x_2)^2 + (y_1 - y_2)^2$$

$$= x_1^2 + x_2^2 - 2x_1x_2 + y_1^2 + y_2^2 - 2y_1y_2$$

$$= x_1^2 + y_1^2 + x_2^2 + y_2^2 - 2x_1x_2 - 2y_1y_2$$

$$|z_1 - z_2|^2 = |z_1|^2 + |z_2|^2 - 2x_1x_2 - 2y_1y_2 \tag{2}$$

Adding equations (1) and (2), we get

$$|z_1 + z_2|^2 + |z_1 - z_2|^2 = 2|z_1|^2 + 2|z_2|^2$$

20. Show that the sum and product of a complex number and its conjugate are both real.
➡ Let $z = x + iy$ be any complex number and it conjugate be $\bar{z} = x - iy$

$$\text{Sum} = z + \bar{z} = x + iy + x - iy = 2x = \text{Real}$$

$$\text{Product} = z \cdot \bar{z} = (x + iy)(x - iy) = x^2 - i^2y^2 = x^2 + y^2 = \text{Real}$$

Exercises

I. *Express the following numbers in the form $x + iy$*

(1) $\dfrac{1}{4+3i}$ (2) $\dfrac{1}{(2+i)^2} - \dfrac{1}{(2-i)^2}$

(3) $\dfrac{1}{1-\cos\theta + 2i\sin\theta}$ (4) $\dfrac{1+i}{1-i} - \dfrac{1-i}{1+i}$

(5) $\dfrac{2+5i}{3-2i} + \dfrac{2-5i}{3+2i}$ (6) $\dfrac{(1-i)^3}{1-i^3}$

(7) $\dfrac{1+i}{1-i}$ (8) $\dfrac{\sqrt{3}+i}{\sqrt{3}-i}$

II. *Find the conjugate of the complex number.*

(1) $\dfrac{(3-2i)\,(2+3i)}{(1+2i)\,(2-i)}$ (2) $\dfrac{(1+i)^2}{3-i}$

(3) $\dfrac{(2-3i)\,(2+i)^2}{1+i}$ (4) $\dfrac{2+5i}{3-2i} + \dfrac{2-5i}{3+2i}$

(5) $\dfrac{3-i}{2+i} + \dfrac{3+i}{2-i}$ (6) $\dfrac{3}{1+i} - \dfrac{2}{2-i} + \dfrac{2}{1-i}$

(7) $\dfrac{1+i}{1-i}$ (8) $\dfrac{\sqrt{5+12i}+\sqrt{5-12i}}{\sqrt{5+12i}-\sqrt{5-12i}}$

III. (1) *If* $(1-i)\,x + (1+i)\,y = 1$, *then find real values of* x *and* y

(2) *If* $(x+iy)\,(i-4) = 8+15i$, *then find real values of* x *and* y

(3) *If* $\dfrac{(1+i)\,(x-2i)}{3+i} + \dfrac{(2-3i)\,y+i}{3-i} = i$, *then find real values of* x *and* y

(4) *If* $z^2 = -4-3i$ *Find* z *(or find the value of* $\sqrt{-4-3i}$*)*

(5) *Find the real value of* θ *for which* $\dfrac{1+i\cos\theta}{1-2i\cos\theta}$ *is a real number.*

(6) *Find* z *if* $(x+iy)\,(2-3i)\,, = 4+i$ *where* $z = x+iy$

(7) *Evaluate* $\left(i^{19} + \dfrac{1}{i^{25}}\right)^2$

(8) *Evaluate* $\left(i^{17} - \dfrac{1}{i^{34}}\right)^3$

(9) *Find* $\sqrt{7-24i}$

(10) *Find the square root of 8–15i*

(11) *If* $z^2 + 5 = 12\sqrt{-1}$ *find the complex number z*

(12) *Find all complex numbers satisfying* $\overline{z} = z^2$

(13) *Find the number of solutions to the equation* $z^2 + \overline{z} = 0$

(14) *If* $\left(\frac{1-i}{1+i}\right)^{100} = a + ib$ *then find a and b*

(15) *Prove that* $\left(\frac{3}{2} + \frac{i\sqrt{3}}{2}\right)^{50} = 3^{25}\left(\frac{1}{2} - i\frac{\sqrt{3}}{2}\right)$

IV. *Express the following complex numbers in polar form and hence find their modulus and amplitude.*

(1) $\frac{1-i}{1+i}$ (2) 2i

(3) -12 (4) $\frac{(2+i)^2}{3i}$

(5) $\left(\frac{2+i}{3-i}\right)^2$ (6) $\left(\frac{1+i}{1-i}\right)^3 - \left(\frac{1-i}{1+i}\right)^3$

(7) $-i\sqrt{2} - \sqrt{2}$ (8) $\frac{1+i}{2-(1-i)^2}$

(9) $\frac{z(z+2i)}{z+4i}$ *where* $z = 1 + i$

(10) $\frac{i + i^2 - i^3 + i^4 + 2}{i^5 + i^6 + 2}$ (11) $4 - 4i\sqrt{3}$

Answers

I. (1) $\frac{4}{25} + \left(\frac{-3}{25}\right)i$ (2) $\frac{17}{2} - \frac{15}{2}i$

(3) $\frac{1}{(5+3\cos\theta)} - i\frac{2\cot\left(\frac{\theta}{2}\right)}{(5+3\cos\theta)}$ (4) $0 + 2i$

(5) $-\frac{8}{13} + i0$ (6) $-2 + i.0$

(7) $0 + i$ (8) $\frac{1}{2} + \left(\frac{\sqrt{3}}{2}\right)i$

II. (1) $\frac{63}{25}+i\frac{16}{25}$ (2) $-\frac{1}{5}-\frac{3}{5}i$

(3) $\frac{17}{2}+\frac{15i}{2}$ (4) $-\frac{8}{13}-i.0$

(5) 2 (6) $\frac{17}{10}+i\frac{9}{10}$

(7) $-i$ (8) $\frac{3}{2}i$

III. (1) $x=\frac{1}{2},\ y=\frac{1}{2}$ (2) $x=-1,\ y=-4$

(3) $x=3,\ y=-1$ (4) $\frac{1}{\sqrt{2}}-\frac{3}{\sqrt{2}}i,-\frac{1}{\sqrt{2}}+\frac{3}{\sqrt{2}}i$

(5) $\frac{\pi}{2}$ (6) $\frac{5}{13}+\frac{14}{13}i$

(7) -4 (8) $-2(1-i)$

(9) $\pm 4-3i$ (10) $\pm\frac{1}{\sqrt{2}}(5-3i)$

(11) $\pm(2+3i)$ (12) $0,1,\frac{-1}{2}+\frac{\sqrt{3}}{2}i,-\frac{1}{2}-\frac{\sqrt{3}}{2}i$

(13) 4 (14) $a=1,\ b=0$

IV. (1) $1,-\frac{\pi}{2}$ (2) $2,\frac{\pi}{2}$

(3) $12,\ \pi$ (4) $\frac{5}{3},\tan^{-1}\left(-\frac{3}{4}\right)$

(5) $\frac{1}{2},\frac{\pi}{2}$ (6) $2,-\frac{\pi}{2}$

(7) $2,\frac{-3\pi}{4}$ (8) $\frac{1}{2},0$

(9) $\sqrt{\frac{10}{13}},\tan^{-1}\frac{7}{9}$ (10) 2, 0

(11) $8,\frac{-\pi}{3}$

1.5 De Moivre's Theorem

If n is any integer, then $(\cos\theta + i\sin\theta)^n = \cos n\theta + i\sin n\theta$ and if n is a rational number say p/q, then $(\cos\theta + i\sin\theta)^{p/q}$ has q values and one of its values is $\cos\left(\frac{p\theta}{q}\right) + i\sin\left(\frac{p\theta}{q}\right)$

Proof

Case (1) Let n be a positive integer.

In this case we will prove the result by mathematical induction.

If $n = 1$ then $(\cos\theta + i\sin\theta)^1 = \cos 1\cdot\theta + i\sin 1\cdot\theta = \cos\theta + i\sin\theta$

Therefore, the result is true for $n = 1$

Let us assume that the result is true for $n = m$.

$$\text{ie., } (\cos\theta + i\sin\theta)^m = \cos m\theta + i\sin m\theta \tag{1}$$

Multiplying both sides of (1) by $\cos\theta + i\sin\theta$, we get

$$\begin{aligned}(\cos\theta + i\sin\theta)^{m+1} &= (\cos m\theta + i\sin m\theta)(\cos\theta + i\sin\theta)\\ &= (\cos m\theta\cos\theta - \sin m\theta\sin\theta) + i(\sin m\theta\cos\theta + \cos m\theta\sin\theta)\\ &= \cos(m\theta + \theta) + i\sin(m\theta + \theta)\\ &= \cos(m+1)\theta + i\sin(m+1)\theta\end{aligned}$$

Therefore, the result is true for $n = m + 1$

Hence, the result is true for all the value of n

Case (2) Let n be a negative integer i.e., $n = -m$ where m is a positive integer. Consider

$$\begin{aligned}(\cos\theta + i\sin\theta)^n &= (\cos\theta + i\sin\theta)^{-m}\\ &= \frac{1}{(\cos\theta + i\sin\theta)^m} = \frac{1}{\cos m\theta + i\sin m\theta} \quad \text{(from case (1))}\\ &= \frac{\cos m\theta - i\sin m\theta}{(\cos m\theta + i\sin m\theta)(\cos m\theta - i\sin m\theta)}\end{aligned}$$

$$= \frac{\cos m\theta - i \sin m\theta}{\cos^2 m\theta + \sin^2 m\theta}$$
$$= \cos m\theta - i \sin m\theta$$
$$= \cos(-m)\theta + i \sin(-m)\theta$$
$$= \cos n\theta + i \sin n\theta$$

Case (3) Let n be a rational number i.e., $n = \frac{P}{q}$, where p and q are integers and $q \neq 0$

Let $z = \cos\left(\frac{p}{q}\theta\right) + i \sin\left(\frac{p}{q}\theta\right)$

Therefore,

$$z^q = \left[\cos\left(\frac{p}{q}\theta\right) + i \sin\left(\frac{p}{q}\theta\right)\right]^q$$
$$= \cos q.\left(\frac{p}{q}\theta\right) + i \sin q\left(\frac{p}{q}\theta\right)$$
$$= \cos p\theta + i \sin p\theta$$
$$= (\cos\theta + i \sin\theta)^p \quad \text{(From case (1) and (2))}$$
$$z^q = (\cos\theta + i \sin\theta)^P$$

Taking q^{th} root on both sides we get q values of z and one of these q values is equal to $(\cos\theta + i \sin\theta)^{\frac{P}{q}}$

Therefore, $z = (\cos\theta + i \sin\theta)^{\frac{P}{q}}$

$$\text{i.e., } \cos\left(\frac{P}{q}\theta\right) + i \sin\left(\frac{P}{q}\theta\right) = (\cos\theta + i \sin\theta)^{\frac{P}{q}}$$

Hence, $(\cos\theta + i \sin\theta)^n = \cos n\theta + i \sin n\theta$ is true for all the values of n

i.e., $(\cos\theta + i \sin\theta)^n = \cos n\theta + i \sin n\theta$.

Note

(1) By replacing $-\theta$ in (1), we get

$$(\cos\theta - i\sin\theta)^n = \cos n\theta - i\sin n\theta$$

(2) $\cos\theta + i\sin\theta = \text{cis}\ \theta$

(3) $\cos\theta - i\sin\theta = \text{cis}\ (-\theta)$

(4) $(\text{cis}\ \theta)^n = \text{cis}\ n\theta$

Prove the following (i) $\text{cis}\ \alpha \text{cis}\ \beta = \text{cis}\ (\alpha+\beta)$ (ii) $\frac{\text{cis}\ \alpha}{\text{cis}\ \beta} = \text{cis}\ (\alpha-\beta)$

Proof

(i)

$$\begin{aligned}\text{cis}\ \alpha \text{cis}\ \beta &= (\cos\alpha + i\sin\alpha)(\cos\beta + i\sin\beta)\\ &= \cos\alpha\cos\beta + i\sin\alpha\cos\beta + i\cos\alpha\sin\beta + i^2\sin\alpha\sin\beta\\ &= \cos\alpha\cos\beta - \sin\alpha\sin\beta + i(\sin\alpha\cos\beta + \cos\alpha\sin\beta)\\ &= \cos(\alpha+\beta) + i\sin(\alpha+\beta)\\ \text{cis}\ \alpha \text{cis}\ \beta &= \text{cis}\ (\alpha+\beta)\end{aligned}$$

(ii)

$$\begin{aligned}\frac{\text{cis}\alpha}{\text{cis}\beta} &= \frac{\cos\alpha + i\sin\alpha}{\cos\beta + i\sin\beta} \times \frac{\cos\beta - i\sin\beta}{\cos\beta - i\sin\beta}\\ &= \frac{\cos\alpha\cos\beta + i\sin\alpha\cos\beta - i\cos\alpha\sin\beta - i^2\sin\alpha\sin\beta}{\cos^2\beta - i^2\sin^2\beta}\\ &= \frac{\cos\alpha\cos\beta + \sin\alpha\sin\beta + i[\sin\alpha\cos\beta - \cos\alpha\sin\beta]}{\cos^2\beta + \sin^2\beta}\\ &= \cos(\alpha-\beta) + i\sin(\alpha-\beta)\\ \frac{\text{cis}\alpha}{\text{cis}\beta} &= \text{cis}\ (\alpha-\beta)\end{aligned}$$

Similarly $\text{cis}\ \alpha_1 \cdot \text{cis}\ \alpha_2 \cdot \text{cis}\ \alpha_3 \ldots \text{cis}\ \alpha_n = \text{cis}\ (\alpha_1 + \alpha_2 + \alpha_3 \ldots \alpha_n)$

Worked Examples

1. *Simplify* $\dfrac{(\cos 6\theta - i\sin 6\theta)^3\,(\cos 2\theta + i\sin + i\sin 2\theta)^7}{(\cos 4\theta - i\sin)^3}$

➡

$$\frac{(\cos 6\theta - i\sin 6\theta)^3\,(\cos 2\theta + i\sin 2\theta)^7}{(\cos 4\theta - i\sin 4\theta)^3} = \frac{(\text{cis}\,(-6\theta))^3\,(\text{cis}2\theta)^7}{[\text{cis}\,(-4\theta)]^3}$$

$$= \frac{(\text{cis}\,\theta)^{-6\times 3} \times (\text{cis}\,\theta)^{2\times 7}}{(\text{cis}\,\theta)^{-4\times 3}} = (\text{cis}\,\theta)^{-18+14+12}$$

$$= (\text{cis}\,\theta)^8 = \text{cis}\,8\theta = \cos 8\theta + i\sin 8\theta$$

2. *Simplify* $\left[\dfrac{(\cos 3\theta + i\sin 3\theta)^4(\cos 4\theta - i\sin 4\theta)^5}{(\cos 4\theta + i\sin 4\theta)^3(\cos 5\theta + i\sin 5\theta)^{-4}}\right]$

➡

$$\left[\frac{(\cos 3\theta + i\sin 3\theta)^4(\cos 4\theta - i\sin 4\theta)^5}{(\cos 4\theta + i\sin 4\theta)^3(\cos 5\theta + i\sin 5\theta)^{-4}}\right] = \frac{(\text{cis}\,3\theta)^4[\text{cis}(-4\theta)]^5}{(\text{cis}\,4\theta)^3(\text{cis}\,5\theta)^{-4}}$$

$$= \frac{(\text{cis}\,\theta)^{3\times 4}(\text{cis}\,\theta)^{-4\times 5}}{(\text{cis}\,\theta)^{4\times 3}(\text{cis}\,\theta)^{5x-4}}$$

$$= (\text{cis}\,\theta)^{12-20-12+20}$$

$$= (\text{cis}\,\theta)^0$$

$$= 1$$

3. *Prove that* $\left(\dfrac{\cos\theta + i\sin\theta}{\sin\theta + i\cos\theta}\right)^4 = \cos 8\theta + i\sin 8\theta$

➡

$$\left(\frac{\cos\theta + i\sin\theta}{\sin\theta + i\cos\theta}\right)^4 = \frac{(\cos\theta + i\sin\theta)^4}{\left[\cos\left(\frac{\pi}{2} - \theta\right) + i\sin\left(\frac{\pi}{2} - \theta\right)\right]^4}$$

$$= \frac{(\cos\theta + i\sin\theta)^4}{\cos 4\left(\frac{\pi}{2} - \theta\right) + i\sin 4\left(\frac{\pi}{2} - \theta\right)}$$

$$= \frac{(\cos\theta + i\sin\theta)^4}{\cos(2\pi - 4\theta) + i\sin(2\pi - 4\theta)}$$

$$= \frac{(\cos\theta + i\sin\theta)^4}{\cos 4\theta - i\sin 4\theta} = \frac{(\text{cis }\theta)^4}{\text{cis}(-4\theta)} = \frac{(\text{cis }\theta)^4}{(\text{cis }\theta)^{-4}}$$

$$= (\text{cis }\theta)^8 = \text{cis } 8\theta = \cos 8\theta + i\sin 8\theta$$

4. *Prove that* $(-1+i\sqrt{3})^{3n} + (-1-i\sqrt{3})^{3n} = 2^{3n+1}$, *where n is an integer.*

➡ $-1+i\sqrt{3} = (-1, \sqrt{3})$

$$r = \sqrt{(-1)^2 + (\sqrt{3})^2} = 2$$

$$\alpha = \tan^{-1}\left|\frac{\sqrt{3}}{-1}\right| = \tan^{-1}\sqrt{3} = \frac{\pi}{3}$$

Here $(-1, \sqrt{3})$ is in 2nd quadrant

$$\theta = \pi - \alpha = \pi - \frac{\pi}{3} = \frac{2\pi}{3}$$

Therefore, $-1+i\sqrt{3} = 2\left(\cos\left(\frac{2\pi}{3}\right) + i\sin\left(\frac{2\pi}{3}\right)\right)$

$$(-1+i\sqrt{3})^{3n} = \left[2\left(\cos\frac{2\pi}{3} + i\sin\frac{2\pi}{3}\right)\right]^{3n}$$

$$= 2^{3n}\left[\cos 2n\pi + i\sin 2n\pi\right] \quad (1)$$

Similarly $-1-i\sqrt{3} = 2\left(\cos\frac{2\pi}{3} - i\sin\frac{2\pi}{3}\right)$

$$\Rightarrow (-1-i\sqrt{3})^{3n} = 2^{3n}\left[\cos 2n\pi - i\sin 2n\pi\right] \quad (2)$$

Adding equations (1) and (2), we get

$$(-1+i\sqrt{3})^{3n} + (-1-i\sqrt{3})^{3n} = 2.2^{3n}\cos 2n\pi$$

$$= 2^{3n+1} \qquad \because \cos 2n\pi = (-1)^{2n} = 1$$

5. *If n is a positive integer, prove that* $(\sqrt{3}+i)^n + (\sqrt{3}-i)^n = 2^{n+1}\cos\left(\frac{n\pi}{6}\right)$

➡

$$\sqrt{3}+i = (\sqrt{3}, 1)$$

$$r = \sqrt{(\sqrt{3})^2 + 1^2} = \sqrt{3+1} = 2$$

$$\alpha = \tan^{-1}\left|\frac{1}{\sqrt{3}}\right| = \tan^{-1}\left(\frac{1}{\sqrt{3}}\right) = \frac{\pi}{6}$$

Here $(\sqrt{3}, 1)$ is in 1st quadrant

$$\theta = \alpha = \frac{\pi}{6}$$

Therefore,

$$\sqrt{3}+i = r(\cos\theta + i\sin\theta) = 2\left(\cos\left(\frac{\pi}{6}\right) + i\sin\left(\frac{\pi}{6}\right)\right)$$

$$(\sqrt{3}+i)^n = 2^n\left(\cos\left(\frac{\pi}{6}\right) + i\sin\left(\frac{\pi}{6}\right)\right)^n$$

$$= 2^n\left(\cos\left(\frac{n\pi}{6}\right) + i\sin\left(\frac{n\pi}{6}\right)\right) \quad (1)$$

Similarly

$$(\sqrt{3}-i)^n = 2^n\left(\cos\left(\frac{n\pi}{6}\right) - i\sin\left(\frac{n\pi}{6}\right)\right) \quad (2)$$

Adding equations (1) and (2), we get

$$(\sqrt{3}+i)^n + (\sqrt{3}-i)^n = 2^n\left[\cos\left(\frac{n\pi}{6}\right) + i\sin\left(\frac{n\pi}{6}\right) + \cos\left(\frac{n\pi}{6}\right) - i\sin\left(\frac{n\pi}{6}\right)\right]$$

$$= 2^n\left[2\cos\left(\frac{n\pi}{6}\right)\right] = 2^{n+1}\cos\left(\frac{n\pi}{6}\right)$$

6. *If α and β are the roots of the equation $x^2 - 2x + 4 = 0$, then prove that $\alpha^n + \beta^n = 2^{n+1} \cos \dfrac{n\pi}{3}$*

➡ $x^2 - 2x + 4 = 0$

$$x = \frac{2 \pm \sqrt{4 - 4\,(1)\;(4)}}{2\,(1)} = \frac{2 \pm \sqrt{-12}}{2} = \frac{2 \pm 2i\sqrt{3}}{2} = 1 \pm i\sqrt{3} = \alpha, \beta$$

Therefore, $\alpha = 1 + i\sqrt{3}, \beta = 1 - i\sqrt{3}$

$$1 + i\sqrt{3} = (1, \sqrt{3})$$

$$r = \sqrt{1^2 + (\sqrt{3})^2} = 2$$

$$\alpha = \tan^{-1}\left|\frac{\sqrt{3}}{-1}\right| = \tan^{-1}\sqrt{3} = \frac{\pi}{3}$$

Here $(1, \sqrt{3})$ is in first quadrant

$$\theta = \alpha_1 = \frac{\pi}{3}$$

$$\alpha = 1 + i\sqrt{3} = 2\left(\cos\frac{\pi}{3} + i\sin\frac{\pi}{3}\right)$$

$$\alpha^n = \left(1 + i\sqrt{3}\right)^n = 2^n\left(\cos\frac{\pi}{3} + i\sin\frac{\pi}{3}\right)^n$$

$$\alpha^n = 2^n\left(\cos\frac{n\pi}{3} + i\sin\frac{n\pi}{3}\right) \tag{1}$$

Similarly

$$\beta = 1 - i\sqrt{3} = 2\left(\cos\frac{\pi}{3} - i\sin\frac{\pi}{3}\right)$$

$$\therefore\ \beta^n = \left(1 - i\sqrt{3}\right)^n = 2^n\left(\cos\frac{\pi}{3} - i\sin\frac{\pi}{3}\right)^n$$

$$\beta^n = 2^n\left(\cos\frac{n\pi}{3} - i\sin\frac{n\pi}{3}\right) \tag{2}$$

Adding equations (1) and (2), we get

$$\alpha^n + \beta^n = 2.2^n\cos\frac{n\pi}{3} = 2^{n+1}\cos\frac{n\pi}{3}$$

7. *Prove that*

$$(1+\cos\theta+i\sin\theta)^n+(1+\cos\theta-i\sin\theta)^n=2^{n+1}\cos\frac{n\theta}{2}\cos\frac{n\theta}{2}$$

➡

$$\begin{aligned}
&(1+\cos\theta+i\sin\theta)^n+(1+\cos\theta-i\sin\theta)^n\\
&=\left[2\cos^2\frac{\theta}{2}+2i\sin\frac{\theta}{2}\cos\frac{\theta}{2}\right]^n+\left[\cos^2\left(\frac{\theta}{2}\right)-2i\sin\frac{\theta}{2}\cos\frac{\theta}{2}\right]^n\\
&=2^n\cos^n\frac{\theta}{2}\left[\cos\frac{\theta}{2}+i\sin\frac{\theta}{2}\right]^n+2^n\cos^n\frac{\theta}{2}\left[\cos\frac{\theta}{2}-i\sin\frac{\theta}{2}\right]^n\\
&=2^n\cos^n\frac{\theta}{2}\left[\cos\frac{n\theta}{2}+i\sin\frac{n\theta}{2}\right]+2^n\cos^n\frac{\theta}{2}\left[\cos\frac{n\theta}{2}-i\sin\frac{n\theta}{2}\right]\\
&=2^n\cos^n\frac{\theta}{2}\left[\cos\frac{n\theta}{2}+i\sin\frac{n\theta}{2}+\cos\frac{n\theta}{2}-i\sin\frac{n\theta}{2}\right]\\
&=2^n\cos^n\left(\frac{\theta}{2}\right)\left[2\cos\left(\frac{n\theta}{2}\right)\right]\\
&=2^{n+1}\cos^n\frac{\theta}{2}\cos\left(\frac{n\theta}{2}\right)
\end{aligned}$$

8. *Show that* $(a+ib)^n+(a-ib)^n=2\left(a^2+b^2\right)^{\frac{n}{2}}\cos\left(n\tan^{-1}\left(\frac{b}{a}\right)\right)$

➡ If $a=r\cos\theta$ and $b=r\sin\theta$ then

$$a^2+b^2=r^2\Rightarrow r=\left(a^2+b^2\right)^{\frac{1}{2}}$$

and

$$\frac{b}{a}=\tan\theta\Rightarrow\theta=\tan^{-1}\left(\frac{b}{a}\right)$$

Therefore, $(a+ib)=r(\cos\theta+i\sin\theta)$

$$(a+ib)^n=r^n(\cos n\theta+i\sin n\theta) \tag{1}$$

and

$$(a - ib)^n = r^n (\cos n\theta - i \sin n\theta)$$
$$(a - ib) = r (\cos\theta - i \sin\theta) \quad (2)$$

Adding equations (1) and (2), we get

$$(a + ib)^n + (a - ib)^n = 2r^n \cos n\theta$$
$$(a + ib)^n + (a - ib)^n = 2\left(a^2 + b^2\right)^{\frac{n}{2}} \cos\left(n \tan^{-1}\left(\frac{b}{a}\right)\right)$$

9. *If* $x + \frac{1}{x} = 2\cos\alpha,\ y + \frac{1}{y} = 2\cos\beta$ *and* $z + \frac{1}{z} = 2\cos\gamma$, *then prove the following*

(i) $x^n + \dfrac{1}{x^n} = 2\cos n\alpha$ (ii) $x^n - \dfrac{1}{x^n} = 2i \sin n\alpha$

(iii) $\dfrac{(x^n)}{(y^m)} + \dfrac{(y^m)}{(x^n)} = 2\cos(n\alpha - m\beta)$

(iv) $\dfrac{(x^n y^m)}{z^l} + \dfrac{z^l}{x^n y^m} = 2\cos(n\alpha + m\beta - lx)$

➡

$$x + \frac{1}{x} = 2\cos\alpha$$
$$x^2 - 2x\cos\alpha + 1 = 0$$
$$x = \frac{2\cos\alpha \pm \sqrt{4\cos^2\alpha - 4(1)(1)}}{2(1)}$$
$$= \frac{2\cos^2\alpha \pm \sqrt{4\left(\cos^2\alpha - 1\right)}}{2} = \frac{2\cos^2\alpha \pm 2\sqrt{-\sin^2\alpha}}{2}$$
$$x = \cos\alpha \pm i \sin\alpha$$

Let $x = \cos\alpha + i \sin\alpha = \text{cis}\,\alpha$
Similarly $y = \cos\beta + i \sin\beta = \text{cis}\,\beta,\ z = \cos\gamma + i \sin\gamma = \text{cis}\,\gamma$
(i)

$$x^n = (\text{cis}\,\alpha)^n = \text{cis}\,n\alpha = \cos n\alpha + i \sin n\alpha \quad (1)$$
$$\Rightarrow \frac{1}{x^n} = \cos n\alpha - i \sin n\alpha \quad (2)$$

Adding equations (1) and (2), we get

$$\therefore\ x^n + \frac{1}{x^n} = 2\cos n\alpha$$

(ii) Subtracting (2) from (1), we get

$$x^n - \frac{1}{x^n} = 2i\sin n\alpha$$

(iii) $x = \text{cis}\,\alpha \Rightarrow x^n = \text{cis}\,n\alpha$

$$y = \text{cis}\,\beta \Rightarrow y^m = \text{cis}\,m\beta$$

$$\begin{aligned}\frac{x^n}{y^m} + \frac{y^m}{x^n} &= \frac{\text{cis}\,n\alpha}{\text{cis}\,m\beta} + \frac{\text{cis}\,m\beta}{\text{cis}\,n\alpha}\\ &= \text{cis}\,(n\alpha - m\beta) + \frac{1}{\text{cis}\,(n\alpha - m\beta)}\\ &= \cos(n\alpha - m\beta) + i\sin(n\alpha - m\beta) + \cos(n\alpha - m\beta) - i\sin(n\alpha - m\beta)\\ &= 2\cos(n\alpha - m\beta)\end{aligned}$$

(iv)

$$\begin{aligned}\frac{x^n y^m}{z^l} + \frac{z^l}{x^n y^m} &= \frac{\text{cis}\,n\alpha\text{cis}\,m\beta}{\text{cis}\,l\gamma} + \frac{\text{cis}\,l\gamma}{\text{cis}\,n\alpha\text{cis}\,m\beta}\\ &= \text{cis}\,(n\alpha + m\beta - l\gamma) + \frac{1}{\text{cis}\,(n\alpha + m\beta - l\gamma)}\\ &= \cos(n\alpha + m\beta - l\gamma) + i\sin(n\alpha + m\beta - l\gamma)\\ &\quad + \cos(n\alpha + m\beta - l\gamma) - i\sin(n\alpha + m\beta - l\gamma)\\ &= 2\cos(n\alpha + m\beta - l\gamma)\end{aligned}$$

10. *If* $\cos\alpha + \cos\beta + \cos\gamma = 0$ *and* $\sin\alpha + \sin\beta + \sin\gamma = 0$, *then prove the following*

(i) $\cos 3\alpha + \cos 3\beta + \cos 3\gamma = 3\cos(\alpha + \beta + \gamma)$

$\sin 3\alpha + \sin 3\beta + \sin 3\gamma = 3\sin(\alpha + \beta + \gamma)$

(ii) $\cos 2\alpha + \cos 2\gamma + \cos 2\gamma = 0$

$\sin 2\alpha + \sin 2\beta + \sin 2\gamma = 0$

(iii) $\cos(\alpha+\beta)+\cos(\beta+\gamma)+\cos(\gamma+\alpha)=0$

$\sin(\alpha+\beta)+\sin(\beta+\gamma)+\sin(\gamma+\alpha)=0$

(iv) $\cos^2\alpha+\cos^2\beta+\cos^2\gamma=\dfrac{3}{2}$

$\sin^2\alpha+\sin^2\beta+\sin^2\gamma=\dfrac{3}{2}$

➡ (i)

$$\cos\alpha+\cos\beta+\cos\gamma=0 \quad (1)$$

$$\sin\alpha+\sin\beta+\sin\gamma=0 \quad (2)$$

Take equation (1) + i (2), we get

$$(\cos\alpha+\cos\beta+\cos\gamma)+i(\sin\alpha+\sin\beta+\sin\gamma)=0$$

$$\text{cis }\alpha+\text{cis }\beta+\text{cis }\gamma=0$$

Put $x=\text{cis }\alpha$, $y=\text{cis }\beta$ and $z=\text{cis }\gamma$

$$\therefore\ x+y+z=0$$

$$\Rightarrow\ x^3+y^3+z^3=3xyz$$

i.e.,

$$(\text{cis }\alpha)^3+(\text{cis }\beta)^3+(\text{cis }\gamma)^3=3\text{cis }\alpha\text{cis }\beta\text{cis }\gamma$$

$$\text{cis }3\alpha+\text{cis }3\beta+\text{cis }3\gamma=3\text{cis }(\alpha+\beta+\gamma)$$

$$\cos 3\alpha+i\sin 3\alpha+\cos 3\beta+i\sin 3\beta+\cos 3\gamma+i\sin 3\gamma$$

$$=3(\cos(\alpha+\beta+\gamma)+i\sin(\alpha+\beta+\gamma))$$

$$(\cos 3\alpha+\cos 3\beta+\cos 3\gamma)+i(\sin 3\alpha+\sin 3\beta+\sin 3\gamma)$$

$$=3\cos(\alpha+\beta+\gamma)+3i\sin(\alpha+\beta+\gamma)$$

$$\Rightarrow\ \cos 3\alpha+\cos 3\beta+\cos 3\gamma=3\cos(\alpha+\beta+\gamma)$$

$$\sin 3\alpha+\sin 3\beta+\sin 3\gamma=3\sin(\alpha+\beta+\gamma)$$

(ii) Let $x=\text{cis }\alpha,\quad y=\text{cis }\beta,\quad z=\text{cis }\gamma$

$$\frac{1}{x}+\frac{1}{y}+\frac{1}{z}=\frac{1}{\text{cis }\alpha}+\frac{1}{\text{cis }\beta}+\frac{1}{\text{cis }\gamma}$$

$$= \text{cis }(-\alpha) + \text{cis }(-\beta) + \text{cis }(-\gamma)$$
$$= (\cos\alpha - i\sin\alpha) + (\cos\beta - i\sin\beta) + (\cos\gamma - i\sin\gamma)$$
$$= (\cos\alpha + \cos\beta + \cos\gamma) - i\,(\sin\alpha + \sin\beta + \sin\gamma)$$
$$= 0 + i0 = 0$$

$$\frac{1}{x} + \frac{1}{y} + \frac{1}{z} = 0 \qquad (3)$$

Since $x + y + z = 0$

$$\Rightarrow (x + y + z)^2 = 0$$
$$x^2 + y^2 + z^2 + 2xy + 2yz + 2zx = 0$$
$$x^2 + y^2 + z^2 + 2xyz\left(\frac{1}{z} + \frac{1}{x} + \frac{1}{y}\right) = 0$$
$$x^2 + y^2 + z^2 + 2xyz\,(0) = 0$$
$$(\text{cis }\alpha)^2 + (\text{cis }\beta)^2 + (\text{cis }\gamma)^2 = 0$$
$$\text{cis }2\alpha + \text{cis }2\beta + \text{cis }2\gamma = 0$$
$$(\cos 2\alpha + \cos 2\beta + \cos 2\gamma) + i\,(\sin 2\alpha + \sin 2\beta + \sin 2\gamma) = 0$$
$$\Rightarrow \cos 2\alpha + \cos 2\beta + \cos 2\gamma = 0$$
$$\sin 2\alpha + \sin 2\beta + \sin 2\gamma = 0$$

(iii) From equation (3), we have

$$\frac{1}{x} + \frac{1}{y} + \frac{1}{z} = 0$$
$$\frac{yz + zx + xy}{xyz} = 0$$
$$xy + yz + xz = 0$$
$$\text{cis }\alpha\text{cis }\beta + \text{cis }\beta\text{cis }\gamma + \text{cis }\alpha\text{cis }\gamma = 0$$
$$\text{cis }(\alpha + \beta) + \text{cis }(\beta + \gamma) + \text{cis }(\alpha + \gamma) = 0$$
$$\cos(\alpha + \beta) + \cos(\beta + \gamma) + \cos(\alpha + \gamma) + i\,(\sin(\alpha + \beta) + \sin(\beta + \gamma) + \sin(\alpha + \gamma)) = 0$$

$$\Rightarrow \cos(\alpha+\beta)+\cos(\beta+\gamma)+\cos(\alpha+\gamma)=0$$
$$\sin(\alpha+\beta)\sin(\beta+\gamma)+\sin(\alpha+\gamma)=0$$

(iv) From (ii), we have

$$\cos 2\alpha+\cos 2\beta+\cos 2\gamma=0$$
$$\left(2\cos^2\alpha-1\right)+\left(2\cos^2\beta-1\right)+\left(2\cos^2\gamma-1\right)=0$$
$$2\left(\cos^2\alpha+\cos^2\beta+\cos^2\gamma\right)-3=0$$
$$\cos^2\alpha+\cos^2\beta+\cos^2\gamma=3/2$$
$$(1-\sin^2\alpha)+(1-\sin^2\beta)+(1-\sin^2\gamma)=3/2$$
$$3-\left(\sin^2\alpha+\sin^2\beta+\sin^2\gamma\right)=3/2$$
$$3-\frac{3}{2}=\sin^2\alpha+\sin^2\beta+\sin^2\gamma$$

Therefore, $\sin^2\alpha+\sin^2\beta+\sin^2\gamma=\dfrac{3}{2}$.

11. *Prove that* $\left(\dfrac{1+\cos\theta+i\sin\theta}{1+\cos\theta-i\sin\theta}\right)^n=\cos n\theta+i\sin n\theta$

➡ Let $z=\cos\theta+i\sin\theta$ and $\frac{1}{z}=\cos\theta-i\sin\theta$
Therefore,

$$\left(\frac{1+\cos\theta+i\sin\theta}{1+\cos\theta-i\sin\theta}\right)^n=\left(\frac{1+z}{1+1/z}\right)^n=\left(\frac{1+z}{(z+1)/z}\right)^n=\left(\frac{1}{1/z}\right)^n=z^n$$
$$=(\cos\theta+i\sin\theta)^n=\cos n\theta+i\sin n\theta$$

12. *If n is a positive integer, then show that*
$$\left(\frac{1+\sin\theta+i\cos\theta}{1+\sin\theta-i\cos\theta}\right)^n=\cos n\left(\frac{\pi}{2}-\theta\right)+i\sin n\left(\frac{\pi}{2}-\theta\right)$$
➡
$$\left(\frac{1+\sin\theta+i\cos\theta}{1+\sin\theta-i\cos\theta}\right)=\left[\frac{1+\cos\left(\frac{\pi}{2}-\theta\right)+i\sin\left(\frac{\pi}{2}-\theta\right)}{1+\cos\left(\frac{\pi}{2}-\theta\right)-i\sin\left(\frac{\pi}{2}-\theta\right)}\right]^n \quad (1)$$

Let $z=\cos\left(\dfrac{\pi}{2}-\theta\right)+i\sin\left(\dfrac{\pi}{2}-\theta\right)$

Then $\frac{1}{z} = \cos\left(\frac{\pi}{2} - \theta\right) - i \sin\left(\frac{\pi}{2} - \theta\right)$

Therefore, equation (1) becomes,

$$\left(\frac{1 + \sin\theta + i\cos\theta}{1 + \sin\theta - i\cos\theta}\right) = \left(\frac{1+z}{1+\frac{1}{z}}\right)^n = \left(\frac{1+z}{(z+1)/z}\right)^n = \left(\frac{1}{1/z}\right)^n = z^n$$
$$= \left[\cos\left(\frac{\pi}{2} - \theta\right) + i\sin\left(\frac{\pi}{2} - \theta\right)\right]^n$$
$$= \left[\cos n\left(\frac{\pi}{2} - \theta\right) + i\sin n\left(\frac{\pi}{2} - \theta\right)\right]$$

13. *If* $a + ib = \frac{1}{\alpha + i\beta}$, *prove that* $(\alpha^2 + \beta^2)(a^2 + b^2) = 1$

➡

$$a + ib = \frac{1}{\alpha + i\beta}$$
$$|a + ib| = \frac{1}{|\alpha + i\beta|}$$
$$\sqrt{a^2 + b^2} = \frac{1}{\sqrt{\alpha^2 + \beta^2}}$$
$$a^2 + b^2 = \frac{1}{\alpha^2 + \beta^2}$$
$$(a^2 + b^2)(\alpha^2 + \beta^2) = 1$$

14. *If* $(a_1 + ib_1)(a_2 + ib_2)\cdots(a_n + ib_n) = A + iB$, *prove that*

(i) $(a_1^2 + b_1^2)(a_2^2 + b_2^2)\cdots(a_n^2 + b_n^2) = A^2 + B^2$

(ii) $\tan^{-1}\frac{b_1}{a_1} + \tan^{-1}\frac{b_2}{a_2} + \cdots + \tan^{-1}\frac{b_n}{a_n} = \tan^{-1}\frac{B}{A}$

➡ Let

$$a_1 + ib_1 = r_1 \text{cis}\,\theta_1 \Rightarrow r_1 = \sqrt{a_1^2 + b_1^2} \quad \text{and} \quad \theta_1 = \tan^{-1}\frac{b_1}{a_1}$$
$$a_2 + ib_2 = r_2 \text{cis}\,\theta_2 \Rightarrow r = \sqrt{a_2^2 + b_2^2} \quad \text{and} \quad \theta_2 = \tan^{-1}\frac{b_2}{a_2}$$

$$\vdots$$

$$a_n + ib_n = r_n \text{cis}\ \theta_\text{n} \Rightarrow r_n = \sqrt{a_n^2 + b_n^2} \quad \text{and} \quad \theta_n = \tan^{-1}\frac{b_n}{a_n}$$

and

$$A + iB = r \text{cis}\ \theta \Rightarrow r = \sqrt{A^2 + B^2} \quad \text{and} \quad \theta = \tan^{-1}\frac{B}{A}$$

Therefore,

$$\begin{aligned}
&(a_1 + ib_1)(a_2 + ib_2)\cdots(a_n + ib_n) = A + iB \\
&\Rightarrow r_1 \text{cis}\ \theta_2 r_2 \text{cis}\ \theta_2 \cdots r_n \text{cis}\ \theta_n = r \text{cis}\ \theta \\
&\Rightarrow r_1 r_2 \cdots r_n \text{cis}\ (\theta_1 + \theta_2 + \cdots + \theta_n) = r \text{cis}\ \theta \\
&\Rightarrow r = r_1 r_2 \cdots r_n \quad \text{and} \quad \theta = \theta_1 + \theta_2 + \cdots + \theta_n \\
&\Rightarrow \sqrt{A^2 + B^2} = \sqrt{a_1^2 + b_1^2}\sqrt{a_2^2 + b_2^2}\cdots\sqrt{a_n^2 + b_n^2} \\
&\Rightarrow A^2 + B^2 = \left(a_1^2 + b_1^2\right)\left(a_2^2 + b_2^2\right)\cdots\left(a_n^2 + b_n^2\right)
\end{aligned}$$

and $\theta_1 + \theta_2 + \cdots + \theta_n = \theta$

$$\tan^{-1}\frac{b_1}{a_1} + \tan^{-1}\frac{b^2}{a^2} + \cdots + \tan^{-1}\frac{b_n}{a_n} = \tan^{-1}\frac{B}{A}$$

15. *If* $x = \cos\theta + i\sin\theta$, *then* $\frac{x^{2n}-1}{x^{2n}+1} = i\tan n\theta$

➡ $x = \cos\theta + i\sin\theta$

$$\begin{aligned}
\frac{1}{x} &= \cos\theta - i\sin\theta \\
x^n &= \cos n\theta + i\sin n\theta \\
\frac{1}{x^n} &= \cos n\theta - i\sin n\theta \\
x^n + \frac{1}{x^n} &= 2\cos n\theta \\
x^n - \frac{1}{x^n} &= 2i\sin n\theta
\end{aligned}$$

Consider,

$$\frac{x+\frac{1}{x^n}}{x^n-\frac{1}{x^n}} = \frac{2i\sin n\theta}{2\cos n\theta}$$

$$\frac{\frac{x^{2n}+1}{x^n}}{\frac{x^{2n}-1}{x^n}} = i\tan n\theta$$

$$\frac{x^{2n}+1}{x^{2n}-1} = i\tan n\theta$$

16. *Prove that* $\cos^4\theta = \frac{1}{8}(\cos 4\theta + 4\cos 2\theta + 3)$

➡ Let $z = \cos\theta + i\sin\theta \Rightarrow \frac{1}{z} = \cos\theta - i\sin\theta$

$$z^n = \cos n\theta + i\sin n\theta \Rightarrow \frac{1}{z^n} = \cos n\theta - i\sin n\theta$$

$$z + \frac{1}{z} = 2\cos\theta \Rightarrow z^n + \frac{1}{z^n} = 2\cos n\theta$$

Therefore,

$$\begin{aligned}
\cos^4\theta &= \left[\frac{1}{2}\left(z+\frac{1}{z}\right)\right]^4 \\
&= \frac{1}{2^4}\left(z+\frac{1}{z}\right)^4 \\
&= \frac{1}{16}\left[z^4 + 4z^3\cdot\frac{1}{z} + 6z^2\cdot\frac{1}{z^2} + 4z\cdot\frac{1}{z^3} + \frac{1}{z^4}\right] \\
&= \frac{1}{16}\left[z^4 + \frac{1}{z^4} + 4\left(z^2+\frac{1}{z^2}\right) + 6\right] \\
&= \frac{1}{16}[2\cos 4\theta + 4\cdot 2\cos 2\theta + 6] \\
&= \frac{1}{8}(\cos 4\theta + 4\cos 2\theta + 3)
\end{aligned}$$

17. *Expand* $\cos^8\theta$ *in a series of cosines multiples of* θ

➡ Let

$$z = \cos\theta + i\sin\theta \Rightarrow \frac{1}{z} = \cos\theta - i\sin\theta$$

$$z^n = \cos n\theta + i\sin n\theta \quad \text{and} \quad \frac{1}{z^n} = \cos n\theta - i\sin n\theta$$

$$z^n + \frac{1}{z^n} = 2\cos n\theta \Rightarrow z + \frac{1}{z} = 2\cos\theta \Rightarrow \frac{1}{2}\left(z + \frac{1}{z}\right) = \cos\theta$$

Therefore,

$$\begin{aligned}
\cos^2\theta &= \left[\frac{1}{2}\left(z + \frac{1}{z}\right)\right]^8 \\
&= \frac{1}{2^8}\left(z + \frac{1}{z}\right)^8 \\
&= \frac{1}{256}\left[z^8 + 8z^7\frac{1}{z} + 28z^6\frac{1}{z^2} + 56z^5\frac{1}{z^3} + 70z^4\frac{1}{z^4} + 56z^3\frac{1}{z^5}\right. \\
&\quad \left. + 28z^2\frac{1}{z^6} + 8z\frac{1}{z^7} + \frac{1}{z^8}\right] \\
&= \frac{1}{256}\left[\left(z^8 + \frac{1}{z^8}\right) + 8\left(z^6 + \frac{1}{z^6}\right) + 28\left(z^4 + \frac{1}{z^4}\right)\right. \\
&\quad \left. + 56\left(z^2 + \frac{1}{z^2}\right) + 70\right] \\
&= \frac{1}{256}[2\cos 8\theta + 8(2\cos 6\theta) + 28(2\cos 4\theta) + 56(2\cos 2\theta) + 70] \\
&= \frac{2}{256}[\cos 8\theta + 8\cos 6\theta + 28\cos 4\theta + 56\cos 2\theta + 35] \\
&= \frac{1}{128}[\cos 8\theta + 8\cos 6\theta + 28\cos 4\theta + 56\cos 2\theta + 35]
\end{aligned}$$

18. *Prove that* $\sin^7\theta = -\frac{1}{64}(\sin 7\theta - 7\sin 5\theta + 21\sin 3\theta - 35\sin\theta)$

➡ Let

$$z = \cos\theta + i\sin\theta, \frac{1}{z} = \cos\theta - i\sin\theta$$

$$z^n = \cos n\theta + i\sin n\theta, \frac{1}{z^n} = \cos n\theta - i\sin n\theta$$

$$\Rightarrow z - \frac{1}{z} = 2i\sin\theta \quad \text{and} \quad z^n - \frac{1}{z^n} = 2i\sin n\theta$$

Therefore,

$$\begin{aligned}
\sin^7\theta &= \left[\frac{1}{2i}\left(z - \frac{1}{z}\right)\right]^7 \\
&= \frac{1}{2^7 i^7}\left(z - \frac{1}{z}\right)^7 \\
&= \frac{1}{-128i}\left[z^7 - 7z^6\frac{1}{z} + 21z^5\frac{1}{z^2} - 35z^4\frac{1}{z^3} + 35z^3\frac{1}{z^4}\right. \\
&\quad \left. - 21z^2\frac{1}{z^5} + 7z\frac{1}{z^6} - \frac{1}{z^7}\right] \\
&= \frac{i}{128}\left[\left(z^7 - \frac{1}{z^7}\right) - 7\left(z^5 - \frac{1}{z^5}\right) + 21\left(z^3 - \frac{1}{z^3}\right) - 35\left(z - \frac{1}{z}\right)\right] \\
&= \frac{i}{128}[2i\sin 7\theta - 7\cdot 2i\sin 5\theta + 21\cdot 2i\sin 3\theta - 35\cdot 2i\sin\theta] \\
&= \frac{2i^2}{128}[\sin 7\theta - 7\sin 5\theta + 21\sin 3\theta - 35\sin\theta] \\
\sin^7\theta &= -\frac{1}{64}[\sin 7\theta - 7\sin 5\theta + 21\sin 3\theta - 35\sin\theta]
\end{aligned}$$

19. *Express* $\sin^4\theta\cos^3\theta$ *in terms of cosines of multiples of* θ

➡

$$\sin^4\theta\cos^3\theta = \left(\frac{1}{2i}\left(z - \frac{1}{z}\right)\right)^4\left(\frac{1}{2}\left(z + \frac{1}{z}\right)\right)^3$$

$$= \frac{1}{128}\left(z-\frac{1}{z}\right)\left(z-\frac{1}{z}\right)^3\left(z+\frac{1}{z}\right)^3$$

$$= \frac{1}{128}\left(z-\frac{1}{z}\right)\left[z^2-\frac{1}{z^2}\right]^3$$

$$= \frac{1}{128}\left(z-\frac{1}{z}\right)\left[\left(z^2\right)^3-3\left(z^2\right)^2\frac{1}{z^2}+3z^2\left(\frac{1}{z^2}\right)^2-\left(\frac{1}{z^2}\right)^3\right]$$

$$= \frac{1}{128}\left(z-\frac{1}{z}\right)\left[z^6-3\cdot z^2+\frac{3}{z^2}-\frac{1}{z^6}\right]$$

$$= \frac{1}{128}\left[z^7-3\cdot z^3+\frac{3}{z}-\frac{1}{z^5}-z^5+3\cdot z-\frac{3}{z^3}+\frac{1}{z^7}\right]$$

$$= \frac{1}{128}\left[\left(z^7+\frac{1}{z^7}\right)-3\left(z^3+\frac{1}{z^3}\right)-\left(z^5+\frac{1}{z^5}\right)+3\left(z+\frac{1}{z}\right)\right]$$

$$= \frac{1}{128}\left[2\cos 7\theta-3\left(2\cos 3\theta\right)-2\cos 5\theta+3\left(2\cos\theta\right)\right]$$

$$= \frac{1}{64}\left[\cos 7\theta-\cos 5\theta-3\cos 3\theta+3\cos\theta\right]$$

20. *Expand* $\sin^7\theta\cos^3\theta$ *in series of sines of multiples of* θ

➡ Let $z=\cos\theta+i\sin\theta \Rightarrow \frac{1}{z}=\cos\theta-i\sin\theta$

$$z^n=\cos n\theta+i\sin n\theta \Rightarrow \frac{1}{z^n}=\cos n\theta-i\sin n\theta$$

$$z^n+\frac{1}{z^n}=2\cos n\theta \quad \text{and} \quad z^n-\frac{1}{z^n}=2i\sin n\theta$$

$$z+\frac{1}{z}=2\cos\theta \quad \text{and} \quad z-\frac{1}{z}=2i\sin\theta$$

$$\sin^7\theta\cos^3\theta=\left[\frac{1}{2i}\left(z-\frac{1}{z}\right)\right]^7\left[\frac{1}{2}\left(z+\frac{1}{z}\right)\right]^3$$

$$= \frac{1}{2^7i^7}\left(z-\frac{1}{z}\right)^4\left(z-\frac{1}{z}\right)^3\frac{1}{2^3}\left(z+\frac{1}{z}\right)^3$$

$$= \frac{i}{2^{10}i^8}\left(z-\frac{1}{z}\right)^4\left(z^2-\frac{1}{z^2}\right)^3$$

$$= \frac{i}{2^{10}(i^4)^2}\left[z^4-4z^3\frac{1}{z}+6z^2\frac{1}{z^2}-4z\frac{1}{z^3}+\frac{1}{z^4}\right]$$

$$\times\left[(z^2)^3-3(z^2)^2\frac{1}{z^2}+3z^2\frac{1}{(z^2)^2}-\frac{1}{(z^2)^3}\right]$$

$$= \frac{i}{2^{10}(1)^2}\left[z^4-4z^2+6-\frac{4}{z^2}+\frac{1}{z^4}\right]\left[z^6-3z^2+\frac{3}{z^2}-\frac{1}{z^6}\right]$$

$$= \frac{i}{2^{10}}\left[z^{10}-3z^6+3z^2-\frac{1}{z^2}-4z^8+12z^4-12+\frac{4}{z^4}+6z^6\right.$$

$$\left.-18z^2+\frac{18}{z^2}-\frac{6}{z^6}-4z^4+12-\frac{12}{z^4}-\frac{4}{z^8}+z^2-\frac{3}{z^2}+\frac{3}{z^6}-\frac{1}{z^{10}}\right]$$

$$= \frac{i}{2^{10}}\left[\left(z^{10}-\frac{1}{z^{10}}\right)-4\left(z^8-\frac{1}{z^8}\right)+3\left(z^6-\frac{1}{z^6}\right)+8\left(z^4-\frac{1}{z^4}\right)\right.$$

$$\left.-14\left(z^2-\frac{1}{z^2}\right)\right]$$

$$= \frac{i}{2^{10}}[2i\sin 10\theta-4(2i\sin 8\theta)+3(2i\sin 6\theta)+8(2i\sin 4\theta)$$

$$-14(2i\sin 2\theta)]$$

$$= \frac{2i^2}{2^{10}}[\sin 10\theta-4\sin 8\theta+3\sin 6\theta+8\sin 4\theta-14\sin 2\theta]$$

$$= -\frac{1}{2^9}[\sin 10\theta-4\sin 8\theta+3\sin 6\theta+8\sin 4\theta-14\sin 2\theta]$$

21. *Prove that following* (i) $\cos x = \dfrac{e^{ix}+e^{-ix}}{2}$, (ii) $\sin x = \dfrac{e^{ix}-e^{-ix}}{2i}$

➡ We have

$$e^{ix} = \cos x + i\sin x \qquad (1)$$

$$e^{-ix} = \cos x - i\sin x \qquad (2)$$

Adding equations (1) and (2), we get

$$e^{ix} + e^{-ix} = 2\cos x \Rightarrow \frac{e^{ix} + e^{-ix}}{2} = \cos x$$

Subtracting equation (2) from (1), we get

$$e^{ix} - e^{-ix} = 2i\sin x \Rightarrow \frac{e^{ix} - e^{-ix}}{2i} = \sin x$$

Exercises

I. *Simplify the following using De Moivre's theorem*

(1) $(\cos 2\theta + i\sin 2\theta)^4 (\cos 3\theta - i\sin 3\theta)^2$

(2) $\left(\cos\frac{5\theta}{2} + i\sin\frac{5\theta}{2}\right)^4$

(3) $\dfrac{(\cos 3\theta + \sin 3\theta)^6 (\cos 2\theta - i\sin 2\theta)^{-4}}{(\cos 4\theta + i\sin 4\theta)^{-2}\cos(5\theta + i\sin 5\theta)^2}$

(4) $\left(\cos\frac{2\pi}{3} + i\sin\frac{2\pi}{3}\right)^{30}$

(5) $\dfrac{(\cos 4\theta + i\sin 4\theta)^3}{(\sin 3\theta + i\cos 3\theta)^2 (\cos 5\theta + i\sin 5\theta)^3}$

(6) $(\sin\theta + i\cos\theta)^n$

(7) $\dfrac{(\cos 3\alpha + \sin 3\alpha)^2 (\cos n2\beta - i\sin n2\beta)^3}{(\cos 3\alpha - i\sin 3\gamma)^4}$

(8) $(\cos\theta + i\sin\theta)^5 (\cos\theta - i\sin\theta)^4$

(9) $\dfrac{(\cos\theta + i\sin\theta)^7}{(\cos\theta - i\sin\theta)^4}$

(10) $\dfrac{(\sin\theta + i\cos\theta)^3}{(\cos\alpha + i\sin\alpha)}$

II. *Prove the following*

(1) $\left(i + \sqrt{3}\right)^4 - \left(-i + \sqrt{3}\right)^4 = 16\sqrt{3i}$

(2) $\left(1+i\sqrt{3}\right)^5+\left(1-i\sqrt{3}\right)^5=32$

(3) $(-1+i)^7+(-1-i)^7=-16$

III. *If n is a positive integer, prove the following*

(1) $\left(1+i\sqrt{3}\right)^n+\left(1-i\sqrt{3}\right)^n=2^{n+1}\cos\dfrac{(n\pi)}{3}$

(2) $(1+i)^n+(1-i)^n=2^{\frac{n}{2}+1}\cos\left(\dfrac{n\pi}{4}\right)$

IV. *If* $\cos\alpha+\cos\beta+\cos\gamma=0$ *and* $\sin\alpha+\sin\beta+\sin\gamma=0$ *prove that,*

(1) $(\cos 3\alpha+\cos 3\beta+\cos 3\gamma)=3\cos(\alpha+\beta+\gamma)$

(2) $\sin 3\alpha+\sin 3\beta+\sin 3\gamma=3\sin(\alpha+\beta+\gamma)$

(3) $\cos^2\alpha+\cos^2\beta+\cos^2\gamma=\sin^2\alpha+\sin^2\beta+\sin^2\gamma=3/2$

(4) $\cos 2\alpha+\cos 2\beta+\cos 2\gamma=0$

V. *If* $\cos\alpha+2\cos\beta+3\cos\gamma=0$ *and* $\sin\alpha+2\sin\beta+3\sin\gamma=0$ *prove that*

(1) $\sin 3\alpha+8\sin 3\beta+27\sin 3\gamma=18\sin(\alpha+\beta+\gamma)$

(2) $\cos 3\alpha+8\cos 3\beta+27\cos 3\gamma=18\cos(\alpha+\beta+\gamma)$

VI. (1) *Prove that* $\left(\dfrac{1+\sin\theta+i\cos\theta}{1+\sin\theta-i\cos\theta}\right)^n=\cos\left(\dfrac{n\pi}{2}-n\theta\right)+i\sin\left(\dfrac{n\pi}{2}-n\theta\right)$

(2) *Prove that* $\left(\dfrac{1+\cos\theta+i\sin\theta}{1+\cos\theta-i\sin\theta}\right)^n=\cos n\theta+i\sin n\theta$

(3) $\left(\dfrac{1-\cos\theta+i\sin\theta}{1-\cos\theta-i\sin\theta}\right)=\cos n(\pi-\theta)+i\sin n(\pi-\theta)$

(4) $\left(\dfrac{1+i\tan\theta}{1-i\tan\theta}\right)^n=\dfrac{1+i\tan n\theta}{1-i\tan n\theta}$, where n is a positive integer.

(5) *Prove that* $\left(\dfrac{1-\cos\frac{\pi}{10}+i\sin\frac{\pi}{10}}{1-\cos\frac{\pi}{10}-i\sin\frac{\pi}{10}}\right)^{10}=-1$

(6) *Prove that* $\left(\dfrac{1+\sin\frac{\pi}{8}+i\cos\frac{\pi}{8}}{1+\sin\frac{\pi}{8}-i\cos\frac{\pi}{8}}\right)^{\frac{1}{2}}=-1$

VII. (1) *If* $x=\cos\theta+i\sin\theta$, *then show that* $x^2+\dfrac{1}{x^2}=2\cos 2\theta$ *and* $x^3-\dfrac{1}{x^3}=2i\sin 3\theta$

(2) *If* $x = \cos\theta + i\sin\theta$ *and* $y = \cos\varphi + i\sin\varphi$, *then prove that* $\frac{x}{y} + \frac{y}{x} = 2\cos(\theta - \varphi)$ *and* $\frac{x}{y} - \frac{y}{x} = 2i\sin(\theta - \varphi)$

(3) *If* $x = \cos\alpha + i\sin\alpha$ *and* $y = \cos\beta + i\sin\beta$, *then prove the following*

(i) $xy + \frac{1}{xy} = 2\cos(\alpha + \beta)$ (ii) $xy - \frac{1}{xy} = 2i\sin(\alpha + \beta)$

(iii) $x^2y^3 + \frac{1}{x^2y^3} = 2\cos(2\alpha + 3\beta)$

VIII. *If* $x = \cos\alpha + i\sin\alpha$, $y = \cos\beta + i\sin\beta$, $z = \cos\gamma + i\sin\gamma$ *then prove the following.*

(1) $xyz + \frac{1}{xyz} = 2\cos(\alpha + \beta + \gamma)$

(2) $\frac{xy}{z} + \frac{z}{xy} = 2\cos(\alpha + \beta - \gamma)$

(3) $\frac{x^l y^n}{z^n} + \frac{z^n}{x^l y^m} = 2\cos(l\alpha + m\beta - n\gamma)$

(4) $\sqrt{\frac{x}{yz}} + \sqrt{\frac{yz}{x}} = 2\cos(\alpha - \beta - \gamma)$

IX. (1) *If* $x + \frac{1}{x} = 2\cos\theta$, *prove that* $x = \cos\theta \pm i\sin\theta$

(2) *If* $x + \frac{1}{x} = 2\cos\alpha$ *and* $y + \frac{1}{y} = 2\cos\beta$, *then prove the following*

(i) $\frac{x^m}{y^n} + \frac{y^n}{x^n} = 2\cos(m\alpha - n\beta)$

(ii) $\frac{x^n}{y^m} - \frac{y^m}{x^n} = 2i\sin(n\alpha - m\beta)$

(iii) $3\sqrt{\frac{x}{y}} + 3\sqrt{\frac{y}{x}} = 2\cos(\alpha - \beta)$

X. *Prove the following*

(a) $\sin ix = i\sinh x$,

(b) $\cos ix = \cosh x,$

(c) $\tan ix = i \tanh x$

(d) $\sin (x + iy) = \sin x \cosh y + i \cos x \sinh y$

(e) $\cos (x + iy) = \cos x \cosh y - i \sin x \sinh y$

(f) $\tan (x + iy) = \dfrac{\sin 2x}{\cos 2x + \cosh 2y} + i\dfrac{\sinh 2y}{\cos 2x + \cosh 2y}$

(g) $\cot (x + iy) = \dfrac{\sin 2x}{\cosh 2y - \cos 2x} - i\dfrac{\sinh 2y}{\cosh 2y - \cos 2x}$

(h) $\sec (x + iy) = \dfrac{2 \cos x \cosh y}{\cos 2x + \cosh 2y} + i\dfrac{2 \sin x \sinh y}{\cos 2x + \cosh 2y}$

(i) $\operatorname{cosec} (x + iy) = \dfrac{2 \sin x \cosh y}{\cosh 2y - \cos 2x} - i\dfrac{2 \cos x \sinh y}{\cosh 2y - \cos 2x}$

(j) $\sinh (x + iy) = \sinh x \cos y + i \cosh x \sin y$

(k) $\cosh (x + iy) = \cosh x \cos y + i \sinh x \sin y$

(l) $\tanh (x + iy) = \dfrac{\sinh 2x}{\cosh 2x + \cos 2y} + i\dfrac{\sin 2y}{\cosh 2x + \cos 2y}$

(m) $\tan^{-1} (x + iy) = \dfrac{1}{2} \tan^{-1}\left(\dfrac{2x}{1 - x^2 - y^2}\right) + i\dfrac{1}{2} \tan^{-1}\left(\dfrac{2y}{1 + x^2 + y^2}\right)$

(n) $\cot^{-1} (x + iy) = \dfrac{1}{2} \cot^{-1}\left(\dfrac{x^2 + y^2 - 1}{2x}\right) - i\dfrac{1}{2} \cot^{-1}\left(\dfrac{x^2 + y^2 + 1}{2y}\right)$

(o) $\sinh^{-1} x = \log_e(x + \sqrt{x^2 + 1})$

(p) $\cosh^{-1} x = \log_e(x + \sqrt{x^2 - 1})$

(q) $\tanh^{-1} x = \dfrac{1}{2} \log\left(\dfrac{1 + x}{1 - x}\right)$

Answers

I. (1) $\cos 2\theta + i \sin 2\theta$

(2) $\cos 10\theta + i \sin 10\theta$

(3) $\cos (24\theta) + i \sin (24\theta)$

(4) 1

(5) $-\cos 15\theta + i \sin 15\theta$

(6) $\cos n\left(\dfrac{\pi}{2} - \theta\right) + i \sin\left(\dfrac{\pi}{2} - \theta\right)$

(7) $\cos (6\alpha - 6\beta + 12\gamma) + i \sin (6\alpha - 6\beta + 12\gamma)$

(8) $\cos\theta + i\sin\theta$

(9) $\cos 11\theta + i\sin 11\theta$

(10) $-[\sin(3\theta + 2\alpha) + i\cos(3\theta + 2\alpha)]$

1.6 nth Roots of a Complex Number

Let $z = x + iy$ be a complex number and $z = r(\cos\theta + i\sin\theta)$ be its polar form.

Where $r = \sqrt{x^2 + y^2}$ and $\theta = \tan^{-1}\left(\frac{y}{x}\right)$

$\therefore$ n^{th} root of a complex number is

$$z^{\frac{1}{n}} = r^{\frac{1}{n}}(\cos\theta + i\sin\theta)^{\frac{1}{n}}$$

Write the general value of the amplitude

$$\theta + 2k\pi, k \in I$$

$$\therefore\ (z)^{\frac{1}{n}} = (r)^{\frac{1}{n}}[\cos(\theta + 2k\pi) + i\sin(\theta + 2k\pi)]^{\frac{1}{n}}$$

By using De Moivre's theorem, we get

$$z_k = z^{\frac{1}{n}} = r^{\frac{1}{n}}\left[\cos\left(\frac{\theta + 2k\pi}{n}\right) + i\sin\left(\frac{\theta + 2k\pi}{n}\right)\right]$$

$$\Rightarrow z_k = r^{\frac{1}{n}}\text{cis}\left(\frac{\theta + 2k\pi}{n}\right) \quad k = 0, 1, 2\ldots(n-1)$$

This gives the n-distinct n^{th} roots of given complex number.

Worked Examples

1. *Find the cube roots of* $1 - i$

➡ Let $z = x + iy = 1 - i \Rightarrow r = \sqrt{x^2 + y^2} = \sqrt{1+1} = \sqrt{2}$

$$\alpha = \tan^{-1}\left|\frac{y}{x}\right| = \tan^{-1}\left|\frac{-1}{1}\right| = \frac{\pi}{4}$$

Here $z = 1 - i = (1, -1)$ is in the 4th quadrant

$$\theta = 2\pi - \alpha = 2\pi - \frac{\pi}{4} = \frac{7\pi}{4}$$

Therefore,

$$z = \sqrt{2}\left[\cos\left(\frac{7\pi}{4}\right) + i\sin\left(\frac{7\pi}{4}\right)\right]$$

or

$$z = \sqrt{2}\left[\cos\left(2k\pi + \frac{7\pi}{4}\right) + i\sin\left(2k\pi + \frac{7\pi}{4}\right)\right]$$

$$z = 2^{\frac{1}{2}}\left[\cos\left(\frac{8k+7}{4}\right)\pi + i\sin\left(\frac{8k+7}{4}\right)\pi\right]$$

$$\Rightarrow z^{\frac{1}{3}} = 2^{\frac{1}{6}}\left[\cos\left(\frac{8k+7}{4}\right)\pi + i\sin\left(\frac{8k+7}{4}\right)\pi\right]^{\frac{1}{3}}$$

$$z_k = z^{\frac{1}{3}} = 2^{\frac{1}{6}}\left[\cos\left(\frac{8k+7}{12}\right)\pi + i\sin\left(\frac{8k+7}{12}\right)\pi\right] \quad \text{where} \quad k = 0, 1, 2$$

$$z_0 = 2^{\frac{1}{6}}\left[\cos\frac{7\pi}{12} + i\sin 12 + i\sin\frac{7\pi}{12}\right]$$

$$z_1 = 2^{\frac{1}{6}}\left[\cos\frac{15\pi}{12} + i\sin\frac{15\pi}{12}\right]$$

$$z_2 = 2^{\frac{1}{6}}\left[\cos\frac{23\pi}{12} + i\sin\frac{23\pi}{12}\right]$$

2. *Find the fourth roots of* $1 - i\sqrt{3}$ *and represent them on an argand plane.*

➡ Let $z = 1 - i\sqrt{3} = x + iy$

$$r = \sqrt{x^2 + y^2} = \sqrt{1+3} = 2$$

$$\alpha = \tan^{-1}\left|\frac{y}{x}\right| = \tan^{-1}\left|\frac{-\sqrt{3}}{1}\right| = \tan^{-1}\sqrt{3} = \frac{\pi}{3}$$

Here $z = 1 - i\sqrt{3} = \left(1, -\sqrt{3}\right)$ is in the 4th quadrant

$$\theta = 2\pi - \alpha = 2\pi - \frac{\pi}{3} = \frac{5\pi}{3}$$

Therefore, $z = 2\left[\cos\frac{5\pi}{3} + i\sin\frac{5\pi}{3}\right]$

$$z = 2\left[\cos\left(2k\pi + \frac{5\pi}{3}\right) + i\sin\left(2k\pi + \frac{5\pi}{3}\right)\right]$$
$$z = 2\left[\cos\left(\frac{6k+5}{3}\right)\pi + i\sin\left(\frac{6k+5}{3}\right)\pi\right]$$

Therefore,

$$z_k = z^{\frac{1}{4}} = 2^{\frac{1}{4}}\left[\cos\left(\frac{6k+5}{3}\right)\pi + i\sin\left(\frac{6k+5}{3}\right)\pi\right]^{\frac{1}{4}}$$
$$z_k = 2^{\frac{1}{4}}\left[\cos\left(\frac{6k+5}{12}\right)\pi + i\sin\left(\frac{6k+5}{12}\right)\pi\right] \quad \text{where} \quad k = 0, 1, 2, 3$$
$$z_0 = 2^{\frac{1}{4}}\left[\cos\frac{5\pi}{12} + i\sin\frac{5\pi}{12}\right]$$
$$z_1 = 2^{\frac{1}{4}}\left[\cos\frac{11\pi}{12} + i\sin\frac{11\pi}{12}\right]$$
$$z_2 = 2^{\frac{1}{4}}\left[\cos\frac{17\pi}{12} + i\sin\frac{17\pi}{12}\right]$$
$$z_3 = 2^{\frac{1}{4}}\left[\cos\frac{23\pi}{12} + i\sin\frac{23\pi}{12}\right]$$

These are four roots of a given complex number. To represents those on argand plane, draw a circle centered at origin and radius $2^{\frac{1}{4}}$ and mark all the 4 roots on the circle.

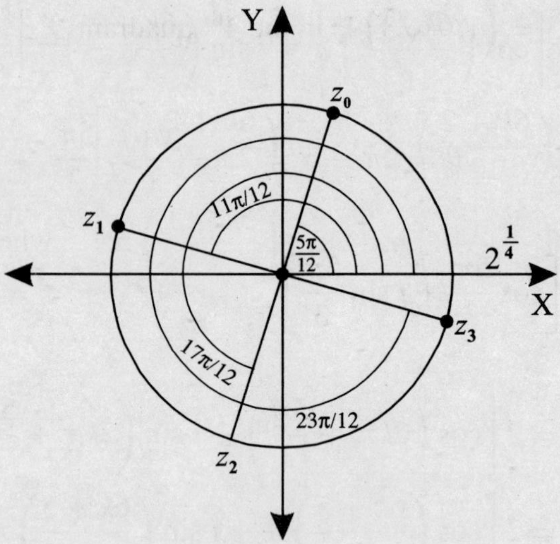

Figure 1.6

3. *Find the fourth roots of $-1 + i\sqrt{3}$ and represent them on the argand diagram.*

➡ Let $z = -1 + i\sqrt{3} = x + iy \Rightarrow r = \sqrt{1+3} = 2$

$$\alpha = \tan^{-1}\left|\frac{y}{x}\right| = \tan^{-1}\left|\frac{\sqrt{3}}{-1}\right| = \tan^{-1}\left(\sqrt{3}\right) = \frac{\pi}{3}$$

Here $z = -1 + i\sqrt{3} = \left(-1, \sqrt{3}\right)$ is in the 2nd quadrant.

$$\theta = \pi - \alpha = \pi - \frac{\pi}{3} = \frac{2\pi}{3}$$

Therefore,

$$\begin{aligned} z &= 2\left(\cos\frac{2\pi}{3} + i\sin\frac{2\pi}{3}\right) \\ &= 2\left[\cos\left(2k\pi + \frac{2\pi}{3}\right) + i\sin\left(2k\pi + \frac{2\pi}{3}\right)\right] \\ z &= 2\left[\cos\left(\frac{6k+2}{3}\right)\pi + i\sin\left(\frac{6k+2}{3}\right)\pi\right] \end{aligned}$$

$$z_k = z^{\frac{1}{4}} = 2^{\frac{1}{4}}\left[\cos\left(\frac{6k+2}{3}\right)\pi + i\sin\left(\frac{6k+2}{3}\right)\pi\right]^{\frac{1}{4}}$$

$$= 2^{\frac{1}{4}}\left[\cos\left(\frac{6k+2}{12}\right)\pi + i\sin\left(\frac{6k+2}{12}\right)\pi\right]$$

$$z_k = 2^{\frac{1}{4}}\left[\cos\left(\frac{3k+1}{6}\right)\pi + i\sin\left(\frac{3k+1}{6}\right)\pi\right] \quad \text{where} \quad k = 0, 1, 2, 3$$

$$z_0 = 2^{\frac{1}{4}}\left(\cos\frac{\pi}{6} + i\sin\frac{\pi}{6}\right)$$

$$z_1 = 2^{\frac{1}{4}}\left(\cos\frac{4\pi}{6} + i\sin\frac{4\pi}{6}\right) = 2^{\frac{1}{4}}\left(\cos\frac{2\pi}{3} + i\sin\frac{2\pi}{3}\right)$$

$$z_2 = 2^{\frac{1}{4}}\left(\cos\frac{7\pi}{6} + i\sin\frac{7\pi}{6}\right)$$

$$z_3 = 2^{\frac{1}{4}}\left(\cos\frac{10\pi}{6} + i\sin\frac{10\pi}{6}\right) = 2^{\frac{1}{4}}\left(\cos\frac{5\pi}{3} + i\sin\frac{5\pi}{3}\right)$$

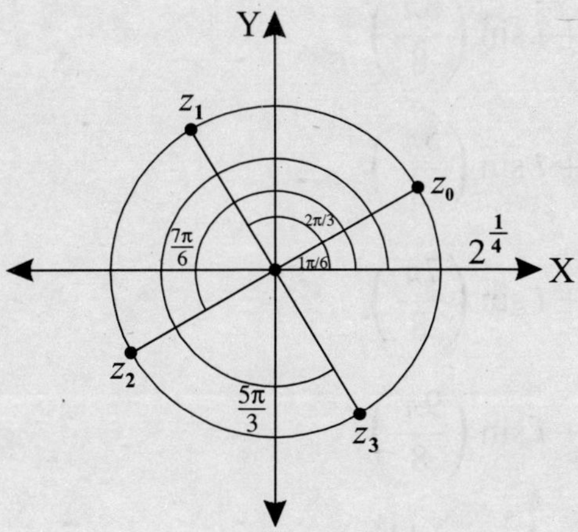

Figure 1.7

4. *Solve* $z^8 + 1 = 0$

➡ $z^8 + 1 = 0 \Rightarrow z^8 = -1 = x + iy$

$$r = \sqrt{x^2 + y^2} = \sqrt{(-1)^2 + 0} = 1$$

$$\alpha = \tan^{-1}\left|\frac{y}{x}\right| = \tan^{-1}\left|\frac{0}{-1}\right| = 0$$

Here $-1 = (-1, 0)$ is in the 2nd quadrant

$$\theta = \pi - \alpha = \pi$$

Therefore, $z^8 = 1\,(\cos\pi + i\sin\pi)$

$$z^8 = \cos(2k\pi + \pi) + \sin(2k\pi + \pi)$$

$$z_K = z = [\cos(2k+1)\pi + i\sin(2k+1)\pi]^{\frac{1}{8}}$$

$$z_k = \cos\left(\frac{2k+1}{8}\right)\pi + i\sin\left(\frac{2k+1}{8}\right)\pi \quad \text{where} \quad k = 0, 1, 2, 3, 4, 5, 6, 7$$

$$z_0 = \cos\left(\frac{\pi}{8}\right) + i\sin\left(\frac{\pi}{8}\right)$$

$$z_1 = \cos\left(\frac{3\pi}{8}\right) + i\sin\left(\frac{3\pi}{8}\right)$$

$$z_2 = \cos\left(\frac{5\pi}{8}\right) + i\sin\left(\frac{5\pi}{8}\right)$$

$$z_3 = \cos\left(\frac{7\pi}{8}\right) + i\sin\left(\frac{7\pi}{8}\right)$$

$$z_4 = \cos\left(\frac{9\pi}{8}\right) + i\sin\left(\frac{9\pi}{8}\right)$$

$$z_5 = \cos\left(\frac{11\pi}{8}\right) + i\sin\left(\frac{11\pi}{8}\right)$$

$$z_6 = \cos\left(\frac{13\pi}{8}\right) + i\sin\left(\frac{13\pi}{8}\right)$$

$$z_7 = \cos\left(\frac{15\pi}{8}\right) + i\sin\left(\frac{15\pi}{8}\right)$$

5. *Find all the values of* $\left(1+i\sqrt{3}\right)^{\frac{2}{3}}$

➡ Let $z = 1+\sqrt{3}i = x+iy$

$$\Rightarrow r = \sqrt{x^2+y^2} = \sqrt{1+3} = 2$$

$$\alpha = \tan^{-1}\left|\frac{y}{x}\right| = \tan^{-1}\left|\frac{\sqrt{3}}{1}\right| = \frac{\pi}{3}$$

Here $z = 1+i\sqrt{3} = \left(1,\sqrt{3}\right)$ is in the 1st quadrant

$$\theta = \alpha = \frac{\pi}{3}$$

Therefore,

$$z = 2\left[\cos\left(\frac{\pi}{3}\right)+i\sin\left(\frac{\pi}{3}\right)\right]$$

$$= 2\left[\cos\left(2k\pi+\frac{\pi}{3}\right)+i\sin\left(2k\pi+\frac{\pi}{3}\right)\right]$$

$$z = 2\left[\cos\left(\frac{6k+1}{3}\right)+\sin\left(\frac{6k+1}{3}\right)\pi\right]$$

$$z^{\frac{2}{3}} = 2^{\frac{2}{3}}\left[\cos\left(\frac{6k+1}{3}\right)\pi+i\sin\left(\frac{6k+1}{3}\right)\pi\right]^{\frac{2}{3}}$$

$$= 2^{\frac{2}{3}}\left[\cos\frac{2}{3}\left(\frac{6k+1}{3}\right)\pi+i\sin\frac{2}{3}\left(\frac{6k+1}{3}\right)\pi\right]$$

$$z^{\frac{2}{3}} = 2^{\frac{2}{3}}\left[\cos\left(\frac{12k+2}{9}\right)\pi+i\sin\left(\frac{12k+2}{9}\right)\pi\right] \quad \text{where} \quad k = 0,1,2$$

$$z_0 = 2^{\frac{2}{3}}\left(\cos\frac{2\pi}{9}+i\sin\frac{2\pi}{9}\right) = 2^{\frac{2}{3}}\text{cis}\,\frac{2\pi}{9}$$

$$z_1 = 2^{\frac{2}{3}}\left[\cos\frac{14\pi}{9}+i\sin\frac{14\pi}{9}\right] = 2^{\frac{2}{3}}\text{cis}\,\frac{14\pi}{9}$$

$$z_2 = 2^{\frac{2}{3}}\left[\cos\frac{26\pi}{9}+i\sin\frac{26\pi}{9}\right] = 2^{\frac{2}{3}}\text{cis}\,\frac{26\pi}{9}$$

6. *Find the fifth root of unity*

➡ Let $z = 1 = 1 + i0 = (1, 0)$

$$r = \sqrt{1^2 + 0^2} = 1 \quad \alpha = \tan^{-1}\left|\frac{0}{1}\right| = \tan^{-1} 0 = 0$$

$$\theta = \alpha = 0$$

Therefore,

$$\begin{aligned}
z &= 1(\cos 0 + i \sin 0) \\
&= \cos(2k\pi + 0) + i \sin(2k\pi + 0) \\
z &= \cos 2k\pi + i \sin 2k\pi \\
z_k &= 2^{1/5}[\cos 2k\pi + i \sin 2k\pi]^{1/5} \\
z_k &= \cos\left(\frac{2k\pi}{5}\right) + i \sin\left(\frac{2k\pi}{5}\right), \qquad k = 0, 1, 2, 3, 4 \\
z_0 &= \cos 0 + i \sin 0 \\
z_1 &= \cos\frac{2\pi}{5} + i \sin\frac{2\pi}{5} \\
z_2 &= \cos\frac{4\pi}{5} + i \sin\frac{4\pi}{5} \\
z_3 &= \cos\frac{6\pi}{5} + i \sin\frac{6\pi}{5} \\
z_4 &= \cos\frac{8\pi}{5} + i \sin\frac{8\pi}{5}
\end{aligned}$$

7. *The centre of a regular hexagon is at the origin and one vertex is given by* $\sqrt{3} + i$ *on the Argand diagram. Determine the other vertex*

Let $A = \sqrt{3} + i$

$$OA = \sqrt{3 + 1} = 2$$

$$X\hat{O}A = \tan^{-1}\left(\frac{1}{\sqrt{3}}\right) = 30°$$

Therefore,

$$X\hat{O}B = 30° + 60° = 90°$$

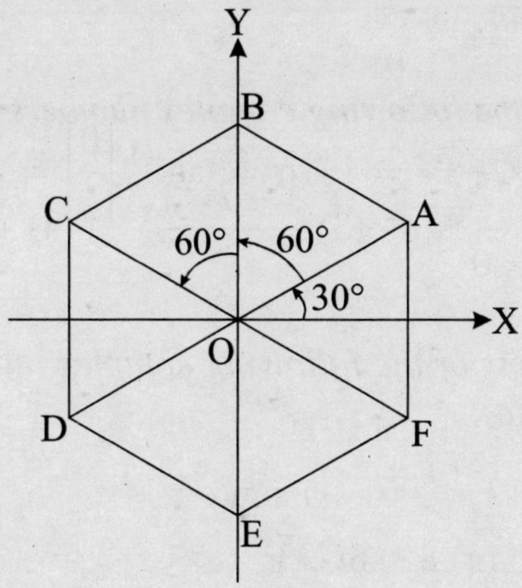

Figure 1.8

$$X\hat{O}C = 90^\circ + 60^\circ = 150^\circ$$

$$X\hat{O}D = 150^\circ + 60^\circ = 210^\circ$$

$$X\hat{O}E = 210^\circ + 60^\circ = 270^\circ$$

$$X\hat{O}F = 270^\circ + 60^\circ = 330^\circ$$

Hence,

$$B = 2\left(\cos 90^\circ + i \sin 90^\circ\right) = 2i$$

$$C = 2\left(\cos 150^\circ + i \sin 150^\circ\right) = 2\left(-\frac{\sqrt{3}}{2} + i\frac{1}{2}\right) = -\sqrt{3} + i$$

$$D = 2\left(\cos 210^\circ + i \sin 210\right) = 2\left(-\frac{\sqrt{3}}{2} + i\left(-\frac{1}{2}\right)\right) = -\sqrt{3} - i$$

$$E = 2\left(\cos 270^\circ + i \sin 270^\circ\right) = 2\left(0 + i\left(-1\right)\right) = -2i$$

$$F = 2\left(\cos 330^\circ + i \sin 330^\circ\right) = 2\left(\frac{\sqrt{3}}{2} + i\left(-\frac{1}{2}\right)\right) = \sqrt{3} - i$$

Exercises

I. *Find the cube roots of the following complex numbers and represent them on the argand plane*

(1) $\sqrt{3}-i$ (2) $-1-i$ (3) $\dfrac{1-i\sqrt{3}}{2}$ (4) $\dfrac{-1+i}{2}$

(5) 8 (6) $-2i$

II. *Find the fourth roots of the following complex numbers and represent them on the argand plane*

(1) $\sqrt{3}+i$ (2) $1-i$

(3) $\dfrac{-1-i\sqrt{3}}{2}$ (4) $8+8i\sqrt{3}$

III. *Find all the values of the following and find their continued product.*

(1) $(\sqrt{3}+i)^{\frac{1}{3}}$ (2) $\left(\dfrac{-1-i\sqrt{3}}{2}\right)^{\frac{3}{4}}$

(3) $27^{\frac{1}{3}}$ (4) $(8i)^{\frac{1}{3}}$

(5) $(\sqrt{3}-i)^{\frac{4}{3}}$ (6) $(1+i)^{\frac{5}{4}}$

Answers

I. (1) $(2)^{\frac{1}{3}}\text{ cis }\left(\dfrac{12k+11}{18}\right)\pi \quad k=0,1,2$

(2) $(2)^{\frac{1}{6}}\text{ cis }\left(\dfrac{8k+5}{12}\right)\pi \quad k=0,1,2$

(3) $\text{cis }\left(\dfrac{6k+5}{9}\right)\pi \quad k=0,1,2$

(4) $\left(\dfrac{1}{2}\right)^{\frac{1}{6}}\text{ cis }\left(\dfrac{8k+3}{12}\right)\pi \quad k=0,1,2$

(5) $2\text{cis }\left(\dfrac{2k\pi}{3}\right) \quad k=0,1,2$

(6) $2^{\frac{1}{3}}\text{cis }\left(\dfrac{4k+3}{6}\right)\pi \quad k=0,1,2$

II. (1) $2^{\frac{1}{4}}\text{cis}\left(\frac{12k+1}{24}\right)\pi\ k=0,1,2,3$

(2) $2^{\frac{1}{8}}\text{cis}\left(\frac{8k+7}{6}\right)\pi\ k=0,1,2,3$

(3) $\text{cis}\left(\frac{3k+2}{6}\right)\pi\quad k=0,1,2,3$

(4) $2\text{cis}\left(\frac{6k+1}{12}\right)\pi\quad k=0,1,2,3$

III. (1) $2^{\frac{1}{3}}\text{cis}\left(\frac{12k+1}{18}\right)\pi k=0,1,2,3$ Product $=\sqrt{3}+i=P$

(2) $\text{cis}\,\frac{K\pi}{2}\quad k=0,1,2,3\quad P=-1$

(3) $3\text{cis}\left(\frac{2k\pi}{3}\right)\quad k=0,1,2\quad P=27$

(4) $2\text{cis}\left(\frac{4k+1}{6}\right)\pi\quad k=0,1,2,\quad P=8i$

(5) $2^{\frac{4}{3}}\text{cis}\left(\frac{12k+11}{9}\right)\pi\ k=0,1,2,\ P=8\left(-1-i\sqrt{3}\right)$

(6) $2^{\frac{5}{8}}\text{cis}\left(\frac{8k+5}{16}\right)\pi\quad k=0,1,2,3,\ P=4(1+i)$

1.7 Vector Algebra

Scalars

The physical quantities, which have only magnitude and no direction, are known as *scalars*. For example mass, volume, distance, speed, temperature, time etc.

Vectors

The physical quantities, which have magnitude and direction both, are known as *vectors*. For example force, displacement, velocity, acceleration, momentum weight etc.

Geometrical Representation of Vectors

A vector is represented by a straight line drawn in a given direction and magnitude to some unit of scale.

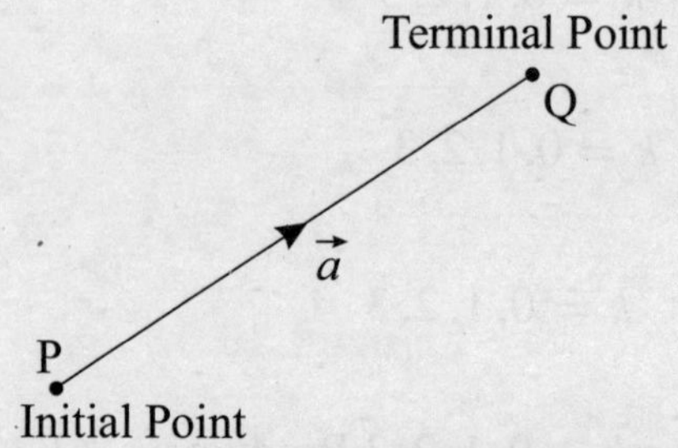

Figure 1.9

If $\overrightarrow{PQ}$ represents a vector with a magnitude which is equal to the length PQ and the direction is from P to Q. Then P is called initial (starting) point and Q is called terminal (end) point. A vector may be represented by a bold letter '**a**' or $\vec{a}$ or $\overrightarrow{PQ}$. The magnitude of a vector is written as $|\overrightarrow{PQ}|$ or a or $|\vec{a}|$, which is a scalar.

1.7.1 Types of Vectors

Unit Vector

The vector whose magnitude is unity is called the *unit vector*. A unit vector is denoted by $\hat{a}$, hence $\left|\hat{a}\right| = 1$. The idea of Unit Vector is usually used to represent the direction of any vector. We can write this as $\hat{a} = \frac{\vec{a}}{|\vec{a}|}$.

Zero (Null) Vector

A vector whose magnitude is zero (which can have no direction associated with it or which may have any direction) is called a *Zero* (*Null*) *Vector*. A zero vector is represented by '**0**' a bold zero or $\vec{0}$. The initial and terminal points of a zero vector are same.

Co-initial Vectors

The vectors, which have the same initial point, are called the *Co-initial Vectors*. For example

$\overrightarrow{PQ}$, $\overrightarrow{PR}$, $\overrightarrow{PS}$ are co-initial vectors with the same initial point P.

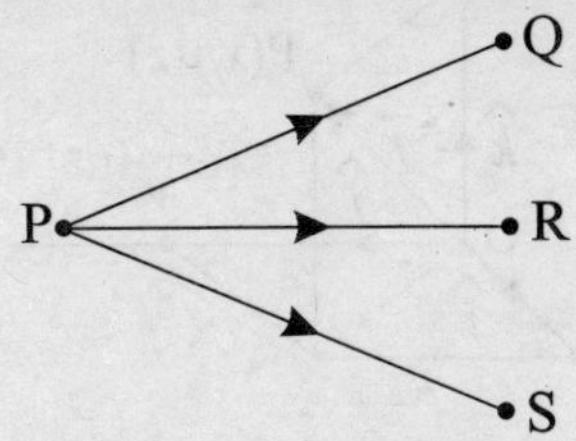

Figure 1.10

Collinear or Parallel Vectors

Two or more vectors are said to be *collinear* or *parallel* if they are parallel to the same line. If $\overrightarrow{PQ}$ and $\overrightarrow{RS}$ are two collinear vectors then $\overrightarrow{PQ} = \lambda\overrightarrow{RS}$, where λ is a Scalar. The angle between the parallel vectors is either zero or 180 degrees.

Coplanar Vectors

If two or more vectors lies on the same plane then they are called *Coplanar Vectors*.

Negative of a Vector

A vector $\overrightarrow{PQ}$ is said to be a *negative vector* of $\overrightarrow{RS}$ if the direction of $\overrightarrow{PQ}$ is opposite to the direction of $\overrightarrow{RS}$ but the magnitude of both the vectors is same, i.e., $\overrightarrow{PQ} = -\overrightarrow{RS}$.

Equal Vectors

If two vectors $\overrightarrow{PQ}$and $\overrightarrow{RS}$ have the same magnitude and the same direction then they are called *equal vectors*, i.e., $\overrightarrow{PQ} = \overrightarrow{RS}$.

Unit Vectors $\hat{i}$, $\hat{j}$, $\hat{k}$

The vectors $\hat{i}$, $\hat{j}$, $\hat{k}$ are three unit vectors along x, y and z-axes respectively where each pair of axes are mutually perpendicular.

$$\therefore\ |\hat{i}| = |\hat{j}| = |\hat{k}| = 1$$

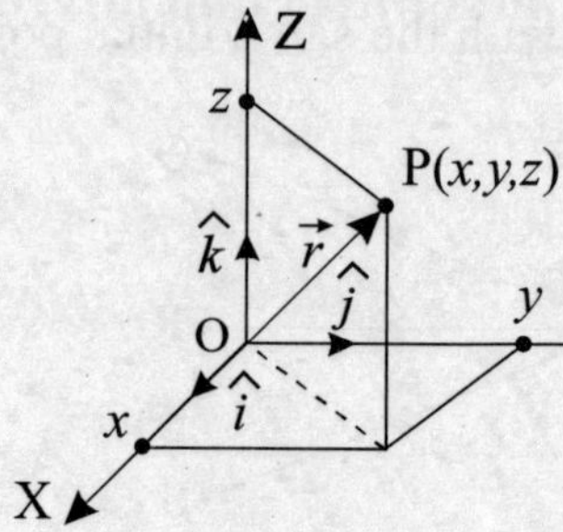

Figure 1.11

1.7.2 Vector Addition and Subtraction

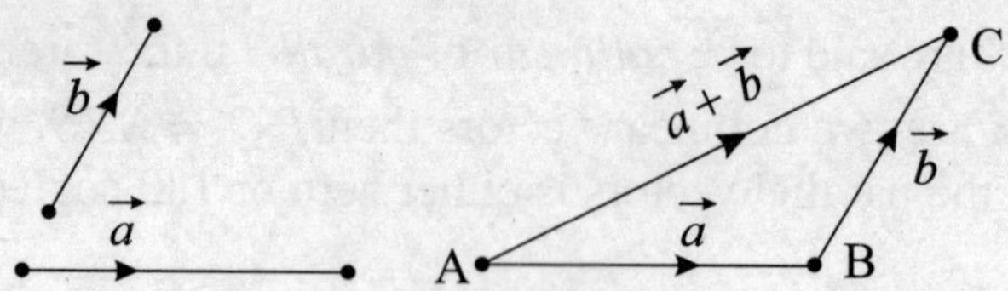

Figure 1.12

Let $\vec{a}$ and $\vec{b}$ be two vectors. Assume a point A and draw line segments AB and BC such that $\overrightarrow{AB} = \vec{a}$ and $\overrightarrow{BC} = \vec{b}$. If we join AC then $\overrightarrow{AC} = \vec{a} + \vec{b}$, which is called the *sum* or *resultant* of vectors $\vec{a}$ and $\vec{b}$. Hence $\overrightarrow{AB} + \overrightarrow{BC} = \vec{a} + \vec{b} = \overrightarrow{AC}$, which is known as triangle law of addition of vectors, i.e., in a triangle ABC, if $\overrightarrow{AB}$ and $\overrightarrow{BC}$ represents the vectors $\vec{a}$ and $\vec{b}$ respectively, the $\overrightarrow{AC}$ represents the vector $\vec{a} + \vec{b}$.

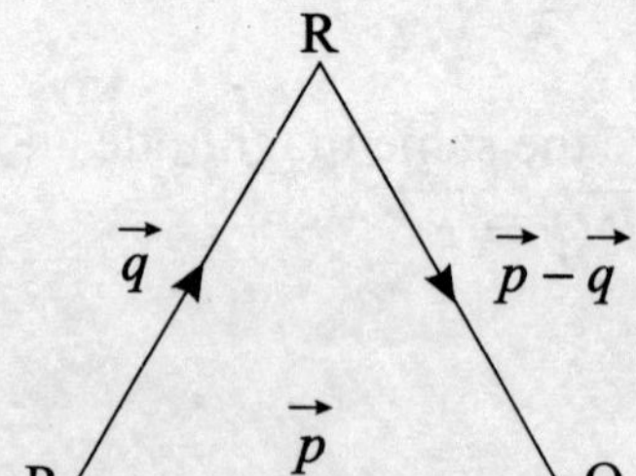

Figure 1.13

Similarly if $\vec{p}$ and $\vec{q}$ are two vectors represented by line segments $\overrightarrow{PQ}$ and $\overrightarrow{PR}$ respectively, then $\overrightarrow{RQ}$ represents the vector $\vec{p} - \vec{q}$ i.e., $\overrightarrow{PQ} - \overrightarrow{PR} = \vec{p} - \vec{q} = \overrightarrow{RQ}$.

Parallelogram law of Addition and Subtraction of Vectors

In a parallelogram $ABCD$, if $\overrightarrow{AB}$ and $\overrightarrow{BC}$ represent vectors $\vec{a}$ and $\vec{b}$ respectively, then $\overrightarrow{AC}$ represents $\vec{a}+\vec{b}$, which is known as *parallelogram law of addition of vectors* and $\overrightarrow{DB}$ represents $\vec{a}-\vec{b}$, which is known as *parallelogram law of subtraction of vectors.*

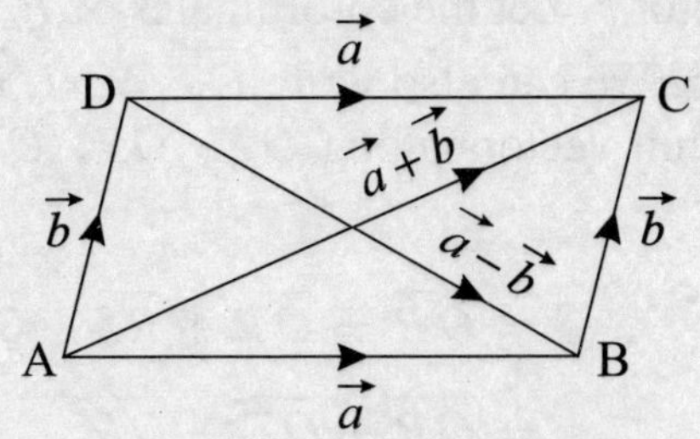

Figure 1.14

Any vector in terms of Unit Vectors $\hat{i}$, $\hat{j}$, $\hat{k}$

1. Let $\vec{a}$ be a vector in xy-plane. Through the origin O we draw a line segment OP such that $\overrightarrow{OP}$ represents the vector $\vec{a}$. Let the co-ordinates of the point P be (x, y), i.e., $OQ = x$ and $QP = y$

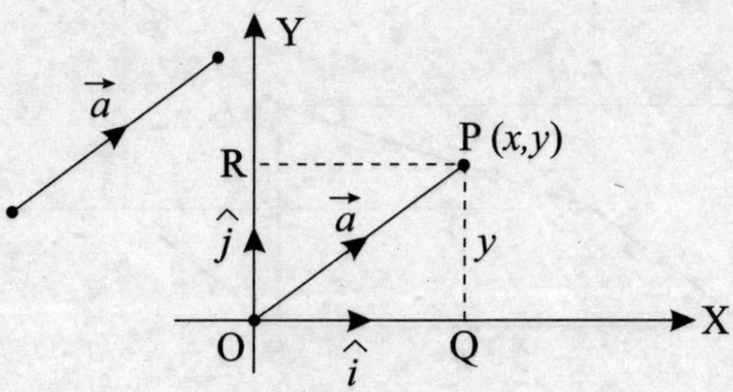

Figure 1.15

We can write $\overrightarrow{OQ} = x\hat{i}$ and $\overrightarrow{QP} = y\hat{j}$, where $\hat{i}$ and $\hat{j}$ are the unit vectors along OX and OY. Therefore we can write

$$\vec{a} = \overrightarrow{OP} = \overrightarrow{OQ} + \overrightarrow{QP} \text{ (By triangle law)}$$

$$\vec{a} = x\hat{i} + y\hat{j},$$

and

$$|\vec{a}| = \left|\overrightarrow{OP}\right| = OP = \sqrt{x^2 + y^2}$$

2. Let $\vec{r}$ be a vector in space. From the origin O we draw a line segment OP such that $\overrightarrow{OP}$ represents the vector $\vec{r}$. Let the co-ordinates of P be (x, y, z), i.e., $OT = x$, $OM = y$ and $OR = z$. We can also write $\overrightarrow{OT} = x\hat{i}$, $\overrightarrow{OM} = y\hat{j}$ and $\overrightarrow{OR} = z\hat{k}$, where $\hat{i},\ \hat{j},\ \hat{k}$ are the unit vectors along $OX,\ OY,\ OZ$ respectively. Hence we can write

$$\begin{aligned}\vec{r} &= \overrightarrow{OP} = \overrightarrow{OR} + \overrightarrow{RS} + \overrightarrow{SP}\\ &= \overrightarrow{OR} + \overrightarrow{OT} + \overrightarrow{OM}\\ &= z\hat{k} + x\hat{i} + y\hat{j}\end{aligned}$$

$$\vec{r} = x\hat{i} + y\hat{j} + z\hat{k}$$

$$\therefore\ |\vec{r}| = |\overrightarrow{OP}| = \sqrt{x^2 + y^2 + z^2}$$

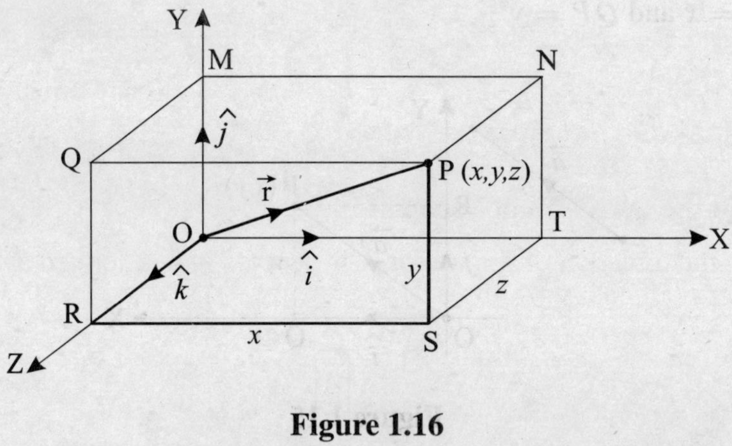

Figure 1.16

Addition or Subtraction of any Two Vectors

If $\vec{A}$ and $\vec{B}$ are any two vectors then their sum or difference is obtained by adding or subtracting the corresponding components of the vectors.

i.e., If $\vec{A} = a_1\hat{i} + a_2\hat{j} + a_3\hat{k}$ and $\vec{B} = b_1\hat{i} + b_2\hat{j} + b_3\hat{k}$

then $\vec{A}+\vec{B}=(a_1+b_1)\ \hat{i}+(a_2+b_2)\ \hat{j}+(a_3+b_3)\ \hat{k}$

and $\vec{A}-\vec{B}=(a_1-b_1)\ \hat{i}+(a_2-b_2)\ \hat{j}+(a_3-b_3)\ \hat{k}$

1.7.3 Multiplication of a Vector by Scalar

Multiplication of a vector by a scalar is obtained by multiplying the components of the vector by the scalar.
i.e., if $\vec{A}=a_1\hat{i}+a_2\hat{j}+a_3\hat{k}$ then

$$k\vec{A}=ka_1\hat{i}+ka_2\hat{j}+ka_3\hat{k}$$

Magnitude (length) of a Vector

Let $\vec{A}=a_1\hat{i}+a_2\hat{j}+a_3\hat{k}$ be any vector then its magnitude is denoted and defined by

$$|\vec{a}|=\sqrt{a_1^2+a_2^2+a_3^2}$$

Equality of Two Vectors

Two vectors $\vec{A}=a_1\hat{i}+a_2\hat{j}+a_3\hat{k}$, $\vec{B}=b_1\hat{i}+b_2\hat{j}+b_3\hat{k}$ are equal if and only if $a_1=b_1,\ \ a_2=b_2,\ \ a_3=b_3$.

Unit Vector in the Direction of Vector $\vec{A}$

Unit vector in the direction of the vector $\vec{A}$ is denoted and is defined as

$$\hat{A}=\frac{\vec{A}}{\left|\vec{A}\right|}$$

Ordered Pairs and Ordered Triplets

If x and y are any two real numbers then the ordered pair (x,y) is called a two dimensional vector, i.e.,

$$x\hat{i}+y\hat{j}=(x,y)$$

If x, y and z are any three real numbers then the ordered triplet (x, y, z) is called a three dimensional vector, i.e.,

$$x\hat{i} + y\hat{j} + z\hat{k} = (x, y, z)$$

1.7.4 Product of Two Vectors

Unlike the product of two scalars, the product of two vectors sometimes yields a scalar quantity and sometimes a vector quantity, the former is known as *scalar product* or *dot product* and the later is known as *vector product* or *cross product*.

If $\vec{a}$ and $\vec{b}$ are two vectors, then the scalar product is written as $\vec{a} \cdot \vec{b}$, read as $\vec{a}$ dot $\vec{b}$ and the vector product is written as $\vec{a} \times \vec{b}$, read as $\vec{a}$ cross $\vec{b}$. It should be noted that the division of a vector by another vector is not defined.

Scalar or Dot Product

The *scalar* or *dot product* of two vectors $\vec{a}$ and $\vec{b}$ is defined as

$$\vec{a} \cdot \vec{b} = |\vec{a}||\vec{b}| \cos\theta,$$

where θ is the angle between $\vec{a}$ and $\vec{b}$.

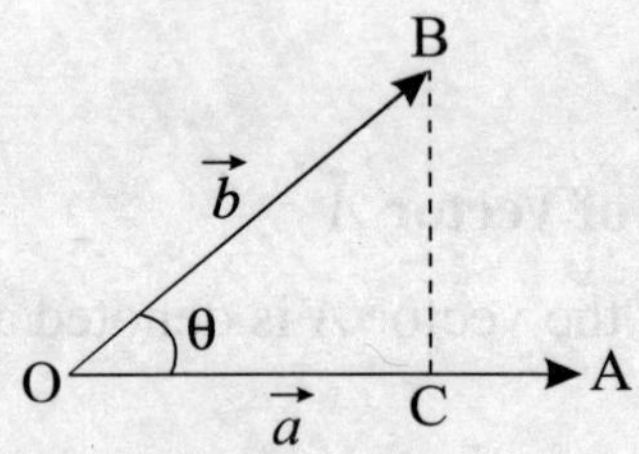

Figure 1.17

Geometrically, if $\vec{a} = \overrightarrow{OA}$, $\vec{b} = \overrightarrow{OB}$, and θ is the angle between $\overrightarrow{OA}$ and $\overrightarrow{OB}$ then,

$$\begin{aligned}\vec{a} \cdot \vec{b} &= |\overrightarrow{OA}||\overrightarrow{OB}| \cos\theta \\ &= |\overrightarrow{OA}|(OC) \quad (\because\ OB\cos\theta = OC) \\ &= |\overrightarrow{OA}| \text{ (Projection of } \vec{b} \text{ in the direction of } \vec{a})\end{aligned}$$

Similarly, we can write

$$\vec{b} \cdot \vec{a} = |\vec{b}| \text{ (Projection of } \vec{a} \text{ in the direction of } \vec{b})$$

We can also define the scalar or dot product of two vectors

$$\vec{a} = (a_1, a_2, a_3) \quad \text{and} \quad \vec{b} = (b_1, b_2, b_3) \text{ as}$$
$$\vec{a} \cdot \vec{b} = a_1 b_1 + a_2 b_2 + a_3 b_3$$

The scalar product of two vectors is a scalar quantity.

Properties of Scalar Dot Product

(i) $\vec{a} \cdot \vec{b} = |\vec{a}||\vec{b}| \cos\theta \Rightarrow \cos\theta = \frac{\vec{a} \cdot \vec{b}}{|\vec{a}||\vec{b}|}$

(ii) If $\theta = 90°$, then $\cos\theta = 0$ and hence $\vec{a} \cdot \vec{b} = 0$

(iii) Since $\hat{i}$, $\hat{j}$, $\hat{k}$ are unit vectors perpendicular to each other

$$\hat{i} \cdot \hat{j} = \hat{j} \cdot \hat{k} = \hat{k} \cdot \hat{i} = 0$$

and

$$\hat{i} \cdot \hat{i} = \hat{j} \cdot \hat{j} = \hat{k} \cdot \hat{k} = 1$$

(iv) $\overrightarrow{a} \cdot \vec{a} = |\vec{a}||\vec{a}| = |\vec{a}|^2 = a^2$

(v) $\vec{a} \cdot \vec{b} = |\vec{a}||\vec{b}| \cos\theta = |\vec{b}||\vec{a}| \cos\theta = \vec{b} \cdot \vec{a}$

Therefore dot product is commutative

(vi) Dot product is distributive over addition, i.e.,

$$\vec{a} \cdot (\vec{b} + \vec{c}) = \vec{a} \cdot \vec{b} + \vec{a} \cdot \vec{c}$$

Proof: Let $\vec{a} = \overrightarrow{OA}, \quad \vec{b} = \overrightarrow{OB}, \; \vec{c} = \overrightarrow{BC}$
Hence $\vec{b} + \vec{c} = \overrightarrow{OC}$

$$\vec{a} \cdot \left(\vec{b} + \vec{c}\right) = |\vec{a}| \text{ (Projection of } (\vec{b} + \vec{c}) \text{ on } \vec{a})$$

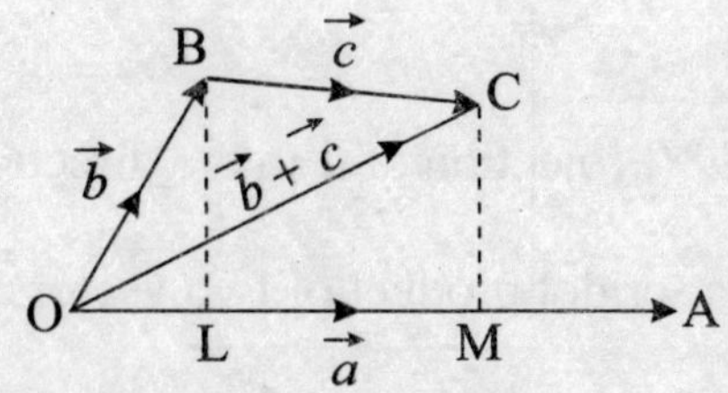

Figure 1.18

$$= |\vec{a}(OM)| = |\vec{a}|(OL + LM) = |\vec{a}|(OL) + |\vec{a}|(LM)$$

$$= |\vec{a}| \text{ (Projection of } \vec{b} \text{ on } \vec{a}) + |\vec{a}| \text{ (Projection of } \vec{c} \text{ on } \vec{a})$$

$$= \vec{a} \cdot \vec{b} + \vec{a} \cdot \vec{c}$$

(vii) $(\vec{a} + \vec{b})^2 = |\vec{a}|^2 + 2\vec{a} \cdot \vec{b} + |\vec{b}|^2$

Proof:

$$(\vec{a} + \vec{b})^2 = (\vec{a} + \vec{b}) \cdot (\vec{a} + \vec{b}) = \vec{a} \cdot \vec{a} + \vec{a} \cdot \vec{b} + \vec{b} \cdot \vec{a} + \vec{b} \cdot \vec{b}$$

$$= |\vec{a}|^2 + 2\vec{a} \cdot \vec{b} + |\vec{b}|^2 \qquad (\because\ \vec{a} \cdot \vec{a} = |\vec{a}|^2 \quad \text{and} \quad \vec{b} \cdot \vec{a}. = \vec{a} \cdot \vec{b})$$

(viii) $(\vec{a} - \vec{b})^2 = |\vec{a}|^2 - 2\vec{a} \cdot \vec{b} + |\vec{b}|^2$

(ix) $(\vec{a} + \vec{b})^2 - (\vec{a} - \vec{b})^2 = 4\vec{a} \cdot \vec{b}$

(x) $(\vec{a} + \vec{b}) \cdot (\vec{a} - \vec{b}) = |\vec{a}|^2 - |\vec{b}|^2$

Vector or Cross Product

The *vector* or *cross product* of two vectors $\vec{a}$ and $\vec{b}$ is defined as

$$\vec{a} \times \vec{b} = |\vec{a}||\vec{b}| \sin\theta\, \hat{n},$$

Where θ is the angle between $\vec{a}$ and $\vec{b}$ and $\hat{n}$ is a unit vector perpendicular to both $\vec{a}$ and $\vec{b}$ such that $\vec{a}$, $\vec{b}$ and $\hat{n}$ form a right-handed system. By a right-handed system we mean that, when a right-handed screw is rotated from $\vec{a}$ to $\vec{b}$, the screw moves along $\hat{n}$. The vector or cross product of two vectors is a vector quantity.

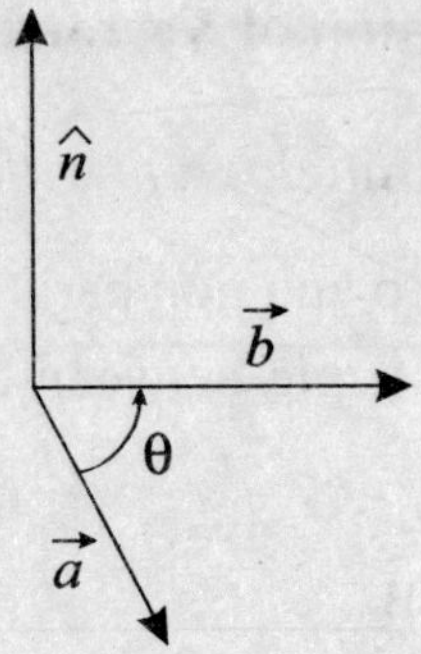

Figure 1.19

Properties of Vector or Cross Product

(i) $|\vec{a} \times \vec{b}| = |\vec{a}||\vec{b}| \sin\theta |\hat{n}| = |\vec{a}||\vec{b}| \sin\theta \qquad (\because |\hat{n}| = 1)$

$$\therefore \sin\theta = \frac{|\vec{a} \times \vec{b}|}{|\vec{a}||\vec{b}|}$$

(ii) If $\theta = 0°$, then $\sin\theta = 0$ and hence $\vec{a} \times \vec{b} = 0$

(iii) $\hat{i} \times \hat{j} = \hat{k},\ \hat{j} \times \hat{k} = \hat{i},\ \hat{k} \times \hat{i} = \hat{j},\ \hat{j} \times \hat{i} = -\hat{k},\ \hat{k} \times \hat{j} = -\hat{i},\ \hat{i} \times \hat{k} = -\hat{j}$

$$\hat{i} \times \hat{i} = \hat{j} \times \hat{j} = \hat{k} \times \hat{k} = \overrightarrow{0}$$

(iv) $\vec{a} \times \vec{a} = \vec{0}$

(v) $\vec{b} \times \vec{a} = |\vec{b}||\vec{a}| \sin\theta(-\hat{n}) = -|\vec{b}||\vec{a}| \sin\theta\, \hat{n} = -|\vec{a}||\vec{b}| \sin\theta\, \hat{n} = -\vec{a} \times \vec{b}$

Therefore cross product is not commutative.

(vi) Cross product is distributive over addition, i.e.,

$$\vec{a} \times \left(\vec{b} + \vec{c}\right) = \vec{a} \times \vec{b} + \vec{a} \times \vec{c}$$

(vii) If $\vec{a} = a_1\hat{i} + a_2\hat{j} + a_3\hat{k}, \quad \vec{b} = b_1\hat{i} + b_2\hat{j} + b_3\hat{k}$, then

$$\vec{a} \times \vec{b} = \begin{vmatrix} \hat{i} & \hat{j} & \hat{k} \\ a_1 & a_2 & a_3 \\ b_1 & b_2 & b_3 \end{vmatrix}$$

$$= (a_2b_3 - a_3b_2)\, \hat{i} - (a_1b_3 - a_3b_1)\, \hat{j} + (a_1b_2 - a_2b_1)\, \hat{k}$$

1.7.5 Geometrical Interpretation of Vector Product

Theorem: *Prove that area of a parallelogram with adjacent sides $\vec{a}$ and $\vec{b}$ is $|\vec{a} \times \vec{b}|$.*

Proof: Let $\vec{a}$ and $\vec{b}$ be two non zero and non parallel vectors represented by $\overrightarrow{OA}$ and $\overrightarrow{OB}$ respectively and let θ be the angle between them. Complete the parallelogram *OACB*, join *BA*.

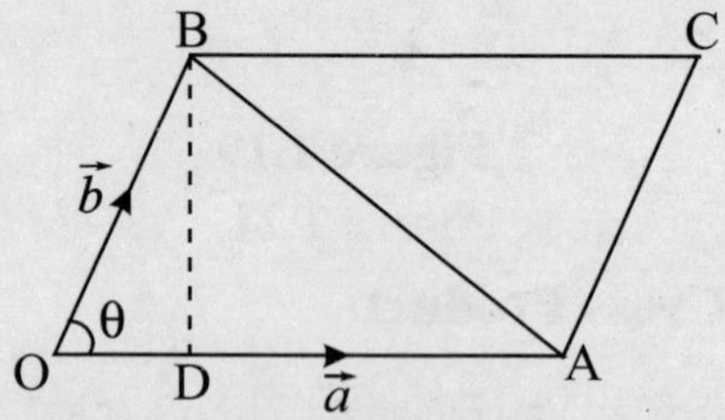

Figure 1.20

Draw *BD* perpendicular to *OA*

In triangle *OAB*, we have base $OA = |\vec{a}|$ and, altitude $= BD = OB \sin\theta = |\vec{b}| \sin\theta$

Area of triangle

$$\begin{aligned} OAB &= \frac{1}{2} \times \text{base} \times \text{altitude} \\ &= \frac{1}{2}|\vec{a}|(|\vec{b}| \sin\theta) \qquad \because \sin\theta = \frac{|\vec{a} \times \vec{b}|}{|\vec{a}||\vec{b}|} \\ &= \frac{1}{2}|\vec{a}||\vec{b}| \sin\theta = \frac{1}{2}|\vec{a} \times \vec{b}| \end{aligned}$$

Therefore, area of parallelogram

$$\begin{aligned} OACB &= 2(\text{area of triangle } OAB) \\ &= |\vec{a} \times \vec{b}| \end{aligned}$$

Hence, the area of parallelogram with adjacent sides $\vec{a}$ and $\vec{b}$ is $|\vec{a} \times \vec{b}|$.

Theorem: *Prove that the area of a triangle with adjacent sides* $\vec{a}$ *and* $\vec{b}$ *is* $\frac{1}{2}|\vec{a} \times \vec{b}|$.

Proof:

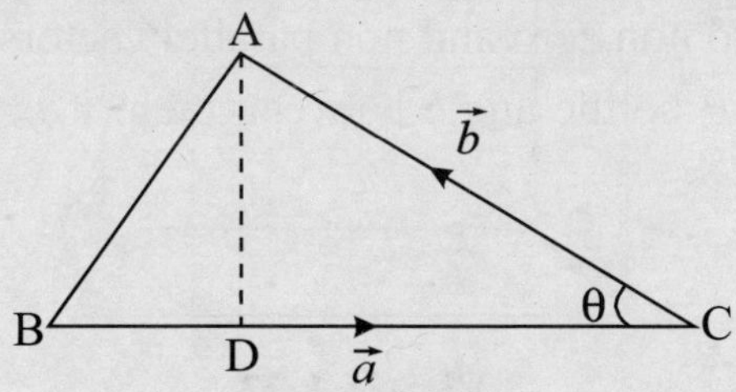

Figure 1.21

Let ABC be a given triangle with $\overrightarrow{BC} = \vec{a}$ and $\overrightarrow{CA} = \vec{b}$, draw AD perpendicular to BC. Then,

$$\text{base} = BC = |\vec{a}|$$

and, height $= AD = CA \sin\theta = |\vec{b}| \sin\theta$

Therefore, area of the triangle ABC is

$$= \frac{1}{2} \times \text{base} \times \text{height}$$

$$= \frac{1}{2}|\vec{a}||\vec{b}| \sin\theta \qquad \because \sin\theta = \frac{|\vec{a} \times \vec{b}|}{|\vec{a}||\vec{b}|}$$

$$= \frac{1}{2}|\vec{a} \times \vec{b}|$$

Thus, the area of the triangle $ABC = \frac{1}{2}|\vec{a} \times \vec{b}|$.

Scalar Triple Product of Vectors

If $\vec{a},\ \vec{b},\ \vec{c}$ are any three vectors then the *scalar triple product* of three vectors is defined as $(\vec{a} \times \vec{b}) \cdot \vec{c}$ and denoted by $[\vec{a}\,\vec{b}\,\vec{c}]$ or $[\vec{a},\ \vec{b},\ \vec{c}]$. It is a scalar quantity.

Properties of Scalar Triple Product

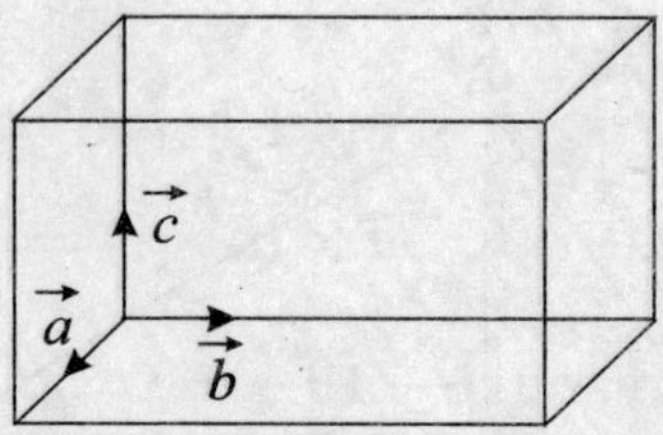

Figure 1.22

(i) The magnitude of $(\vec{a} \times \vec{b}) \cdot \vec{c}$ is equal to the *volume of a parallelopiped* whose three concurrent edges are represented by $\vec{a}$, $\vec{b}$, and $\vec{c}$, as shown in the figure 2.14.

(ii) $(\vec{a} \times \vec{b}) \cdot \vec{c} = \vec{a} \cdot (\vec{b} \times \vec{c})$, i.e., dot and cross can be interchanged in a scalar triple product.

(iii) $[\vec{a}, \vec{b}, \vec{c}] = [\vec{b}, \vec{c}, \vec{a}] = [\vec{c}, \vec{a}, \vec{b}]$

(iv) $[\vec{a}, \vec{b}, \vec{c}] = -[\vec{b}, \vec{a}, \vec{c}] = -[\vec{a}, \vec{c}, \vec{b}] = -[\vec{c}, \vec{b}, \vec{a}]$

(v) $[\vec{a}, \vec{b}, \vec{c}] = 0$ if $\vec{a} = \vec{b}$ or $\vec{b} = \vec{c}$ or $\vec{c} = \vec{a}$

or at least one vector $= \vec{0}$

or $\vec{a}$, $\vec{b}$ and $\vec{c}$ are coplanar.

(vi) $[\hat{i}, \hat{j}, \hat{k}] = 1$

(vii) If $\vec{a} = a_1\hat{i} + a_2\hat{j} + a_3\hat{k}$, $\vec{b} = b_1\hat{i} + b_2\hat{j} + b_3\hat{k}$, $\vec{c} = c_1\hat{i} + c_2\hat{j} + c_3\hat{k}$ then

$$(\vec{a} \times \vec{b}) \cdot \vec{c} = [\vec{a}, \vec{b}, \vec{c}] = \begin{vmatrix} a_1 & a_2 & a_3 \\ b_1 & b_2 & b_3 \\ c_1 & c_2 & c_3 \end{vmatrix}$$

Vector Triple Product

If $\vec{a}, \vec{b}, \vec{c}$ are any three vectors, then the vector triple product of these vectors are defined as $(\vec{a} \times \vec{b}) \times \vec{c}$ and $\vec{a} \times (\vec{b} \times \vec{c})$. It is a vector quantity and perpendicular to both $\vec{a}$ and $\vec{b} \times \vec{c}$ i.e., $\vec{a} \times (\vec{b} \times \vec{c})$ is in the plane determined by $\vec{b}$ and $\vec{c}$.

Properties of Vector Triple Product

(i) $\vec{a} \times (\vec{b} \times \vec{c}) = (\vec{a} \cdot \vec{c})\,\vec{b} - (\vec{a} \cdot \vec{b})\,\vec{c}$

Proof: Let $\vec{a} = a_1\hat{i} + a_2\hat{j} + a_3\hat{k},\ \ \vec{b} = b_1\hat{i} + b_2\hat{j} + b_3\hat{k},\ \ \vec{c} = c_1\hat{i} + c_2\hat{j} + c_3\hat{k}$

And $\vec{b} \times \vec{c} = \overrightarrow{d} = d_1\hat{i} + d_2\hat{j} + d_3\hat{k},\ \ \ \vec{a} \times (\vec{b} \times \vec{c}) = \overrightarrow{e} = e_1\hat{i} + e_2\hat{j} + e_3\hat{k}$

$$\therefore\ \vec{d} = (\vec{b} \times \vec{c}) = \begin{vmatrix} \hat{i} & \hat{j} & \hat{k} \\ b_1 & b_2 & b_3 \\ c_1 & c_2 & c_3 \end{vmatrix}$$

$$= (b_2c_3 - b_3c_2)\,\hat{i} - (b_1c_3 - b_3c_1)\,\hat{j} + (b_1c_2 - b_2c_1)\,\hat{k}$$

$$= d_1\hat{i} + d_2\hat{j} + d_3\hat{k}$$

$$\vec{e} = \vec{a} \times (\vec{b} \times \vec{c}) = \vec{a} \times \vec{d} = \begin{vmatrix} \hat{i} & \hat{j} & \hat{k} \\ a_1 & a_2 & a_3 \\ d_1 & d_2 & d_3 \end{vmatrix}$$

$$= (a_2d_3 - a_3d_2)\ \hat{i} - (a_1d_3 - a_3d_1)\ \hat{j} + (a_1d_2 - a_2d_1)\ \hat{k}$$

$$= e_1\hat{i} + e_2\hat{j} + e_3\hat{k}$$

$$e_1 = a_2d_3 - a_3d_2 = a_2\,(b_1c_2 - b_2c_1) - a_3\,(b_3c_1 - b_1c_3)$$

$$= (a_2c_2 + a_3c_3)\ b_1 - (a_2b_2 + a_3b_3)\ c_1$$

$$= (a_1c_1 + a_2c_2 + a_3c_3)\ b_1 - (a_1b_1 + a_2b_2 + a_3b_3)\ c_1$$

$$e_1 = (\vec{a} \cdot \vec{c})\ b_1 - (\vec{a} \cdot \vec{b})\,c_1$$

Similarly

$$e_2 = (\vec{a} \cdot \vec{c})\,b_2 - (\vec{a} \cdot \vec{b})\,c_2,\ e_3 = (\vec{a} \cdot \vec{c})\,b_3 - (\vec{a} \cdot \vec{b})\,c_3$$

$$\therefore\ \vec{a} \times (\vec{b} \times \vec{c}) = \overrightarrow{e} = e_1\hat{i} + e_2\hat{j} + e_3\hat{k}$$

$$= [(\vec{a} \cdot \vec{c})b_1 - (\vec{a} \cdot \vec{b})\,c_1]\hat{i} + [(\vec{a} \cdot \vec{c})\,b_2 - (\vec{a} \cdot \vec{b})\,c_2]\hat{j} + [(\vec{a} \cdot \vec{c})\,b_3 - (\vec{a} \cdot \vec{b})c_3]\hat{k}$$

$$= (\vec{a} \cdot \vec{c})\,(b_1\hat{i} + b_2\hat{j} + b_3\hat{k}) - (\vec{a} \cdot \vec{b})\,(c_1\hat{i} + c_2\hat{j} + c_3\hat{k})$$

$$\therefore\ \vec{a} \times (\vec{b} \times \vec{c}) = (\vec{a} \cdot \vec{c})\,\vec{b} - (\vec{a} \cdot \vec{b})\,\vec{c}$$

(ii) $(\vec{b} \times \vec{c}) \times \vec{a} = -\vec{a} \times (\vec{b} \times \vec{c}) = (\vec{b} \cdot \vec{a})\,\vec{c} - (\vec{c} \cdot \vec{a})\,\vec{b}$

Reciprocal System of Vectors

If $\vec{a}, \vec{b}, \vec{c}$ are three non-coplanar vectors i.e., $[\vec{a}, \vec{b}, \vec{c}] \neq 0$ then the vectors

$$\vec{a'} = \frac{\vec{b} \times \vec{c}}{[\vec{a}, \vec{b}, \vec{c}]}, \quad \vec{b'} = \frac{\vec{c} \times \vec{a}}{[\vec{a}, \vec{b}, \vec{c}]} \quad \text{and} \quad \vec{c'} = \frac{\vec{a} \times \vec{b}}{[\vec{a}, \vec{b}, \vec{c}]}$$

are said to form a *reciprocal system of vectors* with the vectors $\vec{a}, \vec{b}, \vec{c}$.

Worked Examples

1. *Express $\overrightarrow{AB}$ in terms of unit vectors $\hat{i}$, $\hat{j}$ and $\hat{k}$ and find $|\overrightarrow{AB}|$, where $A = (1, 2, 3)$ and $B = (-6, 5, 3)$.*

   ➡ Given,

$$\overrightarrow{OA} = \hat{i} + 2\hat{j} + 3\hat{k}$$
$$\overrightarrow{OB} = -6\hat{i} + 5\hat{j} + 3\hat{k}$$
$$\overrightarrow{AB} = \overrightarrow{OB} - \overrightarrow{OA} = -6\hat{i} + 5\hat{j} + 3\hat{k} - (\hat{i} + 2\hat{j} + 3\hat{k}) = -7\hat{i} + 3\hat{j}$$
$$\therefore\ |\overrightarrow{AB}| = \sqrt{(-7)^2 + 3^2} = \sqrt{58}$$

2. *If $\vec{a} = 2\hat{i} + 3\hat{j} - \hat{k}$, $\vec{b} = \hat{i} - 2\hat{j} + \hat{k}$ and $\vec{c} = 3\hat{i} - \hat{j} + 2\hat{k}$, find*

   (i) $2\vec{a} + 3\vec{b} - 2\vec{c}$, (ii) $\frac{1}{2}\vec{a} + 3\vec{b} - \frac{3}{2}\vec{c}$, (iii) $\vec{a} + \vec{b} - \frac{\vec{c}}{7}$

   ➡ (i)

$$\begin{aligned} 2\vec{a} + 3\vec{b} - 2\vec{c} &= 2\left(2\hat{i} + 3\hat{j} - \hat{k}\right) + 3\left(\hat{i} - 2\hat{j} + \hat{k}\right) - 2\left(3\hat{i} - \hat{j} + 2\hat{k}\right) \\ &= 4\hat{i} + 6\hat{j} - 2\hat{k} + 3\hat{i} - 6\hat{j} + 3\hat{k} - 6\hat{i} + 2\hat{j} - 4\hat{k} \\ &= \hat{i} + 2\hat{j} - 3\hat{k} \end{aligned}$$

(ii)

$$\frac{1}{2}\vec{a} + 3\vec{b} - \frac{3}{2}\vec{c} = \frac{1}{2}\left(2\hat{i} + 3\hat{j} - \hat{k}\right) + 3\left(\hat{i} - 2\hat{j} + \hat{k}\right) - \frac{3}{2}\left(3\hat{i} - \hat{j} + 2\hat{k}\right)$$

$$= \hat{i} + \frac{3}{2}\hat{j} - \frac{1}{2}\hat{k} + 3\hat{i} - 6\hat{j} + 3\hat{k} - \frac{9}{2}\hat{i} + \frac{3}{2}\hat{j} - 3\hat{k}$$
$$= -\frac{\hat{i}}{2} - 3\hat{j} - \frac{1}{2}\hat{k}$$

(iii)

$$\vec{a} + \vec{b} - \frac{\vec{c}}{7} = 2\hat{i} + 3\hat{j} - \hat{k} + \hat{i} - 2\hat{j} + \hat{k} - \frac{3}{7}\hat{i} + \frac{1}{7}\hat{j} - \frac{2}{7}\hat{k}$$
$$= \frac{18}{7}\hat{i} + \frac{8}{7}\hat{j} - \frac{2}{7}\hat{k}$$

3. *Show that the position vectors of the vertices of a triangle $\vec{a} = 3(\sqrt{3}\hat{i} - \hat{j})$, $\vec{b} = 6\hat{j}$, $\vec{c} = 3(\sqrt{3}\hat{i} + \hat{j})$ from an isosceles triangle.*

➡ Let A, B, C be the vertices of the triangle

$$\overrightarrow{OA} = \vec{a} = 3\left(\sqrt{3}\hat{i} - \hat{j}\right)$$
$$\overrightarrow{OB} = \vec{b} = 6\hat{j}$$
$$\overrightarrow{OC} = \vec{c} = 3\left(\sqrt{3}\hat{i} + \hat{j}\right)$$
$$\therefore\ \overrightarrow{AB} = \overrightarrow{OB} - \overrightarrow{OA} = 6\hat{j} - 3\sqrt{3}\hat{i} + 3\hat{j} = -3\sqrt{3}\hat{i} + 9\hat{j}$$
$$\overrightarrow{BC} = \overrightarrow{OC} - \overrightarrow{OB} = 3\sqrt{3}\hat{i} + 3\hat{j} - 6\hat{j} = 3\sqrt{3}\hat{i} - 3\hat{j}$$
$$\overrightarrow{CA} = \overrightarrow{OA} - \overrightarrow{OC} = 3\sqrt{3}\hat{i} - 3\hat{j} - 3\sqrt{3}\hat{i} - 3\hat{j} = -6\hat{j}$$
$$\therefore\ \left|\overrightarrow{AB}\right| = \sqrt{\left(3\sqrt{3}\right)^2 + (9)^2} = \sqrt{27 + 81} = \sqrt{108}$$
$$\left|\overrightarrow{BC}\right| = \sqrt{\left(3\sqrt{3}\right)^2 + (-3)^2} = \sqrt{27 + 9} = 6$$
$$\left|\overrightarrow{CA}\right| = \sqrt{(-6)^2} = 6$$

Hence the triangle ABC is an isosceles triangle.

4. *Show that the position vectors of the vertices of a triangle* $2\hat{i} - \hat{j} + \hat{k}$, $\hat{i} - 3\hat{j} - 5\hat{k}$ *and* $3\hat{i} - 4\hat{j} - 4k$ *from a right-angled triangle.*

➡ Let A, B, C be the vertices of the triangle

$$\therefore\ \overrightarrow{OA} = 2\hat{i} - \hat{j} + \hat{k}$$

$$\overrightarrow{OB} = \hat{i} - 3\hat{j} - 5\hat{k}$$

$$\overrightarrow{OC} = 3\hat{i} - 4\hat{j} - 4\hat{k}$$

$$\overrightarrow{AB} = \overrightarrow{OB} - \overrightarrow{OA} = \hat{i} - 3\hat{j} - 5\hat{k} - 2\hat{i} + \hat{j} - \hat{k} = -\hat{i} - 2\hat{j} - 6\hat{k}$$

$$\overrightarrow{BC} = \overrightarrow{OC} - \overrightarrow{OB} = 3\hat{i} - 4\hat{j} - 4\hat{k} - \hat{i} + 3\hat{j} + 5\hat{k} = 2\hat{i} - \hat{j} + \hat{k}$$

$$\overrightarrow{CA} = \overrightarrow{OA} - \overrightarrow{OC} = 2\hat{i} - \hat{j} + \hat{k} - 3\hat{i} + 4\hat{j} + 4\hat{k} = -\hat{i} + 3\hat{j} + 5\hat{k}$$

$$AB = \left|\overrightarrow{AB}\right| = \sqrt{(-1)^2 + (-2)^2 + (-6)^2} = \sqrt{1 + 4 + 36} = \sqrt{41}$$

$$BC = \left|\overrightarrow{BC}\right| = \sqrt{2^2 + (-1)^2 + (1)^2} = \sqrt{6}$$

$$CA = \left|\overrightarrow{CA}\right| = \sqrt{(-1)^2 + 3^2 + 5^2} = \sqrt{35}$$

$$BC^2 + CA^2 = 6 + 35 = 41 = AB^2$$

Therefore the triangle ABC is a right-angled triangle.

5. *If* $\vec{a} = r\cos\theta\sin\phi\,\hat{i} + r\sin\theta\sin\phi\,\hat{j} + r\cos\phi\,\hat{k}$, *then show that* $|\vec{a}| = r$

➡

$$\vec{a} = r\cos\theta\sin\phi\,\hat{i} + r\sin\theta\sin\phi\,\hat{j} + r\cos\phi\,\hat{k}$$

$$|\vec{a}| = \sqrt{(r\cos\theta\sin\phi)^2 + (r\sin\theta\sin\phi)^2 + (r\cos\phi)^2}$$

$$= \sqrt{r^2\cos^2\theta\sin^2\phi + r^2\sin^2\theta\sin^2\phi + r^2\cos^2\phi}$$

$$= \sqrt{r^2\sin^2\phi\left(\cos^2\theta + \sin^2\theta\right) + r^2\cos^2\phi}$$

$$= \sqrt{r^2\sin^2\phi\,(1) + r^2\cos^2\phi} = \sqrt{r^2\left(\sin^2\phi + \cos^2\phi\right)}$$

$$|\vec{a}| = r$$

6. *Find $\vec{a} \cdot \vec{b}$, where $\vec{a} = 3\hat{i} + 2\hat{j} - \hat{k}$, $\vec{b} = \hat{i} + 7\hat{j} - (3/2)\hat{k}$*

➡

$$\vec{a} \cdot \vec{b} = \left(3\hat{i} + 2\hat{j} - \hat{k}\right) \cdot \left(\hat{i} + 7\hat{j} - (3/2)\hat{k}\right)$$

$$= 3(1) + 2(7) + (-1)(-(3/2)) = 3 + 14 + (3/2) = 17 + (3/2)$$

$$\vec{a} \cdot \vec{b} = \frac{37}{2}$$

7. *Find the angle between the vectors $\vec{a} = 5\hat{i} - \hat{j} + \hat{k}$ and $\vec{b} = 2\hat{i} - 3\hat{j} + 6\hat{k}$*

➡ We have

$$\cos\theta = \frac{\vec{a} \cdot \vec{b}}{|\vec{a}|\left|\vec{b}\right|} = \frac{5(2) + (-1)(-3) + (1)(6)}{\sqrt{5^2 + (-1)^2 + 1^2}\sqrt{2^2 + (-3)^2 + 6^2}}$$

$$= \frac{10 + 3 + 6}{\sqrt{27}\sqrt{49}} = \frac{19}{7\sqrt{27}} = \frac{19}{21\sqrt{3}}$$

$$\theta = \cos^{-1}\left(\frac{19}{21\sqrt{3}}\right)$$

8. *If $\vec{a} = \hat{i} + 2\hat{j} - 3\hat{k}$ and $\vec{b} = 3\hat{i} - \hat{j} + 2\hat{k}$ then*

(i) *Show that $\left(\vec{a} + \vec{b}\right)$ and $\left(\vec{a} - \vec{b}\right)$ are orthogonal*

(ii) *Also find the angle between $\left(2\vec{a} + \vec{b}\right)$ and $\left(\vec{a} + 2\vec{b}\right)$*

➡ (i)

$$\vec{a} + \vec{b} = (1 + 3)\hat{i} + (2 - 1)\hat{j} + (-3 + 2)\hat{k}$$

$$\vec{a} + \vec{b} = 4\hat{i} + \hat{j} - \hat{k}$$

$$\vec{a} - \vec{b} = -2\hat{i} + 3\hat{j} - 5\hat{k}$$

$$(\vec{a} + \vec{b}) \cdot (\vec{a} - \vec{b}) = 4(-2) + 1(3) + (-1)(-5) = -8 + 3 + 5 = 0$$

Therefore $(\vec{a} + \vec{b})$ and $(\vec{a} - \vec{b})$ are orthogonal.

(ii)

$$2\vec{a} + \vec{b} = 2\left(\hat{i} + 2\hat{j} - 3\hat{k}\right) + \left(3\hat{i} - \hat{j} + 2\hat{k}\right) = 5\hat{i} + 3\hat{j} - 4\hat{k}$$

$$\vec{a} + 2\vec{b} = \left(\hat{i} + 2\hat{j} - 3\hat{k}\right) + 2\left(3\hat{i} - \hat{j} + 2\hat{k}\right) = 7\hat{i} + \hat{k}$$

Therefore angle between $(2\vec{a}+\vec{b})$ and $(\vec{a}+2\vec{b})$ is given by

$$\cos\theta = \frac{\left(2\vec{a}+\vec{b}\right)\cdot\left(\vec{a}+2\vec{b}\right)}{\left|2\vec{a}+\vec{b}\right|\,\left|\vec{a}+2\vec{b}\right|}$$

$$= \frac{35+0-4}{\sqrt{25+9+16}\sqrt{49+1}} = \frac{31}{50}$$

$$\theta = \cos^{-1}\left(\frac{31}{50}\right)$$

9. *Determine the value of a so that $\vec{A} = 2\hat{i}+a\hat{j}+\hat{k}$ and $\vec{B} = 4\hat{i}-2\hat{j}-2\hat{k}$ are perpendicular.*

➡ We have $\vec{A}\cdot\vec{B} = 0$

$$\left(2\hat{i}+a\hat{j}+\hat{k}\right)\cdot\left(4\hat{i}-2\hat{j}-2\hat{k}\right) = 0$$

$$2(4)+a(-2)+1(-2) = 0$$

$$8-2a-2 = 0$$

$$6-2a = 0$$

$$6 = 2a$$

$$a = 3$$

10. *If $\vec{A} = \hat{i}-2\hat{j}+3\hat{k}$, $\vec{B} = -\hat{i}+2\hat{j}+\hat{k}$ and $\vec{C} = 3\hat{i}+\hat{j}$, find the value of p such that $\vec{A}-p\vec{B}$ is perpendicular to $\vec{C}$*

➡

$$\vec{A}-p\vec{B} = (1+p)\,\hat{i}+(-2-2p)\,\hat{j}+(3-p)\,\hat{k}$$

Since $\vec{A}-p\vec{B}$ is perpendicular to $\vec{C}$

$$\Rightarrow \left(\vec{A}-p\vec{B}\right)\cdot\vec{C} = 0$$

$$\left[(1+p)\,\hat{i}+(-2-2p)\,\hat{j}+(3-p)\,\hat{k}\right]\cdot\left(3\hat{i}+\hat{j}\right) = 0$$

$$3(1+p)+1(-2-2p) = 0$$

$$3 + 3p - 2 - 2p = 0$$
$$p + 1 = 0$$
$$p = -1$$

11. *Find the sine of the angle between $\vec{a} = 2\hat{i} - 2\hat{j} + \hat{k}$ and $\vec{b} = \hat{i} - 2\hat{j} + 2\hat{k}$*

➡ We have

$$\sin\theta = \frac{\left|\vec{a} \times \vec{b}\right|}{|\vec{a}|\left|\vec{b}\right|}$$

$$\vec{a} \times \vec{b} = \begin{vmatrix} \hat{i} & \hat{j} & \hat{k} \\ 2 & -2 & 1 \\ 1 & -2 & 2 \end{vmatrix} = \hat{i}\,(-4+2) - \hat{j}\,(4-1) + \hat{k}\,(-4+2)$$

$$= -2\hat{i} - 3\hat{j} - 2\hat{k}$$

$$\left|\vec{a} \times \vec{b}\right| = \sqrt{(-2)^2 + (-3)^2 + (-2)^2} = \sqrt{17}$$

$$|\vec{a}| = \sqrt{2^2 + (-2)^2 + 1^2} = \sqrt{9} = 3$$

$$\left|\vec{b}\right| = \sqrt{1^2 + (-2)^2 + 2^2} = \sqrt{9} = 3$$

Therefore $\sin\theta = \dfrac{\sqrt{17}}{3 \times 3} = \dfrac{\sqrt{17}}{9}$

12. *If $\vec{a} = 2\hat{i} + 3\hat{j} - 4\hat{k}$ and $\vec{b} = 8\hat{i} - 4\hat{j} + \hat{k}$ then prove that $\vec{a}$ is perpendicular to $\vec{b}$, also find $\left|\vec{a} \times \vec{b}\right|$*

➡ We know that if $\vec{a} \perp \overrightarrow{b}$ then $\vec{a} \cdot \vec{b} = 0$

$$\vec{a} \cdot \vec{b} = 2 \times 8 + 3 \times (-4) + (-4) \times 1$$
$$= 16 - 12 - 4 = 0$$

Hence, $\vec{a}$ is perpendicular to $\vec{b}$

$$\vec{a} \times \vec{b} = \begin{vmatrix} \hat{i} & \hat{j} & \hat{k} \\ 2 & 3 & -4 \\ 8 & -4 & 1 \end{vmatrix} = \hat{i}\,(3-16) - \hat{j}\,(2+32) + \hat{k}\,(-8-24)$$

$$= -13\hat{i} - 34\hat{j} - 32\hat{k}$$

$$\left|\vec{a} \times \vec{b}\right| = \sqrt{(-13)^2 + (-34)^2 + (-32)^2} = \sqrt{169 + 1156 + 1024}$$

$$\therefore \ \left|\vec{a} \times \vec{b}\right| = \sqrt{2349}$$

13. *Find the unit vector perpendicular to both $\vec{a}$ and $\vec{b}$, where $\vec{a} = \hat{i} - 2\hat{j} + 3\hat{k}$ and $\vec{b} = 2\hat{i} + \hat{j} + \hat{k}$*

➡

$$\vec{a} \times \vec{b} = \begin{vmatrix} \hat{i} & \hat{j} & \hat{k} \\ 1 & -2 & 3 \\ 2 & 1 & 1 \end{vmatrix} = \hat{i}\,(-2-3) - \hat{j}\,(1-6) + \hat{k}\,(1+4)$$

$$\vec{a} \times \vec{b} = -5\hat{i} + 5\hat{j} + 5\hat{k}$$

$$\left|\vec{a} \times \vec{b}\right| = \sqrt{25 + 25 + 25} = 5\sqrt{3}$$

Therefore the unit vector perpendicular to both $\vec{a}$ and $\vec{b}$ is

$$\hat{n} = \frac{\vec{a} \times \vec{b}}{\left|\vec{a} \times \vec{b}\right|} = -\frac{1}{\sqrt{3}}\hat{i} + \frac{1}{\sqrt{3}}\hat{j} + \frac{1}{\sqrt{3}}\hat{k}$$

14. *If $\vec{A} = 4\hat{i} + 3\hat{j} + \hat{k}$ and $\vec{B} = 2\hat{i} - \hat{j} + 2\hat{k}$, find a unit vector $\hat{N}$ perpendicular to the vectors $\vec{A}$ and $\vec{B}$ such that $\vec{A}$, $\vec{B}$, $\overrightarrow{N}$ form a right handed system.*

➡

$$\vec{A} \times \vec{B} = \begin{vmatrix} \hat{i} & \hat{j} & \hat{k} \\ 4 & 3 & 1 \\ 2 & -1 & 2 \end{vmatrix} = \hat{i}\,(6+1) - \hat{j}\,(8-2) + \hat{k}\,(-4-6)$$

$$\vec{A} \times \vec{B} = 7\hat{i} - 6\hat{j} - 10\hat{k}$$

$$\left|\vec{A} \times \vec{B}\right| = \sqrt{49 + 36 + 100} = \sqrt{185}$$

Therefore, the unit vector $\hat{N}$ perpendicular to both $\vec{A}$ and $\vec{B}$ is

$$\hat{N} = \frac{\vec{A} \times \vec{B}}{|\vec{A} \times \vec{B}|} = \frac{7\hat{i} - 6\hat{j} - 10\hat{k}}{\sqrt{185}}$$

$$= \frac{7}{\sqrt{185}}\hat{i} - \frac{6}{\sqrt{185}}\hat{j} - \frac{10}{\sqrt{185}}\hat{k}$$

15. *Find the unit normal to both the vectors $4\hat{i} - \hat{j} + 3\hat{k}$ and $-2\hat{i} + \hat{j} - 2\hat{k}$. Find also the sine of the angle between them.*

➡ Let $\vec{a} = 4\hat{i} - \hat{j} + 3\hat{k}$ and $\vec{b} = -2\hat{i} + \hat{j} - 2\hat{k}$

$$\vec{a} \times \vec{b} = \begin{vmatrix} \hat{i} & \hat{j} & \hat{k} \\ 4 & -1 & 3 \\ -2 & 1 & -2 \end{vmatrix} = \hat{i}\,(2-3) - \hat{j}\,(-8+6) + \hat{k}\,(4-2)$$

$$\vec{a} \times \vec{b} = -\hat{i} - 2\hat{j} + 2\hat{k}$$

$$|\vec{a} \times \vec{b}| = \sqrt{1+4+4} = 3$$

Therefore unit normal vector to both the vectors is

$$\hat{n} = \frac{\vec{a} \times \vec{b}}{|\vec{a} \times \vec{b}|} = -\frac{1}{3}\hat{i} - \frac{2}{3}\hat{j} + \frac{2}{3}\hat{k}$$

We have

$$\sin\theta = \frac{|\vec{a} \times \vec{b}|}{|\vec{a}||\vec{b}|} = \frac{3}{\sqrt{16+1+9}\sqrt{4+1+4}} = \frac{3}{\sqrt{26}\sqrt{9}} = \frac{1}{\sqrt{26}}$$

$$\sin\theta = \frac{1}{\sqrt{26}}$$

16. *Find the vector of magnitude 12 units which is perpendicular to the vectors $\vec{a} = 4\hat{i} - \hat{j} + 3\hat{k}$ and $\vec{b} = -2\hat{i} + \hat{j} - 2\hat{k}$*

➡

$$\vec{a} \times \vec{b} = \begin{vmatrix} \hat{i} & \hat{j} & \hat{k} \\ 4 & -1 & 3 \\ -2 & 1 & -2 \end{vmatrix} = \hat{i}\,(2-3) - \hat{j}\,(-8+6) + \hat{k}\,(4-2)$$

$$\vec{a} \times \vec{b} = -\hat{i} + 2\hat{j} + 2\hat{k}$$

$$\left|\vec{a} \times \vec{b}\right| = \sqrt{1+4+4} = 3$$

Therefore, the unit vector perpendicular to both $\vec{a}$ and $\vec{b}$ is

$$\hat{n} = \frac{\vec{a} \times \vec{b}}{\left|\vec{a} \times \vec{b}\right|} = -\frac{1}{3}\hat{i} + \frac{2}{3}\hat{j} + \frac{2}{3}\hat{k}$$

Hence, the vector of magnitude 12 units which is perpendicular to both $\vec{a}$ and $\vec{b}$ is

$$12\hat{n} = -4\hat{i} + 8\hat{j} + 8\hat{k}$$

17. *Find* $\vec{a} \cdot (\vec{b} \times \vec{c})$, $\vec{b} \times (\vec{a} \times \vec{c})$ *and* $\vec{c} \cdot (\vec{a} \times \vec{b})$, *where* $\vec{a} = \hat{i} + \hat{j} - \hat{k}$, $\vec{b} = 2\hat{i} - \hat{j} + 2\hat{k}, \vec{c} = 3\hat{i} - \hat{j} - \hat{k}$

➡ We know that,

$$\vec{a} \cdot \left(\vec{b} \times \vec{c}\right) = \begin{vmatrix} 1 & 1 & -1 \\ 2 & -1 & 2 \\ 3 & -1 & -1 \end{vmatrix} = 1\,(1+2) - 1\,(-2-6) - 1\,(-2+3)$$

$$= 3 + 8 - 1 = 10$$

$$\vec{a} \times \vec{c} = \begin{vmatrix} \hat{i} & \hat{j} & \hat{k} \\ 1 & 1 & -1 \\ 3 & -1 & -1 \end{vmatrix} = \hat{i}\,(-1-1) - \hat{j}\,(-1+3) + \hat{k}\,(-1-3)$$

$$= -2\hat{i} - 2\hat{j} - 4\hat{k}$$

$$\vec{b} \times (\vec{a} \times \vec{c}) = \begin{vmatrix} \hat{i} & \hat{j} & \hat{k} \\ 2 & -1 & 2 \\ -2 & -2 & -4 \end{vmatrix} = \hat{i}\,(4+4) - \hat{j}\,(-8+4) + \hat{k}\,(-4-2)$$

$$\vec{b} \times (\vec{a} \times \vec{c}) = 8\hat{i} + 4\hat{j} - 6\hat{k}$$

$$\vec{c} \cdot \left(\vec{a} \times \vec{b}\right) = \begin{vmatrix} 3 & -1 & -1 \\ 1 & 1 & -1 \\ 2 & -1 & 2 \end{vmatrix} = 3\,(2-1) + 1\,(2+2) - 1\,(-1-2)$$

$$= 3 + 4 + 3 = 10$$

$$\therefore\ \vec{c} \cdot (\vec{a} \times \vec{b}) = 10$$

18. *If $\vec{a}=(3,-1,4)$, $\vec{b}=(1,2,3)$ and $\vec{c}=(4,2,-1)$ find $\vec{a}\times\left(\vec{b}\times\vec{c}\right)$.*

➡

$$\vec{b}\times\vec{c}=\begin{vmatrix}\hat{i} & \hat{j} & \hat{k}\\ 1 & 2 & 3\\ 4 & 2 & -1\end{vmatrix}=\hat{i}\,(-2-6)-\hat{j}\,(-1-12)+\hat{k}\,(2-8)$$

$$=-8\hat{i}+13\hat{j}-6\hat{k}$$

$$\therefore\ \vec{a}\times\left(\vec{b}\times\vec{c}\right)=\begin{vmatrix}\hat{i} & \hat{j} & \hat{k}\\ 3 & -1 & 4\\ -8 & 13 & -6\end{vmatrix}=\hat{i}\,(6-52)-\hat{j}\,(-18+32)+\hat{k}\,(39-8)$$

$$\vec{a}\times\left(\vec{b}\times\vec{c}\right)=-46\hat{i}-14\hat{j}+31\hat{k}$$

19. *Find the volume of the parallelopiped whose co-terminal edges are represented by the vectors $\vec{a}=\hat{i}+\hat{j}+\hat{k}$, $\vec{b}=2\hat{i}+3\hat{j}-\hat{k}$, $\vec{c}=\hat{i}-\hat{j}-\hat{k}$*

➡ Volume of the parallelopiped $=\vec{a}\cdot\left(\vec{b}\times\vec{c}\right)$

$$=\begin{vmatrix}1 & 1 & 1\\ 2 & 3 & -1\\ 1 & -1 & -1\end{vmatrix}=1\,(-3-1)-1\,(-2+1)+1\,(-2-3)$$

$$=-4+1-5=-8=8\text{ units.}$$

20. *Prove that the position vectors of the points A, B, C and D represented by the vectors $-\hat{j}-\hat{k}$, $4\hat{i}+5\hat{j}+\hat{k}$, $3\hat{i}+9\hat{j}+4\hat{k}$ and $-4\hat{i}+4\hat{j}+4\hat{k}$, respectively are coplanar.*

➡ Let $\overrightarrow{OA}=-\hat{j}-\hat{k}$, $\overrightarrow{OB}=4\hat{i}+5\hat{j}+\hat{k}$

$$\overrightarrow{OC}=3\hat{i}+9\hat{j}+4\hat{k},\quad \overrightarrow{OD}=-4\hat{i}+4\hat{j}+4\hat{k}$$

$$\overrightarrow{AB}=\overrightarrow{OB}-\overrightarrow{OA}=4\hat{i}+6\hat{j}+2\hat{k}$$

$$\overrightarrow{AC}=\overrightarrow{OC}-\overrightarrow{OA}=3\hat{i}+10\hat{j}+5\hat{k}$$

$$\overrightarrow{AD}=\overrightarrow{OD}-\overrightarrow{OA}=-4\hat{i}+5\hat{j}+5\hat{k}$$

$$\overrightarrow{AB}\cdot\left(\overrightarrow{AC}\times\overrightarrow{AD}\right)=\begin{vmatrix}4 & 6 & 2\\ 3 & 10 & 5\\ -4 & 5 & 5\end{vmatrix}$$

$$= 4\,[50 - 25] - 6\,[15 + 20] + 2\,[15 + 40]$$
$$= 100 - 210 + 110 = 0$$

Therefore $\overrightarrow{AB}$, $\overrightarrow{AC}$, $\overrightarrow{AD}$ are coplanar.
Hence $\overrightarrow{OA}$, $\overrightarrow{OB}$, $\overrightarrow{OC}$, $\overrightarrow{OD}$ are coplanar.

21. *Show that the four points whose position vectors are* $3\hat{i} - 2\hat{j} + 4\hat{k}$, $6\hat{i} + 3\hat{j} + \hat{k}$, $5\hat{i} + 7\hat{j} + 3\hat{k}$ *and* $2\hat{i} + 2\hat{j} + 6\hat{k}$ *are co-planar.*
Let

$$\overrightarrow{OA} = 3\hat{i} - 2\hat{j} + 4\hat{k}$$
$$\overrightarrow{OB} = 6\hat{i} + 3\hat{j} + \hat{k}$$
$$\overrightarrow{OC} = 5\hat{i} + 7\hat{j} + 3\hat{k}$$
$$\overrightarrow{OD} = 2\hat{i} + 2\hat{j} + 6\hat{k}$$
$$\overrightarrow{AB} = \overrightarrow{OB} - \overrightarrow{OA} = 3\hat{i} + 5\hat{j} - 3\hat{k}$$
$$\overrightarrow{AC} = \overrightarrow{OC} - \overrightarrow{OA} = 2\hat{i} + 9\hat{j} - \hat{k}$$
$$\overrightarrow{AD} = \overrightarrow{OD} - \overrightarrow{OA} = -\hat{i} + 4\hat{j} + 2\hat{k}$$
$$\overrightarrow{AB} \cdot \left(\overrightarrow{AC} \times \overrightarrow{AD}\right) = \begin{vmatrix} 3 & 5 & -3 \\ 2 & 9 & -1 \\ -1 & 4 & 2 \end{vmatrix}$$
$$= 3\,(18 + 4) - 5\,(4 - 1) - 3\,(8 + 9)$$
$$= 3\,(22) - 5\,(3) - 3\,(17)$$
$$= 66 - 15 - 51$$
$$= 66 - 66 = 0$$

Therefore, $\overrightarrow{AB}$, $\overrightarrow{AC}$, $\overrightarrow{AD}$ are coplanar.
Hence, $\overrightarrow{OA}$, $\overrightarrow{OB}$, $\overrightarrow{OC}$, $\overrightarrow{OD}$ are coplanar.

22. *Show that the points* $A(-1,4,-3)$, $B(3,2,-5)$, $C(-3,8,-5)$ *and* $D = (-3,2,1)$ *are coplanar.*

➡ Let $\overrightarrow{OA}$, $\overrightarrow{OB}$, $\overrightarrow{OC}$, $\overrightarrow{OD}$ be the position vectors of the points *A, B, C, D.*

$$\overrightarrow{OA} = -\hat{i} + 4\hat{j} - 3\hat{k}, \quad \overrightarrow{OB} = 3\hat{i} + 2\hat{j} - 5\hat{k}$$

$$\overrightarrow{OC} = -3\hat{i} + 8\hat{j} - 5\hat{k}, \quad \overrightarrow{OD} = -3\hat{i} + 2\hat{j} + \hat{k}$$

$$\overrightarrow{AB} = \overrightarrow{OB} - \overrightarrow{OA} = 4\hat{i} - 2\hat{j} - 2\hat{k}$$

$$\overrightarrow{AC} = \overrightarrow{OC} - \overrightarrow{OA} = -2\hat{i} + 4\hat{j} - 2\hat{k}$$

$$\overrightarrow{AD} = \overrightarrow{OD} - \overrightarrow{OA} = -2\hat{i} - 2\hat{j} + 4\hat{k}$$

$$\overrightarrow{AB} \cdot \left(\overrightarrow{AC} \times \overrightarrow{AD}\right) = \begin{vmatrix} 4 & -2 & -2 \\ -2 & 4 & -2 \\ -2 & -2 & 4 \end{vmatrix} = 4[16-4] + 2[-8-4] - 2[4+8]$$

$$= 48 - 24 - 24 = 0$$

Hence $\overrightarrow{AB}$, $\overrightarrow{AC}$, $\overrightarrow{AD}$ are coplanar. Therefore *A, B, C, D* are coplanar.

23. *Show that the vectors* $\vec{A} = \hat{i} - 2\hat{j} + 3\hat{k}$, $\vec{B} = 2\hat{i} + \hat{j} + \hat{k}$ *and* $\vec{C} = 3\hat{i} + 4\hat{j} - \hat{k}$ *are coplanar.*

➡ We have

$$\vec{A} \cdot \left(\vec{B} \times \vec{C}\right) = \begin{vmatrix} 1 & -2 & 3 \\ 2 & 1 & 1 \\ 3 & 4 & -1 \end{vmatrix} = 1(-1-4) + 2(-2-3) + 3(8-3)$$

$$= -5 - 10 + 15 = 0$$

Hence $\vec{A}, \vec{B}, \vec{C}$ are coplanar.

24. *Find the value of* λ *so that the points* $A(-1,\ 4,\ -3)$, $B(3,\ 2,\ -5)$, $C(-3,\ 8,\ -5)$ *and* $D(-3,\ \lambda,\ 1)$ *may lie on one plane.*

➡ Let $\overrightarrow{OA}$, $\overrightarrow{OB}$, $\overrightarrow{OC}$, $\overrightarrow{OD}$ be the position vectors of the points *A, B, C, D.*

$$\overrightarrow{OA} = -\hat{i} + 4\hat{j} - 3\hat{k}$$

$$\overrightarrow{OB} = 3\hat{i} + 2\hat{j} - 5\hat{k}$$

$$\overrightarrow{OC} = -3\hat{i} + 8\hat{j} - 5\hat{k}$$

$$\overrightarrow{OD} = -3\hat{i} + \lambda\hat{j} + \hat{k}$$

$$\overrightarrow{AB} = \overrightarrow{OB} - \overrightarrow{OA} = 4\hat{i} - 2\hat{j} - 2\hat{k}$$

$$\overrightarrow{AC} = \overrightarrow{OC} - \overrightarrow{OA} = -2\hat{i} + 4\hat{j} - 2\hat{k}$$

$$\overrightarrow{AD} = \overrightarrow{OD} - \overrightarrow{OA} = -2\hat{i} + (\lambda - 4)\,\hat{j} + 4\hat{k}$$

Since $\overrightarrow{AB}$, $\overrightarrow{AC}$ and $\overrightarrow{AD}$ are coplanar
Therefore,

$$\overrightarrow{AB} \cdot \left(\overrightarrow{AC} \times \overrightarrow{AD}\right) = 0$$

$$\begin{vmatrix} 4 & -2 & -2 \\ -2 & 4 & -2 \\ -2 & \lambda - 4 & 4 \end{vmatrix} = 0$$

$$4\,(16 + 2\,(\lambda - 4)) + 2\,(-8 - 4) - 2\,(-2\,(\lambda - 4) + 8) = 0$$

$$4\,(2\lambda + 8) - 24 - 2\,(-2\lambda + 16) = 0$$

$$8\lambda + 32 - 24 + 4\lambda - 32 = 0$$

$$12\lambda - 24 = 0 \Rightarrow \lambda = 2$$

25. *Find the value of λ so that the vectors $\vec{a} = 2\hat{i} - 3\hat{j} + \hat{k}$, $\vec{b} = \hat{i} + 2\hat{j} - 3\hat{k}$ and $\vec{c} = \hat{j} + \lambda\hat{k}$ are coplanar.*

➡

$$\vec{a} \cdot \left(\vec{b} \times \vec{c}\right) = \begin{vmatrix} 2 & -3 & 1 \\ 1 & 2 & -3 \\ 0 & 1 & \lambda \end{vmatrix} = 0$$

$$2\,(2\lambda + 3) + 3\,(\lambda - 0) + 1\,(1 - 0) = 0$$

$$4\lambda + 6 + 3\lambda + 1 = 0$$

$$7\lambda + 7 = 0$$

$$\lambda = -1$$

26. *Find the constant a so that the vectors $2\hat{i} - \hat{j} + \hat{k}$, $\hat{i} + 2\hat{j} - 3\hat{k}$ and $3\hat{i} + a\hat{j} + 5\hat{k}$ are coplanar.*

➡ Let $\vec{A} = 2\hat{i} - \hat{j} + \hat{k}$, $\vec{B} = \hat{i} + 2\hat{j} - 3\hat{k}$

$$\vec{C} = 3\hat{i} + a\hat{j} + 5\hat{k}$$

$$\vec{A} \cdot \left(\vec{B} \times \vec{C}\right) = \begin{vmatrix} 2 & -1 & 1 \\ 1 & 2 & -3 \\ 3 & a & 5 \end{vmatrix} = 0$$

$$2\,(10 + 3a) + 1\,(5 + 9) + 1\,(a - 6) = 0$$

$$20 + 6a + 14 + a - 6 = 0$$

$$7a + 28 = 0$$

$$7a = -28$$

$$a = -4$$

27. *Prove that* $\left[\vec{a} \times \vec{b},\ \vec{b} \times \vec{c},\ \vec{c} \times \vec{a}\right] = \left[\vec{a}, \vec{b}, \vec{c}\right]^2$

➡

$$\begin{aligned}
\text{LHS} &= \left[\vec{a} \times \vec{b},\ \vec{b} \times \vec{c},\ \vec{c} \times \vec{a}\right] \\
&= \left(\vec{a} \times \vec{b}\right) \cdot \left[\left(\vec{b} \times \vec{c}\right) \times (\vec{c} \times \vec{a})\right] \\
&= \left(\vec{a} \times \vec{b}\right) \cdot \left[\left\{\left(\vec{b} \times \vec{c}\right) \cdot \vec{a}\right\} \vec{c} - \left\{\left(\vec{b} \times \vec{c}\right) \cdot \vec{c}\right\} \vec{a}\right] \\
&= \left(\vec{a} \times \vec{b}\right) \cdot \left\{\left[\vec{b}, \vec{c}, \vec{a}\right] \vec{c} - \left[\vec{b}, \vec{c}, \vec{c}\right] \vec{a}\right\} \\
&= \left(\vec{a} \times \vec{b}\right) \cdot \left\{\left[\vec{b}, \vec{c}, \vec{a}\right] \vec{c} - 0\right\} = \left(\vec{a} \times \vec{b}\right) \cdot \left[\vec{b}, \vec{c}, \vec{a}\right] \vec{c} \\
&= \left\{\left(\vec{a} \times \vec{b}\right) \cdot \vec{c}\right\} \left[\vec{a}, \vec{b}, \vec{c}\right] \\
&= \left[\vec{a}, \vec{b}, \vec{c}\right] \left[\vec{a}, \vec{b}, \vec{c}\right] \\
&= \left[\vec{a}, \vec{b}, \vec{c}\right]^2
\end{aligned}$$

Note: $\vec{a} \times (\vec{b} \times \vec{c}) = (\vec{a} \cdot \vec{c})\,\vec{b} - (\vec{a} \cdot \vec{b})\,\vec{c}$

28. *Prove that* $\left[\vec{a}+\vec{b},\ \vec{b}+\vec{c},\ \vec{c}+\vec{a}\right]=2\left[\vec{a},\vec{b},\vec{c}\right]$

➡

$$
\begin{aligned}
\text{LHS} &= \left[\vec{a}+\vec{b},\ \vec{b}+\vec{c},\ \vec{c}+\vec{a}\right] \\
&= \left(\vec{a}+\vec{b}\right)\cdot\left[\left(\vec{b}+\vec{c}\right)\times(\vec{c}+\vec{a})\right] \\
&= \left(\vec{a}+\vec{b}\right)\cdot\left\{\vec{b}\times\vec{c}+\vec{b}\times\vec{a}+\vec{c}\times\vec{c}+\vec{c}\times\vec{a}\right\} \\
&= \left(\vec{a}+\vec{b}\right)\cdot\left\{\vec{b}\times\vec{c}+\vec{b}\times\vec{a}+0+\vec{c}\times\vec{a}\right\} \\
&= \vec{a}\cdot\left(\vec{b}\times\vec{c}\right)+\vec{a}\cdot\left(\vec{b}\times\vec{a}\right)+\vec{a}\cdot(\vec{c}\times\vec{a}) \\
&\quad +\vec{b}\cdot\left(\vec{b}\times\vec{c}\right)+\vec{b}\cdot\left(\vec{b}\times\vec{a}\right)+\vec{b}\cdot(\vec{c}\times\vec{a}) \\
&= \left[\vec{a},\vec{b},\vec{c}\right]+\left[\vec{a},\vec{b},\vec{a}\right]+\left[\vec{a},\vec{c},\vec{a}\right]+\left[\vec{b},\vec{b},\vec{c}\right]+\left[\vec{b},\vec{b},\vec{a}\right]+\left[\vec{b},\vec{c},\vec{a}\right] \\
&= \left[\vec{a},\vec{b},\vec{c}\right]+0+0+0+0+\left[\vec{a},\vec{b},\vec{c}\right] \\
&= 2\left[\vec{a},\vec{b},\vec{c}\right]
\end{aligned}
$$

29. *Prove that* $\left[\vec{a}-\vec{b},\ \vec{b}-\vec{c},\ \vec{c}-\vec{a}\right]=0$

➡

$$
\begin{aligned}
\text{LHS} &= \left[\vec{a}-\vec{b},\ \vec{b}-\vec{c},\ \vec{c}-\vec{a}\right] \\
&= \left(\vec{a}-\vec{b}\right)\cdot\left\{\left(\vec{b}-\vec{c}\right)\times(\vec{c}-\vec{a})\right\} \\
&= \left(\vec{a}-\vec{b}\right)\cdot\left\{\vec{b}\times\vec{c}-\vec{b}\times\vec{a}-\vec{c}\times\vec{c}+\vec{c}\times\vec{a}\right\} \\
&= \left(\vec{a}-\vec{b}\right)\cdot\left\{\vec{b}\times\vec{c}-\vec{b}\times\vec{a}-0+\vec{c}\times\vec{a}\right\} \\
&= \vec{a}\cdot\left(\vec{b}\times\vec{c}\right)-\vec{a}\cdot\left(\vec{b}\times\vec{a}\right)+\vec{a}\cdot(\vec{c}\times\vec{a})-\vec{b}\cdot\left(\vec{b}\times\vec{c}\right)+\vec{b}\cdot\left(\vec{b}\times\vec{a}\right) \\
&\quad -\vec{b}\cdot(\vec{c}\times\vec{a}) \\
&= \left[\vec{a},\vec{b},\vec{c}\right]-\left[\vec{a},\vec{b},\vec{a}\right]+\left[\vec{a},\vec{c},\vec{a}\right]-\left[\vec{b},\vec{b},\vec{c}\right]+\left[\vec{b},\vec{b},\vec{a}\right]-\left[\vec{b},\vec{c},\vec{a}\right]
\end{aligned}
$$

$$= \left[\vec{a},\vec{b},\vec{c}\right] - \left[\vec{a},\vec{b},\vec{c}\right] \quad \because \left[\vec{b},\vec{c},\vec{a}\right] = \left[\vec{a},\vec{b},\vec{c}\right]$$
$$= 0$$

30. *Prove that* $\left(2\vec{a}-\vec{b}\right)\times\left(\vec{a}-2\vec{b}\right) = -3\left(\vec{a}\times\vec{b}\right)$

➠

$$\text{LHS} = \left(2\vec{a}-\vec{b}\right)\times\left(\vec{a}-2\vec{b}\right)$$
$$= 2\vec{a}\times\vec{a} - 2\vec{a}\times 2\vec{b} - \vec{b}\times\vec{a} + \vec{b}\times 2\vec{b}$$
$$= 2\left(\vec{a}\times\vec{a}\right) - 4\left(a\times b\right) - \left[-\vec{a}\times\vec{b}\right] + 2\left(\vec{b}\times\vec{b}\right)$$
$$= 2\,(0) - 4\left(\vec{a}\times\vec{b}\right) + \left(\vec{a}\times\vec{b}\right) + 2\,(0)$$
$$= -3\left(\vec{a}\times\vec{b}\right)$$

31. *Prove that* $\vec{a}\times\left(\vec{b}+\vec{c}\right) + \vec{b}\times\left(\vec{c}+\vec{a}\right) + \vec{c}\times\left(\vec{a}+\vec{b}\right) = 0$

➠

$$\text{LHS} = \vec{a}\times\left(\vec{b}+\vec{c}\right) + \vec{b}\times\left(\vec{c}+\vec{a}\right) + \vec{c}\times\left(\vec{a}+\vec{b}\right)$$
$$= \vec{a}\times\vec{b} + \vec{a}\times\vec{c} + \vec{b}\times\vec{c} + \vec{b}\times\vec{a} + \vec{c}\times\vec{a} + \vec{c}\times\vec{b}$$
$$= \vec{a}\times\vec{b} + \vec{a}\times\vec{c} + \vec{b}\times\vec{c} + \left[-\vec{a}\times\vec{b}\right] + \left[-\vec{a}\times\vec{c}\right] + \left[-\vec{b}\times\vec{c}\right]$$
$$= \vec{a}\times\vec{b} + \vec{a}\times\vec{c} + \vec{b}\times\vec{c} - \vec{a}\times\vec{b} - \vec{a}\times\vec{c} - \vec{b}\times\vec{c}$$
$$= 0$$

32. *Prove that*

(i) $\left(\vec{a}\perp\vec{b}\right) \Rightarrow \left(\vec{a}+\vec{b}\right)^2 = \left(\vec{a}-\vec{b}\right)^2$

(ii) $\left|\vec{a}+\vec{b}\right| = \left|\vec{a}-\vec{b}\right| \Rightarrow \vec{a}\perp\vec{b}$

➡ (i) We have

$$\vec{a} \perp \vec{b} \Rightarrow \vec{a} \cdot \vec{b} = 0$$

$$\left(\vec{a} + \vec{b}\right)^2 = (\vec{a})^2 + \left(\vec{b}\right)^2 + 2\vec{a} \cdot \vec{b}$$

$$= |\vec{a}|^2 + \left|\vec{b}\right|^2 + 2\,(0)$$

$$= |\vec{a}|^2 + \left|\vec{b}\right|^2 - 2\,(0) = |\vec{a}|^2 + \left|\vec{b}\right|^2 - 2\left(\vec{a} \cdot \vec{b}\right)$$

$$\left(\vec{a} + \vec{b}\right)^2 = \left(\vec{a} - \vec{b}\right)^2$$

(ii) we have

$$\left|\vec{a} + \vec{b}\right| = \left|\vec{a} - \vec{b}\right|$$

$$\Rightarrow \left|\vec{a} + \vec{b}\right|^2 = \left|\vec{a} - \vec{b}\right|^2$$

$$\Rightarrow (\vec{a})^2 + \left(\vec{b}\right)^2 + 2\vec{a} \cdot \vec{b} = (\vec{a})^2 + \left(\vec{b}\right)^2 - 2\vec{a} \cdot \vec{b}$$

$$\Rightarrow 2\vec{a} \cdot \vec{b} = -2\vec{a} \cdot \vec{b}$$

$$\Rightarrow 4\vec{a} \cdot \vec{b} = 0 \Rightarrow \vec{a} \cdot \vec{b} = 0$$

$$\Rightarrow \vec{a} \perp \vec{b}$$

33. *If* $\vec{a} \cdot \vec{b} = \vec{a} \cdot \vec{c}$, *show that* $\vec{a} = \overrightarrow{0}$ *or* $\vec{b} = \vec{c}$ *or* $\vec{a} \perp \left(\vec{b} - \vec{c}\right)$

➡

$$\vec{a} \cdot \vec{b} = \vec{a} \cdot \vec{c}$$

$$\vec{a} \cdot \vec{b} - \vec{a} \cdot \vec{c} = 0$$

$$\vec{a} \cdot \left(\vec{b} - \vec{c}\right) = 0$$

$$\Rightarrow \vec{a} = 0 \quad \text{or} \quad \vec{b} - \vec{c} = 0 \quad \text{or} \quad \vec{a} \perp (\vec{b} - \vec{c})$$

$$\Rightarrow \vec{a} = 0 \quad \text{or} \quad \vec{b} = \vec{c} \quad \text{or} \quad \vec{a} \perp (\vec{b} - \vec{c})$$

34. *Prove that* $\vec{a} \times \left(\vec{b} \times \vec{c}\right) + \vec{b} \times (\vec{c} \times \vec{a}) + \vec{c} \times \left(\vec{a} \times \vec{b}\right) = 0$

➡

$$\begin{aligned}
\text{LHS} &= \vec{a} \times \left(\vec{b} \times \vec{c}\right) + \vec{b} \times (\vec{c} \times \vec{a}) + \vec{c} \times \left(\vec{a} \times \vec{b}\right) \\
&= (\vec{a} \cdot \vec{c})\,\vec{b} - \left(\vec{a} \cdot \vec{b}\right)\vec{c} + \left(\vec{b} \cdot \vec{a}\right)\vec{c} - \left(\vec{b} \cdot \vec{c}\right)\vec{a} + \left(\vec{c} \cdot \vec{b}\right)\vec{a} - (\vec{c} \cdot \vec{a})\,\vec{b} \\
&= 0
\end{aligned}$$

35. *If* $\vec{a},\ \vec{b},\ \vec{c}$ *are the position vectors of vertices A, B, C of a triangle ABC, show that the area of the triangle ABC is* $\frac{1}{2}\left|\vec{a} \times \vec{b} + \vec{b} \times \vec{c} + \vec{c} \times \vec{a}\right|$. *Deduce that the condition for points* $\vec{a},\ \vec{b},\ \vec{c}$ *to be collinear is* $\vec{a} \times \vec{b} + \vec{b} \times \vec{c} + \vec{c} \times \vec{a} = \vec{0}$

➡ Let O be the origin. Then,

$$\overrightarrow{OA} = \vec{a},\ \overrightarrow{OB} = \vec{b},\ \overrightarrow{OC} = \vec{c}$$

$$\therefore\ \overrightarrow{AB} = \left(\vec{b} - \vec{a}\right) \quad \text{and} \quad \overrightarrow{AC} = (\vec{c} - \vec{a})$$

So, the vector area of triangle ABC is given by

$$\begin{aligned}
&= \frac{1}{2}\left|\overrightarrow{AB} \times \overrightarrow{AC}\right| = \frac{1}{2}\left|\left(\vec{b} - \vec{a}\right) \times (\vec{c} - \vec{a})\right| \\
&= \frac{1}{2}\left|\left(\vec{b} \times \vec{c} - \vec{b} \times \vec{a} - \vec{a} \times \vec{c} + \vec{a} \times \vec{a}\right)\right| \\
&= \frac{1}{2}\left|\vec{b} \times \vec{c} + \vec{a} \times \vec{b} + \vec{c} \times \vec{a}\right| \qquad \left[\because\ \vec{a} \times \vec{a} = \vec{0}\ \&\ \vec{b} \times \vec{a} = -\vec{a} \times \vec{b}\right] \\
&= \frac{1}{2}\left|\vec{a} \times \vec{b} + \vec{b} \times \vec{c} + \vec{c} \times \vec{a}\right|
\end{aligned}$$

Therefore,

$$\text{Area of triangle } ABC = \frac{1}{2}\left|\vec{a} \times \vec{b} + \vec{b} \times \vec{c} + \vec{c} \times \vec{a}\right|$$

Further, let A, B, C be collinear.
Then, the vector area of triangle ABC is zero.
Hence, $\vec{a} \times \vec{b} + \vec{b} \times \vec{c} + \vec{c} \times \vec{a} = \vec{0}$

36. *If $\vec{a}, \vec{b}, \vec{c}$ are the position vectors of points A, B, C prove that $(\vec{a}\times\vec{b}+\vec{b}\times\vec{c}+\vec{c}\times\vec{a})$ is a vector perpendicular to the plane of triangle ABC.*

➡ In order to prove the required result we have to show that $(\vec{a}\times\vec{b}+\vec{b}\times\vec{c}+\vec{c}\times\vec{a})$ is perpendicular to each one of the vectors $\overrightarrow{AB}$, $\overrightarrow{BC}$ and $\overrightarrow{CA}$.

Now, $\overrightarrow{AB} = (\vec{b}-\vec{a})$, $\overrightarrow{BC} = (\vec{c}-\vec{b})$ and $\overrightarrow{CA} = \vec{a}-\vec{c}$.

Next,

$$
\begin{aligned}
&(\vec{a}\times\vec{b}+\vec{b}\times\vec{c}+\vec{c}\times\vec{a})\cdot(\vec{b}-\vec{a})\\
&= (\vec{a}\times\vec{b})\cdot(\vec{b}-\vec{a}) + (\vec{b}\times\vec{c})\cdot(\vec{b}-\vec{a}) + (\vec{c}\times\vec{a})\cdot(\vec{b}-\vec{a})\\
&= \left(\vec{a}\times\vec{b}\right)\cdot\vec{b} - \left(\vec{a}\times\vec{b}\right)\cdot\vec{a} + \left(\vec{b}\times\vec{c}\right)\cdot\vec{b} - \left(\vec{b}\times\vec{c}\right)\cdot\vec{a} + (\vec{c}\times\vec{a})\cdot\vec{b}\\
&\quad - (\vec{c}\times\vec{a})\cdot\vec{a}\\
&= \left[\vec{a},\vec{b},\vec{b}\right] - \left[\vec{a},\vec{b},\vec{a}\right] + \left[\vec{b},\vec{c},\vec{b}\right] - \left[\vec{b},\vec{c},\vec{a}\right] + \left[\vec{c},\vec{a},\vec{b}\right] - [\vec{c}\vec{a}\vec{a}]\\
&= 0 - 0 + 0 - \left[\vec{b},\vec{c},\vec{a}\right] + \left[\vec{b},\vec{c},\vec{a}\right] + 0\\
&= 0 \quad [\because \text{scalar triple product with two equal vectors is } 0]
\end{aligned}
$$

Similarly,

$$(\vec{a}\times\vec{b}+\vec{b}\times\vec{c}+\vec{c}\times\vec{a})\cdot(\vec{c}-\vec{b}) = 0$$

$$(\vec{a}\times\vec{b}+\vec{b}\times\vec{c}+\vec{c}\times\vec{a})\cdot(\vec{a}-\vec{c}) = 0$$

Thus, $(\vec{a}\times\vec{b}+\vec{b}\times\vec{c}+\vec{c}\times\vec{a})$ is perpendicular to each one of the vectors $\overrightarrow{AB}$, $\overrightarrow{BC}$ and $\overrightarrow{CA}$ and therefore, it is perpendicular to the plane of ABC.

37. *Find the area of a parallelogram whose adjacent sides are determined by the vectors $\vec{a} = \hat{i}+2\hat{j}+3\hat{k}$ and $\vec{b} = -3\hat{i}-2\hat{j}+\hat{k}$*

➡ We have $\vec{a}\times\vec{b} = \begin{vmatrix} \hat{i} & \hat{j} & \hat{k} \\ 1 & 2 & 3 \\ -3 & -2 & 1 \end{vmatrix} = 8\hat{i} - 10\hat{j} + 4\hat{k}$

$$
\begin{aligned}
\text{Required area} &= \left|\vec{a}\times\vec{b}\right| = \sqrt{8^2+(-10)^2+4^2}\\
&= \sqrt{180} = 6\sqrt{5} \text{ square units.}
\end{aligned}
$$

38. *Find with the help of vectors, the area of the triangle with vertices $A\,(3,\ -1,\ 2)$, $B\,(1,\ -1,\ -3)$ and $C\,(4,\ -3,\ 1)$*

➡ The position vectors of A, B, C are given by

$$\vec{A} = 3\hat{i} - \hat{j} + 2\hat{k},\quad \vec{B} = \hat{i} - \hat{j} - 3\hat{k} \quad \text{and} \quad \vec{C} = 4\hat{i} - 3\hat{j} + \hat{k}$$

$$\overrightarrow{BC} = \left[(\text{position vector of } C) - (\text{position vector of } B)\right]$$

$$= \left(4\hat{i} - 3\hat{j} + \hat{k}\right) - \left(\hat{i} - \hat{j} - 3\hat{k}\right) = \left(3\hat{i} - 2\hat{j} + 4\hat{k}\right)$$

and

$$\overrightarrow{BA} = \left[(\text{position vector of } A) - (\text{position vector of } B)\right]$$

$$= \left[\left(3\hat{i} - \hat{j} + 2\hat{k}\right) - \left(\hat{i} - \hat{j} - 3\hat{k}\right)\right] = 2\hat{i} + 5\hat{k}$$

Now,

$$\overrightarrow{BC} \times \overrightarrow{BA} = \begin{vmatrix} \hat{i} & \hat{j} & \hat{k} \\ 3 & -2 & 4 \\ 2 & 0 & 5 \end{vmatrix} = \left(-10\hat{i} - 7\hat{j} + 4\hat{k}\right)$$

$$\text{Required area} = \frac{1}{2}\left|\overrightarrow{BC} \times \overrightarrow{BA}\right|$$

$$= \frac{1}{2}\sqrt{(-10)^2 + (-7)^2 + 4^2} = \frac{1}{2}\sqrt{165} \text{ square units.}$$

39. *Find a set of vectors reciprocal to the set $2\hat{i} + 3\hat{j} - \hat{k},\ \ \hat{i} - \hat{j} - 2\hat{k},\ \ -\hat{i} + 2\hat{j} + 2\hat{k}$*

➡ Let $\vec{a} = 2\hat{i} + 3\hat{j} - \hat{k},\ \ \vec{b} = \hat{i} - \hat{j} - 2\hat{k},\ \ \vec{c} = -\hat{i} + 2\hat{j} + 2\hat{k}$

$$\left[\vec{a}, \vec{b}, \vec{c}\right] = \begin{vmatrix} 2 & 3 & -1 \\ 1 & -1 & -2 \\ -1 & 2 & 2 \end{vmatrix} = 2\,(-2+4) - 3\,(2-2) - 1\,(2-1)$$

$$\left[\vec{a}, \vec{b}.\vec{c}\right] = 4 - 1 = 3$$

$$\vec{a} \times \vec{b} = \begin{vmatrix} \hat{i} & \hat{j} & \hat{k} \\ 2 & 3 & -1 \\ 1 & -1 & -2 \end{vmatrix} = \hat{i}\,(-6-1) - \hat{j}\,(-4+1) + \hat{k}\,(-2-3)$$

$$\vec{a} \times \vec{b} = -7\hat{i} + 3\hat{j} - 5\hat{k}$$

$$\vec{b} \times \vec{c} = \begin{vmatrix} \hat{i} & \hat{j} & \hat{k} \\ 1 & -1 & -2 \\ -1 & 2 & 2 \end{vmatrix} = \hat{i}\,(-2+4) - \hat{j}\,(2-2) - \hat{k}\,(2-1)$$

$$\vec{b} \times \vec{c} = 2\hat{i} - \hat{k}$$

$$\vec{c} \times \vec{a} = \begin{vmatrix} \hat{i} & \hat{j} & \hat{k} \\ -1 & 2 & 2 \\ 2 & 3 & -1 \end{vmatrix} = \hat{i}\,(-2-6) - \hat{j}\,(1-4) + \hat{k}\,(-3-4)$$

$$\vec{c} \times \vec{a} = -8\hat{i} + 3\hat{j} - 7\hat{k}$$

$$\vec{a'} = \frac{\vec{b} \times \vec{c}}{\left[\vec{a}, \vec{b}, \vec{c}\right]} = \frac{2\hat{i} - \hat{k}}{3} = \frac{2}{3}\hat{i} - \frac{1}{3}\hat{k}$$

$$\vec{b'} = \frac{\vec{c} \times \vec{a}}{\left[\vec{a}, \vec{b}, \vec{c}\right]} = \frac{-8\hat{i} + 3\hat{j} - 7\hat{k}}{3} = \frac{-8}{3}\hat{i} + \hat{j} - \frac{7}{3}\hat{k}$$

$$\vec{c'} = \frac{\vec{a} \times \vec{b}}{\left[\vec{a}, \vec{b}, \vec{c}\right]} = \frac{-7\hat{i} + 3\hat{j} - 5\hat{k}}{3} = -\frac{7}{3}\hat{i} + \hat{j} - \frac{5}{3}\hat{k}$$

Exercises

1. *If* $\vec{a} = \hat{i} + \hat{j} - \hat{k}$, $\vec{b} = 4\hat{i} + \hat{j} + 2\hat{k}$ *and* $\vec{c} = \hat{j} - 2\hat{k}$, *show that* $\vec{a} - \vec{b} = 3\vec{c} - 3\vec{a}$.
2. *If* $\vec{a} = \hat{i} - \hat{j} + 2\hat{k}$, $\vec{b} = 4\hat{i} + \hat{j} + 2\hat{k}$*and* $\vec{c} = 3\hat{i} + 3\hat{k}$ *find* $|4\vec{a} + 2\vec{b} - 3\vec{c}|$.
3. *Show that* $(5\vec{a} + \vec{b}) \times (\vec{b} + 2\vec{a}) = 3(\vec{a} \times \vec{b})$.
4. *Show that the vectors* $2\hat{i} + 4\hat{j} - \hat{k}$, $4\hat{i} + 5\hat{j} + \hat{k}$ *and* $3\hat{i} + 6\hat{j} - 3\hat{k}$ *from a right-angled triangle.*
5. *Show that the points* $A\,(1, 2, 3)$, $B\,(2, 3, 1)$ *and* $C\,(3, 1, 2)$ *are the vertices of an isosceles triangle.*
6. *Show that the triangle ABC, the position vectors of whose vertices A, B, C are* $7\hat{j} + 10\hat{k}, -\hat{i} + 6\hat{j} + \hat{k}$ *and* $-4\hat{i} + 9\hat{j} + 6\hat{k}$ *respectively, is an isosceles triangle.*

7. *Find $\vec{a} \cdot \vec{b}$ (scalar product) of the following*

   (i) $\vec{a} = 2\hat{i} + 3\hat{j} - \hat{k} \qquad \vec{b} = \hat{i} - 2\hat{j} - 5\hat{k}$

   (ii) $\vec{a} = 3\hat{i} - 4\hat{j} \qquad \vec{b} = 2\hat{i} - \hat{j}$

8. *Find the angle between the following vectors*

   (i) $3\hat{i} + \hat{j} - 2\hat{k}, \quad 3i - 5\hat{j} - 2\hat{k}$

   (ii) $2\hat{i} - \hat{j} + \hat{k}, \quad 3\hat{i} + 4\hat{j} - \hat{k}$

   (iii) $\hat{i} + 3\hat{j} - 8\hat{k}, \quad -3\hat{i} - 5\hat{j} - 4\hat{k}$

9. *Show that the following vectors are orthogonal*

   (i) $3\hat{i} - 2\hat{j} - 5\hat{k}, \quad 6\hat{i} - \hat{j} + 4\hat{k}$

   (ii) $3\hat{i} - 2\hat{j} + \hat{k}, \quad 2\hat{i} + \hat{j} - 4\hat{k}$

10. *If $\vec{a} = \hat{i} + 2\hat{j} - 3\hat{k}$ and $\vec{b} = 3\hat{i} - \hat{j} + 2\hat{k}$ then show that $\vec{a} + \vec{b}$ and $\vec{a} - \vec{b}$ are orthogonal.*

11. *Show that $\vec{a} = 2\hat{i} + 3\hat{j} - \hat{k}$, $\vec{b} = \hat{i} + \hat{j} + 5\hat{k}$ and $\vec{c} = 16\hat{i} - 11\hat{j} - \hat{k}$ from a set of mutually perpendicular vectors.*

12. *Find the unit vector perpendicular to both $\vec{a}$ and $\vec{b}$ if $\vec{a} = 3\hat{i} - 2\hat{j} + 4\hat{k}$ and $\vec{b} = 4\hat{i} - 3\hat{j} - \hat{k}$.*

13. *Find the unit vector perpendicular to both $\vec{a}$ and $\vec{b}$ if $\vec{a} = 2\hat{i} - \hat{j} + \hat{k}$ and $\vec{b} = 3\hat{i} - 4\hat{j} - \hat{k}$.*

14. *Find the unit vector perpendicular to both $\vec{a} + \vec{b}$ and $\vec{b} + \vec{c}$ if $\vec{a} = \hat{i} + \hat{j} - \hat{k}, \vec{b} = -\hat{i} + 2\hat{j} + \hat{k}$ and $\vec{c} = \hat{i} - 2\hat{j} + 3\hat{k}$*

15. *If $\vec{a} = \hat{i} + 2\hat{j}$, $\vec{b} = \hat{j} + 2\hat{k}$, $\vec{c} = \hat{i} + 2\hat{k}$ find $\vec{a} \cdot (\vec{b} \times \vec{c})$.*

16. *Find $\vec{a} \times (\vec{b} \times \vec{c})$, where*

   (i) $\vec{a} = \hat{i} + \hat{j} + \hat{k}, \quad \vec{b} = -\hat{i} + 2\hat{j} + 3\hat{k}, \quad \vec{c} = 4\hat{i} - \hat{j} - \hat{k}$

   (ii) $\vec{a} = (2, 3, -1), \quad \vec{b} = (1, -1, 2), \quad \vec{c} = (1, 2, 2)$

17. *If $\vec{a} = (3, -1, 2)$, $\vec{b} = (2, 1, -1)$ and $\vec{c} = (1, -2, 2)$ find $\vec{a} \times (\vec{b} \times \vec{c})$ and $(\vec{a} \times \vec{b}) \times \vec{c}$.*

18. *If $\vec{a} = 2\hat{i} + \hat{j} + \hat{k}$, $\vec{b} = \hat{i} + 2\hat{j} + \hat{k}$ and $\vec{c} = \hat{i} + \hat{j} + 2\hat{k}$ find $\vec{a} \cdot (\vec{b} \times \vec{c})$ and $\vec{a} \times (\vec{b} \times \vec{c})$.*

19. *Find the volume of the parallelopiped whose coterminous edges are represented by,*

(i) $\vec{a} = \hat{i} + \hat{j} + \hat{k}, \quad \vec{b} = \hat{i} - \hat{j} + \hat{k}, \quad \vec{c} = \hat{i} + 2\hat{j} - \hat{k}$

(ii) $\vec{a} = -3\hat{i} + 7\hat{j} + 5\hat{k}, \quad \vec{b} = -5\hat{i} + 7\hat{j} - 3\hat{k}, \quad \vec{c} = 7\hat{i} - 5\hat{j} - 3\hat{k}$

(iii) $\vec{a} = 11\hat{i}, \quad \vec{b} = 2\hat{j}, \quad \vec{c} = 13\hat{k}$

20. *Show that the four points whose position vectors are* $(6\hat{i} - 7\hat{j}), \quad (16\hat{i} - 19\hat{j} - 4\hat{k}), (3\hat{j} - 6\hat{k}), (2\hat{i} - 5\hat{j} + 10\hat{k})$ *are coplanar.*

21. *Show that the points whose position vectors are* $(-6\hat{i} + 3\hat{j} + 2\hat{k}), \quad (3\hat{i} - 2\hat{j} + 4\hat{k}), (5\hat{i} + 7\hat{j} + 3\hat{k})$ *and* $(-13\hat{i} + 17\hat{j} - \hat{k})$ *are coplanar.*

22. *Show that the points A, B, C, D are coplanar*

(i) $A = (4, 5, 1), \quad B = (0, -1, -1), \quad C = (3, 9, 4), \quad D = (-4, 4, 4)$

(ii) $A = (2, 1, -5), \quad B = (-3, -2, -4), \quad C = (5, 3, -5), \quad D = (6, 7, 5)$

23. *Prove that the points with position vectors* $4\hat{i} + 5\hat{j} + \hat{k}, \quad \hat{j} + \hat{k}, \quad 3\hat{i} + 9\hat{j} + 4\hat{k}$ *and* $-\hat{i} + 5\hat{j} + 4\hat{k}$ *are coplanar.*

24. *Show that the following vectors are coplanar,*

(i) $5\hat{i} + 6\hat{j} + 7\hat{k}, \quad 3\hat{i} + 20\hat{j} + 5\hat{k}$ *and* $7\hat{i} - 8\hat{j} + 9\hat{k}$

(ii) $\hat{i} + \hat{j} + \hat{k}, \quad 3\hat{i} + 4\hat{j} + 2\hat{k}$ *and* $3\hat{i} + \hat{j} + 5\hat{k}$

25. *Find the value of m for which the following vectors are coplanar,*

(i) $4\hat{i} - 7\hat{j} + 5\hat{k}, \quad m\hat{i} - \hat{j} + 3\hat{k}$ *and* $\hat{i} - 3\hat{j} + \hat{k}$

(ii) $2\hat{i} - 3\hat{j} + 4\hat{k}, \quad \hat{i} + 2\hat{j} - \hat{k}$ *and* $m\hat{i} - \hat{j} - 2\hat{k}$

(iii) $\hat{i} - 3\hat{j} + \hat{k}, \quad 2\hat{i} + m\hat{j} + \hat{k}$ *and* $3\hat{i} + \hat{j} - 2\hat{k}$

26. *Prove the following,*

(i) $(3\vec{a} - 2\vec{b}) \times (4\vec{a} + 2\vec{b}) = 14(\vec{a} \times \vec{b})$

(ii) $(2\vec{a} + 3\vec{b}) \times (\vec{a} + 4\vec{b}) = 5(\vec{a} \times \vec{b})$

27. *For any vector* $\vec{a}$, *prove that* $\hat{i} \times (\vec{a} \times \hat{i}) + \hat{j} \times (\vec{a} \times \hat{j}) + \hat{k} \times (\vec{a} \times \vec{k}) = 2\vec{a}$

28. *Show that* $\vec{a} = (\vec{a} \cdot \hat{i})\hat{i} + (\vec{a} \cdot \hat{j})\hat{j} + (\vec{a} \cdot \hat{k})\hat{k}$

29. *If* $\vec{a}+\vec{b}+\vec{c}=\overrightarrow{0}$, $|\vec{a}|=3$, $\left|\vec{b}\right|=5$, $|\vec{c}|=7$, *find the angle between* $\vec{a}$ *and* $\vec{b}$.

30. *If* $\vec{a}+\vec{b}+\vec{c}=0$ *and* $\vec{a}$, $\vec{b}$, $\vec{c}$ *are unit vectors, then show that* $\vec{a}\cdot\vec{b}+\vec{b}\cdot\vec{c}+\vec{c}\cdot\vec{a}=-\frac{3}{2}$.

31. *Find* $\vec{a}\times(\vec{b}\times\vec{c})$, *when*

    (i) $\vec{a}=\hat{i}-2\hat{j}+\hat{k}$, $\vec{b}=2\hat{i}+\hat{j}+\hat{k}$, $\vec{c}=\hat{i}+2\hat{j}-\hat{k}$

    (ii) $\vec{a}=3\hat{i}+4\hat{j}+5\hat{k}$, $\vec{b}=\hat{i}+\hat{j}-3\hat{k}$, $\vec{c}=-2\hat{i}+3\hat{j}-\hat{k}$

32. *Obtain a set of vectors reciprocal to the vector,*

$$\vec{a}=2\hat{i}+3\hat{j}-\hat{k},\quad \vec{b}=\hat{i}-\hat{j}-2\hat{k}\quad \textit{and}\quad \vec{c}=-\hat{i}+2\hat{j}+2\hat{k}$$

Answers

2. $\sqrt{22}$

7. (i) 1, (ii) 10

8. (i) $\cos^{-1}\left(\frac{4}{\sqrt{133}}\right)$ (ii) $\cos^{-1}\left(\frac{1}{2\sqrt{39}}\right)$ (iii) $\cos^{-1}\left(\frac{7}{5\sqrt{37}}\right)$

12. $\dfrac{14\hat{i}+19\hat{j}-\hat{k}}{\sqrt{558}}$

13. $\dfrac{\hat{i}+\hat{j}-\hat{k}}{\sqrt{3}}$

14. $\hat{i}$

15. 6

16. (i) $-18\hat{i}+8\hat{j}+10\hat{k}$, (ii) $9\hat{i}+18\hat{k}$

17. $15(2\hat{i}+\hat{j}-\hat{k})$, $24\hat{i}+7\hat{j}-5\hat{k}$

18. 4, $5\hat{j}-5\hat{k}$

19. (i) 4 *cubic units,* (ii) 264 *cubic units,* (iii) 286 *cubic units*

25. (i) 2 (ii) −4 (iii) −4

29. $\dfrac{\pi}{3}$

31. (i) $-9\hat{i} - 6\hat{j} - 3\hat{k}$ (ii) $-15\hat{i} + 25\hat{j} - 11\hat{k}$

32. $\vec{a}' = \dfrac{2}{3}\hat{i} + \dfrac{1}{3}\hat{k}, \vec{b}' = \dfrac{1}{3}(-8\hat{i} + 3\hat{j} - 7\hat{k}), \vec{c}' = \dfrac{1}{3}(-7\hat{i} + 3\hat{j} - 5\hat{k})$

CHAPTER 2

Differential Calculus

2.1 Introduction

Calculus is an important branch of mathematics that has wide applications in engineering. A students who gets admitted to engineering degree program is supposed to be familiar with the notations of limits, continuity and the process of differentiating functions of a single independent variable. Therefore, in this chapter we shall continue our discussion with Successive Differentiation, Polar Curves, Taylor's Series, Maclaurin's Series and Partial Differentiation with some solved problems.

2.2 Successive Differentiation

If $y = f(x)$ be a real valued function of x, its differentiation dy/dx will be in general a function of x which can be differentiated. The differentiation of dy/dx is called the second differentiation of y. Similarly, the differentiation of d^2y/dx^2 is called the third differentiation of y, and so on. The process of doing second and higher order differentiation is called successive differentiation. The successive differentiations of y are denoted by one of the following ways:

(i) $\frac{dy}{dx}, \frac{d^2y}{dx^2}, \frac{d^3y}{dx^3}, \ldots \ldots \ldots, \frac{d^ny}{dx^n}$

(ii) $f'(x), f''(x), f'''(x), \ldots \ldots \ldots, f^{(n)}(x)$

(iii) $y_1, y_2, y_3, \ldots \ldots \ldots, y_n$

(iv) $y', y'', y''', \ldots \ldots \ldots, y^{(n)}$

(v) $Dy, D^2y, D^3y, \ldots \ldots \ldots, D^ny$

The value of a differentiation at $x = x_1$ is usually denoted by adding a suffix, i.e., $(y^{(n)})_{x=x_1}$ or $(y^{(n)})_{x_1}$

2.3 Taylor's Theorem for a Function of Single Variable

Let $f\,(a+x)$ be a function of x which can be expanded in powers of x and let the expansion be differentiable any number of times with respect to x, then

$$f\,(a+x) = f\,(a) + xf'\,(a) + \frac{x^2}{2!}f''\,(a) + \frac{x^3}{3!}f'''\,(a) + \cdots + \frac{x^n}{n!}f^{(n)}\,(a) + \cdots$$

Remarks:

1. If $a = 0$, then

$$f\,(x) = f\,(0) + xf'\,(0) + \frac{x^2}{2!}f''\,(0) + \frac{x^3}{3!}f'''\,(0) + \cdots$$

which is the Maclaurin's series, (it is discussed afterwards)

2. If $x = h$, then the series in powers of h is

$$f\,(a+h) = f\,(a) + hf'\,(a) + \frac{h^2}{2!}f''\,(a) + \frac{h^3}{3!}f'''\,(a) + \cdots$$

3. If $x = h - a$, then

$$f\,(h) = f\,(a) + (h-a)\,f'\,(a) + \frac{(h-a)^2}{2!}f''\,(a) + \cdots$$

4. $f\,(x) = f\,(a) + \dfrac{x-a}{1\,!}f'\,(a) + \dfrac{(x-a)^2}{2\,!}f''\,(a) + \dfrac{(x-a)^3}{3\,!}f'''\,(a) + \cdots$

2.4 Maclaurin's series

Let $f\,(x)$ be a function of x which can be expanded in powers of x and let the expansion be differentiable term by term any number of times, then

$$f\,(x) = f\,(0) + xf'\,(0) + \frac{x^2}{2\,!}f''\,(0) + \frac{x^3}{3\,!}f'''\,(0) + \cdots + \frac{x^n}{n\,!}f^{(n)}\,(0) + \cdots$$

Worked Examples

1. *Expand* sin x *in powers of* $(x - \pi/2)$

➡

$$f(x) = \sin x \Rightarrow f(\pi/2) = 1$$
$$f'(x) = \cos x \Rightarrow f'(\pi/2) = 0$$
$$f''(x) = -\sin x \Rightarrow f''(\pi/2) = -1$$
$$f'''(x) = -\cos x \Rightarrow f'''(\pi/2) = 0$$
$$f^{iv}(x) = \sin x \Rightarrow f^{iv}(\pi/2) = 1$$

Therefore,

$$f(x) = f(\pi/2) + \frac{x - \pi/2}{1\,!} f'(\pi/2) + \frac{(x - \pi/2)^2}{2\,!} f''(\pi/2) + \frac{(x - \pi/2)^3}{3\,!} f'''(\pi/2) + \cdots$$

$$\sin x = 1 - \frac{(x - \pi/2)^2}{2!} + \frac{(x - \pi/2)^4}{4!} + \cdots$$

2. *Expand* $2x^3 + 7x^2 + x - 1$ *in powers of* $x - 2$

➡

$$y(x) = 2x^3 + 7x^2 + x - 1 \Rightarrow y(2) = 45$$
$$y_1(x) = 6x^2 + 14x + 1 \Rightarrow y_1(2) = 53$$
$$y_2(x) = 12x + 14 \Rightarrow y_2(2) = 38$$
$$y_3(x) = 12 \Rightarrow y_3(2) = 12$$
$$y_4(x) = 0 \Rightarrow y_4(2) = 0$$

Therefore,

$$y(x) = y(2) + \frac{x - 2}{1\,!} y_1(2) + \frac{(x - 2)^2}{2\,!} y_2(2) + \frac{(x - 2)^3}{3\,!} y_3(2) + \cdots$$
$$2x^3 + 7x^2 + x - 1 = 45 + 53(x - 2) + 19(x - 2)^2 + 2(x - 2)^3$$

3. *Expand* $\log(1+x)$ *by using Maclaurin's series*

➡ Let

$$y = \log(1+x) \Rightarrow y(0) = 0$$

$$y_1(x) = \frac{1}{1+x} \Rightarrow y_1(0) = 1$$

$$y_2(x) = -\frac{1}{(1+x)^2} \Rightarrow y_2(0) = -1$$

$$y_3(x) = \frac{2}{(1+x)^3} \Rightarrow y_3(0) = 2$$

$$y_4(x) = -\frac{6}{(1+x)^4} \Rightarrow y_4(0) = -6$$

Therefore,

$$y(x) = y(0) + xy_1(0) + \frac{x^2}{2!}y_2(0) + \frac{x^3}{3!}y_3(0) + \cdots$$

$$= 0 + x(1) + \frac{x^2}{2!}(-1) + \frac{x^3}{3!}(2) + \frac{x^4}{4!}(-6) + \cdots$$

$$\log(1+x) = x - \frac{x^2}{2} + \frac{x^3}{3} - \frac{x^4}{4} + \cdots$$

4. *Obtain the Maclaurin's series expansion of the function* e^x

➡ Let

$$y = e^x \quad \Rightarrow y(0) = 1$$

$$y_1 = e^x \quad \Rightarrow y_1(0) = 1$$

$$y_2 = e^x \quad \Rightarrow y_2(0) = 1$$

$$y_3 = e^x \quad \Rightarrow y_3(0) = 1$$

$$y_4 = e^x \quad \Rightarrow y_4(0) = 1$$

Therefore,

$$y = y(0) + \frac{x}{1!}y_1(0) + \frac{x^2}{2!}y_2(0) + \cdots$$

$$= 1 + \frac{x}{1\,!}(1) + \frac{x^2}{2\,!}(1) + \frac{x^3}{3\,!}(1) + \frac{x^4}{4!}(1) + \cdots$$

$$e^x = 1 + \frac{x}{1\,!} + \frac{x^2}{2\,!} + \frac{x^3}{3\,!} + \frac{x^4}{4!} + \cdots$$

5. *Obtain the Maclaurin's series expansion of the function* $\sin x$

➡ Let

$$\begin{aligned}
y &= \sin x && \Rightarrow y(0) = 0 \\
y_1 &= \cos x && \Rightarrow y_1(0) = 1 \\
y_2 &= -\sin x && \Rightarrow y_2(0) = 0 \\
y_3 &= -\cos x && \Rightarrow y_3(0) = -1 \\
y_4 &= \sin x && \Rightarrow y_4(0) = 0 \\
y_5 &= \cos x && \Rightarrow y_5(0) = 1
\end{aligned}$$

Therefore,

$$y = y(0) + \frac{x}{1\,!}y_1(0) + \frac{x^2}{2\,!}y_2(0) + \cdots$$

$$= 0 + \frac{x}{1\,!}(1) + 0 + \frac{x^3}{3\,!}(-1) + 0 + \frac{x^5}{5\,!}(1) + \cdots$$

$$\sin x = x - \frac{x^3}{3\,!} + \frac{x^5}{5\,!} + \cdots$$

6. *Using Maclaurin's series, obtain the expression of* $\tan x$ *upto the terms containing* x^4

➡ Let

$$\begin{aligned}
y &= \tan x && \Rightarrow y(0) = 0 \\
y_1 &= \sec^2 x = 1 + \tan^2 x = 1 + y^2 && \Rightarrow y_1(0) = 1 \\
y_2 &= 2yy_1 && \Rightarrow y_2(0) = 0 \\
y_3 &= 2yy_2 + 2y_1y_1 = 2yy_2 + 2y_1^2 && \Rightarrow y_3(0) = 2 \\
y_4 &= 2yy_3 + 2y_1y_2 + 4y_1y_2 = 2yy_3 + 6y_1y_2 && \Rightarrow y_4(0) = 0
\end{aligned}$$

$$y_5 = 2yy_4 + 2y_1y_3 + 6y_1y_3 + 6y_2y_2$$

$$y_5 = 2yy_4 + 8y_1y_3 + 6y_2^2 \qquad \Rightarrow y_5(0) = 16$$

Therefore,

$$y = y(0) + \frac{x}{1!}y_1(0) + \frac{x^2}{2!}y_2(0) + \frac{x^3}{3!}y_3(0) + \cdots$$

$$= 0 + \frac{x}{1!}(1) + 0 + \frac{x^3}{3!}(2) + 0 + \frac{x^5}{5!}(16) + \cdots$$

$$\tan x = x + \frac{x^3}{3} + \frac{2x^5}{15} + \cdots$$

7. *Obtain the Maclaurin's series expansion of the function* $\sqrt{1+\sin 2x}$

➡

$$y = \sqrt{1+\sin 2x} = \sqrt{\sin^2 x + \cos^2 x + 2\sin x\cos x} = \sqrt{(\sin x + \cos x)^2}$$

$$y = \sin x + \cos x \Rightarrow y(0) = 1$$

$$y_1 = \cos x - \sin x \Rightarrow y_1(0) = 1$$

$$y_2 = -\sin x - \cos x \Rightarrow y_2(0) = -1$$

$$y_3 = -\cos x + \sin x \Rightarrow y_3(0) = -1$$

$$y_4 = \sin x + \cos x \Rightarrow y_4(0) = 1$$

Therefore,

$$y = y(0) + \frac{x}{1\,!}y_1(0) + \frac{x^2}{2\,!}y_2(0) + \frac{x^3}{3\,!}y_3(0) + \cdots$$

$$= 1 + \frac{x}{1\,!}(1) + \frac{x^2}{2\,!}(-1) + \frac{x^3}{3\,!}(-1) + \frac{x^4}{4\,!}(1) + \cdots$$

$$\sqrt{1+\sin 2x} = 1 + x - \frac{x^2}{2} - \frac{x^3}{6} + \frac{x^4}{24} + \cdots$$

8. *Obtain the Maclaurin's series expansion of the function* $e^{\sin^{-1} x}$

➡ Let

$$y = e^{\sin^{-1} x} \qquad \Rightarrow y(0) = 1$$

$$y_1 = e^{\sin^{-1} x} . \frac{1}{\sqrt{1-x^2}} \Rightarrow y_1(0) = 1$$

$$\sqrt{1-x^2} y_1 = e^{\sin^{-1} x}$$

$$\sqrt{1-x^2} y_1 = y$$

$$\left(1-x^2\right) y_1^2 = y^2$$

$$\left(1-x^2\right) 2y_1 y_2 + (-2x)\, y_1^2 = 2yy_1$$

$$\left(1-x^2\right) y_2 - xy_1 = y \tag{1}$$

At $x = 0$, $y_2(0) = 1$

Differentiating (1) with respect to x, we get

$$\left(1-x^2\right) y_3 + (-2x)\, y_2 - xy_2 - y_1 = y_1$$

$$\left(1-x^2\right) y_3 - 3xy_2 - 2y_1 = 0 \tag{2}$$

At $x = 0$,

$$y_3(0) - 2 = 0$$

$$y_3(0) = 2$$

Differentiating (2) with respect to x, we get

$$\left(1-x^2\right) y_4 + (-2x)\, y_3 - 3xy_3 - 3y_2 - 2y_2 = 0$$

$$\left(1-x^2\right) y_4 - 5xy_3 - 5y_2 = 0$$

At $x = 0$

$$y_4(0) - 0 - 5(1) = 0$$

$$y_4(0) = 5$$

Therefore,

$$y = y(0) + \frac{x}{1\,!} y_1(0) + \frac{x^2}{2\,!} y_2(0) + \cdots$$

$$= 1 + \frac{x}{1\,!}(1) + \frac{x^2}{2\,!}(1) + \frac{x^3}{3\,!}(2) + \frac{x^4}{4\,!}(5) + \cdots$$

$$e^{\sin^{-1}x} = 1 + x + \frac{x^2}{2} + \frac{x^3}{3} + \frac{5x^4}{24} + \cdots$$

9. *Obtain the Maclaurin's series expansion of the function* log sec x

➡ Let

$$y = \log\sec x \Rightarrow y\,(0) = 0$$

$$y_1 = \frac{1}{\sec x}\sec x\tan x$$

$$y_1 = \tan x \Rightarrow y_1\,(0) = 0$$

$$y_2 = \sec^2 x \Rightarrow y_2\,(0) = 1$$

$$y_3 = 2\sec x.\sec x\tan x$$

$$y_3 = 2\sec^2 x\tan x \Rightarrow y_3\,(0) = 0$$

$$y_3 = 2y_2y_1 \quad \text{since} \quad y_2 = \sec^2 x, \quad y_1 = \tan x$$

$$y_4 = 2y_2y_2 + 2y_3y_1$$

$$y_4 = 2y_2^2 + 2y_1y_3 \Rightarrow y_4\,(0) = 2$$

$$y_5 = 4y_2y_3 + 2y_1y_4 + 2y_2y_3$$

$$y_5 = 6y_2y_3 + 2y_1y_4 \Rightarrow y_5\,(0) = 0$$

$$y_6 = 6y_2y_4 + 6y_3y_3 + 2y_2y_4 + 2y_1y_5$$

$$y_6 = 8y_2y_4 + 6y_3^2 + 2y_1y_5 \Rightarrow y_6\,(0) = 16$$

Therefore,

$$y = y\,(0) + \frac{x}{1\,!}y_1\,(0) + \frac{x^2}{2\,!}y_2\,(0) + \cdots$$

$$= 0 + 0 + \frac{x^2}{2\,!}(1) + 0 + \frac{x^4}{4\,!}(2) + 0 + \frac{x^6}{6\,!}(16) + \cdots$$

$$\log\sec x = \frac{x^2}{2} + \frac{x^4}{12} + \frac{x^6}{45} + \cdots$$

10. *Obtain the Maclaurin's series expansion of the function* log $(1 + e^x)$

➡ Let

$$y = \log\left(1 + e^x\right) \Rightarrow y\,(0) = \log 2$$

$$y_1 = \frac{1}{1 + e^x} e^x \Rightarrow y_1\,(0) = \frac{1}{2}$$

$$\left(1 + e^x\right)\, y_1 = e^x$$

$$\left(1 + e^x\right)\, y_2 + e^x y_1 = e^x \qquad (1)$$

At $x = 0$

$$2y_2\,(0) + 1 \cdot y_1\,(0) = 1$$

$$2y_2\,(0) + \frac{1}{2} = 1$$

$$y_2\,(0) = \frac{1}{4}$$

Differentiating (1) with respect to x, we get

$$\left(1 + e^x\right)\, y_3 + e^x y_2 + e^x y_2 + e^x y_1 = e^x$$

$$\left(1 + e^x\right)\, y_3 + 2e^x y_2 + e^x y_1 = e^x \qquad (2)$$

At $x = 0$,

$$2y_3\,(0) + 2\,(1)\left(\frac{1}{4}\right) + 1.\frac{1}{2} = 1$$

$$y_3\,(0) = 0$$

Differentiating (2) with respect to x, we get

$$\left(1 + e^x\right)\, y_4 + e^x y_3 + 2e^x y_3 + 2e^x y_2 + e^x y_2 + e^x y_1 = e^x$$

$$\left(1 + e^x\right)\, y_4 + 3e^x y_3 + 3e^x y_2 + e^x y_1 = e^x$$

At $x = 0$,

$$2y_4\,(0) + 0 + 3\,(1)\left(\frac{1}{4}\right) + 1.\frac{1}{2} = 1$$

$$2y_4(0) + \frac{3}{4} + \frac{1}{2} = 1$$
$$y_4(0) = -\frac{1}{8}$$

Therefore,

$$\begin{aligned} y &= y(0) + \frac{x}{1\,!}y_1(0) + \frac{x^2}{2\,!}y_2(0) + \cdots \\ &= \log 2 + \frac{x}{1\,!}\left(\frac{1}{2}\right) + \frac{x^2}{2\,!}\left(\frac{1}{4}\right) + 0 + \frac{x^4}{4\,!}\left(-\frac{1}{8}\right) + \cdots \\ &= \log 2 + \frac{x}{2} + \frac{x^2}{8} - \frac{x^4}{192} + \cdots \end{aligned}$$

11. *Expand* $\log(1 + \cos x)$ *by Maclaurin's series upto the term containing* x^4

➡ Let

$$y = \log(1 + \cos x) \Rightarrow y(0) = \log 2$$
$$y_1 = \frac{1}{1 + \cos x}(-\sin x) = -\frac{\sin x}{1 + \cos x} \Rightarrow y_1(0) = 0$$
$$(1 + \cos x)\, y_1 + \sin x = 0$$

Differentiating with respect to x, we get

$$(1 + \cos x)\, y_2 + (-\sin x)\, y_1 + \cos x = 0$$
$$(1 + \cos x)\, y_2 - y_1 \sin x + \cos x = 0 \tag{1}$$

At $x = 0$, $2y_2(0) - 0 + 1 = 0 \Rightarrow y_2(0) = -\frac{1}{2}$

Differentiating (1) with respect to x, we get

$$(1 + \cos x)\, y_3 + (-\sin x)\, y_2 - y_2 \sin x - y_1 \cos x - \sin x = 0$$
$$(1 + \cos x)\, y_3 - 2y_2 \sin x - y_1 \cos x - \sin x = 0 \tag{2}$$

At $x = 0$, $2y_3(0) - 0 - 0 - 0 = 0 \Rightarrow y_3(0) = 0$

Differentiating (2) with respect to x, we get

$$(1 + \cos x)\, y_4 + (-\sin x)\, y_3 - 2y_3 \sin x - 2y_2 \cos x - y_2 \cos x$$

$$+ y_1 \sin x - \cos x = 0$$

$$(1 + \cos x)\, y_4 - 3y_3 \sin x - 3y_2 \cos x + y_1 \sin x - \cos x = 0$$

At $x = 0$,

$$2y_4\,(0) - 0 - 3\left(-\frac{1}{2}\right)(1) + 0 - 1 = 0$$

$$2y_4\,(0) + \frac{3}{2} - 1 = 0$$

$$2y_4\,(0) + \frac{1}{2} = 0$$

$$y_4\,(0) = -\frac{1}{4}$$

Therefore,

$$y = y\,(0) + \frac{x}{1\,!} y_1\,(0) + \frac{x^2}{2\,!} y_2\,(0) + \frac{x^3}{3\,!} y_3\,(0) + \cdots$$

$$= \log 2 + \frac{x}{1\,!}\,(0) + \frac{x^2}{2\,!}\left(-\frac{1}{2}\right) + \frac{x^3}{3\,!}\,(0) + \frac{x^4}{4\,!}\left(-\frac{1}{4}\right) + \cdots$$

$$\log\,(1 + \cos x) = \log 2 - \frac{x^2}{4} - \frac{x^4}{96} + \cdots$$

Exercises

I. 1. *Expand* $\sin x$ *in ascending powers of* $(x - \pi/2)$

2. *Expand* $\log x$ *in powers of* $(x - 2)$

3. *Obtain Taylor's expansion of* $\tan^{-1} x$ *in powers of* $(x - 1)$ *up to the term containing* $(x - 1)^3$

4. *Expand* $\log \sin x$ *in ascending powers of* $(x - 3)$

5. *Expand* $\log x$ *in powers of* $(x - 1)$

6. *Obtain Taylor's series for the function* $\cos x$ *about* $\pi/4$

7. *Expand* $\tan x$ *in powers of* $(x - \pi/4)$ *upto third degree term.*

8. *Expand* $\log\ \sin x$ *in powers of* $(x - 2)$

9. *Find the Taylor's series expansion of e^x about 1*
10. *Expand* $\log x$ *in ascending powers of* $(x-1)$
11. *Expand* $\log\cos x$ *in ascending powers of* $(x-\pi/3)$

II. *Obtain the Maclaurin's expansions of the following functions*

1. $\sec x$ 2. $\sin^{-1} x$ 3. $\log(1+\cos x)$
4. $\log(1+\tan x)$ 5. $e^{\cos x}$
6. $e^{\tan^{-1} x}$ 7. $e^{x\cos x}$ 8. $\sec^2 x$
9. $e^x \sec x$ 10. $\log(1+\sin x)$
11. $\log(1+e^x)$ 12. $\log(\sec x+\tan x)$
13. $\log\cos x$ 14. $e^x\cos x$ 15. $e^{\sin x}$

Answers

I. 1. $\sin x = 1 - \frac{1}{2!}\left(x-\frac{\pi}{2}\right)^2 + \frac{1}{4!}\left(x-\frac{\pi}{2}\right)^4 + \cdots$

2. $\log x = \log 2 + \frac{1}{2}(x-2) - \frac{1}{8}(x-2) + \frac{1}{24}(x-3)^3 + \cdots$

3. $\tan^{-1} x = \frac{\pi}{4} + \frac{1}{2}(x-1) - \frac{1}{4}(x-1)^2 + \frac{1}{12}(x-1)^3$

4. $\log\sin x = \log\sin 3 - (x-3)\cot 3 - \frac{(x-3)^2}{2!}\text{cosec}^2 3$
$+2\frac{(x-3)}{3!}\text{cosec}^2 3\cot 3 + \cdots$

5. $\log x = (x-1) - \frac{1}{2}(x-1)^2 + \frac{1}{3}(x-1)^3 - \frac{1}{4}(x-1)^4 + \cdots$

6. $\cos x = \frac{1}{\sqrt{2}}\left\{1 - \frac{(x-\pi/4)}{1\,!} - \frac{(x-\pi/4)^2}{2\,!} + \frac{(x-\pi/4)^3}{3\,!} + \cdots\right\}$

7. $x = 1 + 2\left(x-\frac{\pi}{4}\right) + 2\left(x-\frac{\pi}{4}\right)^2 + \frac{8}{3}\left(x-\frac{\pi}{4}\right)^3 + \cdots$

8. $\log\sin x = \log\sin 2 + (x-2)\cot 2 - \frac{(x-2)^2}{2}\text{cosec}^2 2 + \frac{(x-2)^3}{3}\text{cosec}^2 2\cot 2 + \cdots$

9. $e^x = e\left\{1 + \frac{(x-1)}{1\,!} + \frac{(x-1)^2}{2\,!} + \frac{(x-1)^3}{3\,!} + \frac{(x-1)^4}{4!} + \cdots\right\}$

10. $\log x = \frac{x-1}{1} - \frac{(x-1)^2}{2} + \frac{(x-1)^3}{3} - \frac{(x-1)^4}{4} + \cdots$

11. $\log \cos x = \log\left(\frac{1}{2}\right) - \sqrt{3}\left(x - \frac{\pi}{3}\right) - 2\left(x - \frac{\pi}{3}\right)^2 - \frac{4}{\sqrt{3}}\left(x - \frac{\pi}{3}\right)^3 + \cdots$

II. 1. $1 + \frac{x^2}{2!} + \frac{5x^4}{4!} + \cdots$ 2. $x + \frac{x^3}{6} + \frac{3x^5}{40} + \cdots$

3. $\log 2 - \frac{x^2}{4} - \frac{x^4}{96}$ 4. $x - \frac{x^2}{2!} + \frac{4x^3}{3!}$

5. $e\left\{1 - \frac{x^2}{2} + \frac{x^4}{6} + \cdots\right\}$ 6. $1 + x + \frac{x^2}{2} - \frac{x^3}{6} - \frac{7x^4}{24} + \cdots$

7. $1 + x + \frac{x^2}{2} - \frac{x^3}{3} - \frac{11x^4}{24} - \frac{x^5}{5} + \cdots$

8. $1 + x^2 + \frac{2}{3}x^4 + \cdots$ 9. $1 + x + x^2 + \frac{2}{3}x^3 + \cdots$

10. $1 - \frac{x^2}{2} + \frac{x^3}{6}$ 11. $\log 2 + \frac{x}{2} + \frac{x^2}{8} - \frac{x^4}{196} + \cdots$

12. $x + \frac{x^3}{6} + \frac{x^5}{24} + \cdots$ 13. $-\frac{x^2}{2} - \frac{x^4}{12} - \frac{x^6}{45} + \cdots$

14. $1 + x - \frac{2x^3}{3!} - \frac{4x^4}{4!} + \frac{4x^5}{5!} + \cdots$

15. $1 + x + \frac{x^2}{2} - \frac{x^4}{8} + \cdots$

2.5 Partial Differentiation

Functions of Two or More Variables

So far, we have been dealing with the functions of a single independent variable. We often come across quantities, which depend on two or more variables. For example, the volume (V) of a gas is a function of pressure (P) and temperature (T), i.e., $V = V(P, T)$

Partial Derivatives

Consider a function $f(x, y)$ which depends on two independent variables x and y, denoted by $f = f(x, y)$. The partial derivative of $f(x, y)$ with respect to x is the ordinary derivative of $f(x, y)$ when y is regarded as a constant. It is written as $\partial f/\partial x$ or $D_x f$ or f_x.

Thus,

$$\frac{\partial f}{\partial x} = \lim_{h \to 0} \frac{f(x+h, y) - f(x, y)}{h}.$$

Similarly, the partial derivative of $f(x, y)$ with respect to y is the ordinary derivative of $f(x, y)$ when x is regarded as a constant.

Thus,

$$\frac{\partial f}{\partial y} = \lim_{k \to o} \frac{f(x, y+k) - f(x, y)}{k}$$

The partial derivatives of f_x and f_y are $f_{xx}, f_{xy}, f_{yx}, f_{yy}$ or $\frac{\partial^2 f}{\partial x^2}, \frac{\partial^2 f}{\partial y \partial x}, \frac{\partial^2 f}{\partial x \partial y}, \frac{\partial^2 f}{\partial y^2}$ respectively

It should be noted that

$$\frac{\partial^2 f}{\partial y \partial x} = \frac{\partial}{\partial y}\left(\frac{\partial f}{\partial x}\right), \quad \frac{\partial^2 f}{\partial x \partial y} = \frac{\partial}{\partial x}\left(\frac{\partial f}{\partial y}\right),$$

$$\frac{\partial^2 f}{\partial x^2} = \frac{\partial}{\partial x}\left(\frac{\partial f}{\partial x}\right) \quad and \quad \frac{\partial^2 f}{\partial y^2} = \frac{\partial}{\partial y}\left(\frac{\partial f}{\partial y}\right)$$

The student will be able to convince himself/herself that in all ordinary cases,

$$\frac{\partial^2 f}{\partial x \partial y} = \frac{\partial^2 f}{\partial y \partial x}$$

Worked Examples

1. *If* $z = e^{ax+by} f(ax - by)$, *prove that* $b\frac{\partial z}{\partial x} + a\frac{\partial z}{\partial y} = 2abz$

➡ Let

$$u = ax + by \qquad v = ax - by$$

$$\frac{\partial u}{\partial x} = a \ , \ \frac{\partial u}{\partial y} = b \qquad \frac{\partial v}{\partial x} = a, \ \frac{\partial v}{\partial y} = -b$$

Therefore, $z = e^u f(v)$

$$\frac{\partial z}{\partial x} = e^u \frac{\partial u}{\partial x} f(v) + e^u . f'(v) \frac{\partial v}{\partial x} = e^u (a) f(v) + e^u f'(v)(a)$$

$$\frac{\partial z}{\partial x} = ae^u \left[f(v) + f'(v)\right] \tag{1}$$

$$\frac{\partial z}{\partial y} = e^u . f'(v) \frac{\partial v}{\partial y} + e^u \frac{\partial u}{\partial y} . f(v) = e^u f'(v)(-b) + e^u f(v) b.$$

$$\frac{\partial z}{\partial y} = e^u b \left[f(v) - f'(v)\right] \tag{2}$$

$$\therefore \ b\frac{\partial z}{\partial x} + a\frac{\partial z}{\partial y} = abe^u \left[f(v) + f'(v)\right] + abe^u \left[f(v) - f'(v)\right]$$

$$= abe^u \left[f(v) + f'(v) + f(v) - f'(v)\right] = abe^u \left[2f(v)\right]$$

$$= 2abz \qquad \left[\because z = e^u f(v)\right]$$

2. *If* $u = e^{xy}$, *prove that* $\frac{\partial^2 u}{\partial x^2} + \frac{\partial^2 u}{\partial y^2} = \frac{1}{u}\left[\left(\frac{\partial u}{\partial x}\right)^2 + \left(\frac{\partial u}{\partial y}\right)^2\right]$

➡ $u = e^{xy}$

$$\frac{\partial u}{\partial x} = ye^{xy} \qquad \frac{\partial u}{\partial y} = xe^{xy}$$

$$\frac{\partial^2 u}{\partial x^2} = y^2 e^{xy} \qquad \frac{\partial^2 u}{\partial y^2} = x^2 e^{xy}$$

$$\frac{1}{u}\left[\left(\frac{\partial u}{\partial x}\right)^2 + \left(\frac{\partial u}{\partial y}\right)^2\right] = \frac{1}{e^{xy}}\left[\left(ye^{xy}\right)^2 + \left(xe^{xy}\right)^2\right]$$

$$= \frac{\left(y^2 + x^2\right)\left(e^{xy}\right)^2}{e^{xy}} = y^2 e^{xy} + x^2 e^{xy}$$

$$= \frac{\partial^2 u}{\partial x^2} + \frac{\partial^2 u}{\partial y^2}$$

Therefore, $\frac{\partial^2 u}{\partial x^2} + \frac{\partial^2 u}{\partial y^2} = \frac{1}{u}\left[\left(\frac{\partial u}{\partial x}\right)^2 + \left(\frac{\partial u}{\partial y}\right)^2\right]$

3. *If* $u = \frac{x}{y+z} + \frac{y}{z+x} + \frac{z}{x+y}$, *prove that* $x\frac{\partial u}{\partial x} + y\frac{\partial u}{\partial y} + z\frac{\partial u}{\partial z} = 0$

➡ $u = \frac{x}{y+z} + \frac{y}{z+x} + \frac{z}{x+y}$

$$\frac{\partial u}{\partial x} = \frac{1}{y+z} + y\left(\frac{-1}{(z+x)^2}\right) + z\left(\frac{-1}{(x+y)^2}\right)$$

$$\frac{\partial u}{\partial x} = \frac{1}{y+z} - \frac{y}{(z+x)^2} - \frac{z}{(x+y)^2}$$

Similarly,

$$\frac{\partial u}{\partial y} = -\frac{x}{(y+z)^2} + \frac{1}{z+x} - \frac{z}{(x+y)^2}$$

$$\frac{\partial u}{\partial z} = -\frac{x}{(y+z)^2} - \frac{y}{(z+x)^2} + \frac{1}{(x+y)}$$

$$x\frac{\partial u}{\partial x} + y\frac{\partial u}{\partial y} + z\frac{\partial u}{\partial z} = \frac{x}{y+z} - \frac{xy}{(z+x)^2} - \frac{xz}{(x+y)^2} - \frac{xy}{(y+z)^2} + \frac{y}{z+x}$$
$$- \frac{yz}{(x+y)^2} - \frac{xz}{(y+z)^2} - \frac{yz}{(z+x)^2} + \frac{z}{(x+y)}$$
$$= \left(\frac{x}{y+z} + \frac{y}{z+x} + \frac{z}{x+y}\right) - \left(\frac{y(z+x)}{(z+x)^2} + \frac{z(x+y)}{(x+y)^2} + \frac{x(y+z)}{(y+z)^2}\right)$$
$$= \left(\frac{x}{y+z} + \frac{y}{z+x} + \frac{z}{x+y}\right) - \left(\frac{y}{(z+x)} + \frac{z}{(x+y)} + \frac{x}{(y+z)}\right) = 0$$

4. *If* $u(x+y) = x^2 + y^2$, *then prove that* $\left(\frac{\partial u}{\partial x} - \frac{\partial u}{\partial y}\right)^2 = 4\left(1 - \frac{\partial u}{\partial x} - \frac{\partial u}{\partial y}\right)$

➡ $u(x+y) = x^2 + y^2$

$$\Rightarrow u = \frac{x^2 + y^2}{x+y} \qquad (1)$$

Differentiating (1) partially with respect to x, we get

$$\frac{\partial u}{\partial x} = \frac{(x+y)(2x) - (x^2+y^2)}{(x+y)^2} = \frac{x^2 + 2xy - y^2}{(x+y)^2}$$

Differentiating (1) partially with respect to y, we get

$$\frac{\partial u}{\partial y} = \frac{(x+y)(2y) - \left(x^2+y^2\right)}{(x+y)^2} = \frac{y^2+2xy-x^2}{(x+y)^2}$$

$$\left(\frac{\partial u}{\partial x} - \frac{\partial u}{\partial y}\right)^2 = \left[\frac{x^2+2xy-y^2}{(x+y)^2} - \frac{y^2+2xy-x^2}{(x+y)^2}\right]^2$$

$$= \left[\frac{2\left(x^2-y^2\right)}{(x+y)^2}\right]^2 = \left[\frac{2(x+y)(x-y)}{(x+y)^2}\right]^2$$

$$= \frac{4(x-y)^2}{(x+y)^2}$$

$$4\left(1 - \frac{\partial u}{\partial x} - \frac{\partial u}{\partial y}\right) = 4\left[1 - \frac{x^2+2xy-y^2}{(x+y)^2} - \frac{y^2+2xy-x^2}{(x+y)^2}\right]$$

$$= 4\left[\frac{(x+y)^2 - \left(x^2+2xy-y^2\right) - \left(y^2+2xy-x^2\right)}{(x+y)^2}\right]$$

$$= 4\left[\frac{(x+y)^2 - x^2 - 2xy + y^2 - y^2 - 2xy + x^2}{(x+y)^2}\right]$$

$$= 4\left[\frac{(x+y)^2 - 4xy}{(x+y)^2}\right] = \frac{4(x-y)^2}{(x+y)^2}$$

Therefore, $\left(\frac{\partial u}{\partial x} - \frac{\partial u}{\partial y}\right)^2 = 4\left(1 - \frac{\partial u}{\partial x} - \frac{\partial u}{\partial y}\right)$

5. *If* $z = 2(ax+by)^2 - \left(x^2+y^2\right)$ *and* $a^2+b^2=1$, *then prove that* $\frac{\partial^2 z}{\partial x^2} + \frac{\partial^2 z}{\partial y^2} = 0$

➡

$$z = 2(ax+by)^2 - \left(x^2+y^2\right) \tag{1}$$

Differentiating partially with respect to x, we get

$$\frac{\partial z}{\partial x} = 4(a)(ax+by) - (2x) = 4a^2x + 4aby - 2x$$

Differentiating again, we get

$$\frac{\partial^2 z}{\partial x^2} = 4a^2 - 2$$

Now differentiating (1) partially with respect to y, we get

$$\frac{\partial z}{\partial y} = 4\,(ax + by)\,(b) - (2y) = 4abx + 4b^2 y - 2y$$

Differentiating again, we get

$$\frac{\partial^2 z}{\partial y^2} = 4b^2 - 2$$

Therefore,

$$\frac{\partial^2 z}{\partial x^2} + \frac{\partial^2 z}{\partial y^2} = 4a^2 - 2 + 4b^2 - 2 = 4\left(a^2 + b^2\right) - 4 = 4\,(1) - 4 = 0$$

6. *If* $u = x^2 y + y^2 z + z^2 x$, *prove that* $\frac{\partial u}{\partial x} + \frac{\partial u}{\partial y} + \frac{\partial u}{\partial z} = (x + y + z)^2$

➡

$$u = x^2 y + y^2 z + z^2 x \tag{1}$$

Differentiating (1) partially with respect to x, we get

$$\frac{\partial u}{\partial x} = 2xy + z^2 \tag{2}$$

Differentiating (1) partially with respect to y, we get

$$\frac{\partial u}{\partial y} = 2yz + x^2 \tag{3}$$

Differentiating (1) partially with respect to z, we get

$$\frac{\partial u}{\partial z} = 2zx + y^2 \tag{4}$$

Adding equations (2), (3) and (4), we get

$$\frac{\partial u}{\partial x}+\frac{\partial u}{\partial y}+\frac{\partial u}{\partial z}=2xy+z^2+2yz+x^2+2zx+y^2$$

$$=x^2+y^2+z^2+2xy+2yz+2zx$$

$$\therefore\ \frac{\partial u}{\partial x}+\frac{\partial u}{\partial y}+\frac{\partial u}{\partial x}=(x+y+z)^2$$

7. *If* $u=(y-z)(z-x)(x-y)$ *show that* $\frac{\partial u}{\partial x}+\frac{\partial u}{\partial y}+\frac{\partial u}{\partial z}=0$

➡

$$u=(y-z)(z-x)(x-y) \tag{1}$$

Differentiating (1) partially with respect to x, we get

$$\frac{\partial u}{\partial x}=(y-z)\{(z-x)1+(-1)(x-y)\}$$

$$=(y-z)(z-x)-(y-z)(x-y)$$

Differentiating (1) partially with respect to y, we get

$$\frac{\partial u}{\partial y}=(z-x)(y-z)(-1)+(z-x)(x-y).1$$

$$=-(z-x)(y-z)+(z-x)(x-y)$$

Differentiating (1) partially with respect to z, we get

$$\frac{\partial u}{\partial z}=(x-y)(y-z)1+(x-y)(z-x)(-1)$$

$$=(x-y)(y-z)-(x-y)(z-x)$$

Adding equations (2), (3) and (4), we get

$$\frac{\partial u}{\partial x}+\frac{\partial u}{\partial y}+\frac{\partial u}{\partial z}=(y-z)(z-x)-(y-z)(x-y)$$

$$-(z-x)(y-z)+(z-x)(x-y)$$

$$+(x-y)(y-z)-(x-y)(z-x)$$

$$\frac{\partial u}{\partial x}+\frac{\partial u}{\partial y}+\frac{\partial u}{\partial z}=0$$

8. *If* $u = (x - y)^n + (y - z)^n + (z - x)^n$, *show that* $\dfrac{\partial u}{\partial x} + \dfrac{\partial u}{\partial y} + \dfrac{\partial u}{\partial z} = 0$

➡

$$u = (x - y)^n + (y - z)^n + (z - x)^n \tag{1}$$

Differentiating (1) partially with respect to x, we get

$$\frac{\partial u}{\partial x} = n\,(x - y)^{n-1} + n\,(z - x)^{n-1}\,(-1) = n\,(x - y)^{n-1} - n\,(z - x)^{n-1} \tag{2}$$

Differentiating (1) partially with respect to y, we get

$$\frac{\partial u}{\partial y} = n\,(x - y)^{n-1}\,(-1) + n\,(y - z)^{n-1} = -n\,(x - y)^{n-1} + n\,(y - z)^{n-1} \tag{3}$$

Differentiating (1) partially with respect to z, we get

$$\frac{\partial u}{\partial z} = n\,(y - z)^{n-1}\,(-1) + n\,(z - x)^{n-1} = -n\,(y - z)^{n-1} + n\,(z - x)^{n-1} \tag{4}$$

Adding equations (2), (3) and (4), we get

$$\begin{aligned}\frac{\partial u}{\partial x} + \frac{\partial u}{\partial y} + \frac{\partial u}{\partial z} &= n\left[(x - y)^{n-1} - (z - x)^{n-1} - (x - y)^{n-1} + (y - z)^{n-1}\right.\\ &\qquad \left.- (y - z)^{n-1} + (z - x)^{n-1}\right]\\ &= n\,[0] = 0\end{aligned}$$

9. *If* $u = f\,(x + ay) + g\,(x - ay)$, *prove that* $\dfrac{\partial^2 u}{\partial y^2} = a^2 \dfrac{\partial^2 u}{\partial x^2}$

➡

$$u = f\,(x + ay) + g\,(x - ay) \tag{1}$$

Differentiating (1) partially with respect to x, we get

$$\frac{\partial u}{\partial x} = f'\,(x + ay)\cdot 1 + g'\,(x - ay)\cdot 1,$$

Differentiating again, we get

$$\frac{\partial^2 u}{\partial x^2} = f''(x+ay).1 + g''(x-ay).1 \qquad (2)$$

Differentiating (1) partially with respect to y, we get

$$\frac{\partial u}{\partial y} = f'(x+ay).a + g'(x-ay)(-a)$$

$$\frac{\partial u}{\partial y} = af'(x+ay) - ag'(x-ay),$$

Differentiating again, we get

$$\frac{\partial^2 u}{\partial y^2} = af''(x+ay)\,a - ag''(x-ay)(-a)$$

$$= a^2 f''(x+ay) + a^2 g''(x-ay)$$

$$= a^2\left[f''(x+ay) + g''(x-ay)\right]$$

$$\frac{\partial^2 u}{\partial y^2} = a^2 \frac{\partial^2 u}{\partial x^2}$$

10. *If* $z = \cos(x+ay) + \sin(x-ay)$, *prove that* $\frac{\partial^2 z}{\partial y^2} = a^2 \frac{\partial^2 z}{\partial x^2}$

➡

$$z = \cos(x+ay) + \sin(x-ay) \qquad (1)$$

Differentiating (1) partially with respect to x we get

$$\frac{\partial z}{\partial x} = -\sin(x+ay) + \cos(x-ay)$$

Differentiating again with respect to x, we get

$$\frac{\partial^2 z}{\partial x^2} = -\cos(x+ay) - \sin(x-ay)$$

$$= -[\cos(x+ay) + \sin(x-ay)] \qquad (2)$$

Differentiating (1) partially with respect to y, we get

$$\frac{\partial z}{\partial y} = -\sin(x + ay).a + \cos(x - ay)\cdot(-a)$$

$$= -a\sin(x + ay) - a\cos(x - ay)$$

Differentiating again with respect to y, we get

$$\frac{\partial^2 z}{\partial y^2} = -\left(a^2\right)\cos(x + ay) - a\left[-\sin(x - ay)(-a)\right]$$

$$= -a^2\left[\cos(x + ay) + \sin(x - ay)\right] \quad (3)$$

Therefore, from equations (2) and (3), we get

$$\frac{\partial^2 z}{\partial y^2} = a^2\frac{\partial^2 z}{\partial x^2}$$

11. *If* $u = \log(x^3 + y^3 + z^3 - 3xyz)$ *show that* (i) $\frac{\partial u}{\partial x} + \frac{\partial u}{\partial y} + \frac{\partial u}{\partial z} = \frac{3}{x + y + z}$

(ii) $\left(\frac{\partial}{\partial x} + \frac{\partial}{\partial y} + \frac{\partial}{\partial z}\right)^2 u = \frac{-9}{(x + y + z)^2}$

➡

$$u = \log(x^3 + y^3 + z^3 - 3xyz)$$

$$\frac{\partial u}{\partial x} = \frac{1}{x^3 + y^3 + z^3 - 3xyz}(3x^2 - 3yz) = \frac{3x^2 - 3yz}{x^3 + y^3 + z^3 - 3xyz}$$

Similarly,

$$\frac{\partial u}{\partial y} = \frac{3y^2 - 3xz}{x^3 + y^3 + z^3 - 3xyz}$$

$$\frac{\partial u}{\partial z} = \frac{3z^2 - 3xy}{x^3 + y^3 + z^3 - 3xyz}$$

$$\frac{\partial u}{\partial x} + \frac{\partial u}{\partial y} + \frac{\partial u}{\partial z} = \frac{3x^2 - 3yz + 3y^2 - 3xz + 3z^2 - 3xy}{x^3 + y^3 + z^3 - 3xyz}$$

$$= \frac{3[x^2 + y^2 + z^2 - xy - yz - xz]}{(x + y + z)(x^2 + y^2 + z^2 - xy - yz - xz)}$$

$$\frac{\partial u}{\partial x} + \frac{\partial u}{\partial y} + \frac{\partial u}{\partial z} = \frac{3}{x + y + z} \tag{1}$$

$$\left(\frac{\partial}{\partial x} + \frac{\partial}{\partial y} + \frac{\partial}{\partial z}\right)^2 u = \left(\frac{\partial}{\partial x} + \frac{\partial}{\partial y} + \frac{\partial}{\partial z}\right)\left(\frac{\partial}{\partial x} + \frac{\partial}{\partial y} + \frac{\partial}{\partial z}\right) u$$

$$= \left(\frac{\partial}{\partial x} + \frac{\partial}{\partial y} + \frac{\partial}{\partial z}\right)\left(\frac{\partial u}{\partial x} + \frac{\partial u}{\partial y} + \frac{\partial u}{\partial z}\right)$$

$$= \left(\frac{\partial}{\partial x} + \frac{\partial}{\partial y} + \frac{\partial}{\partial z}\right)\left(\frac{3}{x + y + z}\right)$$

$$= 3\left(\frac{-1}{(x + y + z)^2}\right) + 3\left(\frac{-1}{(x + y + z)^2}\right) + 3\left(\frac{-1}{(x + y + z)^2}\right)$$

$$= \frac{-9}{(x + y + z)^2}$$

Exercises

1. *Find* $\dfrac{\partial f}{\partial x}$ *and* $\dfrac{\partial f}{\partial y}$ *when,*

   (i) $f = \log\left(x^2 + y^2\right)$ (ii) $f = x^y$
   (iii) $f = \sin^{-1}(y/z)$

2. *Prove the relation* $\dfrac{\partial^2 u}{\partial x \partial y} = \dfrac{\partial^2 f}{\partial y \partial x}$ *for the following functions,*

   (i) $f = ax^2 - 2hxy + by^2$ (ii) $f = x \log x$
   (iii) $f = x \sin y + y \sin x$ (iv) $f = x^3 + y^3 - 3axy$
   (v) $f = \sin^{-1}\left(\frac{x}{y}\right)$ (vi) $f = \log(x \sin y + y \sin x)$

3. *If* $u = e^{xyz}$, *show that* $\dfrac{\partial^3 u}{\partial x \partial y \partial z} = \left(1 + 3xyz + x^2y^2z^2\right) e^{xyz}$

4. *If* $f = f\left(\frac{y}{x}\right)$, *prove that* $x\dfrac{\partial f}{\partial x} + y\dfrac{\partial f}{\partial y} = 0$

5. *If* $x^x y^y z^z = c$, *show that at*

$$x = y = z, \frac{\partial^2 z}{\partial x \partial y} = -(x \log ex)^{-1}$$

6. *If* $u = \frac{x^2 + y^2}{\sqrt{x + y}}$, *show that* $x\frac{\partial u}{\partial x} + y\frac{\partial u}{\partial y} = \frac{3}{2}u.$

7. *If* $u = e^{(x^3+y^3)}$, *prove that* $x\frac{\partial u}{\partial x} + y\frac{\partial u}{\partial y} = 3u \log u$

8. *If* $u = \frac{xy}{x+y}$, *show that*

$$\text{(i) } x\frac{\partial u}{\partial x} + y\frac{\partial u}{\partial y} = u, \quad \text{(ii) } x^2\frac{\partial^2 u}{\partial x^2} + 2xy\frac{\partial^2 u}{\partial x \partial y} + y^2\frac{\partial^2 u}{\partial y^2} = 0$$

9. *If prove that* $x\frac{\partial u}{\partial x} + y\frac{\partial u}{\partial y} = 0$

10. *If* $u = \tan(y + ax) + (y - ax)^{\frac{3}{2}}$, *show that* $\frac{\partial^2 u}{\partial x^2} = a^2\frac{\partial^2 u}{\partial y^2}$

11. *If* $z = \cos(x + y) + \sin(x - y)$, *prove that* $\frac{\partial^2 z}{\partial x^2} = \frac{\partial^2 z}{\partial y^2}$

12. *If* $z = \frac{x^2+y^2}{x+y}$, *prove that* $\left(\frac{\partial z}{\partial x} - \frac{\partial z}{\partial y}\right)^2 = 4\left[\frac{\partial z}{\partial x} - \frac{\partial z}{\partial y}\right]$

13. *If* $u = \log(\tan x + \tan y + \tan z)$, *prove that*

$$\sin 2x\frac{\partial u}{\partial x} + \sin 2y\frac{\partial u}{\partial y} + \sin 2z\frac{\partial u}{\partial z} = 2$$

14. *If* $z = f(y - 3x) + y(y + 2x) + \sin x - y \cos x$, *prove that*

$$\frac{\partial^2 u}{\partial x^2} + \frac{\partial^2 u}{\partial x \partial y} - 6\frac{\partial^2 u}{\partial y^2} = y \cos x$$

15. *If* $u = r^n$ *where* $r^2 = x^2 + y^2 + z^2$, *prove that*

$$\frac{\partial^2 u}{\partial x^2} + \frac{\partial^2 u}{\partial y^2} + \frac{\partial^2 u}{\partial z^2} = n(n + 1) r^{n-2}$$

16. If $u = \left(1 - 2x + y^2\right)^{-\frac{1}{2}}$, *prove that* $x\frac{\partial u}{\partial x} - y\frac{\partial u}{\partial y} = y^2 u^3$

Answers

1. (i) $\dfrac{\partial f}{\partial x} = \dfrac{\partial x}{x^2+y^2}, \quad \dfrac{\partial f}{\partial y} = \dfrac{2y}{x^2+y^2}$

   (ii) $\dfrac{\partial f}{\partial x} = x^y \dfrac{y}{x}, \quad \dfrac{\partial f}{\partial y} = x^y \log x$

   (iii) $\dfrac{\partial f}{\partial x} = -\dfrac{y}{x\sqrt{x^2-y^2}}, \quad \dfrac{\partial u}{\partial y} = \dfrac{1}{\sqrt{x^2-y^2}}$

2.6 Homogeneous Functions

A function $f(x, y)$ of two independent variables x and y is called *homogeneous function of degree n* if the function can be written in the form $x^n g(y/x)$ or $y^n h(x/y)$

Illustrations

(a) $f(x, y) = x^2+xy+2y^2 = x^2\left(1+\dfrac{y}{x}+2\left(\dfrac{y}{x}\right)^2\right) = x^2 g\left(\dfrac{y}{x}\right)$ is a homogeneous function of degree 2.

(b) $f(x, y) = \dfrac{x^4-y^4}{x+y} = \dfrac{x^4\left(1-(y/x)^4\right)}{x\left(1+(y/x)\right)} = x^3 g\left(\dfrac{y}{x}\right)$ is a homogeneous of degree 3.

(c) $f(x, y) = \cos(y/x) = x^0\cos(y/x) = x^0 g(y/x)$ is a homogeneous function of degree 0.

2.6.1 Euler's Theorem of Homogeneous Functions

If $f(x, y)$ is a homogeneous function of x and y of degree n, then

$$x\frac{\partial f}{\partial x} + y\frac{\partial f}{\partial y} = nf$$

Proof: *If $f(x, y)$ is homogenous function of degree n, then*

$$f(x, y) = f = x^n g\left(\frac{y}{x}\right)$$

Differentiating, f with respect to x, we get

$$\frac{\partial f}{\partial x} = x^n g'\left(\frac{y}{x}\right)\left(\frac{-y}{x^2}\right) + nx^{n-1} g\left(\frac{y}{x}\right)$$

$$x\frac{\partial f}{\partial x} = -yx^{n-1} g\left(\frac{y}{x}\right) + nx^n g\left(\frac{y}{x}\right) \tag{1}$$

Next, differentiating f with respect y, we get

$$\frac{\partial f}{\partial y} = x^n g'\left(\frac{y}{x}\right)\left(\frac{1}{x}\right) = x^{n-1} g'\left(\frac{y}{x}\right)$$

Therefore,

$$y\frac{\partial f}{\partial y} = yx^{n-1} g'\left(\frac{y}{x}\right) \tag{2}$$

Adding equations (1) and (2), we get

$$x\frac{\partial f}{\partial x} + y\frac{\partial f}{\partial y} = -yx^{n-1} g'\left(\frac{y}{x}\right) + nx^n g\left(\frac{y}{x}\right) + yx^{n-1} g'\left(\frac{y}{x}\right)$$

$$= nx^n g\,(y/x) = nf$$

Hence the proof.

In general if $f\,(x_1, x_2, ...x_m)$ is a homogenous function of degree n, then

$$x_1\frac{\partial f}{\partial x_1} + x_2\frac{\partial f}{\partial x_2} + x_3\frac{\partial f}{\partial x_3} + \ldots\ \ldots\ \ldots + x_m\frac{\partial f}{\partial x_m} = nf$$

Worked Examples

1. *Verify the Euler's theorem for* $u = \dfrac{xy}{x+y}$

➡

$$u = \frac{xy}{x+y} = x\left(\frac{y/x}{1+y/x}\right) = xg\left(\frac{y}{x}\right)$$

Therefore, the given function is homogeneous with degree 1, hence by Euler's theorem, we have

$$x\frac{\partial u}{\partial x} + y\frac{\partial u}{\partial y} = 1.u$$

$$u = \frac{xy}{x+y}$$

$$\frac{\partial u}{\partial x} = \frac{(x+y)\,y - xy\,(1)}{(x+y)^2} = \frac{xy + y^2 - xy}{(x+y)^2} = \frac{y^2}{(x+y)^2}$$

$$\frac{\partial u}{\partial y} = \frac{(x+y)\,x - xy\,(1)}{(x+y)^2} = \frac{x^2}{(x+y)^2}$$

$$\therefore\ x\frac{\partial u}{\partial x} + y\frac{\partial u}{\partial y} = \frac{xy^2}{(x+y)^2} + \frac{yx^2}{(x+y)^2} = \frac{xy^2 + yx^2}{(x+y)^2} = \frac{xy\,(y+x)}{(x+y)^2}$$

$$= \frac{xy}{(x+y)} = u$$

$$\therefore\ x\frac{\partial u}{\partial x} + y\frac{\partial u}{\partial y} = u$$

Hence verified.

2. *Verify Euler's theorem for the function* $u = x\tan^{-1}(y/x)$

➡ $u = x\tan^{-1}(y/x)$

Here u is homogeneous function with degree 1, hence by Euler's theorem, we have

$$x\frac{\partial u}{\partial x} + y\frac{\partial u}{\partial y} = 1.u$$

$$u = x\tan^{-1}(y/x)$$

$$\frac{\partial u}{\partial x} = x\frac{1}{1+(y/x)^2}\left(-\frac{y}{x^2}\right) + 1.\tan^{-1}\left(\frac{y}{x}\right)$$

$$\frac{\partial u}{\partial x} = -\frac{xy}{x^2+y^2} + \tan^{-1}\left(\frac{y}{x}\right)$$

$$x\frac{\partial u}{\partial x} = -\frac{x^2y}{x^2+y^2} + x\tan^{-1}\left(\frac{y}{x}\right)$$

and

$$\frac{\partial u}{\partial y} = x\frac{1}{1+(y/x)^2}\left(\frac{1}{x}\right) = \frac{x^2}{x^2+y^2}$$

$$y\frac{\partial u}{\partial y} = \frac{x^2y}{x^2+y^2}$$

$$\therefore\ x\frac{\partial u}{\partial x} + y\frac{\partial u}{\partial y} = -\frac{x^2y}{x^2+y^2} + x\tan^{-1}\left(\frac{y}{x}\right) + \frac{x^2y}{x^2+y^2}$$

$$= x\tan^{-1}\left(\frac{y}{x}\right) = u$$

$$\therefore\ x\frac{\partial u}{\partial x} + y\frac{\partial u}{\partial y} = u$$

Hence verified.

3. *If* $u = \sin^{-1}\left[\frac{x^3+y^3}{x+y}\right]$ *prove that* $x\frac{\partial u}{\partial x} + y\frac{\partial u}{\partial y} = 2\tan u$

➡

$$u = \sin^{-1}\left[\frac{x^3+y^3}{x+y}\right]$$

$$\sin u = \frac{x^3+y^3}{x+y} = \frac{x^3\left(1+(y/x)^3\right)}{x\left[1+(y/x)\right]} = x^2\left[\frac{1+(y/x)^3}{1+(y/x)}\right] = x^2 g\left(\frac{y}{x}\right) = f$$

Now f is homogeneous function with degree 2, by using Euler's theorem, we get

$$x\frac{\partial f}{\partial x} + y\frac{\partial f}{\partial y} = 2f$$

$$x\frac{\partial}{\partial x}(\sin u) + y\frac{\partial}{\partial x}(\sin u) = 2\sin u$$

$$x\cos u\frac{\partial u}{\partial x} + y\cos u\frac{\partial u}{\partial y} = 2\sin u$$

$$\left(x\frac{\partial u}{\partial x} + y\frac{\partial u}{\partial y}\right)\cos u = 2\sin u$$

$$x\frac{\partial u}{\partial x} + y\frac{\partial u}{\partial y} = 2\tan u$$

4. *If* $u = \tan^{-1}\left(\frac{x^3+y^3}{x-y}\right)$, *prove that* $x\dfrac{\partial u}{\partial x} + y\dfrac{\partial u}{\partial y} = \sin 2u$

➡

$$\tan u = \frac{x^3\left(1+(y/x)^3\right)}{x\left(1-(y/x)\right)} = \frac{x^2\left(1+(y/x)^3\right)}{\left(1-(y/x)\right)} = x^2 g\,(y/x) = f\,(say)$$

Now f is homogeneous function with degree 2, hence using Euler's theorem, we get

$$x\frac{\partial f}{\partial x} + y\frac{\partial f}{\partial y} = 2f$$

$$x\frac{\partial\,(\tan u)}{\partial x} + y\frac{\partial\,(\tan u)}{\partial y} = 2\tan u$$

$$x\sec^2 u\frac{\partial u}{\partial x} + y\sec^2 u\frac{\partial u}{\partial y} = 2\tan u$$

$$x\frac{\partial u}{\partial x} + y\frac{\partial u}{\partial y} = 2\tan u \times \cos^2 u = 2\frac{\sin u}{\cos u}.\cos^2 u = 2\sin u\cos u$$

$$x\frac{\partial u}{\partial x} + y\frac{\partial u}{\partial y} = \sin 2u$$

5. *If* $f\,(x,y) = \dfrac{1}{x^2} + \dfrac{1}{xy} + \dfrac{\log x - \log y}{x^2+y^2}$, *prove that* $x\dfrac{\partial f}{\partial x} + y\dfrac{\partial f}{\partial y} + 2f = 0$

➡

$$f\,(x,y) = \frac{1}{x^2} + \frac{1}{xy} + \frac{\log x - \log y}{x^2+y^2} = \frac{1}{x^2} + \frac{1}{xy} + \frac{\log\,(x/y)}{x^2+y^2}$$

$$= \frac{1}{y^2\,(x/y)^2} + \frac{1}{y^2\,(x/y)} + \frac{\log\,(x/y)}{y^2\left[(x/y)^2+1\right]}$$

$$= \frac{1}{y^2}\left[\frac{1}{(x/y)^2} + \frac{1}{x/y} + \frac{\log\,(x/y)}{(x/y)^2+1}\right] = y^{-2} g\left(\frac{x}{y}\right)$$

Therefore, $f\,(x,y)$ is homogeneous function with degree -2, hence by using Euler's theorem, we have

$$x\frac{\partial f}{\partial x} + y\frac{\partial f}{\partial y} = -2f$$

i.e.,

$$x\frac{\partial f}{\partial x} + y\frac{\partial f}{\partial y} + 2f = 0$$

6. *If* $u = \text{cosec}^{-1}\left(\dfrac{x^{\frac{1}{2}} + y^{\frac{1}{2}}}{x^{\frac{1}{3}} + y^{\frac{1}{3}}}\right)$, *prove that* $x\dfrac{\partial u}{\partial x} + y\dfrac{\partial u}{\partial y} = -\dfrac{1}{6}\tan u$

➡

$$u = \text{cosec}^{-1}\left(\frac{x^{\frac{1}{2}} + y^{\frac{1}{2}}}{x^{\frac{1}{3}} + y^{\frac{1}{3}}}\right)$$

$$\text{cosec}u = \frac{x^{\frac{1}{2}} + y^{\frac{1}{2}}}{x^{\frac{1}{3}} + y^{\frac{1}{3}}} = \frac{x^{\frac{1}{2}}\left(1 + (y/x)^{\frac{1}{2}}\right)}{x^{\frac{1}{3}}\left(1 + (y/x)^{\frac{1}{3}}\right)}$$

$$\text{cosec } u = x^{\frac{1}{6}}\left(\frac{1 + (y/x)^{\frac{1}{2}}}{1 + (y/x)^{\frac{1}{3}}}\right) = x^{\frac{1}{6}}g\,(y/x) = f$$

Therefore, by Euler's theorem, we get

$$x\frac{\partial f}{\partial x} + y\frac{\partial f}{\partial y} = \frac{1}{6}f$$

$$x\frac{\partial}{\partial x}(\text{cosec } u) + y\frac{\partial}{\partial y}(\text{cosec } u) = \frac{1}{6}\text{cosec } u$$

$$\Rightarrow -x\text{cosec } u \cot u\frac{\partial u}{\partial x} - y\text{cosec } u.\cot u\frac{\partial u}{\partial y} = \frac{1}{6}\text{cosec } u$$

$$-\text{cosec } u \cot u\left\{x\frac{\partial u}{\partial x} + y\frac{\partial u}{\partial y}\right\} = \frac{1}{6}\text{cosec } u$$

$$x\frac{\partial u}{\partial x} + y\frac{\partial u}{\partial y} = -\frac{1}{6}\frac{1}{\cot u}$$

$$\Rightarrow x\frac{\partial u}{\partial x} + y\frac{\partial u}{\partial y} = -\frac{1}{6}\tan u$$

7. *If* $u = e^{\frac{x^2y^2}{x+y}}$, *prove that* $x\dfrac{\partial u}{\partial x} + y\dfrac{\partial u}{\partial y} = 3u \log u$

➡

$$u = e^{\frac{x^2y^2}{x+y}}$$

$$\log u = \frac{x^2y^2}{x+y} = \frac{x^4\left(y^2/x^2\right)}{x\left(1+y/x\right)} = x^3\left[\frac{(y/x)^2}{1+y/x}\right] = x^3 g\left(\frac{y}{x}\right) = f \quad \text{(say)}$$

Therefore, f is homogenous function of degree 3. Hence by Euler's theorem, we get

$$x\frac{\partial f}{\partial x} + y\frac{\partial f}{\partial y} = 3f$$

$$x\frac{\partial}{\partial x}(\log u) + y\frac{\partial}{\partial y}(\log u) = 3\log u$$

$$x.\frac{1}{u}\frac{\partial u}{\partial x} + y.\frac{1}{u}\frac{\partial u}{\partial y} = 3\log u$$

$$\frac{1}{u}\left(x\frac{\partial u}{\partial x} + y\frac{\partial u}{\partial y}\right) = 3\log u$$

$$x\frac{\partial u}{\partial x} + y\frac{\partial u}{\partial y} = 3u\log u$$

Exercises

1. *Verify Euler's theorem in the following cases.*
   (i) $f = ax^2 + 2hxy + by^2$
   (ii) $f = \frac{xy}{x-y}$
   (iii) $f = x^n \log\left(\frac{y}{x}\right)$
   (iv) $f = x^3 + y^3 + 3x^2y$
   (v) $f = \frac{1}{x^2+y^2+xy}$
2. *If* $u = \sin^{-1}\left(\frac{x+y}{\sqrt{x}+\sqrt{y}}\right)$, *prove that*

(i) $x\dfrac{\partial u}{\partial x}+y\dfrac{\partial u}{\partial y}=\dfrac{1}{2}\tan u$

(ii) $x^2\dfrac{\partial^2 u}{\partial x^2}+2xy\dfrac{\partial^2 u}{\partial x\partial y}+y^2\dfrac{\partial^2 u}{\partial y^2}=\dfrac{1}{4}\left(\tan^3 u-\tan u\right)$

3. *If* $u=\tan^{-1}\dfrac{x^3+y^3}{x+y}$, *prove that* $x\dfrac{\partial u}{\partial x}+y\dfrac{\partial u}{\partial y}=\sin 2u$

4. *If* $u=\sin^{-1}\left\{\left(x^2+y^2\right)(x+y)\right\}$, *show that* $x\dfrac{\partial u}{\partial x}+y\dfrac{\partial u}{\partial y}=\tan u$

5. *If* $u=\sin^{-1}\left(\dfrac{x}{y}\right)+\tan^{-1}\left(\dfrac{y}{x}\right)$, *prove that* $x\dfrac{\partial u}{\partial x}+y\dfrac{\partial u}{\partial y}=0$

6. *If u be a homogeneous function of degree n, show that*

(i) $x\dfrac{\partial^2 u}{\partial x^2}+y\dfrac{\partial^2 u}{\partial x\partial y}=(n-1)\dfrac{\partial u}{\partial x}$

(ii) $x\dfrac{\partial^2 u}{\partial x\partial y}+y\dfrac{\partial^2 u}{\partial y^2}=(n-1)\dfrac{\partial u}{\partial y}$

7. *If* $u=xyf\left(\dfrac{x}{y}\right)$, *prove that* $x\dfrac{\partial u}{\partial x}+y\dfrac{\partial u}{\partial y}=2u$

8. *If* $u=x^3y^2\sin^{-1}\left(\dfrac{y}{x}\right)$, *prove that* $x\dfrac{\partial u}{\partial x}+y\dfrac{\partial u}{\partial y}=5u$

9. *If* $u=\sin^{-1}\left(\dfrac{x^3-y^3}{x-y}\right)$, *show that* $x\dfrac{\partial u}{\partial x}+y\dfrac{\partial u}{\partial y}=2\tan u.$

10. *If* $u=e^{x^3+y^3}$, *prove that* $x\dfrac{\partial u}{\partial x}+y\dfrac{\partial u}{\partial y}=3u\log u.$

11. *If* $u=\sin^{-1}\left(\dfrac{\sqrt{x}-\sqrt{y}}{\sqrt{x}+\sqrt{y}}\right)$, *prove that* $x\dfrac{\partial u}{\partial x}+y\dfrac{\partial u}{\partial y}=0.$

12. *If* $u=\sin^{-1}\left(\dfrac{x^2y^2}{x+y}\right)$, *prove that* $x\dfrac{\partial u}{\partial x}+y\dfrac{\partial u}{\partial y}=3\tan u$

13. *If* $u=\tan^{-1}\left(\frac{x^2+y^2}{x+y}\right)$, *prove that* $x\dfrac{\partial u}{\partial x}+y\dfrac{\partial u}{\partial y}=\dfrac{1}{2}\sin 2u$

14. *If* $u=\cos^{-1}\left(\dfrac{x+y}{\sqrt{x}+\sqrt{y}}\right)$, *prove that* $x\dfrac{\partial u}{\partial x}+y\dfrac{\partial u}{\partial y}=-\dfrac{1}{2}\cot u$

15. *If* $u = \tan^{-1}\left(\frac{x^3y^3}{x^3+y^3}\right)$, *prove that* $x\dfrac{\partial u}{\partial x} + y\dfrac{\partial u}{\partial y} = \dfrac{3}{2}\sin 2u.$

16. *If* $u = \tan^{-1}\sqrt{x^3y + xy^3 + y^4 + x^4}$, *prove that* $x\dfrac{\partial u}{\partial x} + y\dfrac{\partial u}{\partial y} = \sin 2u$

17. *If* $u = x^4y^6\cos^{-1}\left(\dfrac{y}{x}\right)$, *prove that*

(i) $x\dfrac{\partial u}{\partial x} + y\dfrac{\partial u}{\partial y} = 10u$

(ii) $x^2\dfrac{\partial^2 u}{\partial x^2} + 2xy\dfrac{\partial^2 u}{\partial x \partial y} + y^2\dfrac{\partial^2 u}{\partial y^2} = 9u$

18. *If* $u = \sin^{-1}\left(\dfrac{3x^2 + 4y^2}{3x + 4y}\right)$, *prove that*

(i) $x\dfrac{\partial u}{\partial x} + y\dfrac{\partial u}{\partial y} = \tan u$

(ii) $x^2\dfrac{\partial^2 u}{\partial x^2} + 2xy\dfrac{\partial^2 u}{\partial x \partial y} + y^2\dfrac{\partial^2 u}{\partial y^2} = \tan^3 u$

19. *If* $u = \log\left(\dfrac{x^2 + y^2}{x + y}\right)$, *prove that* $x\dfrac{\partial u}{\partial x} + y\dfrac{\partial u}{\partial y} = 1$

20. *If* $u = \sqrt{x^2 - y^2}\sin^{-1}\left(\dfrac{y}{x}\right)$, *prove that* $x\dfrac{\partial u}{\partial x} + y\dfrac{\partial u}{\partial y} = u$

21. *If* $u = \dfrac{x^2y^2z^2}{x^2 + y^2 + z^2}$, *prove that* $x\dfrac{\partial u}{\partial x} + y\dfrac{\partial u}{\partial y} + z\dfrac{\partial u}{\partial z} = 4u$

22. *If* $u = \dfrac{x^3 + y^3 + z^3}{xyz + x^2y + y^2z}$, *prove that* $x\dfrac{\partial u}{\partial x} + y\dfrac{\partial u}{\partial y} + z\dfrac{\partial u}{\partial z} = 0$

23. *If* $u = \sin^{-1}\left(\dfrac{x^3 + y^3 + z^3}{\sqrt{x + y + z}}\right)$, *prove that* $x\dfrac{\partial u}{\partial x} + y\dfrac{\partial u}{\partial y} + z\dfrac{\partial u}{\partial z} = 2\tan u$

24. *If* $u = \cos^{-1}\left(\frac{x^3+y^3+z^3}{\sqrt{x^4+y^4+z^4}}\right)$, *prove that* $x\dfrac{\partial u}{\partial x} + y\dfrac{\partial u}{\partial y} + z\dfrac{\partial u}{\partial z} = -\cot u$

25. *If* $u = x\Phi\left(\dfrac{y}{x}\right) + \phi\left(\dfrac{x}{y}\right)$, *prove that* $x^2\dfrac{\partial^2 u}{\partial x^2} + 2xy\dfrac{\partial^2 u}{\partial x \partial y} + y^2\dfrac{\partial^2 u}{\partial y^2} = 0$

2.7 Total Differential and Total Derivative

If $f = f(x, y)$ is a function of two independent variables x and y, then the total differential is defined as

$$df = \frac{\partial f}{\partial x}dx + \frac{\partial f}{\partial y}dy$$

Let $f = f(x, y)$ be a function such that $x = x(t)$ and $y = y(t)$ then we can find the value of f in terms of t by substituting from the last two equations in the first equation. Hence we can regard f as a function of the single variable t, and we can find the ordinary differentiation or the total derivative df/dt by using

$$\frac{df}{dt} = \frac{\partial f}{\partial x}\frac{dx}{dt} + \frac{\partial f}{\partial y}.\frac{dy}{dt}$$

Similarly, if $f = f(x_1, x_2, x_3 \ldots\ldots, x_n)$ then total differential

$$df = \frac{\partial f}{\partial x_1}dx_1 + \frac{\partial f}{\partial x_2}dx_2 + \ldots\ldots + \frac{\partial f}{\partial x_n}dx_n$$

and if $f = f(x_1, x_2, x_3 \ldots\ldots, x_n)$ and $x_1, x_2, \ldots\ldots, x_n$ are all functions of t, then total derivative

$$\frac{df}{dt} = \frac{\partial f}{\partial x_1}\frac{dx_1}{dt} + \frac{\partial f}{\partial x_2}.\frac{dx_2}{dt} + \ldots\ldots + \frac{\partial f}{\partial x_n}.\frac{dx_n}{dt}$$

2.8 Differentiation of Implicit Functions

If $f(x, y)$ is a function of x and y, and y is a function of x, then differentiation of f with respect to x is

$$\frac{df}{dx} = \frac{\partial f}{\partial x} + \frac{\partial f}{\partial y}.\frac{dy}{dx}$$

2.9 Differentiation of Composite Functions

Let $f(x, y)$ be a function of x and y, where x and y are themselves functions of two other variables u and v, then

$$\frac{\partial f}{\partial u} = \frac{\partial f}{\partial x}.\frac{\partial x}{\partial u} + \frac{\partial f}{\partial y}.\frac{\partial y}{\partial u}$$

and

$$\frac{\partial f}{\partial v} = \frac{\partial f}{\partial x}.\frac{\partial x}{\partial v} + \frac{\partial f}{\partial y}.\frac{\partial y}{\partial v}$$

Similarly, if f is a function of u and v, where u and v are themselves functions of x and y, then

$$\frac{\partial f}{\partial x} = \frac{\partial f}{\partial u}.\frac{\partial u}{\partial x} + \frac{\partial f}{\partial v}.\frac{\partial v}{\partial x}$$
$$\frac{\partial f}{\partial y} = \frac{\partial f}{\partial u}.\frac{\partial u}{\partial y} + \frac{\partial f}{\partial v}.\frac{\partial v}{\partial y}$$

Worked Examples

1. *If* $f = e^x [x \sin y + y \cos y]$ *find the total differential.*

➡ $f = e^x . [x \sin y + y \cos y]$

$$\frac{\partial f}{\partial x} = e^x [\sin y] + e^x [x \sin y + y \cos y] = e^x [(1 + x) \sin y + y \cos y]$$

$$\frac{\partial f}{\partial y} = e^x [x \cos y + y(-\sin y) + 1 \cdot \cos y] = e^x [(x + 1) \cos y - y \sin y]$$

$$df = \frac{\partial f}{\partial x} dx + \frac{\partial f}{\partial y} dy$$

$$\Rightarrow df = e^x [(1 + x) \sin y + y \cos y] dx + e^x [(x + 1) \cos y - y \sin y] dy$$

2. *Find the total differential of* $u = x^2 y + y^2 z + z^2 x$

➡

$$\frac{\partial u}{\partial x} = 2xy + z^2, \quad \frac{\partial u}{\partial y} = 2yz + x^2, \quad \frac{\partial u}{\partial z} = 2zx + y^2$$

$$du = \frac{\partial u}{\partial x}.dx + \frac{\partial u}{\partial y}dy + \frac{\partial u}{\partial z}.dz$$

$$du = \left(2xy + z^2\right) dx + \left(2yz + x^2\right) dy + \left(2zx + y^2\right) dz$$

3. *Find the total differentiation of* $u = x^3y^2$, *where* $x = e^t, \ y = \log t$

➡ $u = x^3y^2$,

$$\frac{du}{dt} = \frac{\partial u}{\partial x}.\frac{dx}{dt} + \frac{\partial u}{\partial y}.\frac{dy}{dt}$$

$$\frac{du}{dt} = \left(3x^2y^2\right) e^t + \left(2x^3y\right) \frac{1}{t}$$

$$= 3e^{2t} (\log t)^2 .e^t + 2e^{3t} \log t.\frac{1}{t}$$

$$= e^{3t} \log t \left[3 \log t + \frac{2}{t}\right]$$

4. *If* $u = x^2 + y^2 + z^2$ *where* $x = e^t, y = e^t \sin t, z = e^t \cos t$ *show that without actually substituting that* $\frac{du}{dt} = 4e^{2t}$

➡ $u = x^2 + y^2 + z^2$

$$x = e^t \qquad y = e^t \sin t \qquad z = e^t \cos t$$

$$\frac{dx}{dt} = e^t \qquad \frac{dy}{dt} = e^t \cos t + e^t \sin t \qquad \frac{dz}{dt} = e^t (-\sin t) + e^t \cos t$$

$$\frac{dy}{dt} = e^t (\cos t + \sin t) \qquad \frac{dz}{dt} = e^t (\cos t - \sin t)$$

We have

$$\frac{du}{dt} = \frac{\partial u}{\partial x}\frac{dx}{dt} + \frac{\partial u}{\partial y}\frac{dy}{dt} + \frac{\partial u}{\partial z}\frac{dz}{dt}$$

$$= 2x \left(e^t\right) + 2ye^t (\cos t + \sin t) + 2ze^t (\cos t - \sin t)$$

$$= 2e^t [x + y (\cos + \sin t) + z (\cos t - \sin t)]$$

$$= 2e^t\left[e^t + e^t \sin t\,(\cos t + \sin t) + e^t \cos t\,(\cos t - \sin t)\right]$$
$$\doteq 2e^{2t}\left[1 + \sin t \cos t + \sin^2 t + \cos^2 t - \cos t \sin t\right]$$
$$= 2e^{2t}\,[1 + 1] = 4e^{2t}$$

5. *If* $x^y + y^x = c$ *find* $\frac{dy}{dx}$

➡ $f = x^y + y^x = c$

$$\therefore\ \frac{\partial f}{\partial x} = yx^{y-1} + y^x \log y$$
$$\frac{\partial f}{\partial y} = x^y \log x + xy^{x-1}$$

We have,

$$\frac{df}{dx} = \frac{\partial f}{\partial x} + \frac{\partial f}{\partial y}.\frac{dy}{dx}$$
$$0 = \frac{\partial f}{\partial x} + \frac{\partial f}{\partial y}.\frac{dy}{dx}$$
$$\frac{dy}{dx} = -\frac{\partial f/\partial x}{\partial f/\partial y}$$
$$\therefore\ \frac{dy}{dx} = -\frac{\left(yx^{y-1} + y^x \log y\right)}{\left(xy^{x-1} + x^4 \log x\right)}$$

6. *If* $z = z\,(x, y)$ *and* $x = u - v,\ y = uv$, *show that*

(i) $\frac{\partial z}{\partial u} + \frac{\partial z}{\partial v} = (u + v)\,\frac{\partial z}{\partial y}$

(ii) $u\frac{\partial z}{\partial u} - v\frac{\partial z}{\partial v} = (u + v)\,\frac{\partial z}{\partial x}$

➡

$$x = u - v \qquad y = u.v$$
$$\frac{\partial x}{\partial u} = 1 \qquad \frac{\partial y}{\partial u} = v$$
$$\frac{\partial x}{\partial v} = -1 \qquad \frac{\partial y}{\partial v} = u$$

$$\frac{\partial z}{\partial u} = \frac{\partial z}{\partial x}.\frac{\partial x}{\partial u} + \frac{\partial z}{\partial y}.\frac{\partial y}{\partial u} = \frac{\partial z}{\partial x} + \frac{\partial z}{\partial y}(v) \quad (1)$$

$$\frac{\partial z}{\partial v} = \frac{\partial z}{\partial x}.\frac{\partial x}{\partial v} + \frac{\partial z}{\partial y}.\frac{\partial y}{\partial v} = -\frac{\partial z}{\partial x} + u\frac{\partial z}{\partial y} \quad (2)$$

(i) Adding equations (1) and (2), we get

$$\frac{\partial z}{\partial u} + \frac{\partial z}{\partial v} = \frac{\partial z}{\partial x} + v\frac{\partial z}{\partial y} - \frac{\partial z}{\partial x} + u\frac{\partial z}{\partial y} = (u+v)\frac{\partial z}{\partial y}$$

(ii) Taking $u \times (1) - v \times (2)$, we get

$$u\frac{\partial z}{\partial u} - v\frac{\partial z}{\partial v} = u\frac{\partial z}{\partial x} + uv\frac{\partial z}{\partial y} + v\frac{\partial z}{\partial x} - uv\frac{\partial z}{\partial y} = (u+v)\frac{\partial z}{\partial x}$$

7. *If* $z = f(x, y)$ *and* $x = e^u \cos v,\ y = e^u \sin v$, *show that*

$$\left(\frac{\partial z}{\partial u}\right)^2 + \left(\frac{\partial z}{\partial v}\right)^2 = e^{2u}\left\{\left(\frac{\partial z}{\partial x}\right)^2 + \left(\frac{\partial z}{\partial y}\right)^2\right\}$$

➡

$$x = e^u \cos v \qquad y = e^u \sin v,$$

$$\frac{\partial x}{\partial u} = e^u \cos v \qquad \frac{\partial y}{\partial u} = e^u \sin v$$

$$\frac{\partial x}{\partial v} = -e^u \sin v \qquad \frac{\partial y}{\partial v} = e^u \cos v$$

$$\frac{\partial z}{\partial u} = \frac{\partial z}{\partial x}.\frac{\partial x}{\partial u} + \frac{\partial z}{\partial y}.\frac{\partial y}{\partial u} = e^u \cos v\frac{\partial z}{\partial x} + e^u \sin v\frac{\partial z}{\partial y}$$

$$= e^u\left[\cos v\frac{\partial z}{\partial x} + \sin v\frac{\partial z}{\partial y}\right] \quad (1)$$

$$\frac{\partial z}{\partial v} = \frac{\partial z}{\partial x}.\frac{\partial x}{\partial v} + \frac{\partial z}{\partial y}.\frac{\partial y}{\partial v} = -e^u \sin v\frac{\partial z}{\partial x} + e^u \cos v\frac{\partial z}{\partial y}$$

$$= e^u\left[\cos v\frac{\partial z}{\partial y} - \sin v\frac{\partial z}{\partial x}\right] \quad (2)$$

Squaring and adding equations (1) and (2), we get

$$\left(\frac{\partial z}{\partial u}\right)^2 + \left(\frac{\partial z}{\partial v}\right)^2 = e^{2u}\left[\cos v\frac{\partial z}{\partial x} + \sin v\frac{\partial z}{\partial y}\right]^2 + e^{2u}\left[\cos v\frac{\partial z}{\partial y} - \sin v\frac{\partial z}{\partial x}\right]^2$$

$$= e^{2u}\left[\cos^2 v\left(\frac{\partial z}{\partial x}\right)^2 + \sin^2 v\left(\frac{\partial z}{\partial y}\right)^2 + 2\cos v\frac{\partial z}{\partial x}.\sin v\frac{\partial z}{\partial y}\right.$$

$$\left. + \cos^2 v\left(\frac{\partial z}{\partial y}\right)^2 + \sin^2 v\left(\frac{\partial z}{\partial x}\right)^2 - 2\cos v\frac{\partial z}{\partial y}.\sin v\frac{\partial z}{\partial x}\right]$$

$$= e^{2u}\left[\left(\frac{\partial z}{\partial x}\right)^2(\cos^2 v + \sin^2 v) + \left(\frac{\partial z}{\partial y}\right)^2(\sin^2 v + \cos^2 v)\right]$$

$$\left(\frac{\partial z}{\partial u}\right)^2 + \left(\frac{\partial z}{\partial v}\right)^2 = e^{2u}\left[\left(\frac{\partial z}{\partial x}\right)^2 + \left(\frac{\partial z}{\partial y}\right)^2\right]$$

8. *If* $u = f(x - y, y - z, z - x)$, *prove that* $\frac{\partial u}{\partial x} + \frac{\partial u}{\partial y} + \frac{\partial u}{\partial z} = 0$

➡ Let

$$\begin{array}{lll} v = x - y & t = y - z & s = z - x \\ \frac{\partial v}{\partial x} = 1 & \frac{\partial t}{\partial x} = 0 & \frac{\partial s}{\partial x} = -1 \\ \frac{\partial v}{\partial y} = -1 & \frac{\partial t}{\partial y} = 1 & \frac{\partial s}{\partial y} = 0 \\ \frac{\partial v}{\partial z} = 0 & \frac{\partial t}{\partial z} = -1 & \frac{\partial s}{\partial z} = 1 \end{array}$$

Therefore, $u = f(v, t, s)$

$$\frac{\partial u}{\partial x} = \frac{\partial u}{\partial v}.\frac{\partial v}{\partial x} + \frac{\partial u}{\partial t}.\frac{\partial t}{\partial x} + \frac{\partial u}{\partial s}.\frac{\partial s}{\partial x} = \frac{\partial u}{\partial v} - \frac{\partial u}{\partial s} \tag{1}$$

$$\frac{\partial u}{\partial y} = \frac{\partial u}{\partial v}.\frac{\partial v}{\partial y} + \frac{\partial u}{\partial t}.\frac{\partial t}{\partial y} + \frac{\partial u}{\partial s}.\frac{\partial s}{\partial y} = -\frac{\partial u}{\partial v} + \frac{\partial u}{\partial t} \tag{2}$$

$$\frac{\partial u}{\partial z} = \frac{\partial u}{\partial v}.\frac{\partial v}{\partial z} + \frac{\partial u}{\partial t}.\frac{\partial t}{\partial z} + \frac{\partial u}{\partial s}.\frac{\partial s}{\partial z} = -\frac{\partial u}{\partial t} + \frac{\partial u}{\partial s} \tag{3}$$

Adding equations (1), (2) and (3), we get

$$\frac{\partial u}{\partial x} + \frac{\partial u}{\partial y} + \frac{\partial u}{\partial z} = \frac{\partial u}{\partial v} - \frac{\partial u}{\partial s} - \frac{\partial u}{\partial v} + \frac{\partial u}{\partial t} - \frac{\partial u}{\partial t} + \frac{\partial u}{\partial s}$$

$$\frac{\partial u}{\partial x} + \frac{\partial u}{\partial y} + \frac{\partial u}{\partial z} = 0$$

9. *If* $u = f\left(\frac{x}{y}, \frac{y}{z}, \frac{z}{x}\right)$, *prove that* $x\frac{\partial u}{\partial x} + y\frac{\partial u}{\partial y} + z\frac{\partial u}{\partial z} = 0$

➡ Let

$$v = \frac{x}{y} \qquad t = \frac{y}{z} \qquad s = \frac{z}{x}$$

$$\frac{\partial v}{\partial x} = \frac{1}{y} \qquad \frac{\partial t}{\partial x} = 0 \qquad \frac{\partial s}{\partial x} = -\frac{z}{x^2}$$

$$\frac{\partial v}{\partial y} = -\frac{x}{y^2} \qquad \frac{\partial t}{\partial y} = \frac{1}{z} \qquad \frac{\partial s}{\partial y} = 0$$

$$\frac{\partial v}{\partial z} = 0 \qquad \frac{\partial t}{\partial z} = -\frac{y}{z^2} \qquad \frac{\partial s}{\partial z} = \frac{1}{x}$$

Therefore, $u = f(v, t, s)$

$$\frac{\partial u}{\partial x} = \frac{\partial u}{\partial v}.\frac{\partial v}{\partial x} + \frac{\partial u}{\partial t}.\frac{\partial t}{\partial x} + \frac{\partial u}{\partial s}.\frac{\partial s}{\partial x}$$

$$\frac{\partial u}{\partial x} = \frac{1}{y}\frac{\partial u}{\partial v} - \frac{z}{x^2}\frac{\partial u}{\partial s} \tag{1}$$

$$\frac{\partial u}{\partial y} = \frac{\partial u}{\partial v}.\frac{\partial v}{\partial y} + \frac{\partial u}{\partial t}.\frac{\partial t}{\partial y} + \frac{\partial u}{\partial s}.\frac{\partial s}{\partial y}$$

$$\frac{\partial u}{\partial y} = -\frac{x}{y^2}\frac{\partial u}{\partial v} + \frac{1}{z}\frac{\partial u}{\partial t} \tag{2}$$

$$\frac{\partial u}{\partial z} = \frac{\partial u}{\partial v}.\frac{\partial v}{\partial z} + \frac{\partial u}{\partial t}.\frac{\partial t}{\partial z} + \frac{\partial u}{\partial s}.\frac{\partial s}{\partial z}$$

$$\frac{\partial u}{\partial z} = -\frac{y}{z^2}\frac{\partial u}{\partial t} + \frac{1}{x}\frac{\partial u}{\partial s} \tag{3}$$

Adding the equations $x \times (1)$, $y \times (2)$ and $z \times (3)$, we get

$$x\frac{\partial u}{\partial x} + y\frac{\partial u}{\partial y} + z\frac{\partial u}{\partial z} = \frac{x}{y}\frac{\partial u}{\partial v} - \frac{z}{x}\frac{\partial u}{\partial s} - \frac{x}{y}\frac{\partial u}{\partial v} + \frac{y}{z}\frac{\partial u}{\partial t} - \frac{y}{z}\frac{\partial u}{\partial t} + \frac{z}{x}\frac{\partial u}{\partial s}$$

$$\therefore\ x\frac{\partial u}{\partial x} + y\frac{\partial u}{\partial y} + z\frac{\partial u}{\partial z} = 0$$

10. *If* $u = \dfrac{x}{z}$, $v = \dfrac{y}{z}$, $w = z$ *and* $f = f(u, v, w)$, *prove that*

$$x\frac{\partial f}{\partial x} + y\frac{\partial f}{\partial y} + z\frac{\partial f}{\partial z} = w\frac{\partial f}{\partial w}$$

➡ Let

$$u = \frac{x}{z} \qquad v = \frac{y}{z} \qquad w = z$$

$$\frac{\partial u}{\partial x} = \frac{1}{z} \qquad \frac{\partial v}{\partial x} = 0 \qquad \frac{\partial w}{\partial x} = 0$$

$$\frac{\partial u}{\partial y} = 0 \qquad \frac{\partial v}{\partial y} = \frac{1}{z} \qquad \frac{\partial w}{\partial y} = 0$$

$$\frac{\partial u}{\partial z} = -\frac{x}{z^2} \qquad \frac{\partial v}{\partial z} = -\frac{y}{z^2} \qquad \frac{\partial w}{\partial z} = 1$$

Therefore, $f = f(u, v, w)$

$$\frac{\partial f}{\partial x} = \frac{\partial f}{\partial u}.\frac{\partial u}{\partial x} + \frac{\partial f}{\partial v}.\frac{\partial v}{\partial x} + \frac{\partial f}{\partial w}.\frac{\partial w}{\partial x} = \frac{1}{z}\frac{\partial f}{\partial u} \tag{1}$$

$$\frac{\partial f}{\partial y} = \frac{\partial f}{\partial u}.\frac{\partial u}{\partial y} + \frac{\partial f}{\partial v}.\frac{\partial v}{\partial y} + \frac{\partial f}{\partial w}.\frac{\partial w}{\partial y} = \frac{1}{z}.\frac{\partial f}{\partial v} \tag{2}$$

$$\frac{\partial f}{\partial z} = \frac{\partial f}{\partial u}.\frac{\partial u}{\partial z} + \frac{\partial f}{\partial v}.\frac{\partial v}{\partial z} + \frac{\partial f}{\partial w}.\frac{\partial w}{\partial z} = -\frac{x}{z^2}\frac{\partial f}{\partial u} - \frac{y}{z^2}\frac{\partial f}{\partial v} + \frac{\partial f}{\partial w} \tag{3}$$

Adding the equations $x \times (1)$, $y \times (2)$, and $z \times (3)$, we get

$$x\frac{\partial f}{\partial x} + y\frac{\partial f}{\partial y} + z\frac{\partial f}{\partial z} = \frac{x}{z}\frac{\partial f}{\partial u} + \frac{y}{z}\frac{\partial f}{\partial v} - \frac{x}{z}\frac{\partial f}{\partial u} - \frac{y}{z}\frac{\partial f}{\partial v} + \frac{\partial f}{\partial w}.z$$

$$x\frac{\partial f}{\partial x} + y\frac{\partial f}{\partial y} + z\frac{\partial f}{\partial z} = z\frac{\partial f}{\partial w}$$

11. *If* $u = u\left(\dfrac{y-x}{xy}, \dfrac{z-x}{xz}\right)$ *find the value of* $x^2\dfrac{\partial u}{\partial x} + y^2\dfrac{\partial u}{\partial y} + z^2\dfrac{\partial u}{\partial z}$

➡ $u = u\left(\dfrac{y-x}{xy}, \dfrac{z-x}{xz}\right)$

Let $v = \dfrac{y-x}{xy}$ and $w = \dfrac{z-x}{xz}$

$$v = \frac{1}{x} - \frac{1}{y} \qquad w = \frac{1}{x} - \frac{1}{z}$$

$$\frac{\partial v}{\partial x} = -\frac{1}{x^2} \qquad \frac{\partial w}{\partial x} = -\frac{1}{x^2}$$

$$\frac{\partial v}{\partial y} = \frac{1}{y^2} \qquad \frac{\partial w}{\partial y} = 0$$

$$\frac{\partial w}{\partial z} = 0 \qquad \frac{\partial w}{\partial z} = \frac{1}{z^2}$$

Therefore, $u = u\,(v, w)$

$$\frac{\partial u}{\partial x} = \frac{\partial u}{\partial v}\frac{\partial v}{\partial x} + \frac{\partial u}{\partial w}\frac{\partial w}{\partial x}$$

$$\frac{\partial u}{\partial x} = \frac{\partial u}{\partial v}\left(-\frac{1}{x^2}\right) + \frac{\partial u}{\partial w}\left(-\frac{1}{x^2}\right)$$

Multiplying x^2 on both sides, we get

$$x^2\frac{\partial u}{\partial x} = -\frac{\partial u}{\partial v} - \frac{\partial u}{\partial w} \tag{1}$$

$$\frac{\partial u}{\partial y} = \frac{\partial u}{\partial v}\frac{\partial v}{\partial y} + \frac{\partial u}{\partial w}\frac{\partial w}{\partial y}$$

$$\frac{\partial u}{\partial y} = \frac{\partial u}{\partial v}\left(\frac{1}{y^2}\right) + \frac{\partial u}{\partial w}(0)$$

Multiplying y^2 on both sides, we get

$$y^2\frac{\partial u}{\partial y} = \frac{\partial u}{\partial v} \tag{2}$$

$$\frac{\partial u}{\partial z} = \frac{\partial u}{\partial v}\frac{\partial v}{\partial z} + \frac{\partial u}{\partial w}\frac{\partial w}{\partial z}$$

$$\frac{\partial u}{\partial z} = \frac{\partial u}{\partial v}(0) + \frac{\partial u}{\partial w}\frac{1}{z^2}$$

Multiplying z^2 on both sides, we get

$$z^2\frac{\partial u}{\partial z} = \frac{\partial u}{\partial w} \tag{3}$$

Adding equations (1), (2) and (3), we get

$$x^2\frac{\partial u}{\partial x} + y^2\frac{\partial u}{\partial y} + z^2\frac{\partial u}{\partial z} = 0$$

12. *If* $z = f(u, v)$, $u = x^2 - y^2$, $v = 2xy$, *prove that*

$$\left(\frac{\partial z}{\partial x}\right)^2 + \left(\frac{\partial z}{\partial y}\right)^2 = 4\left(x^2 + y^2\right)\left[\left(\frac{\partial z}{\partial u}\right)^2 + \left(\frac{\partial z}{\partial v}\right)^2\right]$$

➠ Let

$$u = x^2 - y^2 \qquad v = 2xy$$

$$\frac{\partial u}{\partial x} = 2x \qquad \frac{\partial v}{\partial x} = 2y$$

$$\frac{\partial u}{\partial y} = -2y \qquad \frac{\partial v}{\partial y} = 2x$$

Therefore, $z = f(u, v)$

$$\frac{\partial z}{\partial x} = \frac{\partial z}{\partial u}.\frac{\partial u}{\partial x} + \frac{\partial z}{\partial v}.\frac{\partial v}{\partial x} = 2x\frac{\partial z}{\partial u} + 2y\frac{\partial z}{\partial v} \tag{1}$$

$$\frac{\partial z}{\partial y} = \frac{\partial z}{\partial u}.\frac{\partial u}{\partial y} + \frac{\partial z}{\partial v}.\frac{\partial v}{\partial y} = -2y\frac{\partial z}{\partial u} + 2x\frac{\partial z}{\partial v} \tag{2}$$

Squaring and adding equations (1) and (2), we get

$$\left(\frac{\partial z}{\partial x}\right)^2 + \left(\frac{\partial z}{\partial y}\right)^2 = \left(2x\frac{\partial z}{\partial u} + 2y\frac{\partial z}{\partial v}\right)^2 + \left(2x\frac{\partial z}{\partial v} - 2y\frac{\partial z}{\partial u}\right)^2$$

$$= 4x^2\left(\frac{\partial z}{\partial u}\right)^2 + 4y^2\left(\frac{\partial z}{\partial v}\right)^2 + 8xy\frac{\partial z}{\partial u}.\frac{\partial z}{\partial v}$$

$$+4x^2\left(\frac{\partial z}{\partial v}\right)^2+4y^2\left(\frac{\partial z}{\partial u}\right)^2-8xy\frac{\partial z}{\partial u}.\frac{\partial z}{\partial v}$$

$$\left(\frac{\partial z}{\partial x}\right)^2+\left(\frac{\partial z}{\partial y}\right)^2=4\left(x^2+y^2\right)\left[\left(\frac{\partial z}{\partial u}\right)^2+\left(\frac{\partial z}{\partial v}\right)^2\right]$$

13. *If $u = f(x, y)$ where $x = r\cos\theta$, $y = r\sin\theta$, show that*

$$\left(\frac{\partial u}{\partial x}\right)^2+\left(\frac{\partial u}{\partial y}\right)^2=\left(\frac{\partial u}{\partial r}\right)^2+\frac{1}{r^2}\left(\frac{\partial u}{\partial \theta}\right)^2$$

➡ $x = r\cos\theta \qquad y = r\sin\theta$

$$\frac{\partial x}{\partial r}=\cos\theta \qquad \frac{\partial y}{\partial r}=\sin\theta$$

$$\frac{\partial x}{\partial \theta}=-r\sin\theta \qquad \frac{\partial y}{\partial \theta}=r\cos\theta$$

$$\frac{\partial u}{\partial r}=\frac{\partial u}{\partial x}.\frac{\partial x}{\partial r}+\frac{\partial u}{\partial y}.\frac{\partial y}{\partial r}=\cos\theta\frac{\partial u}{\partial x}+\sin\theta\frac{\partial u}{\partial y} \tag{1}$$

$$\frac{\partial u}{\partial \theta}=\frac{\partial u}{\partial x}.\frac{\partial x}{\partial \theta}+\frac{\partial u}{\partial y}.\frac{\partial y}{\partial \theta}=-r\sin\theta\frac{\partial u}{\partial x}+r\cos\theta\frac{\partial u}{\partial y} \tag{2}$$

Therefore,

$$\left(\frac{\partial u}{\partial r}\right)^2+\frac{1}{r^2}\left(\frac{\partial u}{\partial \theta}\right)^2=\left(\cos\theta.\frac{\partial u}{\partial x}+\sin\theta\frac{\partial u}{\partial y}\right)^2$$

$$+\frac{1}{r^2}\left(r\cos\theta\frac{\partial u}{\partial y}-r\sin\theta\frac{\partial u}{\partial x}\right)^2$$

$$=\cos^2\theta\left(\frac{\partial u}{\partial x}\right)^2+\sin^2\theta\left(\frac{\partial u}{\partial y}\right)^2+2\cos\theta.\sin\theta\frac{\partial u}{\partial x}.\frac{\partial u}{\partial y}$$

$$+\cos^2\theta\left(\frac{\partial u}{\partial y}\right)^2+\sin^2\theta\left(\frac{\partial u}{\partial x}\right)^2-2\cos\theta.\sin\theta\frac{\partial u}{\partial y}.\frac{\partial u}{\partial x}$$

$$=\left(\frac{\partial u}{\partial x}\right)^2\left(\sin^2\theta+\cos^2\theta\right)+\left(\frac{\partial u}{\partial y}\right)^2\left(\sin^2\theta+\cos^2\theta\right)$$

$$=\left(\frac{\partial u}{\partial x}\right)^2+\left(\frac{\partial u}{\partial y}\right)^2$$

Exercises

1. If $u = x^4y^5$, where $x = t^2$ and $y = t^3$, find $\frac{du}{dt}$
2. If $x^3 + 3x^2y + 6xy^2 = 1$, find $\frac{dy}{dx}$
3. If $u = x^2 - y^2 + \sin yz$, where $y = e^x$, find $\frac{du}{dx}$
4. If $u = x\log xy$ and $x^3 + y^2 - 3axy = 1$, find $\frac{du}{dx}$
5. Find $\frac{du}{dx}$ if $u = \sin\left(x^2 + y^2\right)$, where $a^2x^2 + b^2y^2 = e^2$ and $y = v + e^{-v}$
6. If $u = x\log xy$, where $x^3 + y^3 + 3xy = 1$, find $\frac{du}{dx}$
7. Find $\frac{dy}{dx}$ of $y^x + x^y = e$
8. If $u = \tan^{-1}\left(\frac{y}{x}\right)$, where $x = e^t - e^{-t}$ and $y = e^t - e^{-t}$ find $\frac{du}{dt}$
9. If $u = xy^2 + x^2y$, where $x = at^2$ and $y = 2at$, find $\frac{du}{dt}$
10. Find $\frac{du}{dt}$ if $u = e^y \sin x,\ x = t^2,\ y = \log t$
11. Find $\frac{dy}{dx}$ if $xe^{-y} - 2ye^x = 1$
12. Find $\frac{du}{dx}$ if $u = e^{(x^2+y^2)},\ \frac{x^2}{a^2} + \frac{y^2}{b^2} = 1$
13. If $z = f(x, y)$ and $x = e^u$ and $y = e^{-u} - e^v$, show that $\frac{\partial z}{\partial u} - \frac{\partial z}{\partial v} = x\frac{\partial z}{\partial x} - y\frac{\partial z}{\partial u}$
14. If $z = f(u, v)$ where $u = x^2 - y^2$ and $v = 2xy$, prove that $x\frac{\partial z}{\partial x} - y\frac{\partial z}{\partial y} = 2\left(x^2 + y^2\right)\frac{\partial z}{\partial u}$
15. If f is a homogeneous function of x, y, z with degree n, prove that $x\frac{\partial f}{\partial x} + y\frac{\partial f}{\partial y} + z\frac{\partial f}{\partial z} = nf$

16. *If* $u = x + y,\ v = xy,\ f = f(u, v)$, *show that* $x\dfrac{\partial f}{\partial x} + y\dfrac{\partial f}{\partial y} = u\dfrac{\partial f}{\partial u} + 2v\dfrac{\partial f}{\partial v}$

17. *If* $z = \log\left(u^2 + v\right),\ u = e^{x^2+y^2},\ x^2 + y$, *show that* $\dfrac{\partial z}{\partial x} = \dfrac{2x\left(2u^2+1\right)}{u^2+v},\ \dfrac{\partial z}{\partial y} = \dfrac{uyu^2+1}{u^2+v}$

18. *If* $u = x^2,\ x = 2r - 3s,\ y = -r + 8s - 5$, *prove that* $\dfrac{\partial u}{\partial r} = 4x + 2y$

19. *If* $z = f(x, y)$ *and* $u = ax + by,\ v = ay - bx$, *prove that* $\dfrac{\partial^2 z}{\partial x^2} + \dfrac{\partial^2 z}{\partial y^2} = \left(a^2 + b^2\right)\left(\dfrac{\partial^2 z}{\partial u^2} + \dfrac{\partial^2 z}{\partial v^2}\right)$

20. *If u and v are functions of x and y defined by* $x = u + e^{-v}\sin u$, *and* $y = v + e^{-v}$, *prove that* $\dfrac{\partial u}{\partial y} = \dfrac{\partial v}{\partial x}$

Answers

1. $\dfrac{du}{dt} = 23t^{2z}$
2. $\dfrac{dy}{dx} = -\dfrac{x^2 + 2xy + 2y^2}{x^2 + 4xy + y^2}$
3. $\dfrac{du}{dx} = 2x + (-2y + z\cos yz)\,e^x + \dfrac{y\cos yz}{x}$
4. $\dfrac{du}{dx} = 1 + \log xy + \left\{x\left(x^2 - ay\right)\right\} / \left\{y\left(ax - y^2\right)\right\}$
5. $2x\left\{\cos\left(x^2 + y^2\right)\right\}\left(1 - \dfrac{a^2}{b^2}\right)$
6. $1 + \log xy - x\left(x^2 + y\right)/y\left(x + y^2\right)$
7. $-\left(y^x \log y + yx^{y-1}\right) / \left(xy^{x-1} + x^y \log x\right)$
8. $\dfrac{du}{dt} = -\dfrac{2}{e^{2t} + e^{-2t}}$

9. $\dfrac{du}{dt} = y^3 + 2xy^2 + yaxy + 2ax^2$

10. $\dfrac{du}{dt} = \sin t^2 + 2t^2 \cos t^2$

11. $\dfrac{dy}{dx} = \dfrac{e^{-y} - 2ye^x}{xe^{-y} + 2e^x}$

12. $\dfrac{du}{dx} = \dfrac{2x}{a^2}\left(a^2 - b^2\right) e^{(x^2+y^2)}$

2.10 Jacobians

Let u and v be the functions of two independent variables x and y, then *Jacobian* of u and v with respect to x and y is denoted by

$$J \text{ or } \frac{\partial(u, v)}{\partial(x, y)} \text{ or } J\left(\frac{u, v}{x, y}\right)$$

and is defined by

$$\frac{\partial(u, v)}{\partial(x, y)} = \begin{vmatrix} \dfrac{\partial u}{\partial x} & \dfrac{\partial u}{\partial y} \\ \dfrac{\partial v}{\partial x} & \dfrac{\partial v}{\partial y} \end{vmatrix}$$

If u, v, w are functions of three Independent variables x, y, z, then

$$J = \frac{\partial(u, v, w)}{\partial(x, y, z)} = \begin{vmatrix} \dfrac{\partial u}{\partial x} & \dfrac{\partial u}{\partial y} & \dfrac{\partial u}{\partial z} \\ \dfrac{\partial v}{\partial x} & \dfrac{\partial v}{\partial y} & \dfrac{\partial v}{\partial z} \\ \dfrac{\partial w}{\partial x} & \dfrac{\partial w}{\partial y} & \dfrac{\partial w}{\partial z} \end{vmatrix}$$

Properties of Jacobian

1) *If u & v are the functions of s & t, and s & t are the functions of x and y, then*

$$J = \frac{\partial(u, v)}{\partial(x, y)} = \frac{\partial(u, v)}{\partial(s, t)} \cdot \frac{\partial(s, t)}{\partial(x, y)}$$

Proof:

$$\frac{\partial(u,v)}{\partial(s,t)}\cdot\frac{\partial(s,t)}{\partial(x,y)} = \begin{vmatrix} \frac{\partial u}{\partial s} & \frac{\partial u}{\partial t} \\ \frac{\partial v}{\partial s} & \frac{\partial v}{\partial t} \end{vmatrix} \begin{vmatrix} \frac{\partial s}{\partial x} & \frac{\partial s}{\partial y} \\ \frac{\partial t}{\partial x} & \frac{\partial t}{\partial y} \end{vmatrix}$$

$$= \begin{vmatrix} \frac{\partial u}{\partial s}\frac{\partial s}{\partial x} + \frac{\partial u}{\partial t}\frac{\partial t}{\partial x} & \frac{\partial u}{\partial s}\frac{\partial s}{\partial y} + \frac{\partial u}{\partial t}\frac{\partial t}{\partial y} \\ \frac{\partial v}{\partial s}\frac{\partial s}{\partial x} + \frac{\partial v}{\partial t}\frac{\partial t}{\partial x} & \frac{\partial v}{\partial s}\frac{\partial s}{\partial y} + \frac{\partial v}{\partial t}\frac{\partial t}{\partial y} \end{vmatrix}$$

$$= \begin{vmatrix} \frac{\partial u}{\partial x} & \frac{\partial u}{\partial y} \\ \frac{\partial v}{\partial x} & \frac{\partial v}{\partial y} \end{vmatrix} = \frac{\partial(u,v)}{\partial(x,y)}$$

Therefore,

$$\frac{\partial(u,v)}{\partial(x,y)} = \frac{\partial(u,v)}{\partial(s,t)}\cdot\frac{\partial(s,t)}{\partial(x,y)}$$

Inverse Jacobians

If $J = \frac{\partial(u,v)}{\partial(x,y)}$, then the *inverse Jacobian* of the Jacobian J is denoted and defined by $J' = \frac{\partial(x,y)}{\partial(u,v)}$

2) *Prove that* $JJ' = 1$

Proof:

$$JJ' = \frac{\partial(u,v)}{\partial(x,y)}\cdot\frac{\partial(x,y)}{\partial(u,v)} = \begin{vmatrix} \frac{\partial u}{\partial x} & \frac{\partial u}{\partial y} \\ \frac{\partial v}{\partial x} & \frac{\partial v}{\partial y} \end{vmatrix} \begin{vmatrix} \frac{\partial x}{\partial u} & \frac{\partial x}{\partial v} \\ \frac{\partial y}{\partial u} & \frac{\partial y}{\partial v} \end{vmatrix}$$

$$= \begin{vmatrix} \frac{\partial u}{\partial x}\frac{\partial x}{\partial u} + \frac{\partial u}{\partial y}\frac{\partial y}{\partial u} & \frac{\partial u}{\partial x}\frac{\partial x}{\partial v} + \frac{\partial u}{\partial y}\frac{\partial y}{\partial v} \\ \frac{\partial v}{\partial x}\frac{\partial x}{\partial u} + \frac{\partial v}{\partial y}\frac{\partial y}{\partial u} & \frac{\partial v}{\partial x}\frac{\partial x}{\partial v} + \frac{\partial v}{\partial y}\frac{\partial y}{\partial v} \end{vmatrix}$$

$$= \begin{vmatrix} \frac{\partial u}{\partial u} & \frac{\partial u}{\partial v} \\ \frac{\partial v}{\partial u} & \frac{\partial v}{\partial v} \end{vmatrix} = \begin{vmatrix} 1 & 0 \\ 0 & 1 \end{vmatrix} = 1$$

Null or Zero Jacobian

A Jacobian J is said to be *null* or *zero Jacobian* if $J = 0$.

Remark: If $u = u\,(x, y)$ and $v = v\,(x, y)$ are mutually independent, then the Jacobian $J \neq 0$. If u and v are not independent or functionally dependent, then Jacobian $J = 0$.

Worked Examples

1. *If* $u = e^x \cos y,\ v = e^x \sin y$ *find* $\dfrac{\partial\,(u, v)}{\partial\,(x, y)}$

➡

$$u = e^x \cos y \qquad v = e^x \sin y$$

$$\frac{\partial u}{\partial x} = e^x \cos y \qquad \frac{\partial v}{\partial x} = e^x \sin y$$

$$\frac{\partial u}{\partial y} = -e^x \sin y \qquad \frac{\partial v}{\partial y} = e^x \cos y$$

$$\therefore\ J = \begin{vmatrix} \frac{\partial u}{\partial x} & \frac{\partial u}{\partial y} \\ \frac{\partial v}{\partial x} & \frac{\partial v}{\partial y} \end{vmatrix} = \begin{vmatrix} e^x \cos y & -e^x \sin y \\ e^x \sin y & e^x \cos y \end{vmatrix}$$

$$= e^{2x} \cos^2 y + e^{2x} \sin^2 y$$

$$= e^{2x} (\cos^2 y + \sin^2 y) = e^{2x}$$

2. *If* $u = 1 - x,\ v = x(1-y),\ w = xy(1-z)$ *find* $\dfrac{\partial(u,v,w)}{\partial(x,y,z)}$

➡

$$u = 1 - x \qquad v = x(1-y) \qquad w = xy(1-z)$$

$$\frac{\partial u}{\partial x} = -1 \qquad \frac{\partial v}{\partial x} = (1-y) \qquad \frac{\partial w}{\partial x} = y(1-z)$$

$$\frac{\partial u}{\partial y} = 0 \qquad \frac{\partial v}{\partial y} = -x \qquad \frac{\partial w}{\partial y} = x(1-z)$$

$$\frac{\partial u}{\partial z} = 0 \qquad \frac{\partial v}{\partial z} = 0 \qquad \frac{\partial w}{\partial z} = -xy$$

$$\frac{\partial(u,v,w)}{\partial(x,y,z)} = \begin{vmatrix} \frac{\partial u}{\partial x} & \frac{\partial u}{\partial y} & \frac{\partial u}{\partial z} \\ \frac{\partial v}{\partial x} & \frac{\partial v}{\partial y} & \frac{\partial v}{\partial z} \\ \frac{\partial w}{\partial x} & \frac{\partial w}{\partial y} & \frac{\partial w}{\partial z} \end{vmatrix} = \begin{vmatrix} -1 & 0 & 0 \\ 1-y & -x & 0 \\ y(1-z) & x(1-z) & -xy \end{vmatrix}$$

$$= -x^2 y$$

3. *If* $u = x(1-y),\ v = xy,$ *find* $J = \dfrac{\partial(u,v)}{\partial(x,y)}$ *and* $J' = \dfrac{\partial(x,y)}{\partial(u,v)}$ *verify that* $JJ' = 1$

➡

$$u = x(1-y) \qquad v = xy$$

$$\frac{\partial u}{\partial x} = 1 - y \qquad \frac{\partial v}{\partial x} = y$$

$$\frac{\partial u}{\partial y} = -x \qquad \frac{\partial v}{\partial y} = x$$

$$J = \frac{\partial(u,v)}{\partial(x,y)} = \begin{vmatrix} \frac{\partial u}{\partial x} & \frac{\partial u}{\partial y} \\ \frac{\partial v}{\partial x} & \frac{\partial v}{\partial y} \end{vmatrix} = \begin{vmatrix} 1-y & -x \\ y & x \end{vmatrix} = (1-y)x + xy = x$$

$$u = x - xy \qquad v = xy$$

$$u = x - v \qquad y = v/x$$

$$x = u + v \qquad y = \frac{v}{u+v}$$

$$\frac{\partial x}{\partial u} = 1 \qquad \frac{\partial y}{\partial u} = \frac{-v}{(u+v)^2}$$

$$\frac{\partial x}{\partial v} = 1 \qquad \frac{\partial y}{\partial v} = \frac{(u+v) - v}{(u+v)^2} = \frac{u}{(u+v)^2}$$

$$J' = \begin{vmatrix} 1 & 1 \\ \frac{-v}{(u+v)^2} & \frac{u}{(u+v)^2} \end{vmatrix}$$

$$= \frac{u}{(u+v)^2} + \frac{v}{(u+v)^2}$$

$$= \frac{u+v}{(u+v)^2} = \frac{1}{u+v} = \frac{1}{x}$$

$$J.J' = x.\frac{1}{x} = 1$$

4. *If* $u = x^2 - 2y, \quad v = x + y$ *find J and J′, verify that* $JJ' = 1$

➡

$$u = x^2 - 2y \qquad v = x + y$$

$$\frac{\partial u}{\partial x} = 2x \qquad \frac{\partial v}{\partial x} = 1$$

$$\frac{\partial u}{\partial y} = -2 \qquad \frac{\partial v}{\partial y} = 1$$

$$J = \frac{\partial (u, v)}{\partial (x, y)} = \begin{vmatrix} \frac{\partial u}{\partial x} & \frac{\partial u}{\partial y} \\ \frac{\partial v}{\partial x} & \frac{\partial v}{\partial y} \end{vmatrix} = \begin{vmatrix} 2x & -2 \\ 1 & 1 \end{vmatrix} = 2x + 2 = 2(x+1)$$

$$u = x^2 - 2y \qquad v = x + y \Rightarrow y = v - x$$

$$u = x^2 - 2(v - x)$$

$$u + 2(v - x) = x^2$$

$$x^2 + 2x - (u + 2v) = 0$$

It is quadratic equation in x

$$x = \frac{-2 \pm \sqrt{4 - 4\,(1)\,(-\,(u+2v))}}{2\,(1)} = \frac{-2 \pm 2\sqrt{1+u+2v}}{2}$$

$$x = -1 \pm \sqrt{1+u+2v}$$

Let $x = -1 + \sqrt{1+u+2v} \quad \therefore\; y = v + 1 - \sqrt{1+u+2v}$

$$\frac{\partial x}{\partial u} = \frac{1}{2\sqrt{1+u+2v}} \qquad \frac{\partial y}{\partial u} = -\frac{1}{2\sqrt{1+u+2v}}$$

$$\frac{\partial x}{\partial v} = \frac{1}{2\sqrt{1+u+2v}}.2 \qquad \frac{\partial y}{\partial v} = 1 - \frac{1}{2\sqrt{1+u+2v}}.2$$

$$\frac{\partial x}{\partial v} = \frac{1}{\sqrt{1+u+2v}} \qquad \frac{\partial y}{\partial v} = 1 - \frac{1}{\sqrt{1+u+2v}}$$

$$J' = \begin{vmatrix} \dfrac{1}{2\sqrt{1+u+2v}} & \dfrac{1}{\sqrt{1+u+2v}} \\ \dfrac{-1}{2\sqrt{1+u+2v}} & 1 - \dfrac{1}{\sqrt{1+u+2v}} \end{vmatrix}$$

$$= \frac{1}{2\sqrt{1+u+2v}}\left(1 - \frac{1}{\sqrt{1+u+2v}}\right) + \frac{1}{2\,(1+u+2v)}$$

$$J' = \frac{1}{2\sqrt{1+u+2v}} = \frac{1}{2\,(x+1)}$$

$$\therefore\; J\,J' = (2x+2)\,\frac{1}{2\,(x+1)} = 2\,(x+1)\,\frac{1}{2\,(x+1)} = 1$$

5. *If* $x = e^{u}\sec v, \quad y = e^{u}\tan v$*, prove that* $J\,J' = 1$

➡

$$x = e^{u}\sec v \qquad y = e^{u}\tan v$$

$$\frac{\partial x}{\partial u} = e^{u}\sec v \qquad \frac{\partial y}{\partial u} = e^{u}\tan v$$

$$\frac{\partial x}{\partial v} = e^{u}.\sec v.\tan v \qquad \frac{\partial y}{\partial v} = e^{u}\sec^{2} v$$

$$J = \frac{\partial (x, y)}{\partial (u, v)} = \begin{vmatrix} \dfrac{\partial x}{\partial u} & \dfrac{\partial x}{\partial v} \\ \dfrac{\partial y}{\partial u} & \dfrac{\partial y}{\partial v} \end{vmatrix} = \begin{vmatrix} e^u \sec v & e^u \sec v.\tan v \\ e^u \tan v & e^u \sec^2 v \end{vmatrix}$$

$$= e^{2u} \sec^3 v - e^{2u} \sec v.\tan^2 v$$

$$= e^{2u} \sec v \left(\sec^2 v - \tan^2 v\right)$$

$$= e^{2u} \sec v$$

From the given equations, we have

$$\frac{y}{x} = \frac{e^u \tan v}{e^u \sec v} = \sin v \qquad x^2 - y^2 = e^{2u} \sec^2 v - e^{2u} \tan^2 v$$

$$v = \sin^{-1}(y/x) \qquad x^2 - y^2 = e^{2u} \Rightarrow u = \frac{1}{2} \log\left(x^2 - y^2\right)$$

$$\frac{\partial u}{\partial x} = \frac{1}{2}.\frac{1}{x^2 - y^2}.(2x) = \frac{x}{x^2 - y^2}$$

$$\frac{\partial u}{\partial y} = \frac{1}{2}.\frac{1}{x^2 - y^2}.(-2y) = -\frac{y}{x^2 - y^2}$$

$$\frac{\partial v}{\partial x} = \frac{1}{\sqrt{1 - (y/x)^2}}\left(-\frac{y}{x^2}\right) = \frac{-y}{x\sqrt{x^2 - y^2}}$$

$$\frac{\partial v}{\partial y} = \frac{1}{\sqrt{1 - (y/x)^2}}\left(\frac{1}{x}\right) = \frac{1}{\sqrt{x^2 - y^2}}$$

$$J' = \frac{\partial (u, v)}{\partial (x, y)} = \begin{vmatrix} \dfrac{\partial u}{\partial x} & \dfrac{\partial u}{\partial y} \\ \dfrac{\partial v}{\partial x} & \dfrac{\partial v}{\partial y} \end{vmatrix} = \begin{vmatrix} \dfrac{x}{x^2 - y^2} & -\dfrac{y}{x^2 - y^2} \\ -\dfrac{y}{x\sqrt{x^2 - y^2}} & \dfrac{1}{\sqrt{x^2 - y^2}} \end{vmatrix}$$

$$= \frac{x}{\left(x^2 - y^2\right)^{\frac{3}{2}}} - \frac{y^2}{x\left(x^2 - y^2\right)^{\frac{3}{2}}} = \frac{x^2 - y^2}{x\left(x^2 - y^2\right)^{\frac{3}{2}}}$$

$$= \frac{1}{x\sqrt{x^2 - y^2}}$$

Substituting for x and $x^2 - y^2$, we get

$$J' = \frac{1}{e^u \sec v.\sqrt{e^{2u}}} = \frac{1}{e^{2u} \sec v}$$

$$\therefore\ JJ' = e^{2u} \sec v.\frac{1}{e^{2u} \sec v} = 1$$

6. *If* $u = x + y, \quad v = xy$, *verify that* $JJ' = 1$

➡ $u = x + y, \quad v = xy$

$$\frac{\partial u}{\partial x} = 1, \qquad \frac{\partial u}{\partial y} = 1$$

$$\frac{\partial v}{\partial x} = y, \qquad \frac{\partial v}{\partial y} = x$$

$$J = \begin{vmatrix} \frac{\partial u}{\partial x} & \frac{\partial u}{\partial y} \\ \frac{\partial v}{\partial x} & \frac{\partial v}{\partial y} \end{vmatrix} = \begin{vmatrix} 1 & 1 \\ y & x \end{vmatrix}$$

$$J = x - y$$

From the given equations, we have

$$x = \frac{v}{y} \qquad \therefore\ u = \frac{v}{y} + y$$

$$\Rightarrow uy = v + y^2$$

$$\therefore\ y^2 - uy + v = 0$$

$$\Rightarrow y = \frac{u \pm \sqrt{u^2 - 4v}}{2}$$

Considering any one of the roots of y, we get

$$y = \frac{u + \sqrt{u^2 - 4v}}{2}$$

Substituting this in $u = x + y \Rightarrow x = u - y$, we get

$$= u - \frac{u + \sqrt{u^2 - 4v}}{2}$$

$$x = \frac{2u - u - \sqrt{u^2 - 4v}}{2}$$

$$\therefore x = \frac{u - \sqrt{u^2 - 4v}}{2}$$

$$\therefore \frac{\partial x}{\partial u} = \frac{1}{2}\left[1 - \frac{1}{2\sqrt{u^2 - 4v}}(2u)\right] = \frac{\sqrt{u^2 - 4v} - u}{2\sqrt{u^2 - 4v}} = \frac{-x}{\sqrt{u^2 - 4v}}$$

$$\frac{\partial x}{\partial v} = \frac{1}{2}\left[-\frac{1}{2\sqrt{u^2 - 4v}}(-4)\right] = \frac{1}{\sqrt{u^2 - 4v}}$$

$$\frac{\partial y}{\partial u} = \frac{1}{2}\left[1 + \frac{1}{2\sqrt{u^2 - 4v}}(2u)\right] = \frac{1}{2}\left[\frac{\sqrt{u^2 - 4v} + u}{\sqrt{u^2 - 4v}}\right] = \frac{y}{\sqrt{u^2 - 4v}}$$

$$\frac{\partial y}{\partial v} = \frac{1}{2}\left[\frac{1}{2\sqrt{u^2 - 4v}}(-4)\right] = -\frac{1}{\sqrt{u^2 - 4v}}$$

$$\therefore J' = \begin{vmatrix} \dfrac{\partial x}{\partial u} & \dfrac{\partial x}{\partial v} \\ \dfrac{\partial y}{\partial u} & \dfrac{\partial y}{\partial v} \end{vmatrix} = \begin{vmatrix} \dfrac{-x}{\sqrt{u^2 - 4v}} & \dfrac{1}{\sqrt{u^2 - 4v}} \\ \dfrac{y}{\sqrt{u^2 - 4v}} & -\dfrac{1}{\sqrt{u^2 - 4v}} \end{vmatrix}$$

$$= \frac{x}{u^2 - 4v} - \frac{y}{u^2 - 4v} = \frac{x - y}{(x - y)^2} \quad \because x - y = \sqrt{u^2 - 4v}$$

$$\therefore J' = \frac{1}{(x - y)}$$

$$\therefore JJ' = (x - y) \times \frac{1}{(x - y)} = 1$$

7. *If* $x = \dfrac{u^2}{v}$, $y = \dfrac{v^2}{u}$. *Find the associated increase Jacobian*

➡ $x = \frac{u^2}{v}, \qquad y = \frac{v^2}{u}$

$$\Rightarrow u^2 = xv, \qquad v^2 = yu \tag{1}$$

$$v^4 = y^2u^2$$

Substituting for u^2, we get $v^4 = y^2 x v$

$$v^3 = xy^2$$

$$\Rightarrow v = y^{\frac{2}{3}} x^{\frac{1}{3}}$$

$$u^2 = xv = x\left(y^{\frac{2}{3}} x^{\frac{1}{3}}\right) = y^{\frac{2}{3}} x^{\frac{4}{3}}$$

$$u = y^{\frac{1}{3}} x^{\frac{2}{3}} \quad \Rightarrow \frac{\partial u}{\partial x} = \frac{2}{3} x^{-\frac{1}{3}} y^{\frac{1}{3}}, \qquad \frac{\partial u}{\partial y} = \frac{1}{3} .x^{\frac{2}{3}} .y^{-\frac{2}{3}}$$

$$v = y^{\frac{2}{3}} x^{\frac{1}{3}} \quad \Rightarrow \frac{\partial v}{\partial x} = \frac{1}{3} x^{-\frac{2}{3}} y^{\frac{2}{3}}, \qquad \frac{\partial v}{\partial y} = \frac{2}{3} .y^{-\frac{1}{3}} .x^{\frac{1}{3}}$$

$$J' = \frac{\partial (u, v)}{\partial (x, y)} = \begin{vmatrix} \frac{\partial u}{\partial x} & \frac{\partial u}{\partial y} \\ \frac{\partial v}{\partial x} & \frac{\partial v}{\partial y} \end{vmatrix} = \begin{vmatrix} \frac{2}{3} x^{-\frac{1}{3}} .y^{\frac{1}{3}} & \frac{1}{3} x^{\frac{2}{3}} .y^{-\frac{2}{3}} \\ \frac{1}{3} x^{-\frac{2}{3}} y^{\frac{2}{3}} & \frac{2}{3} y^{-\frac{1}{3}} x^{\frac{1}{3}} \end{vmatrix}$$

$$= \frac{4}{9} x^{-\frac{1}{3}} y^{\frac{1}{3}} .x^{\frac{1}{3}} y^{-\frac{1}{3}} - \frac{1}{9} x^{\frac{2}{3}} y^{-\frac{2}{3}} .x^{-\frac{2}{3}} y^{\frac{2}{3}}$$

$$= \frac{4}{9}(1) - \frac{1}{9}(1) = \frac{1}{3}$$

8. *If* $x = r\cos\theta, \quad y = r\sin\theta,$ *find* $\dfrac{\partial (r, \theta)}{\partial (x, y)}$ *in terms of* r

➡ $x = r\cos\theta \qquad y = r\sin\theta$

$$\Rightarrow r = \sqrt{x^2 + y^2} \quad \theta = \tan^{-1}\left(\frac{y}{x}\right)$$

$$\frac{\partial r}{\partial x} = \frac{1}{2\sqrt{x^2 + y^2}} .2x = \frac{x}{\sqrt{x^2 + y^2}}$$

Similarly $\dfrac{\partial r}{\partial y} = \dfrac{y}{\sqrt{x^2 + y^2}}$

$$\frac{\partial \theta}{\partial x} = \frac{1}{1 + (y/x)^2} . \left(-\frac{y}{x^2}\right) = \frac{1}{(x^2 + y^2)/x^2} . \left(-\frac{y}{x^2}\right) = -\frac{y}{x^2 + y^2}$$

$$\frac{\partial \theta}{\partial y} = \frac{1}{1 + (y/x)^2} \left(\frac{1}{x}\right) = \frac{1/x}{(x^2 + y^2)/x^2} = \frac{x}{x^2 + y^2}$$

$$\frac{\partial(r,\theta)}{\partial(x,y)} = \begin{vmatrix} \dfrac{x}{\sqrt{x^2+y^2}} & \dfrac{y}{\sqrt{x^2+y^2}} \\ \dfrac{-y}{x^2+y^2} & \dfrac{x}{x^2+y^2} \end{vmatrix} = \frac{x^2}{\left(x^2+y^2\right)^{\frac{3}{2}}} + \frac{y^2}{\left(x^2+y^2\right)^{\frac{3}{2}}}$$

$$= \frac{x^2+y^2}{\left(x^2+y^2\right)^{\frac{3}{2}}} = \frac{1}{\left(x^2+y^2\right)^{\frac{1}{2}}} = \frac{1}{r}$$

9. *If* $u = x^2 - 2y^2$, $v = 2x^2 - y^2$ *and* $x = r\cos\theta$, $y = r\sin\theta$ *show that* $\dfrac{\partial(u,v)}{\partial(r,\theta)} = 6r^2 \sin 2\theta$

➡ $u = x^2 - 2y^2 \qquad v = 2x^2 - y^2$

$$\frac{\partial u}{\partial x} = 2x \qquad \frac{\partial v}{\partial x} = 4x$$

$$\frac{\partial u}{\partial y} = -4y \qquad \frac{\partial v}{\partial y} = -2y$$

$$\therefore \frac{\partial(u,v)}{\partial(x,y)} = \begin{vmatrix} \dfrac{\partial u}{\partial x} & \dfrac{\partial u}{\partial y} \\ \dfrac{\partial v}{\partial x} & \dfrac{\partial v}{\partial y} \end{vmatrix} = \begin{vmatrix} 2x & -4y \\ 4x & -2y \end{vmatrix} = -4xy + 16xy$$

$$\frac{\partial(u,v)}{\partial(x,y)} = 12xy$$

$$x = r\cos\theta \qquad y = r\sin\theta$$

$$\frac{\partial x}{\partial r} = \cos\theta \qquad \frac{\partial y}{\partial r} = \sin\theta$$

$$\frac{\partial x}{\partial \theta} = -r\sin\theta \qquad \frac{\partial y}{\partial \theta} = r\cos\theta$$

$$\frac{\partial(x,y)}{\partial(r,\theta)} = \begin{vmatrix} \cos\theta & -r\sin\theta \\ \sin\theta & r\cos\theta \end{vmatrix}$$

$$= r\cos^2\theta + r\sin^2\theta$$

$$= r\left(\cos^2\theta + \sin^2\theta\right)$$

$$\frac{\partial(x,y)}{\partial(r,\theta)} = r$$

We have,

$$\frac{\partial (u, v)}{\partial (r, \theta)} = \frac{\partial (u, v)}{\partial (x, y)} . \frac{\partial (x, y)}{\partial (r, \theta)}$$

$$= (12xy)\ (r) = 12r\ (r \cos \theta)\ (r \sin \theta)$$

$$\frac{\partial (u, v)}{\partial (r, \theta)} = 6r^3 \sin 2\theta$$

10. *If* $u = x^2 - y^2$, $v = 2xy$ *and* $x = r \cos \theta$, $y = r \sin \theta$, *then determine the Jacobian* $\frac{\partial (u, v)}{\partial (r, \theta)}$

➡

$$\frac{\partial u}{\partial x} = 2x, \quad \frac{\partial u}{\partial y} = -2y$$

$$\frac{\partial v}{\partial x} = 2y, \quad \frac{\partial v}{\partial y} = 2x$$

$$\therefore \frac{\partial (u, v)}{\partial (x, y)} = \begin{vmatrix} \frac{\partial u}{\partial x} & \frac{\partial u}{\partial y} \\ \frac{\partial v}{\partial x} & \frac{\partial v}{\partial y} \end{vmatrix} = \begin{vmatrix} 2x & -2y \\ 2y & 2x \end{vmatrix} = 4x^2 + 4y^2$$

$$\frac{\partial x}{\partial r} = \cos \theta, \quad \frac{\partial x}{\partial \theta} = -r \sin \theta$$

$$\frac{\partial y}{\partial r} = \sin \theta, \quad \frac{\partial y}{\partial \theta} = r \cos \theta$$

$$\therefore \frac{\partial (x, y)}{\partial (r, \theta)} = \begin{vmatrix} \cos \theta & -r \sin \theta \\ \sin \theta & r \cos \theta \end{vmatrix}$$

$$= r \cos^2 \theta + r \sin^2 \theta = r \left(\cos^2 \theta + \sin^2 \theta\right) = r$$

We have,

$$\frac{\partial (u, v)}{\partial (r, \theta)} = \frac{\partial (u, v)}{\partial (x, y)} . \frac{\partial (x, y)}{\partial (r, \theta)} = \left(4x^2 + 4y^2\right) (r) = 4\left(x^2 + y^2\right) .r$$

$$= 4\left(r^2\right) .r \quad = 4r^3 \quad x^2 + y^2 = r^2$$

11. *If* $x = r\cos\theta,\ \ y = r\sin\theta,\ \ z = z$ *find* $\dfrac{\partial(x,y,z)}{\partial(r,\theta,z)}$

➡ $x = r\cos\theta \qquad y = r\sin\theta \qquad z = z$

$$\frac{\partial x}{\partial r} = \cos\theta \qquad \frac{\partial y}{\partial r} = \sin\theta \qquad \frac{\partial z}{\partial r} = 0$$

$$\frac{\partial x}{\partial \theta} = -r\sin\theta \qquad \frac{\partial y}{\partial \theta} = r\cos\theta \qquad \frac{\partial z}{\partial \theta} = 0$$

$$\frac{\partial x}{\partial z} = 0 \qquad \frac{\partial y}{\partial z} = 0 \qquad \frac{\partial z}{\partial z} = 1$$

$$J = \frac{\partial(x,y,z)}{\partial(r,\theta,z)} = \begin{vmatrix} \frac{\partial x}{\partial r} & \frac{\partial x}{\partial \theta} & \frac{\partial x}{\partial z} \\ \frac{\partial y}{\partial r} & \frac{\partial y}{\partial \theta} & \frac{\partial y}{\partial z} \\ \frac{\partial z}{\partial r} & \frac{\partial z}{\partial \theta} & \frac{\partial z}{\partial z} \end{vmatrix} = \begin{vmatrix} \cos\theta & -r\sin\theta & 0 \\ \sin\theta & r\cos\theta & 0 \\ 0 & 0 & 1 \end{vmatrix}$$

$$= \cos\theta\,(r\cos\theta - 0) + r\sin\theta\,(\sin\theta - 0) + 0$$

$$= r\left(\cos^2\theta + \sin^2\theta\right)$$

$$\frac{\partial(x,y,z)}{\partial(r,\theta,z)} = r$$

12. *If* $u = x - y$ *and* $v = \dfrac{1}{x-y}$*, show that* $\dfrac{\partial(u,v)}{\partial(x,y)} = 0$

➡ $u = x - y \qquad v = \dfrac{1}{x-y}$

$$\frac{\partial u}{\partial x} = 1 \qquad \frac{\partial v}{\partial x} = -\frac{1}{(x-y)^2}$$

$$\frac{\partial u}{\partial y} = -1 \qquad \frac{\partial v}{\partial y} = -\frac{1(-1)}{(x-y)^2} = \frac{1}{(x-y)^2}$$

$$\frac{\partial(u,v)}{\partial(x,y)} = \begin{vmatrix} \frac{\partial u}{\partial x} & \frac{\partial u}{\partial y} \\ \frac{\partial v}{\partial x} & \frac{\partial v}{\partial y} \end{vmatrix} = \begin{vmatrix} 1 & -1 \\ \frac{-1}{(x-y)^2} & \frac{1}{(x-y)^2} \end{vmatrix}$$

$$= \frac{1}{(x-y)^2} - \frac{1}{(x-y)^2}$$

$$\frac{\partial(u,v)}{\partial(x,y)} = 0$$

13. *If* $u = \tan^{-1} x + \tan^{-1} y, \quad v = \frac{x+y}{1-xy}$, *show that*

➡ $u = \tan^{-1} x + \tan^{-1} y$

$$\frac{\partial u}{\partial x} = \frac{1}{1+x^2} \quad \frac{\partial u}{\partial y} = \frac{1}{1+y^2}$$

$$v = \frac{x+y}{1-xy}$$

$$\frac{\partial v}{\partial x} = \frac{(1-xy)\,1-(x+y)\,(-y)}{(1-xy)^2} = \frac{1-xy+xy+y^2}{(1-xy)^2} = \frac{1+y^2}{(1-xy)^2}$$

$$\frac{\partial v}{\partial x} = \frac{(1-xy)\,1-(x+y)\,(-x)}{(1-xy)^2} = \frac{1-xy+x^2+xy}{(1-xy)^2} = \frac{1+x^2}{(1-xy)^2}$$

$$\therefore \frac{\partial\,(u,v)}{\partial\,(x,y)} = \begin{vmatrix} \frac{\partial u}{\partial x} & \frac{\partial u}{\partial y} \\ \frac{\partial v}{\partial x} & \frac{\partial v}{\partial y} \end{vmatrix} = \begin{vmatrix} \frac{1}{1+x^2} & \frac{1}{1+y^2} \\ \frac{1+y^2}{(1-xy)^2} & \frac{1+x^2}{(1-xy)^2} \end{vmatrix}$$

$$= \frac{1}{1+x^2}.\frac{1+x^2}{(1-xy)^2} - \frac{1}{1+y^2}.\frac{1+y^2}{(1-xy)^2}$$

$$= \frac{1}{(1-xy)^2} - \frac{1}{(1-xy)^2} = 0$$

Exercises

1. *Find* $\frac{\partial\,(u,v,w)}{\partial\,(x,y,z)}$ *for the following*

(a) $u = x^2 - 2y, \; v = x+y+z, \; w = x-2y+3z$

(b) $u = xyz, \; v = xy+yz+zx, \; w = x+y+z$

(c) $u = \cos x,\ v = \sin x \cos y,\ w = \sin x \sin y \cos z$

(d) $u = xy^2,\ v = yz^2,\ w = zx^2$

(e) $u = x \cos y \cos z,\ v = x \cos y \sin z,\ w = x \sin y$

2. *If* $u = \sqrt{x^2 + y^2},\ v = \sqrt{x^2 - y^2}$ *then prove that* $JJ' = 1$

3. *If* $u = x + y, v = xy$ *find* $J = \dfrac{\partial(u, v)}{\partial(x, y)}$ & $J' = \dfrac{\partial(x, y)}{\partial(u, v)}$ *and verify* $JJ' = 1$

4. *If* $u = \dfrac{xy}{z}, v = \dfrac{yz}{x}, w = \dfrac{xz}{y}$ *find* $J = \dfrac{\partial(u, v, w)}{\partial(x, y, z)}$ *verify* $JJ' = 1$

5. *Find* $J = \dfrac{\partial(x, y, z)}{\partial(u, v, w)}$ *of*

(a) $x = \dfrac{1}{2}(u^2 - v^2), y = uv, z = w$

(b) $x = u, y = u \tan v, z = w$

6. *If* $u = 2axy$ & $v = a(x^2 - y^2)$ *where* $x = r\cos\theta,\ y = r\sin\theta$ *then, prove that* $\dfrac{\partial(u, v)}{\partial(r, \theta)} = -4a^2r^3$

7. *If* $u = x^2 - y^2$ & $v = 2xy$ *where* $x = r\cos\theta,\ y = r\sin\theta$ *show that* $\dfrac{\partial(u, v)}{\partial(r, \theta)}$

8. *If* $u = a(x + y),\ v = b(x - y)$ & $x = r^2\cos 2\theta,\ y = r^2 \sin 2\theta$ *then find* $\dfrac{\partial(u, v)}{\partial(r, \theta)}$

9. *If* $x = \dfrac{u^2v}{v}, x = \dfrac{v^2}{u}$ *find* $\dfrac{\partial(u, v)}{\partial(x, y)}$

10. *If* $u = x + y, v = \dfrac{1}{x + y}$ *then* $\dfrac{\partial(u, v)}{\partial(x, y)} = 0$

11. *If* $x = u^2, y = v^2 - w^2, z = w^2 - u^2$, *show that* $\dfrac{\partial(x, y, z)}{\partial(u, v, w)} = 0$

12. *If* $ux = 2yz, vy = 2zx, wz = 2xy$, *prove that* $\dfrac{\partial(u, v, w)}{\partial(x, y, z)} = 0$

13. *If* $u = \sin^{-1} y, v = x\sqrt{1 - y^2} + y\sqrt{1 - x^2}$, *show that* $\dfrac{\partial(u, v)}{\partial(x, y)} = 0$

Answers

1.
   (a) $10x + 4$
   (b) $(x - y)(y - z)(z - x)$
   (c) $-\sin^3 x \sin^2 y \sin z$
   (d) $9x^2y^2z^2$
   (e) $-x^2y$
8. $-8abr^3$
9. $\frac{1}{3}$

CHAPTER 3

Vector Differentiation

3.1 Introduction

We come across two types of quantities in physics, mechanics and other branches of applied mathematics, one characterized by both magnitude and direction such as displacement, velocity, force, acceleration etc and the other characterized by only magnitude and no direction such as mass, speed and density etc. The former is known as vector while the later is known as scalar. In this chapter we discuss the vector differentiation in detail.

3.2 Vector Differentiation

Vector Point Function and Vector Field

Let $P(x, y, z)$ be any point in the region R of space. Let $\vec{r}$ be the position vector of P. If there exists a vector function $\vec{F}$ corresponding to each P, then $\vec{F}$ is called a *vector point function* and the region R is called a *vector field*.

Examples

1. $\vec{F} = (x + y)\,\hat{i} + xy\,\hat{j} + z\,\hat{k}$
2. $\vec{A} = (x - y)\,\hat{i} + z\,\hat{j} + (x + y)\,\hat{k}$
3. $\vec{f} = (x + y + z)\,(\hat{i} + \hat{j} + \hat{k})$

Scalar Point Function and Scalar Field

Let $P(x, y, z)$ be any point in the region R of space with the position vector $\vec{r}$. If there exists a scalar function $\phi(x, y, z)$ corresponding to each P, then $\phi(x, y, z)$ is called *scalar point function* and the region R is called *scalar field*.

Examples

1. $\phi = xyz$
2. $\phi = xy + yz + zx$
3. $\phi = x + y + zx + x^2y$

Vector Differentiation

Let $\vec{r} = x\hat{i} + y\hat{j} + z\hat{k}$ be the position vector of the point $P(x, y, z)$ then its derivative is given by

$$\frac{d\vec{r}}{dt} = \lim_{\delta t \to 0} \frac{\delta \vec{r}}{\delta t} = \lim_{\delta t \to 0} \left\{ \frac{\vec{r}\,(t + \delta t) - \vec{r}(t)}{\delta t} \right\}$$

Here $\frac{d\vec{r}}{dt}$ represents a *tangent vector* to curve C whose the position vector at any point is $\vec{r}$ and also called as *velocity* at P.

Differentiation of Scalar Product

$$\frac{d}{dt}\left(\vec{F} \cdot \vec{G}\right) = \vec{F} \cdot \frac{d\vec{G}}{dt} + \frac{d\vec{F}}{dt} \cdot \vec{G}$$

Differentiation of Vector Product

$$\frac{d}{dt}\left[\vec{F} \times \vec{G}\right] = \vec{F} \times \frac{d\vec{G}}{dt} + \frac{d\vec{F}}{dt} \times \vec{G}$$

3.2.1 Tangent Vector to the Space Curve

Let $\vec{r} = x\hat{i} + y\hat{j} + z\hat{k}$ be the position vector to the space curve C at the point $P(x, y, z)$, then the *tangent vector* to the curve at the point P is denoted by $\vec{T}$ and defined by

$$\vec{T} = \frac{d\vec{r}}{dt} = \frac{dx}{dt}\hat{i} + \frac{dy}{dt}\hat{j} + \frac{dz}{dt}\hat{k}$$

Note: Unit tangent vector is $\hat{T} = \vec{T}/|\vec{T}|$.

3.2.2 Normal Vector to the Space Curve

We know that $\hat{T}$ is the unit tangent vector to the space curve at the point $P(x, y, z)$

$$\therefore \left|\hat{T}\right| = 1 \Rightarrow \left|\hat{T}\right|^2 = 1 \Rightarrow \hat{T} \cdot \hat{T} = 1$$

Differentiating with respect to S, we get

$$\hat{T} \cdot \frac{d\hat{T}}{dS} + \frac{d\hat{T}}{dS} \cdot \hat{T} = 0 \Rightarrow 2\hat{T} \cdot \frac{d\hat{T}}{dS} = 0 \Rightarrow \hat{T} \cdot \frac{d\hat{T}}{dS} = 0$$

Therefore, $\hat{T}$ and $d\hat{T}/dS$ are orthogonal (perpendicular). Since $\hat{T}$ is unit tangent vector, therefore, $d\hat{T}/dS$ is the *normal vector* to the space curve.

$$\text{i.e., } \vec{n} = \frac{d\hat{T}}{dS}$$

Note: Unit normal vector to the space curve is $\hat{n} = \frac{\vec{n}}{|\vec{n}|} = \frac{d\hat{T}/dS}{\left|d\hat{T}/dS\right|}$

3.2.3 Application to Space Curve

Let $\vec{r} = x\hat{i} + y\hat{j} + z\hat{k}$ be the position vector to the space curve C at the point $P(x, y, z)$ whose equations are given by $x = x(t), \quad y = y(t)$ and $z = z(t)$, where t is time, then *velocity* and *acceleration* are given by

$$\text{Velocity} = \vec{v} = \frac{d\vec{r}}{dt} = \frac{dx}{dt}\hat{i} + \frac{dy}{dt}\hat{j} + \frac{dz}{dt}\hat{k}$$

$$\text{Acceleration} = \vec{a} = \frac{d^2\vec{r}}{dt^2} = \frac{d^2x}{dt^2}\hat{i} + \frac{d^2y}{dt^2}\hat{j} + \frac{d^2z}{dt^2}\hat{k}$$

3.2.4 Tangential and Normal Components of Acceleration

Let $\vec{r} = x\hat{i} + y\hat{j} + z\hat{k}$ be the position vector of a moving particle at time t and let $\vec{a}$ be the acceleration and $\vec{v}$ be the velocity of a particle at P.

Here, $\overrightarrow{OA}$ is the tangential component and $\overrightarrow{OB}$ is normal component of acceleration

$$\therefore\ OA = \vec{a} \cdot \hat{v} = \text{tangential component}$$

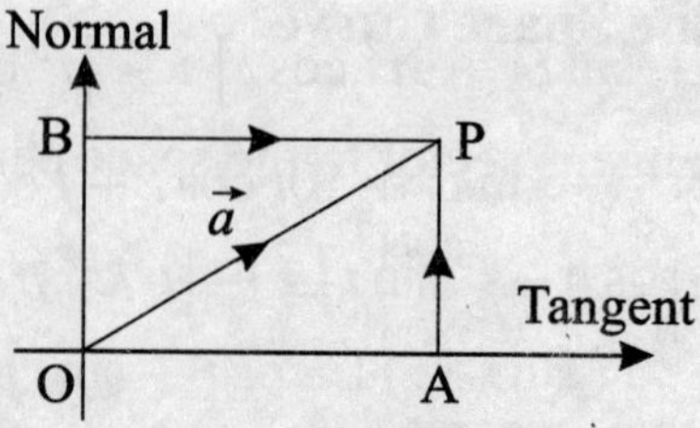

Figure 3.1

and $\overrightarrow{OP} = \overrightarrow{OB} + \overrightarrow{BP}$ $\overrightarrow{OB} = \overrightarrow{OP} - \overrightarrow{BP}$

$$OB = \left|\overrightarrow{OP} - \overrightarrow{OA}\right| = \left|\vec{a} - \left(\vec{a} \cdot \hat{v}\right)\, \hat{v}\right| = \text{normal component}$$

Worked Examples

1. *If* $\vec{A} = 5t^2\hat{i} + t\,\hat{j} - t^3\hat{k}$, $\vec{B} = \sin t\,\hat{i} - \cos t\,\hat{j}$, *find*

(i) $\frac{d}{dt}\left(\vec{A} \cdot \vec{B}\right)$ (ii) $\frac{d}{dt}\left(\vec{A} \times \vec{B}\right)$

➡

(i) $\vec{A} \cdot \vec{B} = 5t^2 \sin t - t \cos t$

$$\frac{d}{dt}\left(\vec{A} \cdot \vec{B}\right) = 5t^2 \cos t + 10t \sin t - [t\,(-\sin t) + 1 \cdot \cos t]$$

$$= 5t^2 \cos t + 10t \sin t + t \sin t - \cos t$$

$$\frac{d}{dt}\left(\vec{A} \cdot \vec{B}\right) = \left(5t^2 - 1\right) \cos t + 11t \sin t$$

(ii)

$$\vec{A} \times \vec{B} = \begin{vmatrix} \hat{i} & \hat{j} & \hat{k} \\ 5t^2 & t & -t^3 \\ \sin t & -\cos t & 0 \end{vmatrix}$$

$$= \hat{i}\left(0 - t^3 \cos t\right) - \hat{j}\left(0 + t^3 \sin t\right) + \hat{k}\left(-5t^2 \cos t - t \sin t\right) \hat{k}$$

$$\vec{A} \times \vec{B} = -t^3 \cos t\hat{i} - t^3 \sin t\,\hat{j} - \left(5t^2 \cos t + t \sin t\right) \hat{k}$$

$$\frac{d}{dt}\left(\vec{A}\times\vec{B}\right) = -\left[t^3(-\sin t) + 3t^2\cos t\right]\hat{i} - \left[t^3\cos t + 3t^2\sin t\right]\hat{j}$$
$$-\left[5t^2(-\sin t) + 10t\cos t + t\cos t + \sin t\right]\hat{k}$$
$$= -\left[3t^2\cos t - t^3\sin t\right]\hat{i} - \left[t^3\cos t + 3t^2\sin t\right]\hat{j}$$
$$-\left[-5t^2\sin t + 11t\cos t + \sin t\right]\hat{k}$$

2. *Find the unit tangent vector of the space curve* $\vec{r} = \cos t\hat{i} + \sin t\hat{j} + t\hat{k}$

➡ $\vec{r} = \cos t\hat{i} + \sin t\hat{j} + t\hat{k}$

$$\therefore\ \vec{T} = \frac{d\vec{r}}{dt} = -\sin t\hat{i} + \cos t\hat{j} + \hat{k}$$
$$|\vec{T}| = \sqrt{(-\sin t)^2 + (\cos t)^2 + 1^2}$$
$$= \sqrt{\sin^2 t + \cos^2 t + 1} = \sqrt{1+1} = \sqrt{2}$$

Therefore, unit tangent vector to the given curve at any point t is

$$\hat{T} = \frac{\vec{T}}{|\vec{T}|} = \frac{1}{\sqrt{2}}\left(-\sin t\hat{i} + \cos t\hat{j} + \hat{k}\right)$$

3. *Find the unit tangent vector of the space curve* $x = 1 + t^3,\ y = 2t^3,\ z = 2 - t^3$

➡ We have,

$$\vec{r} = (1+t^3)\,\hat{i} + 2t^3\hat{j} + (2-t^3)\,\hat{k}$$
$$\therefore\ \vec{T} = \frac{\overrightarrow{dr}}{dt} = 3t^2\hat{i} + 6t^2\hat{j} - 3t^2\hat{k}$$
$$|\vec{T}| = \sqrt{(3t^2)^2 + (6t^2)^2 + (-3t^2)^2}$$
$$= \sqrt{9t^4 + 36t^4 + 9t^4} = \sqrt{54t^4}$$
$$|\vec{T}| = 3\sqrt{6}t^2$$

Therefore, the unit tangent vector to the given curve at the point t is

$$\hat{T} = \frac{\vec{T}}{|\vec{T}|} = \frac{3t^2\hat{i} + 6t^2\hat{j} - 3t^2\hat{k}}{3\sqrt{6}t^2}$$
$$\hat{T} = \frac{1}{\sqrt{6}}\left(\hat{i} + 2\hat{j} - \hat{k}\right)$$

4. *Find the unit tangent vector to the space curve $x = \cos t^2$, $y = \sin t^2$ and $z = 0$*

➡ Let, $\vec{r} = x\hat{i} + y\hat{j} + z\hat{k}$

$$\vec{r} = \cos t^2\hat{i} + \sin t^2\hat{j} + 0.\hat{k}$$

$$\vec{T} = \frac{d\vec{r}}{dt} = -\sin t^2\,(2t)\,\hat{i} + \cos t^2\,(2t)\,\hat{j}$$

$$|\vec{T}| = \sqrt{(-2t\sin t^2)^2 + (2t\cos t^2)^2}$$

$$= \sqrt{4t^2\sin^2 t^2 + 4t^2\cos^2 t^2} = \sqrt{4t^2\left(\sin^2 t^2 + \cos^2 t^2\right)}$$

$$|\vec{T}| = \sqrt{4t^2} = 2t$$

$$\therefore\ \hat{T} = \frac{\vec{T}}{|\vec{T}|} = \frac{-2t\sin t^2\hat{i} + 2t\cos t^2\hat{j}}{2t}$$

$$\hat{T} = -\sin t^2\hat{i} + \cos t^2\hat{j}$$

5. *Find the unit tangent vector and unit normal vector to the curve $\vec{r}(t) = 3\cos 2t\hat{i} +$ $3\sin 2t\,\hat{j}$ at $x = \dfrac{3\sqrt{3}}{2}$*

➡ $\vec{r} = 3\cos 2t\hat{i} + 3\sin 2t\,\hat{j}$

$$\vec{T} = \frac{d\vec{r}}{dt} = -6\sin 2t\,\hat{i} + 6\cos 2t\,\hat{j}$$

$$|\vec{T}| = \sqrt{(-6\sin 2t)^2 + (6\cos 2t)^2} = \sqrt{36\left(\sin^2 2t + \cos^2 2t\right)} = 6$$

$$\therefore\ \hat{T} = \frac{\vec{T}}{|\vec{T}|} = \frac{1}{6}\left(-6\sin 2t\,\hat{i} + 6\cos 2t\,\hat{j}\right)$$

$$\hat{T} = -\sin 2t\,\hat{i} + \cos 2t\,\hat{j}$$

Given, $x = \dfrac{3\sqrt{3}}{2}$ and we know that

$$\vec{r} = x\hat{i} + y\hat{j} + z\hat{k}$$

$$\therefore x = 3\cos 2t$$

$$\therefore \Rightarrow \frac{3\sqrt{3}}{2} = 3\cos 2t \Rightarrow \frac{\sqrt{3}}{2} = \cos 2t$$

$$\Rightarrow 2t = \frac{\pi}{6} \Rightarrow t = \frac{\pi}{12}$$

Therefore, the unit tangent vector at $x = \dfrac{3\sqrt{3}}{2}$ is

$$\hat{T} = -\frac{1}{2}\hat{i} + \frac{\sqrt{3}}{2}\hat{j}$$

$$\hat{T} = -\sin 2t\,\hat{i} + \cos 2t\,\hat{j}$$

$$\frac{d\hat{T}}{dt} = -\cos 2t \cdot 2\hat{i} - \sin 2t \cdot 2\hat{j}$$

$$\therefore \frac{d\hat{T}}{ds} = \frac{d\hat{T}/dt}{ds/dt} = \frac{d\hat{T}/dt}{|d\vec{r}/dt|} = \frac{-2\cos 2t\,\hat{i} - 2\sin 2t\,\hat{j}}{6}$$

$$\frac{d\hat{T}}{ds} = -\frac{1}{3}\cos 2t\,\hat{i} - \frac{1}{3}\sin 2t\,\hat{j}$$

$$\left|\frac{d\hat{T}}{ds}\right| = \sqrt{\frac{1}{9}\cos^2 2t + \frac{1}{9}\sin^2 2t} = \frac{1}{3}$$

We know that the unit normal vector to the space curve is

$$\hat{n} = \frac{d\hat{T}/ds}{\left|d\hat{T}/ds\right|} = \frac{-(1/3)\cos 2t\hat{i} - (1/3)\sin 2t\hat{j}}{1/3}$$

$$\hat{n} = -\cos 2t\hat{i} - \sin 2t\hat{j}$$

6. *Find the unit normal vector to the curve* $\vec{r} = 4\sin t\,\hat{i} + 4\cos t\,\hat{j} + 3t\,\hat{k}$

➡ $\vec{r} = 4\sin t\,\hat{i} + 4\cos t\,\hat{j} + 3t\,\hat{k}$

$$\vec{T} = \frac{d\vec{r}}{dt} = 4\cos t\,\hat{i} - 4\sin t\,\hat{j} + 3\,\hat{k}$$

$$|\vec{T}| = \sqrt{(4\cos t)^2 + (-4\sin t)^2 + 3^2} = \sqrt{16\cos^2 t + 16\sin^2 t + 9}$$

$$= \sqrt{16\left(\cos^2 t + \sin^2 t\right) + 9} = \sqrt{16\,(1) + 9} = 5$$

$$\therefore\ \hat{T} = \frac{\vec{T}}{|\vec{T}|} = \frac{4\cos t\hat{i} - 4\sin t\,\hat{j} + 3\hat{k}}{5}$$

$$\frac{d\hat{T}}{dt} = \frac{1}{5}\left(-4\sin t\hat{i} - 4\cos t\,\hat{j}\right)$$

$$\therefore\ \frac{d\hat{T}}{ds} = \frac{d\hat{T}/dt}{ds/dt} = \frac{d\hat{T}/dt}{|d\vec{r}/dt|} = \frac{1/5\left(-4\sin t\hat{i} - 4\cos t\,\hat{j}\right)}{5}$$

$$\frac{d\hat{T}}{ds} = -\frac{4}{25}\sin t\hat{i} - \frac{4}{25}\cos t\,\hat{j}$$

$$\left|\frac{d\hat{T}}{ds}\right| = \sqrt{\frac{16}{625}\sin^2 t + \frac{16}{625}\cos^2 t} = \frac{4}{25}$$

Therefore, the unit normal vector to given space curve is

$$\hat{n} = \frac{d\hat{T}/ds}{\left|d\hat{T}/ds\right|} = \frac{-(4/25)\sin t\hat{i} - (4/25)\cos t\,\hat{j}}{4/25}$$

$$\hat{n} = -\sin t\hat{i} - \cos t\,\hat{j}$$

7. *Find the angle between the tangents to the curve* $\vec{r} = \left(t - \frac{t^2}{2}\right)\hat{i} + t^2\hat{j} + \left(t + \frac{t^2}{2}\right)\hat{k}$ *at* $t = \pm 1$

➡ $\vec{r} = \left(t - \frac{t^2}{2}\right)\hat{i} + t^2\hat{j} + \left(t + \frac{t^2}{2}\right)\hat{k}$

$$\vec{T} = \frac{d\vec{r}}{dt} = (1 - t)\,\hat{i} + 2t\,\hat{j} + (1 + t)\,\hat{k}$$

Let, $\vec{a} = [\vec{T}]_{t=1} = 2\hat{j} + 2\hat{k}$ and $\vec{b} = [\vec{T}]_{t=-1} = 2\hat{i} - 2\hat{j}$

$$\therefore |\vec{a}| = \sqrt{2^2 + 2^2} = 2\sqrt{2},\quad |\vec{b}| = \sqrt{2^2 + (-2)^2} = 2\sqrt{2}$$

Therefore, angle between the tangents is

$$\cos\theta = \frac{\vec{a}\cdot\vec{b}}{|\vec{a}||\vec{b}|} = \frac{\left(2\hat{j}+2\hat{k}\right)\cdot\left(2\hat{i}-2\hat{j}\right)}{2\sqrt{2}\,2\sqrt{2}} = \frac{-4}{8}$$

$$\cos\theta = -\frac{1}{2} \Rightarrow \theta = \cos^{-1}\left(-\frac{1}{2}\right)$$

$$\therefore\ \theta = 120^\circ = \frac{2\pi}{3}$$

8. *Find the angle between the tangents to the curve $x = t^2$, $y = t^3$, $z = t^4$ at $t = 2$ and $t = 3$*

➡ $\vec{r} = x\hat{i} + y\hat{j} + z\hat{k}$

$$\vec{r} = t^2\hat{i} + t^3\hat{j} + t^4\hat{k}$$

$$\vec{T} = \frac{d\vec{r}}{dt} = 2t\hat{i} + 3t^2\hat{j} + 4t^3\hat{k}$$

Let, $\vec{a} = [\vec{T}]_{t=2} = 4\hat{i} + 12\hat{j} + 32\hat{k} = 4[\hat{i} + 3\hat{j} + 8\hat{k}]$

$$|\vec{a}| = \sqrt{16\,(1+9+64)} = 4\sqrt{74}$$

and $\vec{b} = [\vec{T}]_{t=3} = 6\hat{i} + 27\hat{j} + 108\hat{k} = 3[2\hat{i} + 9\hat{j} + 36\hat{k}]$
$|\vec{b}| = \sqrt{9\,(4+81+1296)} = 3\sqrt{1381}$

$$\cos\theta = \frac{\vec{a}\cdot\vec{b}}{|\vec{a}||\vec{b}|} = \frac{4\left(\hat{i}+3\hat{j}+8\hat{k}\right)\cdot 3\left(2\hat{i}+9\hat{j}+32\hat{k}\right)}{4\sqrt{74}\ 3\sqrt{1381}}$$

$$= \frac{2+27+256}{\sqrt{74}\ \sqrt{1381}}$$

$$\cos\theta = 0.8915$$

$$\theta = \cos^{-1}(0.8915)$$

9. *A particle moves along the curve* $\vec{r} = (1-t^3)\,\hat{i} + (1+t^2)\hat{j} + (2t-5)\,\hat{k}$, *determine the velocity and acceleration.*

➡ $\vec{r} = \left(1-t^3\right)\hat{i} + \left(1+t^2\right)\hat{j} + (2t-5)\,\hat{k}$

$$\text{Velocity} = \frac{d\vec{r}}{dt} = -3t^2\hat{i} + 2t\,\hat{j} + 2\hat{k}$$

$$\text{Acceleration} = \frac{d^2\vec{r}}{dt^2} = -6t\hat{i} + 2\hat{j}$$

10. *A particle moves along a curve with parametric equations* $x = t - \frac{t^3}{3}$, $y = t^2$ *and* $z = t + \frac{t^3}{3}$, *where t is the time. Find the velocity and acceleration at any time t and also find their magnitudes at* $t = 3$.

➡ $\vec{r} = x\hat{i} + y\hat{j} + z\hat{k}$

$$\vec{r} = \left(t - \frac{t^3}{3}\right)\hat{i} + t^2\hat{j} + \left(t + \frac{t^3}{3}\right)\hat{k}$$

$$\text{Velocity} = \vec{v} = \frac{d\vec{r}}{dt} = \left(1-t^2\right)\hat{i} + 2t\hat{j} + \left(1+t^2\right)\hat{k}$$

$$\text{Acceleration} = \vec{a} = \frac{d\vec{v}}{dt} = -2t\hat{i} + 2\hat{j} + 2t\hat{k}$$

$$[\vec{v}]_{t=3} = -8\hat{i} + 6\hat{j} + 10\hat{k}$$

$$|\vec{v}| = \sqrt{64+36+100} = \sqrt{200}$$

$$[\vec{a}]_{t=3} = -6\hat{i} + 2\hat{j} + 6\hat{k}$$

$$|\vec{a}| = \sqrt{36+4+36} = \sqrt{76}$$

11. *A particle moves along the curve* $\vec{r} = \cos 2t\,\hat{i} + \sin 2t\,\hat{j} + t\,\hat{k}$. *Find the velocity and the acceleration at* $t = \frac{\pi}{8}$ *along* $\sqrt{2}\hat{i} + \sqrt{2}\,\hat{j} + \hat{k}$

➡ $\vec{r} = \cos 2t\,\hat{i} + \sin 2t\,\hat{j} + t\,\hat{k}$

$$\vec{v} = \frac{d\vec{r}}{dt} = -2\sin 2t\,\hat{i} + 2\cos 2t\,\hat{j} + \hat{k}$$

$$[\vec{v}]_{t=\frac{\pi}{8}} = -2\frac{1}{\sqrt{2}}\hat{i} + 2\cdot\frac{1}{\sqrt{2}}\hat{j} + \hat{k}$$

$$[\vec{v}]_{t=\frac{\pi}{8}} = -\sqrt{2}\hat{i} + \sqrt{2}\hat{j} + \hat{k}$$

$$\vec{a} = \frac{d\vec{v}}{dt} = -4\cos 2t\,\hat{i} - 4\sin 2t\,\hat{j}$$

$$[\vec{a}]_{t=\frac{\pi}{8}} = -4\frac{1}{\sqrt{2}}\hat{i} - 4\cdot\frac{1}{\sqrt{2}}\hat{j} = -2\sqrt{2}\hat{i} - 2\sqrt{2}\,\hat{j}$$

Let, $\vec{b} = \sqrt{2}\hat{i} + \sqrt{2}\hat{j} + \hat{k}$

$$|\vec{b}| = \sqrt{2+2+1} = \sqrt{5}$$

$$\hat{b} = \frac{\vec{b}}{|\vec{b}|} = \frac{\sqrt{2}\hat{i} + \sqrt{2}\hat{j} + \hat{k}}{\sqrt{5}}$$

Therefore, velocity $\vec{v}$ along the vector $\vec{b}$ is

$$\vec{v}\cdot\hat{b} = \left(-\sqrt{2}\hat{i} + \sqrt{2}\hat{j} + \hat{k}\right)\cdot\frac{\left(\sqrt{2}\hat{i} + \sqrt{2}\hat{j} + \hat{k}\right)}{\sqrt{5}} = \frac{-2+2+1}{\sqrt{5}} = \frac{1}{\sqrt{5}}$$

and acceleration $\vec{a}$ along the vector $\vec{b}$ is

$$\vec{a}\cdot\hat{b} = \left(-2\sqrt{2}\hat{i} - 2\sqrt{2}\hat{j}\right)\cdot\frac{\left(\sqrt{2}\hat{i} + \sqrt{2}\hat{j} + \hat{k}\right)}{\sqrt{5}} = \frac{-4-4}{\sqrt{5}} = -\frac{8}{\sqrt{5}}$$

12. *Find the velocity and acceleration of a particle moves along the curve* $\vec{r} = e^{-2t}\hat{i} + 2\cos 5t\,\hat{j} + 5\sin 2t\,\hat{k}$ *at any time 't'.*

➡ $\vec{r} = e^{-2t}\hat{i} + 2\cos 5t\,\hat{j} + 5\sin 2t\,\hat{k}$

$$\text{Velocity} = \frac{d\vec{r}}{dt} = -2e^{-2t}\hat{i} - 10\sin 5t\,\hat{j} + 10\cos 2t\hat{k}$$

$$\text{Acceleration} = \frac{d^2\vec{r}}{dt^2} = 4e^{-2t}\hat{i} - 50\cos 5t\,\hat{j} - 20\sin 2t\,\hat{k}$$

13. *Find the tangential and normal components of its acceleration at t = 1 of a particle moves along the curve* $\vec{r} = t^2\hat{i} - t^3\hat{j} + t^4\hat{k}$

➡ $\vec{r} = t^2\hat{i} - t^3\hat{j} + t^4\hat{k}$

$$\vec{v} = \frac{d\vec{r}}{dt} = 2t\hat{i} - 3t^2\hat{j} + 4t^3\hat{k}$$

$$(\vec{v})_{t=1} = 2\hat{i} - 3\hat{j} + 4\hat{k}$$

$$|\vec{v}| = \sqrt{4+9+16} = \sqrt{29}$$

$$\vec{a} = \frac{d^2\vec{r}}{dt^2} = 2\hat{i} - 6t\,\hat{j} + 12t^2\hat{k}$$

$$(\vec{a})_{t=1} = 2\hat{i} - 6\hat{j} + 12\hat{k}$$

$$\therefore\ \hat{v} = \frac{\vec{v}}{|\overrightarrow{v}|} = \frac{2\hat{i} - 3\hat{j} + 4\hat{k}}{\sqrt{29}}$$

The tangential component of acceleration is

$$\vec{a}\cdot\hat{v} = \left(2\hat{i} - 6\hat{j} + 12\hat{k}\right)\cdot\frac{\left(2\hat{i} - 3\hat{j} + 4\hat{k}\right)}{\sqrt{29}} = \frac{4+18+48}{\sqrt{29}}$$

$$\vec{a}\cdot\hat{v} = 70/\sqrt{29}$$

The normal component of acceleration is

$$|\vec{a} - (\vec{a}\cdot\hat{v})\,\hat{v}| = \left|\left(2\hat{i} - 6\hat{j} + 12\hat{k}\right) - \frac{70}{\sqrt{29}}\left(\frac{2\hat{i} - 3\hat{j} + 4\hat{k}}{\sqrt{29}}\right)\right|$$

$$= \left|\left(2\hat{i} - 6\hat{j} + 12\hat{k}\right) - \frac{70}{29}\left(2\hat{i} - 3\hat{j} + 4\hat{k}\right)\right|$$

$$= \left|\frac{58\hat{i} - 174\hat{j} + 348\hat{k} - 140\hat{i} + 210\hat{j} - 280\hat{k}}{29}\right|$$

$$= \frac{1}{29}\left|-82\hat{i} + 36\hat{j} + 68\hat{k}\right| = \frac{\sqrt{12644}}{29}$$

Exercises

1. *Find the unit tangent vector to the following space curves.*

   (i) $\vec{r} = 4\sin t\,\hat{i} + 4\cos t\,\hat{j} + 3t\,\hat{k}$

   (ii) $\vec{r} = 2\log t\,\hat{i} + 4t\,\hat{j} + \left(2t^2 + 1\right)\hat{k}$

   (iii) $x = t^2 + 1, \quad y = 4t - 3, \quad z = 2t^2 - 6t$ *at* $t = 2$

2. *Find the unit normal vector to the curve* $\vec{r} = 3\cos t\hat{i} + 3\sin t\hat{j} + 4t\hat{k}$

3. *Find the unit tangent vector and the unit normal vector at the point* $t = 2$ *on the curve whose parametric equations are:*

$$x = t - (t^3/3), \quad y = t^2, \quad z = t + (t^3/3)$$

4. *Find the angle between the tangents to the curve* $\vec{r} = t^2\hat{i} + 2t\,\hat{j} - t^3\hat{k}$ *at the points* $t = \pm 1$

5. *Find the angle between the tangents to the curve* $\vec{r} = t^2\,\hat{i} + 3t^2\,\hat{j} - \left(t^2 + 1\right)\hat{k}$ *at* $t = \pm 1$

6. *Find the angle between the tangents to the curve* $x = t, \quad y = t^2, \quad z = t^3$ *at* $t = \pm 1$

7. *A particle moves along the curve* $\vec{r} = \left(t^3 - 4t\right)\hat{i} + \left(t^2 + 4t\right)\hat{j} + \left(8t^2 - 3t^3\right)\hat{k}$. *Find the velocity and acceleration.*

8. *A particle moves along the curve* $\vec{r} = 3t^2\hat{i} + \left(t^3 - 4t\right)\hat{j} + (3t + 4)\,\hat{k}$. *Find the components of velocity and acceleration at* $t = 2$ *in the direction* $\hat{i} - 2\hat{j} + 2\hat{k}$.

9. *A particle moves along the curve* $\vec{r} = \left(t^3 + 1\right)\hat{i} + t^2\hat{j} + (t + 5)\,\hat{k}$. *Find the components of velocity and acceleration along* $\hat{i} + 3\hat{j} + 2\hat{k}$ *at* $t = 1$.

10. *A particle moves along the curve* $\vec{r} = \left(t^3 - 4t\right)\hat{i} + \left(t^2 + 4t\right)\hat{j} + \left(8t^2 - 3t^3\right)\hat{k}$. *Determine the magnitude of the acceleration at* $t = 1$.

Answers

1. (i) $\frac{1}{5}[4\cos t\hat{i} - 4\sin t\,\hat{j} + 3\hat{k}]$ (ii) $\frac{2}{t(2t^2 + 1)}(\hat{i} + 2t\,\hat{j} + 2t^2\hat{k})$

   (iii) $\frac{1}{3}\left(2\hat{i} + 2\hat{j} + \hat{k}\right)$

2. $-\cos t\hat{i} - \sin t\hat{j}$ 3. $\dfrac{-3\hat{i}+4\hat{j}+5\hat{k}}{5\sqrt{2}}, \quad -\dfrac{(4\hat{i}+3\hat{j})}{5}$

4. $\cos^{-1}\left(\dfrac{9}{17}\right)$ 5. $\cos^{-1}\left(\dfrac{7}{11}\right)$ 6. $\cos^{-1}\left(\dfrac{3}{7}\right)$

7. $(3t^2-4)\,\hat{i} + (2t+4)\hat{j} + (16t-9t^2)\hat{k},\ 6t\hat{i} + 2\hat{j} + (16-18t)\,\hat{k}$

8. $\dfrac{2}{3}, \quad -6$ 9. $\dfrac{11}{\sqrt{14}} \quad \dfrac{6}{\sqrt{10}}$ 10. $\sqrt{44}$.

3.3 The vector differential operator '*Del*' or '*Nabla*'

The vector differential operator '*Del*' or '*Nabla*' is denoted by '∇' and it is defined by

$$\nabla = \frac{\partial}{\partial x}\hat{i} + \frac{\partial}{\partial y}\hat{j} + \frac{\partial}{\partial z}\hat{k}$$

This operator is used in defining *gradient*, *divergence* and *curl*.

The properties of '∇' are similar to those of vectors. The operator is applied to both vector and scalar functions

3.3.1 Gradient of a Scalar Function

Let $\phi = \phi(x, y, z)$ be any scalar function, defined at each point (x, y, z) in a region of space and is differentiable, then *gradient* of ϕ is denoted by "$grad\phi$" or $\nabla\phi$ and is defined by

$$\text{grad}\,\phi = \nabla\phi = \left(\frac{\partial}{\partial x}\hat{i} + \frac{\partial}{\partial y}\hat{j} + \frac{\partial}{\partial z}\hat{k}\right)\phi$$

$$\text{grad}\phi = \nabla\phi = \frac{\partial\phi}{\partial x}\hat{i} + \frac{\partial\phi}{\partial y}\hat{j} + \frac{\partial\phi}{\partial z}\hat{k}$$

which is a vector function.

Therefore, gradient of a scalar function is a vector function.

Geometrical meaning

Let $\phi(x, y, z) = c$ be the equation of surface and $\vec{r} = x\hat{i} + y\hat{j} + z\hat{k}$ be the position vector of the point (x, y, z) on the surface, then we have $d\vec{r} = dx\,\hat{i} + dy\,\hat{j} + dz\,\hat{k}$, which is the *tangent plane* to the surface.

$$\nabla\phi \cdot d\vec{r} = \left(\frac{\partial\phi}{\partial x}\hat{i} + \frac{\partial\phi}{\partial y}\hat{j} + \frac{\partial\phi}{\partial z}\hat{k}\right) \cdot \left(dx\hat{i} + dy\hat{j} + dz\hat{k}\right)$$

$$= \frac{\partial\phi}{\partial x}dx + \frac{\partial\phi}{\partial y}dy + \frac{\partial\phi}{\partial z}dz = d\phi = 0$$

$$\nabla\phi \cdot d\vec{r} = 0 \qquad \phi = c \text{ (constant)}$$

Therefore, vector $\nabla\phi$ is perpendicular to the tangent plane. Hence $\nabla\phi$ is the *normal vector* at the point (x, y, z) to the surface $\phi(x, y, z) = c$.

Unit Normal Vector

We know that $\nabla\phi$ is the normal vector to the surface $\phi(x, y, z) = c$ then *unit normal vector* is denoted by $\hat{n}$ and is defined as

$$\hat{n} = \frac{\vec{n}}{|\vec{n}|} = \frac{\nabla\phi}{|\nabla\phi|}$$

where $\vec{n} = \nabla\phi =$ Normal vector.

Directional Derivative

If $\vec{a}$ is any vector and ϕ is any scalar point function, then $\dfrac{\nabla\phi \cdot \vec{a}}{|a|}$ represents the component of $\nabla\phi$ in the direction of $\vec{a}$, which is known as the *directional derivative* of ϕ in the direction of $\vec{a}$.

$$\text{i.e., D.D (directional derivative)} = \frac{\nabla\phi \cdot \vec{a}}{|a|} = \nabla\phi \cdot \hat{a}.$$

Maximum Directional Derivative (Normal Derivative)

The directional derivative will be maximum in the direction $\nabla\phi$ (i.e., $\vec{a} = \nabla\phi$) and the maximum value of directional derivative $= \dfrac{\nabla\phi \cdot \nabla\phi}{|\nabla\phi|} = \dfrac{|\nabla\phi|^2}{|\nabla\phi|} =$ $|\nabla\phi| \qquad (\vec{a} \cdot \vec{a} = |\vec{a}|^2)$

Note: The *maximum directional derivative* is also called *Normal derivative* i.e., Normal derivative $= |\nabla\phi|$.

Equations of Tangent Plane and Normal Line

Let $\phi(x, y, z) = c$ be any given surface and (x_1, y_1, z_1) be a point on it then

(i) Equation of Tangent plane to $\phi(x, y, z) = c$ at $P\ (x_1, y_1, z_1)$ is

$$(x - x_1)\left(\frac{\partial\phi}{\partial x}\right)_P + (y - y_1)\left(\frac{\partial\phi}{\partial y}\right)_P + (z - z_1)\left(\frac{\partial\phi}{\partial z}\right)_P = 0$$

(ii) Equation of Normal line to $\phi(x, y, z) = c$ at $P\ (x_1, y_1, z_1)$ is

$$\frac{x - x_1}{(\partial\phi/\partial x)_P} = \frac{y - y_1}{(\partial\phi/\partial y)_P} = \frac{z - z_1}{(\partial\phi/\partial z)_P}$$

3.3.2 Divergence of a Vector Function

If $\vec{A} = A_1\hat{i} + A_2\hat{j} + A_3\hat{k}$ is a vector function defined and differentiable at each point (x, y, z), then *divergence* of $\vec{A}$ is denoted by $\text{div}\vec{A}$ or $\nabla \cdot \vec{A}$ and is defined by

$$\text{div}\vec{A} = \nabla \cdot \vec{A} = \left(\frac{\partial}{\partial x}\hat{i} + \frac{\partial}{\partial y}\hat{j} + \frac{\partial}{\partial z}\hat{k}\right) \cdot \left(A_1\hat{i} + A_2\hat{j} + A_3\hat{k}\right)$$

$$\text{div}\vec{A} = \nabla \cdot \vec{A} = \frac{\partial A_1}{\partial x} + \frac{\partial A_2}{\partial y} + \frac{\partial A_3}{\partial z}$$

Hence, divergence of a vector function is a scalar function.

Remark: $\nabla \cdot \vec{A} \neq \vec{A} \cdot \nabla$.

Physical meaning

1. If $\vec{A}$ represents the velocity of fluid in a fluid flow, then $\text{div}\vec{A}$ represents the rate of fluid flow through unit volume
2. If $\vec{A}$ represents the electric flux, then $\text{div}\vec{A}$ represents the amount of electric flux or heat flux that diverges per unit volume in unit time.

Solenoidal Vector

A vector $\vec{A}$ is said to be *solenoidal vector* or *divergence free vector* if div$\vec{A} = 0$ i.e., $\nabla.\vec{A} = 0$

3.3.3 Curl of a Vector Function

If $\vec{A}$ is any vector function differentiable at each point (x, y, z) then *curl* of $\vec{A}$ is denoted by *curl* $\vec{A}$ or $\nabla \times \vec{A}$ and it is defined by

$$\text{curl}\,\vec{A} = \nabla \times \vec{A} = \begin{vmatrix} \hat{i} & \hat{j} & \hat{k} \\ \dfrac{\partial}{\partial x} & \dfrac{\partial}{\partial y} & \dfrac{\partial}{\partial z} \\ A_1 & A_2 & A_3 \end{vmatrix}$$

$$\text{curl}\vec{A} = \nabla \times \vec{A} = \left(\frac{\partial A_3}{\partial y} - \frac{\partial A_2}{\partial z}\right)\hat{i} - \left(\frac{\partial A_3}{\partial x} - \frac{\partial A_1}{\partial z}\right)\hat{j} + \left(\frac{\partial A_2}{\partial x} - \frac{\partial A_1}{\partial y}\right)\hat{k}$$

Hence, curl of a vector function is a vector.

Physical Meaning

Let $\vec{r} = x\hat{i} + y\hat{j} + z\hat{k}$ be the position vector of a particle at $P(x, y, z)$ of a rigid body rotating about the fixed axis about the origin O with an angular velocity $\vec{W} = w_1\hat{i} + w_2\hat{j} + w_3\hat{k}$, then the velocity $\vec{V}$of the particle is given by

$$\begin{aligned} \vec{V} &= \vec{W} \times \vec{r} \\ &= \begin{vmatrix} \hat{i} & \hat{j} & \hat{k} \\ w_1 & w_2 & w_3 \\ x & y & z \end{vmatrix} \\ &= \hat{i}\,(w_2 z - w_3 y) - \hat{j}\,(w_1 z - w_3 x) + \hat{k}\,(w_1 y - w_2 x) \end{aligned}$$

$$\therefore\ \vec{V} = (w_2 z - w_3 y)\,\hat{i} + (w_3 x - w_1 z)\,\hat{j} + (w_1 y - w_2 x)\,\hat{k}$$

$$\therefore\ \text{curl}\vec{V} = \begin{vmatrix} \hat{i} & \hat{j} & \hat{k} \\ \dfrac{\partial}{\partial x} & \dfrac{\partial}{\partial y} & \dfrac{\partial}{\partial z} \\ w_2 z - w_3 y & w_3 x - w_1 z & w_1 y - w_2 x \end{vmatrix}$$

$$= \hat{i}\left[\frac{\partial}{\partial y}(w_1 y - w_2 x) - \frac{\partial}{\partial z}(w_3 x - w_1 z)\right]$$

$$-\hat{j}\left[\frac{\partial}{\partial x}(w_1 y - w_2 x) - \frac{\partial}{\partial z}(w_2 z - w_3 y)\right]$$
$$+\hat{k}\left[\frac{\partial}{\partial x}(w_3 x - w_1 z) - \frac{\partial}{\partial y}(w_2 z - w_3 y)\right]$$
$$= \hat{i}(w_1 + w_1) - \hat{j}(-w_2 - w_2) + \hat{k}(w_3 + w_3)$$
$$= 2\left(w_1\hat{i} + w_2\hat{j} + w_3\hat{k}\right)$$
$$\text{curl}\vec{V} = 2\vec{W}$$

Thus curl of velocity vector is twice the angular velocity of rotation.

Irrotatational Vector (or Conservative Force Field or Potential Field)

A vector field $\vec{A}$ is said to be *irrotatational vector* or *conservative force field* or *potential field* or *curl free vector* if $\nabla \times \vec{A} = 0$or curl$\vec{A} = 0$.

Scalar Potential

A vector field $\vec{A}$ which can be derived from the scalar field ϕ such that $F = \nabla\phi$ is called *conservative force field* and ϕ is called *scalar potential.*

Worked Examples

1.

(i) *If* $\phi = x^2yz$, *find* $\nabla\phi$

(ii) *If* $\phi = xy + x^2y^2z + x^3y^2z$, *find* $grad\phi$

(iii) *Find the gradient of* $x + y + z$

(iv) *If* $\phi = x^2y^2 + y^2z^2 + z^2x^2$, *find* $\nabla\phi$ *at the point* (1,1,1)

(v) *If* $\phi = x^3y^3z^3$, *find* $\nabla\phi$ *at* (1,2,1) *along* $\hat{i} + 2\hat{j} + 2\hat{k}$

➡ (i) $\phi = x^2yz$

$$\nabla\phi = \frac{\partial\phi}{\partial x}\hat{i} + \frac{\partial\phi}{\partial y}\hat{j} + \frac{\partial\phi}{\partial z}\hat{k} = \frac{\partial}{\partial x}(x^2yz)\,\hat{i} + \frac{\partial}{\partial y}(x^2yz)\,\hat{j} + \frac{\partial}{\partial z}(x^2yz)\,\hat{k}$$
$$\nabla\phi = 2xyz\hat{i} + x^2z\hat{j} + x^2y\hat{k}$$

(ii) $\phi = xy + x^2y^2z + x^3y^2z$

$$\nabla\phi = \frac{\partial\phi}{\partial x}\hat{i} + \frac{\partial\phi}{\partial y}\hat{j} + \frac{\partial\phi}{\partial z}\hat{k}$$

$$\therefore\ \nabla\phi = (y + 2xy^2z + 3x^2y^2z)\hat{i} + (x + 2x^2yz + 2x^3yz)\hat{j} + (x^2y^2 + x^3y^2)\hat{k}$$

(iii) Let $\phi = x + y + z$

$$\text{grad}\,\phi = \frac{\partial\phi}{\partial x}\hat{i} + \frac{\partial\phi}{\partial y}\hat{j} + \frac{\partial\phi}{\partial z}\hat{k} = \hat{i} + \hat{j} + \hat{k}$$

(iv) $\phi = x^2y^2 + y^2z^2 + z^2x^2$

We have, $\nabla\phi = \dfrac{\partial\phi}{\partial x}\hat{i} + \dfrac{\partial\phi}{\partial y}\hat{j} + \dfrac{\partial\phi}{\partial z}\hat{k}$

$$\nabla\phi = (2xy^2 + 2xz^2)\,\hat{i} + (2yx^2 + 2yz^2)\,\hat{j} + (2zy^2 + 2zx^2)\,\hat{k}$$

$$[\nabla\phi]_{(1,1,1)} = 4\hat{i} + 4\hat{j} + 4\hat{k}$$

(v) $\phi = x^3y^3z^3$

We have, $\nabla\phi = \dfrac{\partial\phi}{\partial x}\hat{i} + \dfrac{\partial\phi}{\partial y}\hat{j} + \dfrac{\partial\phi}{\partial z}\hat{k}$

$$\nabla\phi = 3x^2y^3z^3\hat{i} + 3x^3y^2z^3\hat{k} + 3x^3y^3z^2\hat{k}$$

$$[\nabla\phi]_{(1,2,1)} = 24\hat{i} + 12\hat{j} + 24\hat{k}$$

Let $\vec{a} = \hat{i} + 2\hat{j} + 2\hat{k} \Rightarrow |\vec{a}| = \sqrt{1+4+4} = 3$

$$\therefore\ \hat{a} = \frac{\vec{a}}{|\vec{a}|} = \frac{\hat{i} + 2\hat{j} + 2\hat{k}}{3} = \frac{1}{3}\left(\hat{i} + 2\hat{j} + 2\hat{k}\right)$$

$\therefore\ \nabla\phi$ at (1,2,1) along $\vec{a}$ is

$$\nabla\phi\cdot\hat{a} = \left(24\hat{i} + 12\hat{j} + 24\hat{k}\right)\cdot\left[\frac{1}{3}\left(\hat{i} + 2\hat{j} + 2\hat{k}\right)\right] = \frac{1}{3}\,(24 + 24 + 48)$$

$$= \frac{1}{3}\,(96)$$

$$\nabla\phi\cdot\hat{a} = 32$$

2. *Find the unit normal vector to the surface $xy^3z^2 = 4$ at the point* $(-1, -1, 2)$

➡ Let $\phi = xy^3z^2 - 4$

$$\therefore \nabla\phi = \frac{\partial\phi}{\partial x}\hat{i} + \frac{\partial\phi}{\partial y}\hat{j} + \frac{\partial\phi}{\partial z}\hat{k} = y^3z^2\hat{i} + 3xy^2z^2\hat{j} + 2xy^3z\hat{k}$$

$$[\nabla\phi]_{(-1,-1,2)} = -4\hat{i} - 12\hat{j} + 4\hat{k}$$

Therefore, the normal vector to the given surface is

$$\vec{n} = \nabla\phi = -4\hat{i} - 12\hat{j} + 4\hat{k}$$

$$|\vec{n}| = \sqrt{16 + 144 + 16} = \sqrt{176} = 4\sqrt{11}$$

$$\therefore \hat{n} = \frac{\vec{n}}{|\vec{n}|} = -\frac{1}{\sqrt{11}}\hat{i} - \frac{3}{\sqrt{11}}\hat{j} + \frac{1}{\sqrt{11}}\hat{k}$$

3. *Find the unit normal vector to the surface $xy + x + zx = 3$ at* $(1, 1, 1)$

➡ Let $\phi = xy + x + zx - 3$

$$\therefore \nabla\phi = \frac{\partial\phi}{\partial x}\hat{i} + \frac{\partial\phi}{\partial y}\hat{j} + \frac{\partial\phi}{\partial z}\hat{k}$$

$$\nabla\phi = (y + 1 + z)\,\hat{i} + x\hat{j} + x\hat{k}$$

$$[\nabla\phi]_{(1,1,1)} = 3\hat{i} + \hat{j} + \hat{k}$$

Therefore, the normal vector of the given surface is

$$\vec{n} = \nabla\phi = 3\hat{i} + \hat{j} + \hat{k} \Rightarrow |\vec{n}| = \sqrt{9 + 1 + 1} = \sqrt{11}$$

$$\therefore \hat{n} = \frac{\vec{n}}{|\vec{n}|} = \frac{1}{\sqrt{11}}\left(3\hat{i} + \hat{j} + \hat{k}\right)$$

4. *Find the angle between the surfaces $x^2 + y^2 + z^2 = 9$ and $x = z^2 + y^2 - 3$ at* $(2, -1, 2)$

➡ Let $\phi = x^2 + y^2 + z^2 - 9$

$$\nabla\phi = 2x\hat{i} + 2y\hat{j} + 2z\hat{k}$$

$$\therefore \overrightarrow{n_1} = [\nabla\phi]_{(2,-1,2)} = 4\hat{i} - 2\hat{j} + 4\hat{k}$$

$$\left(\overrightarrow{n_1}\right) = \sqrt{16+4+16} = \sqrt{36} = 6$$
$$\psi = z^2 + y^2 - x - 3$$
$$\nabla\psi = -\hat{i} + 2y\hat{j} + 2z\hat{k}$$
$$\therefore\ \overrightarrow{n_2} = [\nabla\psi]_{(2,-1,2)} = -\hat{i} - 2\hat{j} + 4\hat{k}$$
$$\left|\overrightarrow{n_2}\right| = \sqrt{1+4+16} = \sqrt{21}$$
$$\therefore\ \cos\theta = \frac{\overrightarrow{n_1}\cdot\overrightarrow{n_2}}{\left|\overrightarrow{n_1}\right|\left|\overrightarrow{n_2}\right|} = \frac{\left(-\hat{i} - 2\hat{j} + 4\hat{k}\right)\cdot\left(4\hat{i} - 2\hat{j} + 4\hat{k}\right)}{6\sqrt{21}}$$
$$= \frac{-4+4+16}{6\sqrt{21}} = \frac{16}{6\sqrt{21}} = \frac{8}{3\sqrt{21}}$$
$$\theta = \cos^{-1}\left(\frac{8}{3\sqrt{21}}\right)$$

5. *Find the angle between the normals to the surface* $x^2y^2 = z^4$ *at* $(1,1,1)$ *and* $(3,3,-3)$.

➡ Let $\phi = x^2y^2 - z^4$

$$\therefore\ \nabla\phi = 2xy^2\hat{i} + 2x^2y\hat{j} - 4z^3\hat{k}$$

The normal vector at (1,1,1) of the surface ϕ is

$$\overrightarrow{n_1} = [\nabla\phi]_{(1,1,1)} = 2\hat{i} + 2\hat{j} - 4\hat{k}$$
$$\left|\overrightarrow{n_1}\right| = \sqrt{4+4+16} = \sqrt{24} = 2\sqrt{6}$$

and the normal vector at $(3,3,-3)$of the surface ϕ is

$$\overrightarrow{n_2} = [\nabla\phi]_{(3,3,-3)} = 54\hat{i} + 54\hat{j} + 108\hat{k}$$
$$\left|\overrightarrow{n_2}\right| = \sqrt{54^2+54^2+108^2} = \sqrt{54^2+54^2+(2\times 54)^2}$$
$$= \sqrt{54^2\left(1+1+2^2\right)} = 54\sqrt{6}$$
$$\therefore\ \cos\theta = \frac{\overrightarrow{n_1}\cdot\overrightarrow{n_2}}{|n_1|\,|n_2|} = \frac{\left(2\hat{i} + 2\hat{j} - 4\hat{k}\right)\cdot\left(54\hat{i} + 54\hat{j} + 108\hat{k}\right)}{2\sqrt{6}\cdot 54\sqrt{6}}$$

$$= \frac{108 + 108 - 432}{2 \cdot 54 \cdot 6} = \frac{-216}{2 \cdot 54 \cdot 6} = -\frac{1}{3}$$

$$\theta = \cos^{-1}\left(-\frac{1}{3}\right)$$

6. *Find the directional derivative of x^2yz^3 at $(1, 1, 1)$ in the direction of $\hat{i} + \hat{j} + 2\hat{k}$*

➡ Let $\phi = x^2yz^3$

We know that the directional derivative of ϕ along the vector $\vec{a}$ is $\nabla\phi \cdot \hat{a}$

$$\therefore\ \nabla\phi = 2xyz^3\hat{i} + x^2z^3\hat{j} + 3x^2yz^2\hat{k}$$

$$\therefore\ [\nabla\phi]_{(1,1,1,)} = 2\hat{i} + \hat{j} + 3\hat{k}$$

let $\vec{a} = \hat{i} + \hat{j} + 2\hat{k} \Rightarrow |\vec{a}| = \sqrt{1 + 1 + 4} = \sqrt{6}$

$$\hat{a} = \frac{\vec{a}}{|\vec{a}|} = \frac{1}{\sqrt{6}}\left(\hat{i} + \hat{j} + 2\hat{k}\right)$$

Therefore, the directional derivative of ϕ along $\vec{a}$ is

$$\nabla\phi \cdot \hat{a} = \left(2\acute{\imath} + \hat{j} + 3\hat{k}\right) \cdot \frac{\left(\hat{i} + \hat{j} + 2\hat{k}\right)}{\sqrt{6}} = \frac{1}{\sqrt{6}}(2 + 1 + 6)$$

$$\nabla\phi \cdot \hat{a} = \frac{9}{\sqrt{6}}$$

7. *Find the directional derivative of $\phi = \dfrac{xz}{x^2 + y^2}$ at $(1, -1, 1)$ in the direction of $\vec{A} = \hat{i} - 2\hat{j} + \hat{k}$.*

➡ $\phi = \dfrac{xz}{x^2 + y^2}$

$$\nabla\phi = \frac{(x^2 + y^2)\ z - xz\ (2x)}{\left(x^2 + y^2\right)^2}\hat{i} + zx\left(\frac{-1}{\left(x^2 + y^2\right)^2}2y\right)\hat{j} + \frac{x}{x^2 + y^2}\hat{k}$$

$$\therefore\ [\nabla\phi]_{(1,-1,1)} = \left(\frac{2-2}{4}\right)\hat{i} + \frac{2}{4}\hat{j} + \frac{1}{2}\hat{k} = \frac{1}{2}\hat{j} + \frac{1}{2}\hat{k}$$

and $\vec{A} = \hat{\imath} - 2\hat{\imath} + \hat{k} \Rightarrow \left|\vec{A}\right| = \sqrt{1+4+1} = \sqrt{6}$

$$\therefore\ \hat{A} = \frac{1}{\sqrt{6}}\left(\hat{\imath} - 2\hat{\jmath} + \hat{k}\right)$$

Therefore, the directional derivative of ϕ in the direction of $\vec{A}$ is

$$\nabla\phi \cdot \hat{A} = \left(\frac{1}{2}\hat{\jmath} + \frac{1}{2}\hat{k}\right) \cdot \frac{1}{\sqrt{6}}\left(\hat{\imath} - 2\hat{\jmath} + k\right) = \frac{1}{\sqrt{6}}\left(0 + \frac{1}{2}(-2) + \frac{1}{2}(1)\right)$$

$$\nabla\phi \cdot \hat{A} = -\frac{1}{2\sqrt{6}}$$

8. *If* $\vec{F} = 2x^2\hat{\imath} - 3yz\hat{\jmath} + xz^2\hat{k}$ *and* $\phi = 2z - x^3y$, *find* $\vec{F} \cdot (\nabla\phi)$ *and* $\vec{F} \times (\nabla\phi)$ *at* $(1, -1, 1)$.

➡ $\phi = 2z - x^3y$

$$\nabla\phi = \frac{\partial\phi}{\partial x}\hat{\imath} + \frac{\partial\phi}{\partial y}\hat{\jmath} + \frac{\partial\phi}{\partial z}\hat{k} = -3x^2y\hat{\imath} - x^3\hat{\jmath} + 2\hat{k}$$

$$[\nabla\phi]_{(1,-1,1)} = 3\hat{\imath} - \hat{\jmath} + 2\hat{k}$$

$$\vec{F} = 2x^2\hat{\imath} - 3yz\hat{\jmath} + xz^2\hat{k}$$

$$\left[\vec{F}\right]_{(1,-1,1)} = 2\hat{\imath} + 3\hat{\jmath} + \hat{k}$$

$$\therefore\ \vec{F} \cdot \nabla\phi = \left(2\hat{\imath} + 3\hat{\jmath} + \hat{k}\right) \cdot \left(3\hat{\imath} - \hat{\jmath} + 2\hat{k}\right) = 6 - 3 + 2 = 5$$

$$\vec{F} \times \nabla\phi = \begin{vmatrix} \hat{\imath} & \hat{\jmath} & \hat{k} \\ 2 & 3 & 1 \\ 3 & -1 & 2 \end{vmatrix} = \hat{\imath}\,(6+1) - \hat{\jmath}\,(4-3) + \hat{k}\,(-2-9)$$

$$\vec{F} \times \nabla\phi = 7\hat{\imath} - \hat{\jmath} - 11\hat{k}$$

9. *If* $\vec{F} = x^2y\hat{\imath} + yz^2\hat{\jmath} + zx^2\hat{k}$ *and* $\phi = xy + yz + zx$, *then find*

(i) grad $\left(\text{div}\vec{F}\right)$ (ii) div $\left(\text{curl}\vec{F}\right)$ (iii) curl (gradϕ)

(iv) div (gradϕ) (v) curl $\left(\text{curl}\vec{F}\right)$ (vi) div $\left(\phi\vec{F}\right)$

(vii) $\text{curl}\vec{F} \times \text{grad}\phi$ at (1,1,1) (viii) $\text{curl}\left(\text{grad}\left(\text{div}\vec{F}\right)\right)$

➡ (i) $\vec{F} = x^2y\hat{i} + yz^2\hat{j} + zx^2\hat{k}$

$$\text{div}\vec{F} = 2xy + z^2 + x^2$$

$$\text{grad}\left(\text{div}\vec{F}\right) = (2y + 2x)\ \hat{i} + 2x\hat{j} + 2z\hat{k}$$

(ii) $\text{curl}\ \vec{F} = \nabla \times \vec{F} = \begin{vmatrix} \hat{i} & \hat{j} & \hat{k} \\ \dfrac{\partial}{\partial x} & \dfrac{\partial}{\partial y} & \dfrac{\partial}{\partial z} \\ x^2y & yz^2 & zx^2 \end{vmatrix}$

$$= \hat{i}\,(0 - 2yz) - \hat{j}\ (2xz - 0) + \hat{k}\left(0 - x^2\right)$$

$$\text{curl}\vec{F} = -2yz\hat{i} - 2xz\hat{j} - x^2\hat{k}$$

$$\therefore\ \text{div}\left(\text{curl}\vec{F}\right) = \frac{\partial}{\partial x}(-2yz) + \frac{\partial}{\partial y}(-2xz) + \frac{\partial}{\partial z}\left(-x^2\right) = 0 + 0 + 0$$

$$\text{div}\left(\text{curl}\vec{F}\right) = 0$$

(iii) $\text{grad}\ \phi = \nabla\phi = \dfrac{\partial\phi}{\partial x}\hat{i} + \dfrac{\partial\phi}{\partial y}\hat{j} + \dfrac{\partial\phi}{\partial z}\hat{k}$

$$= (y + z)\ \hat{i} + (x + z)\,\hat{j} + (x + y)\ \hat{k}$$

$$\text{curl}\,(\text{grad}\phi) = \nabla \times (\nabla\phi) = \begin{vmatrix} \hat{i} & \hat{j} & \hat{k} \\ \dfrac{\partial}{\partial x} & \dfrac{\partial}{\partial y} & \dfrac{\partial}{\partial z} \\ y + z & x + z & x + y \end{vmatrix}$$

$$= \hat{i}\,(1 - 1) - \hat{j}\,(1 - 1) + \hat{k}\,(1 - 1)$$

$$\text{curl}\,(\text{grad}\phi) = 0$$

(iv) We have,

$$\text{grad}\phi = \nabla\phi = (y + z)\ \hat{i} + (x + z)\ \hat{j} + (x + y)\ \hat{k}$$

$$\text{div}\,(\text{grad}\phi) = \nabla\cdot(\nabla\phi) = \frac{\partial}{\partial x}(y + z) + \frac{\partial}{\partial y}(x + z) + \frac{\partial}{\partial z}(x + y)$$

$$\text{div}\,(\text{grad}\phi) = 0$$

(v) From (ii) we have,

$$\text{curl}\vec{F} = -2yz\hat{i} - 2xz\hat{j} - x^2\hat{k}$$

$$\text{curl}(\text{curl}\vec{F}) = \begin{vmatrix} \hat{i} & \hat{j} & \hat{k} \\ \dfrac{\partial}{\partial x} & \dfrac{\partial}{\partial y} & \dfrac{\partial}{\partial z} \\ -2yz & -2xz & -x^2 \end{vmatrix}$$

$$= \hat{i}\ (0 + 2x) - \hat{j}\ (-2x + 2y) + \hat{k}\ (-2z + 2z)$$

$$\text{curl}(\text{curl}\vec{F}) = 2x\hat{i} + (2x - 2y)\ \hat{j}$$

(vi) $\vec{F} = x^2y\hat{i} + yz^2\hat{j} + zx^2\hat{k}$

$$\phi = xy + yz + zx$$

$$\therefore\ \phi\vec{F} = (x^3y^2 + x^2y^2z + x^3yz)\ \hat{i} + (xy^2z^2 + y^2z^3 + xyz^3)\ \hat{j} + (x^3yz + x^2yz^2 + x^3z^2)\ \hat{k}$$

$$\text{div}(\phi\vec{F}) = (3x^2y^2 + 2xy^2z + 3x^2yz) + (2xyz^2 + 2yz^3 + xz^3) + (x^3y + 2x^2yz + 2x^3z)$$

$$= 3x^2y^2 + 2xy^2z + 5x^2yz + 2xyz^2 + 2yz^3 + xz^3 + x^3y + 2x^3z$$

(vii) From (ii) we have, $\text{curl}\vec{F} = \nabla \times \vec{F} = -2yz\hat{i} - 2xz\hat{j} - x^2\hat{k}$

$$\left[\text{curl}\vec{F}\right]_{(1,1,1)} = -2\hat{i} - 2\hat{j} - \hat{k}$$

From (iii) we have, $\text{grad}\phi = \nabla\phi = (y + z)\ \hat{i} + (x + z)\ \hat{j} + (x + y)\ \hat{k}$

$$\left[\text{grad}\phi\right]_{(1,1,1)} = 2\hat{i} + 2\hat{j} + 2\hat{k}$$

$$\therefore\ \text{curl}\vec{F} \times \text{grad}\phi = \begin{vmatrix} \hat{i} & \hat{j} & \hat{k} \\ -2 & -2 & -1 \\ 2 & 2 & 2 \end{vmatrix}$$

$$= \hat{i}\ (-4 + 2) - \hat{j}\ (-4 + 2) + \hat{k}\ (-4 + 4)$$

$$\text{curl}\vec{F} \times \text{grad}\phi = -2\hat{i} + 2\hat{j}$$

(viii) From (i) we have,

$$\text{grad}\left(\text{div}\vec{F}\right) = (2y + 2x)\ \hat{i} + 2x\hat{j} + 2z\hat{k}$$

$$\text{curl}\left[\text{grad}\left(\text{div}\vec{F}\right)\right] = \begin{vmatrix} \hat{i} & \hat{j} & \hat{k} \\ \dfrac{\partial}{\partial x} & \dfrac{\partial}{\partial y} & \dfrac{\partial}{\partial z} \\ 2y + 2x & 2x & 2z \end{vmatrix}$$

$$= \hat{i}\ (0 - 0) - \hat{j}\ (0 - 0) + \hat{k}\ (2 - 2)$$

$$\text{curl}\left[\text{grad}\left(\text{div}\vec{F}\right)\right] = 0$$

10. *Find divergence and curl of the vector* $\vec{F} = \left(xyz + y^2z\right)\ \hat{i} + \left(3x^2 + y^2z\right)\ \hat{j} + \left(xz^2 - y^2z\right)\ \hat{k}$

➡ $\vec{F} = \left(xyz + y^2z\right)\ \hat{i} + \left(3x^2 + y^2z\right)\ \hat{j} + \left(xz^2 - y^2z\right)\ \hat{k}$

$$\text{div}\vec{F} = \frac{\partial}{\partial x}\left(xyz + y^2z\right) + \frac{\partial}{\partial y}\left(3x^2 + y^2z\right) + \frac{\partial}{\partial z}\left(xz^2 - y^2z\right)$$

$$= yz + 2yz + 2xz - y^2$$

$$\text{div}\vec{F} = 3yz + 2xz - y^2$$

$$\text{curl}\vec{F} = \begin{vmatrix} \hat{i} & \hat{j} & \hat{k} \\ \dfrac{\partial}{\partial x} & \dfrac{\partial}{\partial y} & \dfrac{\partial}{\partial z} \\ xyz + y^2z & 3x^2 + y^2z & xz^2 - y^2z \end{vmatrix}$$

$$= \hat{i}\left(-2yz - y^2\right) - \hat{j}\left(z^2 - xy - y^2\right) + \hat{k}\ (6x - xz - 2yz)$$

$$= -\left(2yz + y^2\right)\ \hat{i} - \left(z^2 - xy - y^2\right)\hat{j} + (6x - xz - 2yz)\ \hat{k}$$

11. *Find* $\text{div}\vec{F}$ *and* $\text{curl}\vec{F}$, *where* $\vec{F} = \nabla\left(x^3 + y^3 + z^3 - 3xyz\right)$

➡ $F = \nabla\left(x^3 + y^3 + z^3 - 3xyz\right)$

$$= \frac{\partial}{\partial x}\left(x^3 + y^3 + z^3 - 3xyz\right)\ \hat{i} + \frac{\partial}{\partial y}\left(x^3 + y^3 + z^3 - 3xyz\right)\hat{j}$$

$$+ \frac{\partial}{\partial z}\left(x^3 + y^3 + z^3 - 3xyz\right)\hat{k}$$

$$\vec{F} = \left(3x^2 - 3yz\right)\hat{i} + \left(3y^2 - 3xz\right)\hat{j} + \left(3z^2 - 3xy\right)\hat{k}$$

$$\text{div}\vec{F} = 6x + 6y + 6z$$

and

$$\text{curl}\vec{F} = \begin{vmatrix} \hat{i} & \hat{j} & \hat{k} \\ \dfrac{\partial}{\partial x} & \dfrac{\partial}{\partial y} & \dfrac{\partial}{\partial z} \\ 3x^2 - 3yz & 3y^2 - 3xz & 3z^2 - 3xy \end{vmatrix}$$

$$= \hat{i}\,(-3x + 3x) - \hat{j}\,(-3y + 3y) + \hat{k}\,(-3z + 3z)$$

$$\text{curl}\vec{F} = 0$$

12. *If* $\vec{F} = \text{grad}\left(x^3y + y^3z + z^3x - x^2y^2z^2\right)$ *then find* $\text{div}\vec{F}$ *at* $(1, 1, 1)$

➡ $\vec{F} = \text{grad}\left(x^3y + y^3z + z^3x - x^2y^2z^2\right) = \nabla\left(x^3y + y^3z + z^3x - x^2y^2z^2\right)$

$$\vec{F} = \left(3x^2y + z^3 - 2xy^2z^2\right)\hat{i} + \left(x^3 + 3y^2z - 2x^2yz^2\right)\hat{j} + \left(y^3 + 3z^2x - 2x^2y^2z\right)\hat{k}$$

$$\text{div}\vec{F} = 6xy - 2y^2z^2 + 6yz - 2x^2z^2 + 6zx - 2x^2y^2$$

$$[\text{div}\vec{F}]_{(1,1,1)} = 6 - 2 + 6 - 2 + 6 - 2 = 12$$

13. *If* $\vec{F} = (x + y + 1)\,\hat{i} + \hat{j} - (x + y)\,\hat{k}$, *show that* $\vec{F} \cdot \text{curl}\vec{F} = 0$

➡ $\vec{F} = (x + y + 1)\,\hat{i} + \hat{j} - (x + y)\,\hat{k}$

$$\text{curl}\vec{F} = \nabla \times \vec{F} = \begin{vmatrix} \hat{i} & \hat{j} & \hat{k} \\ \dfrac{\partial}{\partial x} & \dfrac{\partial}{\partial y} & \dfrac{\partial}{\partial z} \\ x + y + 1 & 1 & -(x + y) \end{vmatrix}$$

$$= \hat{i}\,(-1 - 0) - \hat{j}\,(-1 - 0) + \hat{k}\,(0 - 1)$$

$$\text{curl}\vec{F} = -\hat{i} + \hat{j} - \hat{k}$$

$$\therefore\ \vec{F} \cdot \text{curl}\vec{F} = ((x + y + 1)\,\hat{i} + \hat{j} - (x + y)\,\hat{k}) \cdot (-\hat{i} + \hat{j} - \hat{k})$$

$$= -(x + y + 1) + 1 + (x + y)$$

$$\vec{F} \cdot \text{curl}\vec{F} = 0$$

14. *If* $\vec{F} = (3x^2y - z)\,\hat{i} + (xz^3 + y^4)\,\hat{j} - 2x^3z^2\hat{k}$, *then find* $\nabla \cdot \vec{F}$, $\nabla \times \vec{F}$ *and* $\nabla \cdot (\nabla \times \vec{F})$ *at* $(2, -1, 0)$

➡ $\vec{F} = (3x^2y - z)\,\hat{i} + (xz^3 + y^4)\,\hat{j} - 2x^3z^2\hat{k}$

$$\nabla \cdot \vec{F} = 6xy + 4y^3 - 4x^3z$$

$$[\nabla \cdot \vec{F}]_{(2,-1,0)} = -12 - 4 - 0 = -16$$

$$\nabla \times \vec{F} = \begin{vmatrix} \hat{i} & \hat{j} & \hat{k} \\ \dfrac{\partial}{\partial x} & \dfrac{\partial}{\partial y} & \dfrac{\partial}{\partial z} \\ 3x^2y - z & xz^3 + y^4 & -2x^3z^2 \end{vmatrix}$$

$$= \hat{i}(0 - 3xz^2) - \hat{j}(-6x^2z^2 + 1) + \hat{k}(z^3 - 3x^2)$$

$$\nabla \times \vec{F} = -3xz^2\hat{i} + (6x^2z^2 - 1)\,\hat{j} + (z^3 - 3x^2)\,\hat{k}$$

$$\therefore\ [\nabla \times F]_{(2,-1,0)} = -\hat{j} - 12\hat{k}$$

$$\therefore\ \nabla \cdot (\nabla \times \vec{F}) = -3z^2 + 0 + 3z^2 = 0$$

$$\nabla \cdot (\nabla \times \vec{F}) = 0$$

15. *If* $\vec{A} = xz^3\hat{i} - 2x^2yz\hat{j} + 2yz^4\hat{k}$, *then find* $\text{grad}\left(\text{div}\vec{A}\right)$ *at* $(1, -1, 1)$

$$\vec{A} = xz^3\hat{i} - 2x^2yz\hat{j} + 2yz^4\hat{k}$$

$$\text{div}\vec{A} = \nabla \cdot \vec{A} = z^3 - 2x^2z + 8yz^3$$

$$\therefore\ \text{grad}\left(\text{div}\vec{A}\right) = (-4xz)\,\hat{i} + 8z^3\,\hat{j} + \left(3z^2 - 2x^2 + 24yz^2\right)\,\hat{k}$$

$$\left[\text{grad}\left(\text{div}\vec{A}\right)\right]_{(1,-1,1)} = -4\hat{i} + 8\hat{j} - 23\hat{k}$$

16. *Find* $\text{curl}\left(\text{curl}\vec{A}\right)$ *where* $\vec{A} = xy\,\hat{i} + y^2z\,\hat{j} + z^2y\,\hat{k}$

➡ $\vec{A} = xy\,\hat{i} + y^2z\,\hat{j} + z^2y\,\hat{k}$

$$\text{curl}\vec{A} = \begin{vmatrix} \hat{i} & \hat{j} & \hat{k} \\ \dfrac{\partial}{\partial x} & \dfrac{\partial}{\partial y} & \dfrac{\partial}{\partial z} \\ xy & y^2z & z^2y \end{vmatrix} = \hat{i}\ \left(z^2 - y^2\right) - \hat{j}\ (0 - 0) + \hat{k}\ (0 - x)$$

$$\text{curl}\vec{A} = \left(z^2 - y^2\right)\hat{i} - x\hat{k}$$

$$\therefore \text{ curl}\left(\text{curl}\vec{A}\right) = \begin{vmatrix} \hat{i} & \hat{j} & \hat{k} \\ \dfrac{\partial}{\partial x} & \dfrac{\partial}{\partial y} & \dfrac{\partial}{\partial z} \\ z^2 - y^2 & 0 & -x \end{vmatrix}$$

$$= \hat{i}\,(0 - 0) - \hat{j}\,(-1 - 2z) + \hat{k}\,(0 + 2y)$$

$$\text{curl}\left(\text{curl}\vec{A}\right) = (2z + 1)\,\hat{j} + 2y\hat{k}$$

17. *If $\phi = x^2 + y^2 + z^2$, find $\nabla^2\phi$*
➡ $\phi = x^2 + y^2 + z^2$
We have,

$$\nabla^2\phi = \frac{\partial^2\phi}{\partial x^2} + \frac{\partial^2\phi}{\partial y^2} + \frac{\partial^2\phi}{\partial z^2}$$

$$\frac{\partial\phi}{\partial x} = 2x \Rightarrow \frac{\partial^2\phi}{\partial x^2} = 2$$

$$\frac{\partial\phi}{\partial y} = 2y \Rightarrow \frac{\partial^2\phi}{\partial y^2} = 2$$

$$\frac{\partial\phi}{\partial z} = 2z \Rightarrow \frac{\partial^2\phi}{\partial z^2} = 2$$

$$\nabla^2\phi = 2 + 2 + 2$$

$$\nabla^2\phi = 6$$

18. *If $\phi = xy + yz + zx$, find $\nabla \cdot (\nabla\phi)$ and verify that $\nabla \cdot (\nabla\phi) = \nabla^2\phi$*
➡ $\phi = xy + yz + zx$

$$\nabla\phi = \frac{\partial\phi}{\partial x}\hat{i} + \frac{\partial\phi}{\partial y}\hat{j} + \frac{\partial\phi}{\partial z}\hat{k}$$

$$\nabla\phi = (y + z)\,\hat{i} + (x + z)\,\hat{j} + (x + y)\,\hat{k}$$

$$\therefore\ \nabla\cdot(\nabla\phi) = \frac{\partial}{\partial x}(y+z) + \frac{\partial}{\partial y}(x+z) + \frac{\partial}{\partial z}(x+y) = 0+0+0$$

$$\therefore\ \nabla\cdot(\nabla\phi) = 0 \qquad (1)$$

We know that

$$\nabla^2\phi = \left(\frac{\partial^2}{\partial x^2} + \frac{\partial^2}{\partial y^2} + \frac{\partial^2}{\partial z^2}\right)\phi$$

$$= \left(\frac{\partial^2}{\partial x^2} + \frac{\partial^2}{\partial y^2} + \frac{\partial^2}{\partial z^2}\right)(xy+yz+zx)$$

$$= \frac{\partial}{\partial x}(y+z) + \frac{\partial}{\partial y}(x+z) + \frac{\partial}{\partial z}(x+y) = 0+0+0$$

$$\nabla^2\phi = 0 \qquad (2)$$

From equations (1) and (2), we get

$$\therefore\ \nabla\cdot\nabla\phi = \nabla^2\phi$$

19. *Show that the vector field $\vec{F} = yz\hat{i} + xz\hat{j} + xy\hat{k}$ is solenoidal vector.*

➡ We know that a vector field $\vec{F}$ is said to be solenoidal if $\nabla\cdot\vec{F} = 0$

$$\vec{F} = yz\hat{i} + xz\hat{j} + xy\hat{k}$$

$$\nabla\cdot\vec{F} = \frac{\partial}{\partial x}(yz) + \frac{\partial}{\partial y}(xz) + \frac{\partial}{\partial z}(xy) = 0+0+0$$

$$\nabla\cdot\vec{F} = 0$$

Hence, $\vec{F}$ is solenoidal.

20. *Show that the vector field $\vec{F} = (3x+3y+4z)\,\hat{i} + (x-2y+3z)\,\hat{j} + (3x+2y-z)\,\hat{k}$ is solenoidal.*

➡ $\vec{F} = (3x+3y+4z)\,\hat{i} + (x-2y+3z)\,\hat{j} + (3x+2y-z)\,\hat{k}$

$$\nabla\cdot\vec{F} = \frac{\partial}{\partial x}(3x+3y+4z) + \frac{\partial}{\partial y}(x-2y+3z) + \frac{\partial}{\partial z}(3x+2y-z)$$

$$= 3-2-1$$

$$\nabla \cdot \vec{F} = 0$$

Hence, F is solenoidal.

21. *If* $\vec{F} = (ax+3y+4z)\,\hat{i} + (x-2y+3z)\,\hat{j} + (3x+2y-z)\,\hat{k}$ *is solenoidal, find 'a'.*

➡ $\vec{F} = (ax+3y+4z)\,\hat{i} + (x-2y+3z)\,\hat{j} + (3x+2y-z)\,\hat{k}$

$$\nabla \cdot \vec{F} = \frac{\partial}{\partial x}(ax+3y+4z) + \frac{\partial}{\partial y}(x-2y+3z) + \frac{\partial}{\partial z}(3x+2y-z)$$

$$= a - 2 - 1$$

$$\nabla \cdot \vec{F} = a - 3 \qquad (1)$$

It is given that $\vec{F}$ is solenoidal i.e., $\nabla \cdot \vec{F} = 0 \Rightarrow a - 3 = 0$

$$a = 3$$

22. *If* $\vec{f} = x^2\hat{i} + y^2\hat{j} + z^2\hat{k}$, $\vec{g} = yz\hat{i} + zx\hat{j} + xy\hat{k}$ *show that* $\vec{f} \times \vec{g}$ *is solenoidal.*

➡

$$\vec{f} \times \vec{g} = \begin{vmatrix} \hat{i} & \hat{j} & \hat{k} \\ x^2 & y^2 & z^2 \\ yz & zx & xy \end{vmatrix}$$

$$= \hat{i}\left(xy^3 - xz^3\right) - \hat{j}\left(x^3y - yz^3\right) + \hat{k}\left(x^3z - y^3z\right)$$

$$\vec{f} \times \vec{g} = x\left(y^3 - z^3\right)\hat{i} - y\left(x^3 - z^3\right)\hat{j} + z\left(x^3 - y^3\right)\hat{k}$$

$$\nabla \cdot \left(\vec{f} \times \vec{g}\right) = \frac{\partial}{\partial x}\left[x\left(y^3 - z^3\right)\right] - \frac{\partial}{\partial y}\left[y\left(x^3 - z^3\right)\right] + \frac{\partial}{\partial z}\left[z\left(x^3 - y^3\right)\right]$$

$$= y^3 - z^3 - \left(x^3 - z^3\right) + x^3 - y^3$$

$$\nabla \cdot \left(\vec{f} \times \vec{g}\right) = 0$$

Therefore, $\vec{f} \times \vec{g}$ is solenoidal vector field.

23. *Show that the vector* $\vec{F} = \left(3x^2 - 2yz\right)\hat{i} + \left(3y^2 - 2zx\right)\hat{j} + \left(3z^2 - 2xy\right)\hat{k}$ *is irrotational and find* ϕ *such that* $\vec{F} = \text{grad}\phi$.

➡ A vector field $\vec{F}$ is said to be irrotational or conservative force field if curl$\vec{F} = 0$ i.e., $\nabla \times \vec{F} = 0$

$$\vec{F} = \left(3x^2 - 2yz\right)\hat{i} + \left(3y^2 - 2zx\right)\hat{j} + \left(3z^2 - 2xy\right)\hat{k}$$

$$\nabla \times \vec{F} = \begin{vmatrix} \hat{i} & \hat{j} & \hat{k} \\ \dfrac{\partial}{\partial x} & \dfrac{\partial}{\partial y} & \dfrac{\partial}{\partial z} \\ 3x^2 - 2yz & 3y^2 - 2zx & 3z^2 - 2xy \end{vmatrix}$$

$$= \hat{i}\,[-2x + 2x] - \hat{j}\,[-2y + 2y] + \hat{k}\,[-2z + 2z]$$

$$\nabla \times \vec{F} = 0$$

$\therefore$ $\vec{F}$ is irrotational.
To find ϕ given $\vec{F} = \nabla\phi$i.e.,

$$\left(3x^2 - 2yz\right)\hat{i} + \left(3y^2 - 2zx\right)\hat{j} + \left(3z^2 - 2xy\right)\hat{k} = \frac{\partial\phi}{\partial x}\hat{i} + \frac{\partial\phi}{\partial y}\hat{j} + \frac{\partial\phi}{\partial z}\hat{k}$$

$$\therefore \quad \frac{\partial\phi}{\partial x} = 3x^2 - 2yz \qquad (1)$$

$$\frac{\partial\phi}{\partial y} = 3y^2 - 2xz \qquad (2)$$

$$\frac{\partial\phi}{\partial z} = 3z^2 - 2xy \qquad (3)$$

(1) gives $\phi = \int \left(3x^2 - 2yz\right) dx = x^3 - 2xyz + f_1(y, z)$
(treating y and z as constants)

(2) gives $\phi = \int \left(3y^2 - 2xz\right) dy = y^3 - 2xyz + f_2(x, z)$
(treating x and z as constants)

(3) gives $\phi = \int \left(3z^2 - 2xy\right) dz = z^3 - 2xyz + f_3(x, y)$
(treating x and y as constants)

Therefore, $\phi = x^3 + y^3 + z^3 - 2xyz$.

24. *Show that $\vec{F} = \left(2xy + z^2\right)\hat{i} + \left(x^2 + 2yz\right)\hat{j} + \left(y^2 + 2xz\right)\hat{k}$ is conservative force field and find the scalar potential.*

➡ $\vec{F} = (2xy + z^2)\,\hat{i} + (x^2 + 2yz)\,\hat{j} + (y^2 + 2xz)\,\hat{k}$

$$\nabla \times \vec{F} = \begin{vmatrix} \hat{i} & \hat{j} & \hat{k} \\ \dfrac{\partial}{\partial x} & \dfrac{\partial}{\partial y} & \dfrac{\partial}{\partial z} \\ 2xy + z^2 & x^2 + 2yz & y^2 + 2xz \end{vmatrix}$$

$$= \hat{i}\,(2y - 2y) - \hat{j}\,(2z - 2z) + \hat{k}\,(2x - 2x)$$

$$\nabla \times \vec{F} = 0$$

Therefore, $\vec{F}$ is conservative force field.
Hence, $\vec{F} = \nabla\phi$ i.e.,

$$(2xy + z^2)\,\hat{i} + (x^2 + 2yz)\,\hat{j} + (y^2 + 2xz)\,\hat{k} = \frac{\partial\phi}{\partial x}\hat{i} + \frac{\partial\phi}{\partial y}\hat{j} + \frac{\partial\phi}{\partial z}\hat{k}$$

$$\therefore\ \frac{\partial\phi}{\partial x} = 2xy + z^2 \Rightarrow \phi = x^2y + z^2x + f_1(y, z) \tag{1}$$

$$\frac{\partial\phi}{\partial y} = x^2 + 2yz \Rightarrow \phi = x^2y + y^2z + f_2(x, z) \tag{2}$$

$$\frac{\partial\phi}{\partial z} = y^2 + 2xz \Rightarrow \phi = y^2z + xz^2 + f_3(x, y) \tag{3}$$

Therefore, from equations (1), (2) and (3), we get

$$\phi = x^2y + y^2z + z^2x$$

25. *Find the constant 'a' such that the vector field $\vec{F} = 2xy^2z^2\hat{i} + 2x^2yz^2\hat{j} + ax^2y^2z\hat{k}$ is irrotational.*

➡ Given that $\vec{F}$ is irrotational vector.
Therefore, $\nabla \times \vec{F} = 0$

$$\begin{vmatrix} \hat{i} & \hat{j} & \hat{k} \\ \dfrac{\partial}{\partial x} & \dfrac{\partial}{\partial y} & \dfrac{\partial}{\partial z} \\ 2xy^2z^2 & 2yx^2z^2 & ax^2y^2z \end{vmatrix} = 0$$

$$\hat{i}\,(2ax^2yz - 4yx^2z) - \hat{j}\,(2axy^2z - 4xy^2z) + \hat{k}\,(4xyz^2 - 4xyz^2) = 0$$

$$2(a-2)x^2yz\hat{i} - 2(a-2)xy^2z\hat{j} = 0$$
$$\Rightarrow 2(a-2)x^2yz = 0 \text{ and } 2(a-2)xy^2z = 0$$

The above equations are identically substituted when

$$a - 2 = 0 \Rightarrow a = 2$$

26. *Find the constants a, b, c such that the vector* $\vec{F} = (x+y+az)\,\hat{i} + (x+cy+2z)\,\hat{k} + (bx+2y-z)\,\hat{j}$ *is irrotational.*

➡

$$\vec{F} = (x+y+az)\,\hat{i} + (x+cy+2z)\,\hat{k} + (bx+2y-z)\,\hat{j}$$
$$\vec{F} = (x+y+az)\,\hat{i} + (bx+2y-z)\,\hat{j} + (x+cy+2z)\,\hat{k}$$

Given that the vector field is irrotational. Therefore $\nabla \times \vec{F} = 0$

$$\begin{vmatrix} \hat{i} & \hat{j} & \hat{k} \\ \dfrac{\partial}{\partial x} & \dfrac{\partial}{\partial y} & \dfrac{\partial}{\partial z} \\ x+y+az & bx+2y-z & x+cy+2z \end{vmatrix} = 0$$

$$\hat{i}\,(c+1) - \hat{j}\,(1-a) + \hat{k}\,(b-1) = 0$$

This is possible only when

$$c+1 = 0, \quad 1-a = 0, \quad b-1 = 0$$
$$c = -1, \quad a = 1, \quad b = 1$$

27. *Find the constants 'a', 'b', 'c' such that the vector field* $(\sin y + az)\,\hat{i} + (bx\cos y + z)\,\hat{j} + (x+cy)\,\hat{k}$ *is irrotational. Also find the scalar field* ϕ *such that* $\vec{F} = \nabla\phi$.

➡ Given that the vector field

$$\vec{F} = (\sin y + az)\,\hat{i} + (bx\cos y + z)\,\hat{j} + (x+cy)\,\hat{k}$$

irrotational vector field. Therefore, $\nabla \times \vec{F} = 0$

$$\begin{vmatrix} \hat{i} & \hat{j} & \hat{k} \\ \dfrac{\partial}{\partial x} & \dfrac{\partial}{\partial y} & \dfrac{\partial}{\partial z} \\ \sin y + az & bx\cos y + z & x + cy \end{vmatrix} = 0$$

$$\hat{i}\,(c-1) - \hat{j}\,(1-a) + \hat{k}\,(b\cos y - \cos y) = 0$$

$$(c-1)\,\hat{i} - (1-a)\,\hat{j} + (b-1)\cos y\hat{k} = 0$$

This is possible only when

$$c - 1 = 0, \quad 1 - a = 0, \quad b - 1 = 0$$

$$\Rightarrow a = 1, \quad b = 1, \quad c = 1$$

$$\therefore\ \vec{F} = (\sin y + z)\,\hat{i} + (x\cos y + z)\,\hat{j} + (x + y)\,\hat{k}$$

Given that, $\vec{F} = \nabla\phi$

$$(\sin y + z)\,\hat{i} + (x\cos y + z)\,\hat{j} + (x + y)\,\hat{k} = \frac{\partial\phi}{\partial x}\hat{i} + \frac{\partial\phi}{\partial y}\hat{j} + \frac{\partial\phi}{\partial z}\hat{k}$$

$$\Rightarrow \frac{\partial\phi}{\partial x} = \sin y + z \Rightarrow \phi = x\sin y + xz + f_1\,(y,z)$$

$$\frac{\partial\phi}{\partial y} = x\cos y + z \Rightarrow \phi = x\sin y + yz + f_2\,(x,z)$$

$$\frac{\partial\phi}{\partial z} = x + y \Rightarrow \phi = xz + yz + f_3\,(x,y)$$

$$\therefore\ \phi = x\sin y + yz + xz$$

28. *Find the constants 'a' and 'b' so that* $\vec{F} = \left(axy + z^3\right)\hat{i} + \left(3x^2 - z\right)\hat{j} + \left(bxz^2 - y\right)\hat{k}$ *is irrotational and find* ϕ *such that* $\vec{F} = \nabla\phi$.

➡ $\vec{F} = \left(axy + z^3\right)\hat{i} + \left(3x^2 - z\right)\hat{j} + \left(bxz^2 - y\right)\hat{k}$

Given that F is irrotational i.e., $\nabla \times \vec{F} = 0$

$$\begin{vmatrix} \hat{i} & \hat{j} & \hat{k} \\ \dfrac{\partial}{\partial x} & \dfrac{\partial}{\partial y} & \dfrac{\partial}{\partial z} \\ axy + z^3 & 3x^2 - z & bxz^2 - y \end{vmatrix} = 0$$

$$i\,(-1+1) - \hat{j}\left(bz^2 - 3z^2\right) + \hat{k}\,(6x - ax) = 0$$

$$-\,z^2\,(b-3)\,\hat{j} + x\,(6-a)\,\hat{k} = 0$$

$$\Rightarrow b = 3 \quad a = 6$$

$$\therefore\ \vec{F} = \left(6xy + z^3\right)\hat{i} + \left(3x^2 - z\right)\hat{j} + \left(3xz^2 - y\right)\hat{k}$$

Given, $\nabla\phi = \vec{F}$

$$\frac{\partial\phi}{\partial x}\hat{i} + \frac{\partial\phi}{\partial y}\hat{j} + \frac{\partial\phi}{\partial z}\hat{k} = \left(6xy + z^3\right)\hat{i} + \left(3x^2 - z\right)\hat{j} + \left(3xz^2 - y\right)\hat{k}$$

$$\therefore\ \frac{\partial\phi}{\partial x} = 6xy + z^3 \Rightarrow \phi = 3x^2y + xz^3 + f_1(y,z)$$

$$\frac{\partial\phi}{\partial y} = 3x^2 - z \Rightarrow \phi = 3x^2y - yz + f_2(x,z)$$

$$\frac{\partial\phi}{\partial z} = 3xz^2 - y \Rightarrow \phi = xz^3 - yz + f_3(x,y)$$

Hence, $\phi = 3x^2y + xz^3 - yz$

29. *Show that the vector* $\vec{F} = \dfrac{\left(x\hat{i} + y\hat{j} + z\hat{k}\right)}{\sqrt{x^2+y^2+z^2}}$ *is irrotational.*

➡ Let $r^2 = x^2 + y^2 + z^2$

$$2r\frac{\partial r}{\partial x} = 2x \Rightarrow \frac{\partial r}{\partial x} = \frac{x}{r} \text{ Similarly, } \frac{\partial r}{\partial y} = \frac{y}{r}, \quad \frac{\partial r}{\partial z} = \frac{z}{r}$$

$$\therefore\ \vec{F} = \frac{x}{r}\hat{i} + \frac{y}{r}\hat{j} + \frac{z}{r}\hat{k}$$

$$\nabla \times \vec{F} = \begin{vmatrix} \hat{i} & \hat{j} & \hat{k} \\ \dfrac{\partial}{\partial x} & \dfrac{\partial}{\partial y} & \dfrac{\partial}{\partial z} \\ \dfrac{x}{r} & \dfrac{y}{r} & \dfrac{z}{r} \end{vmatrix}$$

$$= \hat{i}\left[\frac{\partial}{\partial y}\left(\frac{z}{r}\right) - \frac{\partial}{\partial z}\left(\frac{y}{r}\right)\right] - \hat{j}\left[\frac{\partial}{\partial x}\left(\frac{z}{r}\right) - \frac{\partial}{\partial z}\left(\frac{x}{r}\right)\right]$$

$$+ \hat{k}\left[\frac{\partial}{\partial x}\left(\frac{y}{r}\right) - \frac{\partial}{\partial y}\left(\frac{x}{r}\right)\right]$$

$$= \hat{i}\left[z\left(-\frac{1}{r^2}\frac{\partial r}{\partial y}\right) - y\left(-\frac{1}{r^2}\frac{\partial r}{\partial z}\right)\right] - \hat{j}\left[z\left(-\frac{1}{r^2}\frac{\partial r}{\partial x}\right) - x\left(-\frac{1}{r^2}\frac{\partial r}{\partial z}\right)\right]$$

$$+ \hat{k}\left[y\left(-\frac{1}{r^2}\frac{\partial r}{\partial x}\right) - x\left(-\frac{1}{r^2}\frac{\partial r}{\partial y}\right)\right]$$

$$= \hat{i}\left[-\frac{z}{r^2}\left(\frac{y}{r}\right) + \frac{y}{r^2}\left(\frac{z}{r}\right)\right] - \hat{j}\left[-\frac{z}{r^2}\left(\frac{x}{r}\right) + \frac{x}{r^2}\left(\frac{z}{r}\right)\right]$$

$$+ \hat{k}\left[-\frac{y}{r^2}\left(\frac{x}{r}\right) + \frac{x}{r^2}\left(\frac{y}{r}\right)\right]$$

$$\nabla \times \vec{F} = 0$$

Hence, $\vec{F}$ is irrotational.

30. *Show that* $\phi(x, y, z) = 2x^2 - 5y^2 + 3z^2$ *satisfies Laplace equation* $\nabla^2\phi = 0$

➡ We have,

$$\nabla^2\phi = \left(\frac{\partial^2}{\partial x^2} + \frac{\partial^2}{\partial y^2} + \frac{\partial^2}{\partial z^2}\right)\phi$$

$$= \left(\frac{\partial^2}{\partial x^2} + \frac{\partial^2}{\partial y^2} + \frac{\partial^2}{\partial z^2}\right)(2x^2 - 5y^2 + 3z^2)$$

$$= \frac{\partial}{\partial x}(4x) + \frac{\partial}{\partial y}(-10y) + \frac{\partial}{\partial z}(6z) = 4 - 10 + 6$$

$$\nabla^2\phi = 0$$

31. *Show that* $\phi = ax^2 + by^2 + cz^2$ *satisfies Laplace equation* $\nabla^2\phi = 0$*, given that* $a + b + c = 0$

➡

$$\nabla^2\phi = \frac{\partial^2\phi}{\partial x^2} + \frac{\partial^2\phi}{\partial y^2} + \frac{\partial^2\phi}{\partial z^2}$$

$$= \frac{\partial}{\partial x}(2ax) + \frac{\partial}{\partial y}(2by) + \frac{\partial}{\partial z}(2cz)$$
$$= 2a + 2b + 2c = 2(a+b+c)$$
$$= 0$$

Exercises

1. *Find* $\nabla\phi$ (*or* grad ϕ) *in the following examples*

   (a) $\phi = 10y\left(x^2 + y^2 + z^2\right)$

   (b) $\phi = x^2 + y^2 + z^2 + 2$ at $(2, 2, 2)$

   (c) $\phi = x^3 + y^3 + z^3 - 3xyz$ at $(1, 1, 1)$

   (d) $\phi = x^2yz + 4xz^2 + xyz$ at $(1, 2, 3)$

   (e) $\phi = x^2y + 2xz^2 - 8$ at $(1, 0, 2)$

   (f) $\phi = x^3 - y^3 + xz^2$ at $(1, -1, 2)$

   (g) $\phi = 3x^2y - y^3z^2$ at $(1, -2, -1)$

   (h) $\phi = 3x^2 + 2y - 3z$ at $(2, 1, -3)$

2. *Find the unit normal vector to the following surfaces*

   (a) $x^2 + y^2 + z^2 = 5$ at $(0, 1, 2)$

   (b) $xy^3z^2 = 4$ at $(-1, -1, 2)$

   (c) $x^2y + 2xy = 4$ at $(2, -2, 3)$

   (d) $x^3 + y^3 + 3xyz = 3$ at $(1, 2, -1)$

   (e) $x^2y + 2xz^2 = 8$ at $(1, 0, 2)$

3. *Find the angle between the following surfaces*

   (a) $x^2 - y^2 - z^2 = 16, \quad xy + yz - zx = 20$ at $(6, 4, 2)$

   (b) $x^2 + yz = 2, \quad x + 2y - z = 2$ at $(1, 1, 1)$

   (c) $x \log z = y^2 - 1, \quad x^2y = 2 - z$ at $(1, 1, 1)$

4. *Find the angle between the normals to the surface* $xy = z^2$ *at the points* $(4, 1, 2)$ *and* $(3, 3, -3)$.

5. *Find the angle between the normals to the surface* $2x^2 + 3y^2 = 5z$ *at the points* $(2, -2, 4)$ *and* $(-1, -1, 1)$.

6. *Find the angle between the normals to the surface* $x \log z = y^2 - 1$ *at* $(1, 1, 1)$ *and* $(2, 1, 1)$.
7. *Show that the surfaces* $4x^2 + z^3 = 4$ *and* $5x^2 - 2yz = 9x$ *intersect orthogonally at the point* $(1, -1, 2)$.
8. *Find the constants A and B so that the surfaces* $Ax^2 - Byz = (A + 2)x$ *and* $4x^2y + z^3 = 4$ *may intersect orthogonally at the point* $(1, -1, 2)$.
9. *Find the constants a and b, so that the surfaces* $bx^2 + z^3 = (b - 8)y$ *and* $x^2 + ayz = 3x$ *are intersect orthogonally at* $(1, 1, -2)$.
10. *Find the directional derivative of* $\phi = 2xy + z^2$ *at* $(1, -1, 3)$ *in the direction* $\hat{i} + 2\hat{j} + 2\hat{k}$.
11. *Find the directional derivative of* $4xz^3 - 3x^2y^2z$ *at* $(2, 1, -2)$ *in the direction of* $3\hat{i} - 2\hat{j} + 6\hat{k}$.
12. *Find the directional derivative of* $x^2yz + 4z^2x$ *at the point* $(1, -2, -1)$ *along the vector* $2\hat{i} - \hat{j} - 2\hat{k}$.
13. *Find the directional derivative of* $x^2y^2z^2$ *at* $(1, 1, -1)$ *in the direction of the tangent to the curve* $\vec{r} = e^t\hat{i} + (2\sin t + 1)\hat{j} + (t - \cos t)\hat{k}$ *at* $t = 0$.
14. *Find the directional derivative of the function* $4xz^2 + x^2yz$ *at* $(1, -2, -1)$ *in the direction of* $2\hat{i} - \hat{j} - 2\hat{k}$.
15. *Find the directional derivative of* $4xz^3 - 3x^2yz^2$ *at* $(2, -1, 2)$ *along y-axis.*
16. *Find the directional derivative of* $xy^2 + yz^2$ *at* $(2, -1, 1)$ *in the direction of* $\hat{i} + 2\hat{j} + 3\hat{k}$.
17. *Find the directional derivative of* $x^2yz + 4xz^2$ *at* $(1, -2, 1)$ *in the direction of* $2\hat{i} - \hat{j} + 2\hat{k}$.
18. *Find the directional derivative of* $x^2yz + 4xz^2 + xyz$ *at* $(1, 2, 3)$ *in the direction* $2\hat{i} + \hat{j} - \hat{k}$.
19. *Find the directional derivative of* $x^2y + y^2z + z^2x$ *at* $(1, 1, 1)$ *along the tangent to the curve* $\vec{r} = t\hat{i} + t^2\hat{j} + t^3\hat{k}$.
20. *Find the directional derivative of* $x^2y + y^3z$ *at* $(2, -1, 1)$ *along the normal to the surface* $xy + yz + zx = 3$ *at the point* $(1, 1, 1)$.
21. *Find the directional derivative of* xyz *along the direction of the normal to the surface* $x^2z + y^2x + yz^2 = 3$ *at the point* $(1, 1, 1)$.
22. *In what direction from the point* $(1, -2, -1)$ *the directional derivative of* $x^2yz + 4xz^2$ *a maximum. Find the magnitude of this maximum.*

23. *In what direction from the point* $(1, 3, 2)$ *the directional derivative of* $2xz - y^2$ *maximum? What is the magnitude of this maximum?*

24. *In what direction from the point* $(1, 2, 3)$ *is the directional derivative of* x^3y^2z *a maximum and find this maximum.*

25. *If the directional derivative of* $ax^2 + by^2 + cz^2$ *at* $(1, 1, 2)$ *has maximum of 4 in the direction parallel to y-axis, find a, b, c.*

26. *Find a, b, c so that the directional derivative of* $axy^2 + byz + cz^2x^3$ *at* $(1, 2, -1)$ *has a magnitude of 64 in the direction parallel to the z-axis.*

27. *Find the normal derivatives of the following:*

(a) $\phi = 3x^2y - y^3z^2$ *at* $(1, -2, -1)$
(b) $\phi = 3x^2 + 2y - 3z$ *at* $(2, 1, -3)$
(c) $\phi = x^3 - y^3 + xz^2$ *at* $(1, -1, 2)$

28. *Find the equations of the tangent plane and normal line to the surface* $xy^2 + yz^2 + zx^2 = 3$ *at the point* $(1, 1, 1)$.

29. *Find the equations to the tangent plane and the normal line to the surface* $xz^2 + x^2y = z - 1$ *at the point* $(1, -3, 2)$.

30. *Find the equations to the tangent plane and normal line to the surface* $y = x^2 + z^2$ *at the point* $(1, 5, -2)$.

31. *If* $\vec{V} = (x^2z)\,\hat{i} - (2y^3z^2)\,\hat{j} + (xy^2z)\,\hat{k}$, *find* div $\vec{V}$ *at the point* $(1, -1, 1)$.

32. *If* $\vec{V} = 2x\hat{i} - 3y^2\hat{j} + z^3\hat{k}$ *and* $\phi = 2xyz - 3z^2$, *find* $\vec{V} \cdot \nabla\phi$ *and* $\vec{V} \times \nabla\phi$ *at the point* $(1, 2, 3)$.

33. *If* $\phi = x^2y + yz^2 + zx^2$, *find* $\nabla \cdot (\nabla\phi)$.

34. *If* $\vec{f} = 3xyz^2\hat{i} + 2xy^2\hat{j} - x^2yz\hat{k}$ *and* $\phi = 3x^3 - yz$, *find*

(i) div $\vec{f}$ (ii) div $\left(\phi\vec{f}\right)$

(iii) div (gradϕ) (iv) $\vec{f} \cdot$ gradϕ *at* $(1, -1, 1)$.

35. *Find* ϕ, *if* $\nabla\phi = (6xy + z^3)\,\hat{i} + (3x^2 - z)\,\hat{j} + (3xz^2 - y)\,\hat{k}$.

36. *Find* div$\vec{f}$, *if* $\vec{f} = \nabla(xy + yz + zx)$.

37. *If* $\vec{f} = 3xyz^2\hat{i} + 4x^3y\hat{j} - xy^2z\hat{k}$, *find* $\nabla\left(\nabla \cdot \vec{f}\right)$ *at the point* $(-1, 2, 1)$.

38. *Find* curl $\left(\text{curl}\,\vec{f}\right)$, *if* $\vec{f} = x^2y\hat{i} + xz\hat{j} + 2yz\hat{k}$ *at the point* $(1, 1, 1)$.

39. *If* $\phi = x^2 + y^2 + z^2$ *and* $\vec{f} = x\hat{i} + y\hat{j} + z\hat{k}$, *show that* div $\left(\phi\vec{f}\right) = 5\phi$.

40. *If* $\phi = x^2 - y^2$, *prove that* $\nabla^2\phi = 0$.

41. *If* $\phi = xy^2 + yz^2 + zx^2$, *verify that* div (gradϕ) $= \nabla^2\phi$.

42. *Show that the following vectors are solenoidal*

(a) $3y^4z^2\hat{i} + 4x^3z^2\hat{j} + 6x^2y^3\hat{k}$

(b) $(x + 3y)\,\hat{i} + (y - 3z)\,\hat{j} + (x - 2z)\,\hat{k}$

(c) $2x^2z\hat{i} - 10xyz\hat{j} + 3xz^2\hat{k}$

43. *Find the constant a such that the vector* $\vec{f} = \left(ayx^2 + yz\right)\hat{i} + \left(xy^2 - xz^2\right)\hat{j} + \left(2xyz - 2x^2y^2\right)\hat{k}$ *is solenoidal.*

44. *Find the constant a such that* $\vec{f} = (x + 3y)\,\hat{i} + (y - 2x)\,\hat{j} + (x + az)\,\hat{k}$ *is solenoidal.*

45. *Determine the constant a such that the vector* $(2x + 3y)\,\hat{i} + (ay - 3z)\,\hat{j} + (6x - 12z)\,\hat{k}$ *is solenoidal.*

46. *Show that the vector field* $\vec{f} = \left(4xy - z^3\right)\hat{i} + 2x^2\hat{j} - 3xz^2\hat{k}$ *is irrational.*

47. *Show that* $\vec{f} = (\sin y + z)\,\hat{i} + (x\cos y - z)\,\hat{j} + (x - y)\,\hat{k}$ *is irrational and also find* ϕ *such that* $\vec{f} = \nabla\phi$.

48. *Show that* $\vec{f} = (2x + yz)\,\hat{i} + (4y + zx)\,\hat{j} - (6z - xy)\,\hat{k}$ *is solenoidal as well as irrational. Also find the scalar potential.*

49. *Find the constants a, b, c if the vector* $\vec{f} = (2x + 3y + az)\,\hat{i} + (bx + 2y + 3z)\,\hat{j} + (2x + cy + 3z)\,\hat{k}$ *is irrational.*

50. *Prove that* div$\vec{r} = 3$

51. *Prove that* curl$\vec{r} = 0$

52. *Prove that* div $\left(\frac{\vec{r}}{r^3}\right) = 0$

53. *Prove that* curl $(r^n\vec{r}) = 0$

[Hint: $\vec{r} = x\hat{i} + y\hat{j} + z\hat{k}, \quad r = |r| = \sqrt{x^2 + y^2 + z^2}$

54. *If* $\vec{a}$ *and* $\vec{b}$ *are any two constant vectors then prove the following:*

(i) div $\left(\vec{a} \times \nabla\left(\frac{1}{r}\right)\right) = 0$

(ii) $\text{div}\left[(\vec{r} \times \vec{a}) \times \vec{b}\right] = -2\vec{a} \cdot \vec{b}$

(iii) $\text{curl}\left[(\vec{r} \times \vec{a}) \times \vec{b}\right] = \vec{b} \times \vec{a}$

Answers

1. (a) $\dfrac{2x\hat{i} + 2y\hat{j} + 2z\hat{k}}{x^2 + y^2 + z^2}$ (b) $4\hat{i} + 4\hat{j} + 4\hat{k}$ (c) 0
   (d) $54\hat{i} + 6\hat{j} + 28\hat{k}$ (e) $8\hat{i} + \hat{j} + 8\hat{k}$ (f) $7\hat{i} - 3\hat{j} + 4\hat{k}$
   (g) $-12\hat{i} - 9\hat{j} - 16\hat{k}$ (h) $12\hat{i} + 2\hat{j} - 3\hat{k}$
2. (a) $\dfrac{1}{\sqrt{11}}\left(\hat{j} + 2\hat{k}\right)$ (b) $-\hat{i} - 3\hat{j} + \hat{k}$ (c) $\dfrac{1}{3}\left(-\hat{i} + 2\hat{j} + 2\hat{k}\right)$
   (d) $\dfrac{1}{\sqrt{14}}\left(-\hat{i} + 3\hat{j} + 2\hat{k}\right)$ (e) $\dfrac{1}{\sqrt{129}}\left(8\hat{i} + \hat{j} + 8\hat{k}\right)$
3. (a) $\cos^{-1}\left(\dfrac{-24}{\sqrt{5246}}\right)$ (b) $\dfrac{\pi}{3}$ (c) $\cos^{-1}\left(\dfrac{1}{\sqrt{30}}\right)$
4. $\cos^{-1}\left(\dfrac{1}{\sqrt{22}}\right)$ 5. $\cos^{-1}\left(\dfrac{65}{\sqrt{233}\sqrt{77}}\right)$
6. $\cos^{-1}\left(\dfrac{3}{\sqrt{10}}\right)$ 8. $a = \dfrac{5}{2},\ \ b = 1$
9. $a = -1,\ \ b = 2$ 10. $\dfrac{14}{3}$ 11. $\dfrac{384}{7}$
12. $\dfrac{29}{3}$ 13. $\dfrac{4}{\sqrt{6}}$ 14. $\dfrac{37}{3}$
15. 144 16. $-\dfrac{11}{3}$ 17. $-\dfrac{13}{3}$
18. $\dfrac{86}{\sqrt{6}}$ 19. $\dfrac{18}{\sqrt{14}}$ 20. $-\dfrac{5}{\sqrt{3}}$
21. $\sqrt{3}$ 22. $8\hat{i} - \hat{j} - 10\hat{k},\ \ \sqrt{165}$
23. $4\hat{i} - 6\hat{j} + 2\hat{k},\ \ 2\sqrt{14}$ 24. $36\hat{i} + 12\hat{j} + 4\hat{k},\ \ 4\sqrt{91}$
25. $a = 0,\ \ b = 2,\ \ c = 0$ 26. $a = 6,\ \ b = 24,\ \ c = -8$

27. $a \cdot \sqrt{481}$, $b \cdot \sqrt{159}$, $c \cdot \sqrt{74}$

28. $x + y + z = 3$, $x - 1 = y - 1 = z - 1$

29. $2x - y - 3z + 1 = 0$, $\dfrac{x-1}{-2} = \dfrac{y+3}{1} = \dfrac{z-2}{3}$

30. $2x - y - 4z = 5$, $\dfrac{x-1}{2} = \dfrac{y-5}{-1} = \dfrac{z+2}{-4}$

31. -3 32. -426, $6\hat{i} + 352\hat{j} + 156\hat{k}$ 33. $4y + 2z$

34. $(a) - 8$ $(b) - 28$ $(c)\ 18$ $(d) - 10$

35. $3x^2y + xz^3 - 4z + c$ 36. 0 37. $8\hat{i} + 7\hat{j} + 12\hat{k}$

38. $4\hat{j}$ 43. $a = -2$ 44. $a = 2$

45. $a = 10$ 47. $xz - yz + x \sin y$

48. $xyz + x^2 + 2y^2 - 3z^2$ 49. $a = 2$, $b = 3$, $c = 3$.

CHAPTER 4

Integral Calculus

4.1 Introduction

An integral can be considered as an antiderivative. Thus, if the derivative of $F(x)$ is $F'(x) = f(x)$, then an integral of $f(x)$ is $F(x)$.

In practice integrals are necessary for finding solution of differential equations, area under the curve, solutions using integral transforms etc.

In this chapter we establish a few reduction formulae for integrals, evaluations of these integrals with standard limits and evaluation of double and triple integrals.

4.2 Reduction Formulae

4.2.1 Reduction Formula for $\int \sin^n x dx$

Let $I_n = \int \sin^n \ x dx$,

Where n is positive integer

$$I_n = \int \sin^{n-1} \ x \ (\sin \ x) \ dx.$$

Applying the method of integration by parts, we get

$$I_n = \sin^{n-1} \ x \, (-\cos \ x) - \int (n-1) \sin^{n-2} \ x \, (\cos x) \ (-\cos x) \ dx$$

$$= -\sin^{n-1} x \cos x + (n-1)\int \sin^{n-2} x \cos^2 x\, dx$$

$$= -\sin^{n-1} x \cos x + (n-1)\int \sin^{n-2} x \left[1 - \sin^2 x\right] dx$$

$$= -\sin^{n-1} x \cos x + (n-1)\int \left(\sin^{n-2} x - \sin^n x\right) dx$$

$$= -\sin^{n-1} x \cos x + (n-1)\int \sin^{n-2} x dx - (n-1)\int \sin^n x\, dx$$

$$I_n = -\sin^{n-1} x \cos x + (n-1)\, I_{n-2} - (n-1)\, I_n$$

$$I_n + (n-1)\, I_n = -\sin^{n-1} x \cos x + (n-1)\, I_{n-2}$$

$$I_n\,[1 + n - 1] = -\sin^{n-1} x \cos x + (n-1)\, I_{n-2}$$

$$nI_n = -\sin^{n-1} x \cos x + (n-1)\, I_{n-2}$$

$$I_n = -\frac{1}{n}\sin^{n-1} x \cos x + \frac{n-1}{n} I_{n-2}.$$

This is the reduction formula for $\int \sin^n x\, dx$.

Evaluation of $\int_0^{\frac{\pi}{2}} \sin^n x\, dx$

Let $I_n = \int_0^{\frac{\pi}{2}} sin^n x\, dx$

We have, $I_n = -\left.\dfrac{\sin^{n-1} x \cos x}{n}\right|_0^{\frac{\pi}{2}} + \dfrac{n-1}{n} I_{n-2}$

$$I_n = \frac{n-1}{n} I_{n-2} \qquad \left[\cos\frac{\pi}{2} = 0 \text{ and } \sin 0 = 0\right]$$

From the above equation, we get

$$I_{n-2} = \frac{n-3}{n-2} I_{n-4}$$

$$I_{n-4} = \frac{n-5}{n-4} I_{n-6}$$

$$I_{n-6} = \frac{n-7}{n-6} I_{n-8}$$

....

$$I_3 = \frac{2}{3} I_1$$

$$I_2 = \frac{1}{2} I_0$$

$$\therefore\ I_n = \frac{n-1}{n} I_{n-2}$$

$$= \frac{(n-1)}{n} \frac{(n-3)}{(n-2)} I_{n-4}$$

$$I_n = \frac{(n-1)}{n} . \frac{(n-3)}{(n-2)} . \frac{(n-5)}{(n-4)} I_{n-6}$$

....

$$\therefore\ I_n = \begin{cases} \frac{(n-1)}{n} . \frac{(n-3)}{(n-2)} . \frac{(n-5)}{(n-4)} - - - \frac{2}{3} I_1 & \text{if } n \text{ is odd} \\ \frac{(n-1)}{n} . \frac{(n-3)}{(n-2)} . \frac{(n-5)}{(n-4)} - - - \frac{1}{2} I_o & \text{if } n \text{ is even} \end{cases}$$

Here $I_1 = \int_0^{\frac{\pi}{2}} sin^1 x\, dx = -\cos x]_0^{\frac{\pi}{2}} = -(0-1) = 1$

$$I_0 = \int_0^{\frac{\pi}{2}} sin^0 x\, dx = \int_0^{\frac{\pi}{2}} dx = x \Big|_0^{\frac{\pi}{2}} = \frac{\pi}{2}$$

$$I_n = \begin{cases} \frac{(n-1)}{n} . \frac{(n-3)}{(n-2)} . \frac{(n-5)}{(n-4)} ...... \frac{2}{3} & \text{if } n \text{ is odd} \\ \frac{(n-1)}{n} . \frac{(n-3)}{(n-2)} . \frac{(n-5)}{(n-4)} .... \frac{1}{2} . \frac{\pi}{2} & \text{if } n \text{ is even} \end{cases}$$

4.2.2 Reduction Formula for $\int \cos^n x dx$

Let $I_n = \int \cos^n\ x dx$ where n is positive integer.

$$I_n = \int \cos^{n-1} x \cos x dx$$

Applying the method of integration by parts, we get

$$I_n = \cos^{n-1} x\,(\sin x) - \int (n-1)\cos^{n-2} x\,(-\sin x)\sin x\,dx$$

$$= \cos^{n-1} x \sin x + (n-1)\int \cos^{n-2} x \sin^2 x\,dx$$

$$= \cos^{n-1} x \sin x + (n-1)\int \cos^{n-2} x\left(1-\cos^2 x\right)dx$$

$$= \cos^{n-1} x \sin x + (n-1)\int \left(\cos^{n-2} x - \cos^n x\right)dx$$

$$= \cos^{n-1} x \sin x + (n-1)\int \cos^{n-2} x\,dx - (n-1)\int \cos^n x\,dx$$

$$I_n = \cos^{n-1} x \sin x + (n-1)\,I_{n-2} - (n-1)\,I_n$$

$$I_n + (n-1)\,I_n = \cos^{n-1} x \sin x + (n-1)\,I_{n-2}$$

$$I_n\,(1+n-1) = \cos^{n-1} x \sin x + (n-1)\,I_{n-2}$$

$$nI_n = \cos^{n-1} x \sin x + (n-1)\,I_{n-2}$$

$$I_n = \frac{1}{n}\cos^{n-1} x \sin x + \frac{n-1}{n}\,I_{n-2}.$$

This is the reduction formula for $\int \cos^n x\,dx$

Evaluation of $\int_0^{\frac{\pi}{2}} \cos^n x\,dx$

Let $I_n = \int_0^{\frac{\pi}{2}} \cos^n x\,dx$

We have, $I_n = \left.\dfrac{\cos^{n-1} x \sin x}{n}\right|_0^{\frac{\pi}{2}} + \dfrac{n-1}{n}\,I_{n-2}$

$$I_n = \frac{n-1}{n}\,I_{n-2} \qquad \left[\because \cos\frac{\pi}{2} = 0, \sin 0 = 0\right]$$

From the above equation, we have

$$I_{n-2} = \frac{n-3}{n-2}I_{n-4}$$

$$I_{n-4} = \frac{n-5}{n-4}I_{n-6}$$

$$I_{n-6} = \frac{n-7}{n-6} I_{n-8}$$

$$\dots\dots\dots\dots\dots\dots$$

$$I_3 = \frac{2}{3} I_1$$

$$I_2 = \frac{1}{2} I_0$$

$$\therefore\ I_n = \frac{n-1}{n} I_{n-2} = \frac{(n-1)}{n} \cdot \frac{(n-3)}{(n-2)} . I_{n-4}$$

$$= \frac{(n-1)}{n} \frac{(n-3)}{(n-2)} \cdot \frac{(n-5)}{(n-4)} I_{n-6} \text{ and so on}$$

$$I_n = \begin{cases} \frac{(n-1)}{n} \cdot \frac{(n-3)}{(n-2)} \cdot \frac{(n-5)}{(n-4)} \dots\dots\dots \frac{2}{3} I_1 & \text{if } n \text{ is odd} \\ \frac{(n-1)}{n} \cdot \frac{(n-3)}{(n-2)} \cdot \frac{(n-5)}{(n-4)} \dots\dots\dots \frac{1}{2} I_0 & \text{if } n \text{ is even} \end{cases}$$

$$I_1 = \int_0^{\frac{\pi}{2}} \cos^1 x dx = \sin x \Big|_0^{\frac{\pi}{2}} = 1 - 0 = 1$$

$$\text{and } I_0 = \int_0^{\frac{\pi}{2}} \cos^0 x dx = \int_0^{\frac{\pi}{2}} dx = x \Big|_0^{\frac{\pi}{2}} = \frac{\pi}{2}$$

$$I_n = \begin{cases} \frac{(n-1)}{n} \cdot \frac{(n-3)}{(n-2)} \cdot \frac{(n-5)}{(n-4)} \dots\dots \frac{2}{3} & \text{if } n \text{ is odd} \\ \frac{(n-1)}{n} \cdot \frac{(n-3)}{(n-2)} \cdot \frac{(n-5)}{(n-4)} \dots\dots \frac{1}{2} \cdot \frac{\pi}{2} & \text{if } n \text{ is even} \end{cases}$$

Worked Examples

1. *Evaluate* $\int \sin^6 x\, dx$

➡ Let $I_6 = \int \sin^6 x\, dx$

We know that $I_n = -\frac{1}{n}\sin^{n-1}x\ \cos x + \frac{n-1}{n}I_{n-2}$

$$I_6 = -\frac{1}{6}\sin^5 x\ \cos x + \frac{5}{6}I_4$$
$$= -\frac{1}{6}\sin^5 x\ \cos x + \frac{5}{6}\left[-\frac{1}{4}\sin^3 x\cos x + \frac{3}{4}I_2\right]$$
$$= -\frac{1}{6}\ \sin^5 x\ \cos x - \frac{5}{24}\sin^3 x\cos x + \frac{15}{24}\left[-\frac{1}{2}\sin\ x\cos x + \frac{1}{2}I_0\right]$$
$$I_6 = -\frac{1}{6}\sin^5 x\cos x - \frac{5}{24}\ \sin^3 x\ \cos x - \frac{15}{48}\sin x\cos x + \frac{15}{48}x + c$$
$$\left[I_0 = \int \sin^0 x\,dx = \int dx = x\right]$$

2. *Evaluate* $\int \cos^5 x\,dx$

➡ We know that $I_n = \frac{1}{n}\cos^{n-1}x\sin x + \frac{n-1}{n}I_{n-2}$

$$\therefore\ I_5 = \frac{1}{5}\cos^4 x\ \sin x + \frac{4}{5}I_3$$
$$= \frac{1}{5}\cos^4 x\ \sin x + \frac{4}{5}\left[\frac{1}{3}\cos^2 x.\ \sin x + \frac{2}{3}I_1\right]$$
$$= \frac{1}{5}\cos^4 x\ \sin x + \frac{4}{15}\cos^2 x\ \sin x + \frac{8}{15}\int \cos x\,dx$$
$$\therefore\ I_5 = \frac{1}{5}\cos^4 x\ \sin x + \frac{4}{15}\cos^2 x\sin x + \frac{8}{15}\ \sin\ x + c.$$

3. *Evaluate* $\int_0^{\frac{\pi}{2}} \sin^8 x dx$

➡ $\int_0^{\frac{\pi}{2}} \sin^8 x dx = \frac{7}{8}.\frac{5}{6}.\frac{3}{4}.\frac{1}{2}.\frac{\pi}{2} = \frac{35\pi}{256}$

4. *Evaluate* $\int_0^{\frac{\pi}{2}} \cos^6 x dx$

➡ $\int_0^{\frac{\pi}{2}} \cos^6 x dx = \frac{5.3.1}{6.4.2}.\frac{\pi}{2} = \frac{5\pi}{32}$

5. *Evaluate* $\int_0^{\frac{\pi}{6}} \sin^6 3x dx$

➡ Let $I = \int_0^{\frac{\pi}{6}} \sin^6 3x dx$

Put $3x = t \Rightarrow 3dx = dt \Rightarrow dx = dt/3$

$x = 0 \Rightarrow t = 0, \quad x = \pi/6 \Rightarrow t = \pi/2$

$$\therefore\ I = \int_0^{\frac{\pi}{2}} \sin^6 t \frac{dt}{3} = \frac{1}{3}\int_0^{\frac{\pi}{2}} \sin^6 t\, dt = \frac{1}{3}.\frac{5}{6}.\frac{3}{4}.\frac{1}{2}.\frac{\pi}{2} = \frac{5\pi}{96}$$

6. *Evaluate* $\int_0^{2\pi} \cos^4 x dx$

➡ Let $I = \int_0^{2\pi} \cos^4 x dx = 2\int_0^{\pi} \cos^4 x dx$

$$I = 4\int_0^{\frac{\pi}{2}} \cos^4 x dx = 4\,\frac{3}{4}.\frac{1}{2}.\frac{\pi}{2} = \frac{3\pi}{4}$$

$$\left[\therefore\ \int_0^{a} f(x)\, dx = 2\int_0^{\frac{a}{2}} f(x) dx \text{ if } f(x) \text{ is even function}\right]$$

7. *Evaluate* $\int_0^{\pi} \sin^4 x dx$

➡ Let $I = \int_0^{\pi} \sin^4 x dx = 2\int_0^{\frac{\pi}{2}} \sin^4 x dx = 2.\frac{3}{4}.\frac{1}{2}.\frac{\pi}{2} = \frac{3\pi}{8}$

8. *Evaluate* $\int_0^{\pi} x \cos^6 x\, dx$

➡ Let $I = \int_0^{\pi} x \cos^6 x\, dx \quad \left[\int_0^{\pi} f(x)\, dx = \int_0^{\pi} f(a - x)\, dx\right]$

$$= \int_0^{\pi} (\pi - x)\ [\cos(\pi - x)]^6\ dx$$

$$= \int_0^{\pi} (\pi - x)\left(\cos^6 x\right) dx = \int_0^{\pi} \pi \cos^6 x dx - \int_0^{\pi} x \cos^6 x\, dx$$

$$I = \pi \int_0^{\pi} \cos^6 x\, dx - I$$

$$\therefore\ 2I = \pi \int_0^{\pi} \cos^6\ x\, dx = \pi\left[2\int_0^{\frac{\pi}{2}} \cos^6 x\, dx\right]$$

$$I = \pi \int_0^{\frac{\pi}{2}} \cos^6 x\,dx = \pi.\frac{5}{6}.\frac{3}{4}.\frac{1}{2}.\frac{\pi}{2} = \frac{5}{32}\pi^2$$

9. *Evaluate* $\int_0^{\pi} \frac{\sin^4\theta}{(1+\cos\theta)^2} d\theta$

➡ Let $I = \int_0^{\pi} \frac{\sin^4\theta}{(1+\cos\theta)^2} d\theta$

$$= \int_0^{\pi} \frac{(2\sin(\theta/2)\cos(\theta/2))^4}{\left(2\cos^2(\theta/2)\right)^2} d\theta \quad \left[\sin\theta = 2\sin\left(\frac{\theta}{2}\right)\cos\left(\frac{\theta}{2}\right)\right]$$

$$= \int_0^{\pi} \frac{2^4\sin^4(\theta/2)\cos^4(\theta/2)}{2^2\cos^4(\theta/2)} d\theta \quad \left[1+\cos\theta = 2\cos^2\frac{\theta}{2}\right]$$

$$I = 2^2 \int_0^{\pi} \sin^4(\theta/2)\,d\theta$$

Put $\frac{\theta}{2} = x \Rightarrow \frac{d\theta}{2} = dx \Rightarrow d\theta = 2dx$
If $\theta = 0 \Rightarrow x = 0$, If $\theta = \pi \Rightarrow x = \pi/2$

$$\therefore\ I = 4\int_0^{\frac{\pi}{2}} \sin^4 x\,2dx = 8\frac{3}{4}.\frac{1}{2}.\frac{\pi}{2} = \frac{3\pi}{2}$$

10. *Evaluate* $\int_0^{\pi} \frac{\sqrt{1-\cos\theta}}{1+\cos\theta}\sin^2\theta\,d\theta$

➡ Let $I = \int_0^{\pi} \frac{\sqrt{1-\cos\theta}}{1+\cos\theta}\sin^2\theta\,d\theta$

$$= \int_0^{\pi} \frac{\sqrt{2\sin^2(\theta/2)}}{2\cos^2(\theta/2)}(2\sin(\theta/2)\cos(\theta/2))^2\,d\theta$$

$$= \int_0^{\pi} \frac{\sqrt{2}\,\sin(\theta/2).4\sin^2(\theta/2)\cos^2(\theta/2)}{2\cos^2(\theta/2)} d\theta$$

$$I = 2\sqrt{2}\int_0^{\pi} \sin^3(\theta/2)\,d\theta$$

Put $(\theta/2) = x \Rightarrow (d\theta/2) = dx \Rightarrow d\theta = 2dx$

If $\theta = 0 \Rightarrow x = 0$, $If\ \theta = \pi \Rightarrow x = \pi/2$

$$I = 2\sqrt{2}\int_0^{\frac{\pi}{2}} \sin^3 x\ 2dx = 4\sqrt{2}\int_0^{\frac{\pi}{2}} \sin^3\ x\,dx = 4\sqrt{2}.\frac{2}{3} = \frac{8\sqrt{2}}{3}$$

11 *Evaluate* $\int_0^a \frac{x^4}{\sqrt{a^2 - x^2}}dx$

➡ Let $I = \int_0^a \frac{x^4}{\sqrt{a^2 - x^2}}dx$

Put $x = a\ \sin\theta \Rightarrow dx = a\cos\theta\,d\theta$

If $x = 0 \Rightarrow \theta = 0$, If $x = a \Rightarrow \theta = \pi/2$

$$\therefore\ I = \int_0^{\frac{\pi}{2}} \frac{a^4 \sin^4\theta}{\sqrt{a^2 - a^2\sin^2\theta}} a\cos\theta\,d\theta = a^5\int_0^{\frac{\pi}{2}} \frac{\sin^4\theta\cos\theta}{\sqrt{a^2\left(1 - \sin^2\theta\right)}}\,d\theta$$

$$= a^5\int_0^{\frac{\pi}{2}} \frac{\sin^4\theta\cos\theta}{a\ \cos\theta}d\theta = a^4\int_0^{\frac{\pi}{2}} \sin^4\theta\,d\theta = a^4\,\frac{3}{4}.\frac{1}{2}.\frac{\pi}{2} = \frac{3a^4\pi}{16}$$

12. *Evaluate* $\int_0^a x^4\sqrt{a^2 - x^2}dx$

➡ Let $I = \int_0^a x^4\sqrt{a^2 - x^2}dx$

Put $x = a\sin\theta \Rightarrow dx = a\cos\theta\,d\theta$

If $x = 0 \Rightarrow \theta = 0$, If $x = a \Rightarrow \theta = \pi/2$

$$I = \int_0^{\frac{\pi}{2}} a^4\sin^4\ \theta\sqrt{a^2 - a^2\sin^2\theta}.a\cos\theta\ d\theta$$

$$= a^6\int_0^{\frac{\pi}{2}} \sin^4\theta\cos^2\theta d\theta = a^6\int_0^{\frac{\pi}{2}} \sin^4\theta\left(1 - \sin^2\theta\right)d\theta$$

$$= a^6\int_0^{\frac{\pi}{2}} \left(\sin^4\theta - \sin^6\theta\right)d\theta = a^6\int_0^{\frac{\pi}{2}} \sin^4\theta\ d\theta - a^6\int_0^{\frac{\pi}{2}} \sin^6\theta\ d\theta$$

$$= a^6\left[\frac{3}{4}.\frac{1}{2}.\frac{\pi}{2}\right] - a^6\left[\frac{5}{6}.\frac{3}{4}.\frac{1}{2}.\frac{\pi}{2}\right]$$

$$= a^6\left[\frac{3}{4}.\frac{1}{2}.\frac{\pi}{2}\right]\left(1 - \frac{5}{6}\right) = \frac{3a^6\pi}{16}\left(\frac{1}{6}\right) = \frac{a^6\pi}{32}$$

13. *Evaluate* $\int_0^\infty \frac{x^2}{(1+x^6)^{7/2}} dx$

➡ Let $I = \displaystyle\int_0^\infty \frac{x^2}{(1+x^6)^{7/2}} dx = \int_0^\infty \frac{x^2}{[1+(x^3)^2]^{7/2}} dx$

Put $x^3 = \tan\theta \Rightarrow 3x^2 dx = \sec^2\theta\, d\theta \Rightarrow x^2 dx = (1/3)\sec^2\theta\, d\theta$
If $x = 0 \Rightarrow \theta = 0$, If $x = \infty \Rightarrow \theta = \pi/2$

$$\therefore\ I = \int_0^{\frac{\pi}{2}} \frac{\frac{1}{3}\sec^2\theta\, d\theta}{(1+\tan^2\theta)^{7/2}} = \frac{1}{3}\int_0^{\frac{\pi}{2}} \frac{\sec^2\theta}{(\sec^2\theta)^{7/2}} d\theta$$

$$= \frac{1}{3}\int_0^{\frac{\pi}{2}} \frac{\sec^2\theta}{\sec^7\theta} d\theta \quad = \frac{1}{3}\int_0^{\frac{\pi}{2}} \cos^5\theta\, d\theta = \frac{1}{3}\frac{4}{5}.\frac{2}{3.} = \frac{8}{45}$$

14. *Evaluate* $\displaystyle\int_0^a \frac{x^n}{\sqrt{ax-x^2}} dx$, *where n is positive integer*

➡ Let $I = \displaystyle\int_0^a \frac{x^n}{\sqrt{ax-x^2}} dx$

Put $x = a\sin^2\theta \Rightarrow dx = 2a\ \sin\theta\ \cos\theta\ d\theta$
If $x = 0 \Rightarrow \theta = 0$, If $x = a \Rightarrow \theta = \pi/2$

$$\therefore\ I = \int_0^{\frac{\pi}{2}} \frac{(a\ \sin^2\theta)^n}{\sqrt{a^2\sin^2\theta - a^2\sin^4\theta}} 2a\ \sin\theta\cos\theta\, d\theta$$

$$= 2a^n \int_0^{\frac{\pi}{2}} \frac{\sin^{2n}\theta\, a\ \sin\theta\cos\theta.d\,\theta}{a\ \sin\theta\sqrt{1-\sin^2\theta}} = 2a^n \int_0^{\frac{\pi}{2}} \sin^{2n}\theta\ d\theta$$

$$= 2a^n \frac{2n-1}{2n}.\frac{2n-3}{2n-2}.\frac{2n-5}{2n-4}....\frac{5}{6}.\frac{3}{4}.\frac{1}{2}\frac{\pi}{2} \qquad [2n \text{ is an even}]$$

$$= \frac{1.3.5.........(2n-1)}{2.4.6.........2n}\pi\, a^n$$

15. *Evaluate* $\displaystyle\int_0^\infty \frac{dx}{(x^2+a^2)^n}$, *where n is positive integer greater than* 1

➡ Let $I = \displaystyle\int_0^\infty \frac{dx}{(x^2+a^2)^n}$

Put $x = a\tan\theta \Rightarrow dx = a\sec^2\theta\, d\,\theta$

If $x = 0 \Rightarrow \theta = 0$, If $x = \infty \Rightarrow \theta = \pi/2$

$$\therefore\ I = \int_0^{\frac{\pi}{2}} \frac{a \sec^2 \theta \, d\theta}{\left[a^2 \tan^2 \theta + a^2\right]^n}$$

$$= \int_0^{\frac{\pi}{2}} \frac{a \sec^2 \theta \, d\theta}{\left(a^2 \sec^2 \theta\right)^n} = \int_0^{\frac{\pi}{2}} \frac{a \sec^2 \theta \, d\theta}{a^{2n} \sec^{2n} \theta}$$

$$= \frac{1}{a^{2n-1}} \int_0^{\frac{\pi}{2}} \frac{1}{\cos^2 \theta} . \cos^{2n} \theta \, d\theta = \frac{1}{a^{2n-1}} \int_0^{\frac{\pi}{2}} \cos^{2n-2} \theta \, d\theta$$

$$= \frac{1}{a^{2n-1}} \frac{2n-3}{2n-2} . \frac{2n-5}{2n-4} .... \frac{5}{6} . \frac{3}{4} . \frac{1}{2} ... \frac{\pi}{2}$$

$$= \frac{1}{a^{2n-1}} \frac{1.3.5 .... (2n-3)}{2.4.6 ...... (2n-2)} . \frac{\pi}{2}$$

16. *Evaluate* $\int_0^1 \frac{x^9}{\sqrt{1-x^2}} dx$

➡ Let $I = \int_0^1 \frac{x^9}{\sqrt{1-x^2}} dx$

Put $x = \sin \theta \Rightarrow dx = \cos \theta \, d\theta$

If $x = 0 \Rightarrow \theta = 0$, If $x = 1 \Rightarrow \theta = \pi/2$

$$\therefore\ I = \int_0^{\frac{\pi}{2}} \frac{\sin^9 \theta}{\sqrt{1 - \sin^2 \theta}} \cos \theta \, d\theta = \int_0^{\frac{\pi}{2}} \frac{\sin^9 \theta}{\sqrt{\cos^2 \theta}} \cos \theta . d\theta$$

$$= \int_0^{\frac{\pi}{2}} \sin^9 \theta \, d\theta = \frac{8}{9} . \frac{6}{7} . \frac{4}{5} . \frac{2}{3} = \frac{128}{315}$$

Exercises

Evaluate the following integrals

(1) $\int \cos^6 x dx$ (2) $\int_0^{\frac{\pi}{2}} \cos^6 x dx$

(3) $\int_0^{\frac{\pi}{2}} \sin^4 x dx$ (4) $\int_0^{\frac{\pi}{2}} \sin^8 3x dx$

(5) $\int_0^{\pi} \cos^6 x dx$ (6) $\int_0^{\frac{\pi}{2}} \cos^7 x dx$

(7) $\int_0^{\pi} x \cos^4 x dx$ (8) $\int_0^{\pi} x \sin^3 x dx$

(9) $\int_0^{\pi} (1 - \cos\theta)^3 d\theta$ (10) $\int_0^{1} \frac{x^7}{\sqrt{1 - x^4}} dx$

(11) $\int_0^{\infty} \frac{dx}{(1 + x^2)^5}$ (12) $\int_0^{\infty} \frac{x^2}{(x^6 + 1)^{9/2}} dx$

Answers

(1) $\frac{1}{48}\left[8\cos^5 x \sin x + 10\cos^3 x \sin x + 15\cos x \sin x + 15x\right] + c$

(2) $\frac{5\pi}{32}$ (3) $\frac{3\pi}{16}$ (4) $\frac{35\pi}{768}$ (5) $\frac{15\pi}{48}$

(6) $\frac{16}{35}$ (7) $\frac{3\pi^2}{16}$ (8) $\frac{2\pi}{3}$ (9) $\frac{5\pi}{2}$

(10) $\frac{1}{3}$ (11) $\frac{35\pi}{256}$ (12) $\frac{16}{105}$

4.2.3 Reduction Formula for $\int \sin^m x \cos^n x\, dx$

Let $I_{m,n} = \int \sin^m x \cos^n x\, dx.$

Where m and n are positive integers

$$I_{m,n} = \frac{cos^{n-1}x sin^{m+1}x}{m+n} + \frac{n-1}{m+n} I_{m,n-2}$$

This is the reduction formula for $\int \sin^m x \cos^n x\, dx$

Evaluation of $\int_0^{\frac{\pi}{2}} \sin^m x \cos^n x\, dx$

Let $I_{m,n} = \int_0^{\frac{\pi}{2}} \sin^m x \cos^n x\, dx$

Case (i) If n is odd and m is odd or even

$$I_{m,n} = \frac{(n-1)}{(m+n)}\frac{(n-3)}{(m+n-2)}.\frac{(n-5)}{(m+n-4)}.............\frac{2}{(m+3)}.\frac{1}{(m+1)}$$

Case (ii) If n is even and m is odd

$$I_{m,n} = \frac{(n-1)}{(m+n)}.\frac{(n-3)}{(m+n-2)}.\frac{(n-5)}{(m+n-4)}...\frac{1}{(m+2)}.\left(\frac{(m-1)}{m}\frac{(m-3)}{(m-2)}...\frac{2}{3}\right)$$

$$= \frac{[(n-1)(n-3)...3.1][(m-1)(m-3)...2]}{(m+n)(m+n-2)(m+n-4)---3}$$

Case (iii) If n is even and m is even

$$I_{m,n} = \frac{n-1}{m+n}.\frac{n-2}{m+n-2}.\frac{n-5}{m+n-4}......\frac{1}{m+2}.\left(\frac{m-1}{m}.\frac{m-3}{m-2}.......\frac{1}{2}.\frac{\pi}{2}\right)$$

$$= \frac{[(n-1)(n-3)...3.1][(m-1)(m-3)...1]}{(m+n)(m+n-2)(m+n-4)---4.2}\cdot\frac{\pi}{2}$$

Note: $I_{m,n} = \dfrac{[(n-1)(n-3)(n-5)\ldots][(m-1)(m-3)(m-5)\ldots]}{(m+n)(m+n-2)(m+n-4)\ldots}K$

where $K = \begin{cases} \dfrac{\pi}{2} & \text{if both } m \text{ and } n \text{ are even} \\ 1 & \text{otherwise} \end{cases}$

Worked Examples

1. *Evaluate* $\int_0^{\frac{\pi}{2}} \sin^3 x \cos^7 x\, dx$

➡ $I_{3,7} = \int_0^{\frac{\pi}{2}} \sin^3 x \cos^7 x\, dx$

Here $m = 3$ $n = 7$ therefore, from case (1), we get

$$I_{3,7} = \frac{(6\cdot4\cdot2)(2)}{10\cdot8\cdot6\cdot4\cdot2} = \frac{1}{40}$$

2. *Evaluate* $\int_0^{\frac{\pi}{2}} \sin^5 x \ \cos^3 x \, dx$

➡ $I_{5,3} = \int_0^{\frac{\pi}{2}} \sin^5 \ x \cos^3 \ x \, dx = \dfrac{(4 \cdot 2)(2)}{8 \cdot 6 \cdot 4 \cdot 2} = \dfrac{1}{24}$

3. *Evaluate* $\int_0^{\frac{\pi}{2}} \sin^6 x \ \cos^8 \ x \, dx$

➡ $I_{6,8} = \dfrac{(7 \cdot 5 \cdot 3 \cdot 1)(5 \cdot 3 \cdot 1)}{14 \cdot 12 \cdot 10 \cdot 8 \cdot 6 \cdot 4 \cdot 2}\left(\dfrac{\pi}{2}\right) = \dfrac{5\pi}{2^{12}}$

4. *Evaluate* $\int_0^{\frac{\pi}{2}} \sin^6 x \ \cos^5 \ x \, dx$

➡ $I_{6,5} = \dfrac{(4 \cdot 2)(5 \cdot 3 \cdot 1)}{11 \cdot 9 \cdot 7 \cdot 5 \cdot 3 \cdot 1} = \dfrac{8}{693}$

5. *Evaluate* $\int_0^{\frac{\pi}{2}} \sin^5 x \ \cos^5 \ x \, dx$

➡ $I_{5,5} = \dfrac{(4 \cdot 2)(4 \cdot 2)}{10 \cdot 8 \cdot 6 \cdot 4 \cdot 2} = \dfrac{1}{60}$

6. *Evaluate* $\int_0^{\frac{\pi}{4}} \sin^4 4\theta \ \cos^2 2\theta \ d\theta$

➡

$$I = \int_0^{\frac{\pi}{4}} \sin^4 4\theta \ \cos^2 2\theta \ d\theta = \int_0^{\frac{\pi}{4}} (2 \sin 2\theta \cos 2\theta)^4 \cos^2 2\theta \ d\theta$$

$$= 2^4 \int_0^{\frac{\pi}{4}} \sin^4 2\theta \ \cos^6 2\theta \ d\theta$$

Put $2\theta = x \Rightarrow d\theta = dx/2$
If $\theta = 0 \Rightarrow x = 0$, If $\theta = \pi/4 \Rightarrow x = \pi/2$

$$\therefore \ I = 2^4 \int_0^{\frac{\pi}{2}} \sin^4 \ x \ \cos^6 \ x \ \frac{dx}{2} = 2^3 \ \frac{(5 \cdot 3 \cdot 1)(3 \cdot 1)}{10 \cdot 8 \cdot 6 \cdot 4 \cdot 2} \ \frac{\pi}{2} = \frac{3\pi}{64}$$

7. *Evaluate* $\int_0^{\pi} x \sin^4 \ x \ \cos^6 x \ dx$

➡ Let

$$I = \int_0^{\pi} x \sin^4 \ x \ \cos^6 \ x \ dx$$

$$= \int_0^{\pi} (\pi - x) \sin^4 (\pi - x) \cos^6 (\pi - x)\, dx$$

$$\left[\because \int_0^a f(x)dx = \int_0^a (a - x)\, dx\right]$$

$$I = \int_0^{\pi} (\pi - x) \sin^4 x \cos^6 x\, dx$$

$$= \pi \int_0^{\pi} \sin^4 x \cos^6 x\, dx - \int_0^{\pi} x \sin^4 x \cos^6 x\, dx$$

$$I = \pi \int_0^{\pi} \sin^4 x \cos^6 x\, dx - I$$

$$2I = \pi \int_0^{\pi} \sin^4 x \cos^6 x\, dx$$

$$2I = 2\pi \int_0^{\frac{\pi}{2}} \sin^4 x \cos^6 x\, dx$$

$$I = \pi \left[\frac{(5 \cdot 3 \cdot 1)\ (3 \cdot 1)}{10 \cdot 8 \cdot 6 \cdot 4 \cdot 2} \cdot \frac{\pi}{2}\right] = \frac{3\pi^2}{512}$$

8. *Evaluate* $\int_0^1 x^6 \sqrt{1 - x^2}\, dx$

➡ Let $I = \int_0^1 x^6 \sqrt{1 - x^2} dx$

Put $x = \sin\theta \Rightarrow dx = \cos\theta\, d\theta$

If $x = 0 \Rightarrow \theta = 0$, If $x = 1 \Rightarrow \theta = \pi/2$

$$\therefore I = \int_0^{\frac{\pi}{2}} \sin^6\theta \sqrt{1 - \sin^2\theta} \cos\theta\, d\theta = \int_0^{\frac{\pi}{2}} \sin^6\theta \cos^2\theta\, d\theta$$

$$= \frac{(5 \cdot 3 \cdot 1)(1)}{8 \cdot 6 \cdot 4 \cdot 2} \cdot \frac{\pi}{2} = \frac{5\pi}{256}$$

9. *Evaluate* $\int_0^1 x^2 \left(1 - x^2\right)^{\frac{3}{2}} dx$

➡ Let $I = \int_0^1 x^2 \left(1 - x^2\right)^{\frac{3}{2}} dx$

Put $x = \sin\theta$

If $x = 0 \Rightarrow \theta = 0$, If $x = 1 \Rightarrow \theta = \pi/2$

$$I = \int_0^{\frac{\pi}{2}} \sin^2\theta\left(1-\sin^2\theta\right)^{\frac{3}{2}}\cos\theta\, d\theta = \int_0^{\frac{\pi}{2}} \sin^2\theta\cos^4\theta\, d\theta$$

$$= \frac{(3\cdot 1)\ (1)}{6\cdot 4\cdot 2}.\frac{\pi}{2} = \frac{\pi}{32}$$

10. *Evaluate* $\int_0^1 x^5\left(1-x^2\right)^{5/2} dx$

➡ Let $I = \int_0^1 x^5\left(1-x^2\right)^{5/2} dx$

Put $x = \sin\theta \Rightarrow dx = \cos\theta\ d\theta$

If $x = 0 \Rightarrow \theta = 0$, If $x = 1 \Rightarrow \theta = \pi/2$

$$I = \int_0^{\frac{\pi}{2}} \sin^5\theta\left(1-\sin^2\theta\right)^{\frac{5}{2}}\cos\theta\, d\theta = \int_0^{\frac{\pi}{2}} \sin^5\theta.\cos^6\theta\, d\theta$$

$$= \frac{(5\cdot 3\cdot 1)\ (4\cdot 2)}{11\cdot 9\cdot 7\cdot 5\cdot 3\cdot 1} = \frac{8}{693}$$

11. *Evaluate* $\int_0^{2a} x^2\sqrt{2ax-x^2}dx$

➡ Let $I = \int_0^{2a} x^2\sqrt{2ax-x^2}dx$

Put $x = 2a\sin^2\theta \Rightarrow dx = 4a\sin\theta.\cos\theta\, d\theta$

If $x = 0 \Rightarrow \theta = 0$, If $x = 2a \Rightarrow \theta = \pi/2$

$$I = \int_0^{\frac{\pi}{2}} \left(2a\sin^2\theta\right)^2\sqrt{2a\left(2a\sin^2\theta\right)-\left(2a\sin^2\theta\right)^2}\,4a\ \cos\theta\sin\theta.d\theta$$

$$= \int_0^{\frac{\pi}{2}} 4a^2\sin^4\theta.2a\sin\theta\sqrt{1-\sin^2\theta}.4a\cos\theta.\sin\theta.d\theta$$

$$= 32a^4\int_0^{\frac{\pi}{2}} \sin^6\theta.\cos^2\theta\, d\theta = 32a^4\frac{(1)\ (5\cdot 3\cdot 1)}{8\cdot 6\cdot 4\cdot 2}.\frac{\pi}{2} = \frac{5a^4\pi}{8}$$

12. *Evaluate* $\int_0^{\infty} \frac{x^6}{\left(1+x^2\right)^{9/2}}dx$

➡ Let $I = \int_0^{\infty} \frac{x^6}{(1+x^2)^{9/2}} dx$

Put $x = \tan\theta \Rightarrow dx = \sec^2\theta\, d\theta$.

If $x = 0 \Rightarrow \theta = 0$, If $x = \infty \Rightarrow \theta = \pi/2$

$$\therefore\ I = \int_0^{\frac{\pi}{2}} \frac{\tan^6\theta}{(\sec^2\theta)^{9/2}} \sec^2\theta\, d\theta = \int_0^{\frac{\pi}{2}} \tan^6\theta, \cos^7\theta\, d\theta$$

$$= \int_0^{\frac{\pi}{2}} \sin^6\theta . \cos\theta\, d\theta = \frac{(5\cdot 3\cdot 1)(1)}{7\cdot 5\cdot 3\cdot 1} = \frac{1}{7}$$

Exercises

Evaluate the following integrals

1. $\int_0^{\frac{\pi}{2}} \sin^6 x \cos^8 x dx$
2. $\int_0^{\frac{\pi}{2}} \sin^3 x \cos^4 x dx$
3. $\int_0^{\frac{\pi}{2}} \sin^5 x \cos^2 x dx$
4. $\int_0^{\pi} x \sin x \cos^4 x\, dx$
5. $\int_0^{\pi} \sin^4(\theta/2) \cos^3(\theta/2)\, d\theta$
6. $\int_0^{\frac{\pi}{2}} \sin^2 x \left(\sin^3 x + \cos^3 x\right) dx$
7. $\int_0^{\frac{\pi}{6}} \sin^2 6\theta \cos^4 3\theta\, d\theta$
8. $\int_0^1 x^{\frac{3}{2}} (1-x)^{\frac{3}{2}}\, dx$
9. $\int_0^{\pi} x \sin^3 x \cos^4 x dx$
10. $\int_0^{\frac{\pi}{2}} \sin^7 x \cos^5 x dx$
11. $\int_0^{\pi} x \sin^6 x \cos^4 x dx$
12. $\int_0^1 x^{\frac{3}{2}} \sqrt{1-x}\, dx$
13. $\int_0^{2a} x^3 \sqrt{2ax - x^2} dx$
14. $\int_0^{\frac{1}{2}} x^3 \sqrt{1-4x^2} dx$
15. $\int_0^{\infty} \frac{x^5}{(1+x^2)^6} dx$
16. $\int_0^{\infty} \frac{x^3}{(x^2+4)^{\frac{3}{2}}} dx$
17. $\int_0^{\infty} \frac{x}{(x^2+a^2)^5} dx$
18. $\int_0^4 x^{\frac{9}{2}} (4-x)^{\frac{-1}{2}}\, dx$

19. $\int_0^2 x^3\sqrt{2-x}\,dx$

20. $\int_0^\infty \frac{x^4}{(1+x^2)^4}dx$

21. *If n is a positive integer, then show that*

$$\int_0^{2a} x^n\sqrt{2ax-x^2}dx = \frac{(2n+1)!}{(n+2)!\,n!}\,\frac{a^{n+2}}{2^n}\pi$$

Answers

1. $\frac{5\pi}{4096}$
2. $\frac{2}{35}$
3. $\frac{8}{105}$
4. $\frac{\pi}{5}$
5. $\frac{4}{35}$
6. $\frac{2}{3}$
7. $\frac{5\pi}{192}$
8. $\frac{3\pi}{128}$
9. 0
10. $\frac{1}{120}$
11. $\frac{3\pi^2}{512}$
12. $\frac{\pi}{16}$
13. $\frac{5\pi a^4}{8}$
14. $\frac{1}{120}$
15. $\frac{1}{7}$
16. $\frac{1}{2}$
17. $\frac{1}{12a^6}$
18. 252π

4.3 Double Integrals

Double integrals can be evaluated by expressing them in terms of two single integrals. If the region R is bounded by curves $x = x_1$, $x = x_2$ and $y = y_1$, $y = y_2$ then

$$I = \iint_R f(x,y)\,dx\,dy = \int_{y_1}^{y_2}\int_{x_1}^{x_2} f(x,y)\,dx\,dy$$

To evaluate this double integral, we proceed as follows:

Case (i) Let x_1, x_2 and y_1, y_2 be constants, then it does not matter, whether we first integrate with respect to x and, then with respect to y or vice versa.

Case (ii) Letx_1, x_2 be constants and y_1, y_2 be functions of x, where $y_1 = f_1(x)$ and $y_2 = f_2(x)$. In this case $f(x, y)$ is first integrated with respect to y treating x as constant between the limits $y_1 = f_1(x)$, and $y_2 = f_2(x)$ and, then the resulting expression is integrated with respect to x between the limits x_1 and x_2,

$$\text{i.e., } I = \int_{x_1}^{x_2} \left[\int_{f_1(x)}^{f_2(x)} f(x, y) dy \right] dx$$

Case (iii) Let y_1, y_2 be constants and x_1, x_2 be functions of y, where $x_1 = g_1(y)$, $x_2 = g_2(y)$. In this case $f\ (x, y)$ is first integrated with respect to x treating y as constant between the limits $x_1 = g_1(y)$ and $x_2 = g_2(y)$ and, then the resulting expression is integrated with respect to y between the limits y_1 and y_2

$$\text{i.e., } I = \int_{y_1}^{y_2} \left[\int_{g_1(y)}^{g_2(y)} f(x, y)\, dx \right] dy$$

Case (iv) Let R be the region bounded by the simple closed curve C as shown in Fig. 3.1.

Let a be the least and b be the greatest values of x in this region. Now, let $y = f_1(x)$ be the equation of the curve ACB and $y = f_2(x)$ be the equation of the curve ADB.

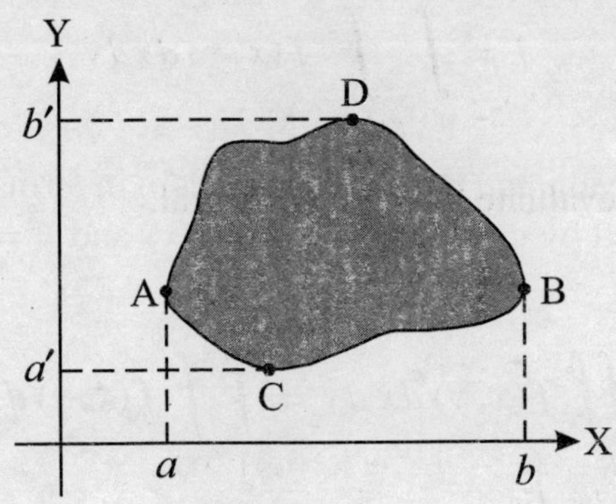

Figure 4.1

Thus x varies from a to b and y varies from $f_1(x)$ to $f_2(x)$. Therefore,

$$I = \int_a^b \int_{f_1(x)}^{f_2(x)} f(x, y)\, dydx$$

Using case (ii), we can evaluate the above integral.

We can construct the integral I in an alternative way by taking constant limits for y as explained below. Refer Fig. 3.2.

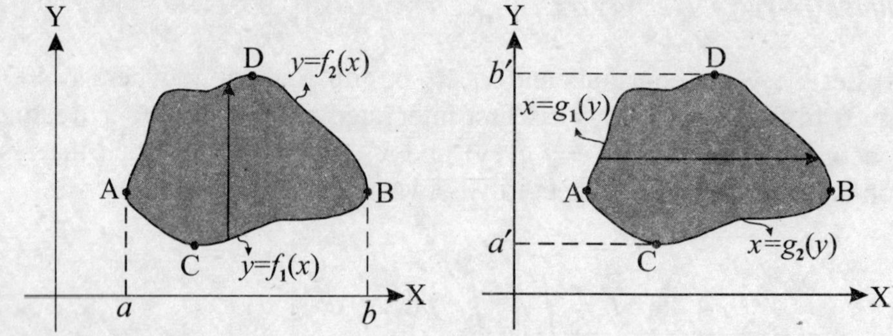

Figure 4.2

Let a' be the least and b' be the greatest values of y in the region. Now let $x = g_1(y)$ be the equation of the curve DAC and $x = g_2(y)$ be the equation of the curve DBC. Therefore, y varies from a' to b' and x varies from $g_1(y)$ to $g_2(y)$

$$I = \int_{a'}^{b'} \int_{g_1(y)}^{g_2(y)} f(x, y)\, dxdy$$

Using case (iii), we can evaluate the above integral.

Worked Examples

1. *Evaluate* $\int_0^1 \int_0^3 x^3 y^3 dx\, dy$

➡ Let

$$I=\int_0^1\int_0^3 x^3y^3dx\,dy=\int_0^1 y^3\frac{x^4}{4}\bigg]_0^3 dy=\frac{1}{4}\int_0^1 y^3(81-0)dy$$

$$=\frac{81}{4}\left[\frac{y^4}{4}\right]_0^1=\frac{81}{16}(1-0)=\frac{81}{16}$$

2. *Evaluate* $\int_1^2\int_3^4 (xy+e^y)dy\,dx$

➡ Let

$$I=\int_1^2\int_3^4 (xy+e^y)dy\,dx=\int_1^2\left[x\frac{y^2}{2}+e^y\right]_3^4 dx$$

$$=\int_1^2\left[\frac{x}{2}(16-9)+(e^4-e^3)\right]dx$$

$$=\left[\frac{7}{2}\left(\frac{x^2}{2}\right)+(e^4-e^3)x\right]_1^2=\frac{7}{4}(4-1)+(e^4-e^3)(2-1)=\frac{21}{4}+e^4-e^3$$

3. *Evaluate* $\int_0^1\int_0^1 \frac{dxdy}{\sqrt{(1-x^2)(1-y^2)}}$

➡ Let

$$I=\int_0^1\int_0^1\frac{dxdy}{\sqrt{(1-x^2)(1-y^2)}}=\int_0^1\int_0^1\frac{dxdy}{\sqrt{1-x^2}.\sqrt{1-y^2}}$$

$$=\int_0^1\frac{1}{\sqrt{1-y^2}}\left[\int_0^1\frac{1}{\sqrt{1-x^2}}dx\right]dy$$

$$= \int_0^1 \frac{1}{\sqrt{1-y^2}} [\sin^{-1} x]_0^1 dy = \int_0^1 \frac{1}{\sqrt{1-y^2}} \left[\frac{\pi}{2} - 0\right] dy$$

$$= \frac{\pi}{2} \sin^1 y]_0^1 = \frac{\pi}{2}\left(\frac{\pi}{2} - 0\right) = \frac{\pi^2}{4}$$

4. *Evaluate* $\int_0^{\pi/2} \int_0^{\pi/2} \sin(x+y)\, dy\, dx$

➡ Let

$$I = \int_0^{\pi/2} \int_0^{\pi/2} \sin(x+y)\, dy\, dx$$

$$= \int_0^{\pi/2} [-\cos(x+y)]_0^{\frac{\pi}{2}}\, dx \quad \left[\int \sin(a+x)\ dx = -\cos(a+x)\right]$$

$$= -\int_0^{\pi/2} \left[\cos\left(x + \frac{\pi}{2}\right) - \cos x\right] dx = -\int_0^{\pi/2} [-\sin x - \cos x]\, dx$$

$$= \int_0^{\pi/2} (\sin x + \cos x)\ dx = -\cos x + \sin x\ ]_0^{\frac{\pi}{2}}$$

$$= -(0-1) + (1-0) = 2$$

5. *Evaluate* $\int_1^5 \int_1^{x^2} x(x^2+y^2)\, dx\, dy$

➡ Let

$$I = \int_1^5 \int_1^{x^2} x(x^2+y^2)\, dx\, dy = \int_1^5 \int_1^{x^2} (x^3 + xy^2)\, dy\, dx$$

$$= \int_1^5 \left[x^3y + \frac{xy^3}{3} \right]_1^{x^2} dx = \int_1^5 \left[x^3(x^2-1) + \frac{x}{3}(x^6-1) \right] dx$$

$$= \int_1^5 \left[x^5 - x^3 + \frac{x^7}{3} - \frac{x}{3} \right] dx = \left[\frac{x^6}{6} - \frac{x^4}{4} + \frac{x^8}{24} - \frac{x^2}{6} \right]_0^1$$

$$= \frac{1}{6}(1-0) - \frac{1}{4}(1-0) + \frac{1}{24}(1-0) - \frac{1}{6}(1-0)$$

$$= \frac{1}{6} - \frac{1}{4} + \frac{1}{24} - \frac{1}{6} = \frac{1}{24} - \frac{1}{4} = \frac{1-6}{24} = -\frac{5}{24}$$

6. *Evaluate* $\int_0^1 \int_x^{\sqrt{x}} (x^2 + y^2)\, dy\, dx$

➡ Let

$$I = \int_0^1 \int_x^{\sqrt{x}} (x^2 + y^2)\, dy\, dx = \int_0^1 \left[x^2y + \frac{y^3}{3} \right]_x^{\sqrt{x}} dx$$

$$= \int_0^1 \left[x^2(\sqrt{x} - x) + \frac{1}{3}((\sqrt{x})^3 - x^3) \right] dx$$

$$= \int_0^1 \left[x^{5/2} - x^3 + \frac{1}{3}x^{3/2} - \frac{1}{3}x^3 \right] dx$$

$$= \int_0^1 \left[x^{5/2} + \frac{1}{3}x^{3/2} - \frac{4}{3}x^3 \right] dx$$

$$= \left[\frac{x^{7/2}}{7/2} + \frac{1}{3}\left(\frac{x^{5/2}}{5/2}\right) - \frac{4}{3}\left(\frac{x^4}{4}\right) \right]_0^1$$

$$= \frac{2}{7}(1-0) + \frac{2}{15}(1-0) - \frac{1}{3}(1-0)$$

$$= \frac{30 + 14 - 35}{7 \times 5 \times 3} = \frac{9}{7 \times 5 \times 3} = \frac{3}{35}$$

7. *Evaluate* $\int_0^a \int_0^{\sqrt{a^2-x^2}} x^2 y \, dy \, dx$

➡ Let

$$I = \int_0^a \int_0^{\sqrt{a^2-x^2}} x^2 y \, dy \, dx = \int_0^a \left[x^2 \frac{y^2}{2} \right]_0^{\sqrt{a^2-x^2}} dx = \frac{1}{2} \int_0^a x^2 \left[a^2 - x^2 - 0 \right] dx$$

$$= \frac{1}{2} \int_0^a \left[a^2 x^2 - x^4 \right] dx = \frac{1}{2} \left[a^2 \frac{x^3}{3} - \frac{x^5}{5} \right]_0^a = \frac{1}{2} \left[\frac{a^2}{3} (a^3 - 0) - \frac{1}{5} (a^5 - 0) \right]$$

$$= \frac{1}{2} \left[\frac{a^5}{3} - \frac{a^5}{5} \right] = \frac{1}{2} \left[\frac{5a^5 - 3a^5}{15} \right] = \frac{a^5}{15}$$

8. *Evaluate* $\int_0^1 \int_{x^2}^{x} \left(x^2 + 3y + 2 \right) dy \, dx$

➡ Let

$$I = \int_0^1 \int_{x^2}^{x} (x^2 + 3y + 2) \, dy \, dx = \int_0^1 (x^2 + 2) y + \frac{3y^2}{2} \Big|_{x^2}^{x} dx$$

$$= \int_0^1 (x^2 + 2)(x - x^2) + \frac{3}{2} (x^2 - x^4) \, dx$$

$$= \int_0^1 \left[(x^3 - x^4 + 2x - 2x^2) + \frac{3}{2} x^2 - \frac{3}{2} x^4 \right] dx$$

$$= \frac{1}{2} \int_0^1 (2x^3 - 2x^4 + 4x - 4x^2 + 3x^2 - 3x^4) \, dx$$

$$= \frac{1}{2} \int_0^1 (-5x^4 + 2x^3 - x^2 + 4x) \, dx$$

$$= \frac{1}{2} \left[\frac{-5x^5}{5} + \frac{2x^4}{4} - \frac{x^3}{3} + \frac{4x^2}{2} \right]_0^1$$

$$= \frac{1}{2} \left[-(1 - 0) + \frac{1}{2} (1 - 0) - \frac{1}{3} (1 - 0) + 2(1 - 0) \right]$$

$$= \frac{1}{2} \left[-1 + \frac{1}{2} - \frac{1}{3} + 2 \right] = \frac{1}{2} \left[\frac{-6 + 3 - 2 + 12}{6} \right] = \frac{7}{12}$$

9. *Evaluate* $\int_0^1 \int_0^{1-x} (x+y)^2 \, dy\, dx$

➡ Let

$$I = \int_0^1 \int_0^{1-x} (x+y)^2 \, dy\, dx = \int_0^1 \left[\frac{(x+y)^3}{3}\right]_0^{(1-x)} dx$$

$$= \frac{1}{3}\int_0^1 \left[(x+1-x)^3 - (x+0)^3\right] dx = \frac{1}{3}\int_0^1 \left(1 - x^3\right) dx$$

$$= \frac{1}{3}\left[x - \frac{x^4}{4}\right]_0^1 = \frac{1}{3}\left[(1-0) - \frac{1}{4}(1-0)\right] = \frac{1}{3}\left(1 - \frac{1}{4}\right) = \frac{1}{4}$$

10. *Evaluate* $\int_1^2 \int_0^{2-y} xy \, dx\, dy$

➡ Let

$$I = \int_1^2 \int_0^{2-y} xy \, dx\, dy = \int_1^2 \left[y\frac{x^2}{2}\right]_0^{2-y} dy = \frac{1}{2}\int_1^2 y\left[(2-y)^2 - 0\right] dy$$

$$= \frac{1}{2}\int_1^2 y\left[4 + y^2 - 4y\right] dy$$

$$= \frac{1}{2}\int_1^2 \left(4y + y^3 - 4y^2\right) dy = \frac{1}{2}\left[\frac{4y^2}{2} + \frac{y^4}{4} - 4\frac{y^3}{3}\right]_1^2$$

$$= \frac{1}{2}\left[2\left(2^2 - 1^2\right) + \frac{1}{4}\left(2^4 - 1^4\right) - \frac{4}{3}\left(2^3 - 1^3\right)\right] = \frac{1}{2}\left[6 + \frac{15}{4} - \frac{28}{3}\right]$$

$$= \frac{1}{2}\left[\frac{72 + 45 - 112}{12}\right] = \frac{5}{24}$$

11. *Evaluate* $\int_0^1 \int_0^{\sqrt{1-x^2}} xye^{x^2}\,dy\,dx$

➡ Let

$$I = \int_0^1 \int_0^{\sqrt{1-x^2}} xye^{x^2}\,dy\,dx$$

$$= \int_0^1 xe^{x^2} \left.\frac{y^2}{2}\right]_0^{\sqrt{1-x^2}} dx = \frac{1}{2}\int_0^1 xe^{x^2}\left(1 - x^2 - 0\right) dx$$

$$= \frac{1}{2}\int_0^1 x\left(1 - x^2\right) e^{x^2}\,dx$$

Put $x^2 = t \Rightarrow 2xdxdt \Rightarrow xdx = \frac{dt}{2}$
If $x = 0 \Rightarrow t = 0$, if $x = 1 \Rightarrow t = 1$

$$\therefore\ I = \frac{1}{2}\int_0^1 (1 - t)\, e^t \frac{dt}{2}$$

$$= \frac{1}{4}\left\{\left[(1-t)\, e^t\right]_0^1 - \int_0^1 (-1)\, e^t dt\right\} \quad \text{[By integration by parts]}$$

$$= \frac{1}{4}\left[(0-1) + e^t\right]_0^1 = \frac{1}{4}\left[-1 + (e-1)\right] = \frac{1}{4}(e-2)$$

12. *Evaluate* $\int_0^1 \int_x^{\sqrt{x}} xy\,dy\,dx$

➡ Let

$$I = \int_0^1 \int_x^{\sqrt{x}} xy\,dy\,dx = \int_0^1 x \left.\frac{y^2}{2}\right|_x^{\sqrt{x}} dx = \frac{1}{2}\int_0^1 x\left(x - x^2\right) dx$$

$$= \frac{1}{2}\int_0^1 (x^2 - x^3)\, dx = \frac{1}{2}\left[\frac{x^3}{3} - \frac{x^4}{4}\right]_0^1 = \frac{1}{2}\left[\frac{1}{3}(1-0) - \frac{1}{4}(1-0)\right]$$

$$= \frac{1}{2}\left[\frac{1}{3} - \frac{1}{4}\right] = \frac{1}{2}\left[\frac{1}{12}\right] = \frac{1}{24}$$

13. *Evaluate* $\int_0^{2a}\int_0^{\sqrt{2ax-x^2}} xy\, dy\, dx$

➡ Let

$$I = \int_0^{2a}\int_0^{\sqrt{2ax-x^2}} xy\, dy\, dx = \int_0^{2a} x \left[\frac{y^2}{2}\right]_0^{\sqrt{2ax-x^2}} dx = \frac{1}{2}\int_0^{2a} x\left[(2ax - x^2) - 0\right] dx$$

$$= \frac{1}{2}\int_0^{2a} (2ax^2 - x^3)\, dx = \frac{1}{2}\left[2a\frac{x^3}{3} - \frac{x^4}{4}\right]_0^{2a}$$

$$= \frac{1}{2}\left[\frac{2a}{3}[\,(2a)^3 - 0] - \frac{1}{4}\left((2a)^4 - 0\right)\right]$$

$$= \frac{1}{2}\left[\frac{16a^4}{3} - \frac{16a^4}{4}\right] = \frac{16a^4}{2}\left[\frac{1}{3} - \frac{1}{4}\right] = 8a^4\left(\frac{4-3}{12}\right) = \frac{2a^4}{3}$$

14. *Evaluate* $\iint_R (x^2 + y^2)\, dx\, dy$ *when R is the triangle bounded by the lines* $y = 0$, $y = x$ *and* $x = 1$

➡ Let $I = \iint_R (x^2 + y^2) dx\, dy$

Here the minimum value of x is 0 and maximum value is 1. Therefore x varies from 0 to 1, and y varies from the line $y = 0$ to the line $y = x$ as shown in Fig. 3.3

$$\text{i.e., } x : 0 \to 1, \quad y : 0 \to x$$

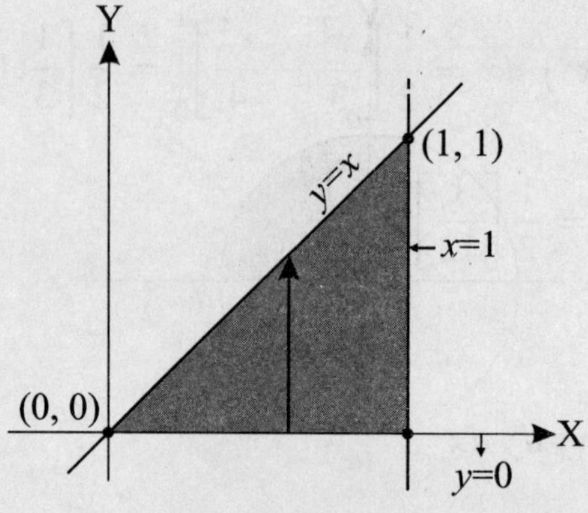

Figure 4.3

Therefore

$$I = \int_{x=0}^{1} \int_{y=0}^{x} \left(x^2 + y^2\right) dy\, dx = \int_{0}^{1} x^2 y + \frac{y^3}{3}\Bigg]_0^x dx$$

$$= \int_{0}^{1} \left[x^2 (x - 0) + \frac{1}{3}\left(x^3 - 0\right)\right] dx$$

$$= \int_{0}^{1} \left(x^3 + \frac{x^3}{3}\right) dx = \int_0^1 \frac{4x^3}{3} dx$$

$$= \frac{4}{3}\int_{0}^{1} x^3\, dx = \frac{4}{3}\ \frac{x^4}{4}\Bigg]_0^1 = \frac{1}{3}(1 - 0) = \frac{1}{3}$$

15. *Evaluate* $\iint_A xy\, dx\, dy$ *when A is area bounded by the circle* $x^2 + y^2 = a^2$ *in the first quadrant.*

➡ Let $I = \iint_A xy\, dx\, dy$

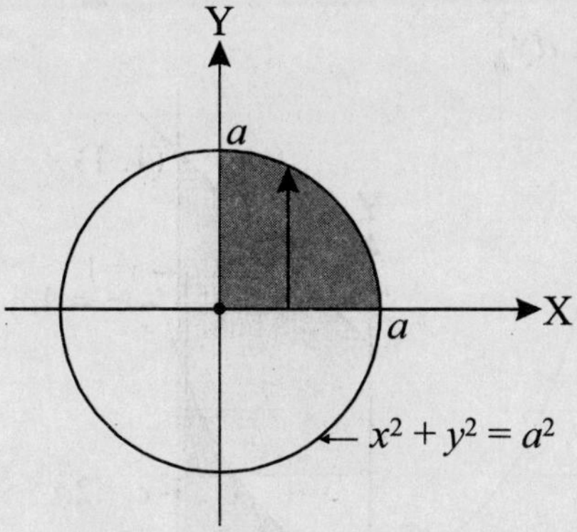

Figure 4.4

Here the minimum value of x is 0 and the maximum value is a. Therefore, x varies from 0 to a and y varies from the line $y = 0$ to the circle $x^2 + y^2 = a^2$

$$\therefore\ y^2 = a^2 - x^2 \Rightarrow y = \pm\sqrt{a^2 - x^2}$$

We take $y = \sqrt{a^2 - x^2}$ because y is positive above the x-axis

$$\text{i.e., } x : 0 \to a \quad \text{and} \quad y : 0 \to \sqrt{a^2 - x^2}$$

Therefore,

$$I = \int_0^a \int_0^{\sqrt{a^2-x^2}} xy\,dy\,dx = \int_0^a x\left[\frac{y^2}{2}\right]_0^{\sqrt{a^2-x^2}} dx$$

$$= \frac{1}{2}\int_0^a x\left[(a^2 - x^2) - 0\right] dx = \frac{1}{2}\int_0^a \left(a^2x - x^3\right) dx$$

$$= \frac{1}{2}\left[a^2\frac{x^2}{2} - \frac{x^4}{4}\right]_0^a = \frac{1}{2}\left[\frac{a^4}{2} - \frac{a^4}{4}\right] = \frac{a^4}{8}$$

16. *Evaluate* $\iint_R xy\,dx\,dy$ *where R is the region bounded by x-axis, the ordinate $x = 2a$ and the parabola $x^2 = 4ay$*

➡ Let $I = \iint_R xy\,dx\,dy$

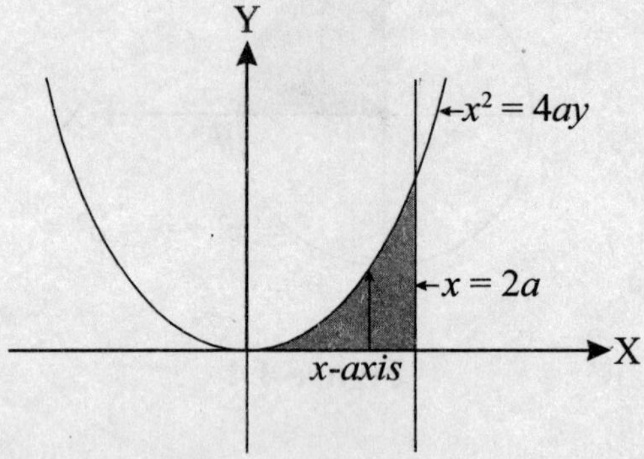

Figure 4.5

Here the minimum value of x is 0 and maximum value is $2a \Rightarrow x : 0 \to 2a$ and y varies from x axis to the parabola $x^2 = 4ay$ (refer Fig. 3.5). $\Rightarrow y : 0 \to \frac{x^2}{4a}$

$$\iint_R xy\,dx\,dy = \int_0^{2a}\int_0^{x^2/4a} xy\,dy\,dx = \int_0^{2a} x\left.\frac{y^2}{2}\right|_0^{x^2/4a} dx = \frac{1}{2}\int_0^{2a} x\left(\frac{x^4}{16a^2} - 0\right)dx$$

$$= \frac{1}{2}\int_0^{2a} \frac{x^5}{16a^2}dx = \frac{1}{32a^2}\left.\frac{x^6}{6}\right|_0^{2a} dx = \frac{1}{32a^2 \times 6}(2a)^6 = \frac{a^4}{3}$$

17. *If R is the region bounded by the parabolas $x = y^2$ and $y = x^2$ show that* $\iint_R xy\,(x + y)\,dx\,dy = \frac{3}{28}$

➡ Let $I = \iint_R xy(x + y)dx\,dy$

The given curves are

$$y = x^2 \qquad (1)$$

$$x = y^2 \qquad (2)$$

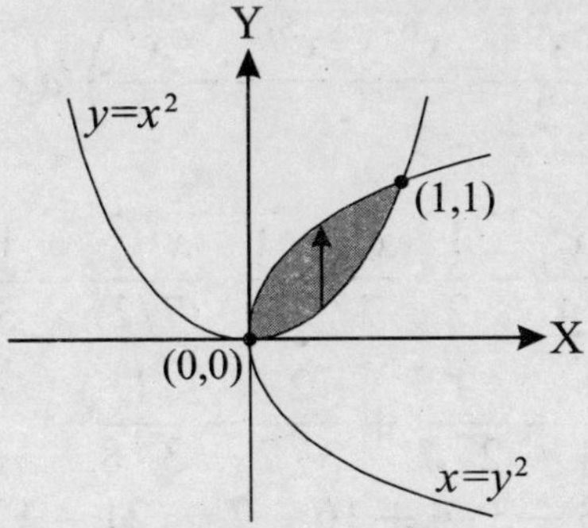

Figure 4.6

To find the points of intersection we substitute (2) in (1)

$$\therefore\ y = \left(y^2\right)^2 = y^4$$
$$y - y^4 = 0$$
$$y\left(1 - y^3\right) = 0$$
$$\therefore\ y = 0 \text{ or } y = 1$$
$$\therefore \text{ If } y = 0 \Rightarrow x = 0 \quad \text{if } y = 1 \Rightarrow x = 1$$

Therefore, the parabolas interacts at (0,0) and (1,1) $x : 0 \to 1$ and y varies from the parabola $y = x^2$ to the parabola $y^2 = x$ as shown in Fig. 3.6.

i.e., $y : x^2 \to \sqrt{x}$

$$I = \int_0^1 \int_{x^2}^{\sqrt{x}} xy\,(x + y)\,dy\,dx$$

$$= \int_0^1 \int_{x^2}^{\sqrt{x}} \left(x^2 y + xy^2\right) dy\,dx = \int_0^1 x^2 \frac{y^2}{2} + x\,\frac{y^3}{3}\Big|_{x^2}^{\sqrt{x}} dx$$

$$= \int_0^1 \left[\frac{x^2}{2}\left(x - x^4\right) + \frac{x}{3}\left(\left(\sqrt{x}\right)^3 - x^6\right)\right] dx$$

$$= \int_0^1 \left(\frac{x^3}{2} - \frac{x^6}{2} + \frac{x^{5/2}}{3} - \frac{x^7}{3} \right) dx$$

$$= \frac{1}{2} \cdot \frac{x^4}{4} - \frac{1}{2} \cdot \frac{x^7}{7} + \frac{1}{3} \cdot \frac{x^{7/2}}{(7/2)} - \frac{1}{3} \cdot \frac{x^8}{8} \Big]_0^1$$

$$= \frac{1}{2 \cdot 4} - \frac{1}{2 \cdot 7} + \frac{2}{3 \cdot 7} - \frac{1}{3 \cdot 8}$$

$$= \frac{7 \cdot 3 - 3 \cdot 4 + 16 - 7}{7 \cdot 3 \cdot 8} = \frac{21 - 12 + 9}{7 \cdot 3 \cdot 8} = \frac{18}{7 \cdot 3 \cdot 8} = \frac{3}{28}$$

18. *Evaluate* $\iint_R y^2 \, dx \, dy$ *where R is the region bounded by the ellipse* $\frac{x^2}{a^2} + \frac{y^2}{b^2} = 1$

➡ Let $I = \iint_R y^2 \, dx \, dy$

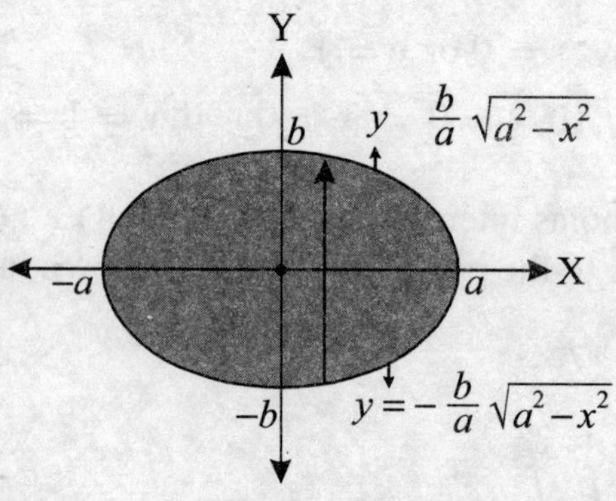

Figure 4.7

Refer Fig. 3.7. Here x varies from $-a$ to a and

$$\frac{x^2}{a^2} + \frac{y^2}{b^2} = 1$$

$$\frac{y^2}{b^2} = 1 - \frac{x^2}{a^2}$$

$$y^2 = \frac{b^2}{a^2}\left(a^2 - x^2\right)$$
$$y = \pm\frac{b}{a}\sqrt{a^2 - x^2}$$
$$y : -\frac{b}{a}\sqrt{a^2 - x^2} \Rightarrow \frac{b}{a}\sqrt{a^2 - x^2}$$

Therefore,

$$I = \int_{-a}^{a} \int_{-\frac{b}{a}\sqrt{a^2-x^2}}^{\frac{b}{a}\sqrt{a^2-x^2}} y^2\, dy\, dx = \int_{-a}^{a} \frac{y^3}{3}\bigg|_{-\frac{b}{a}\sqrt{a^2-x^2}}^{\frac{b}{a}\sqrt{a^2-x^2}} dx$$

$$= \frac{1}{3}\int_{-a}^{a} \left[\frac{b^3}{a^3}\left(a^2 - x^2\right)^{\frac{3}{2}} + \frac{b^3}{a^3}\left(a^2 - x^2\right)^{\frac{3}{2}}\right] dx$$

$$= \frac{1}{3}\int_{-a}^{a} \frac{2b^3}{a^3}\left(a^2 - x^2\right)^{3/2} dx = \frac{2b^3}{3a^3}\int_{-a}^{a} \left(a^2 - x^2\right)^{3/2} dx$$

$$= \frac{2b^3}{3a^3} 2\int_{0}^{a} \left(a^2 - x^2\right)^{3/2} dx = \frac{4b^3}{3a^3}\int_{0}^{a} \left(a^2 - x^2\right)^{3/2} dx$$

Put $x = a\sin\theta \Rightarrow dx = a\cos\theta\, d\theta$
If $x = 0 \Rightarrow \theta = 0$, if $x = a \Rightarrow \theta = \pi/2$

$$= \frac{4b^3}{3a^3}\int_{0}^{\pi/2} \left(a^2 - a^2\sin^2\theta\right)^{\frac{3}{2}} a\cos\theta\, d\theta$$

$$= \frac{4b^3}{3a^3}\int_{0}^{\pi/2} a^3\cos^3\theta a\cos\theta\, d\theta$$

$$= \frac{4b^3}{3} a\int_{0}^{\pi/2} \cos^4\theta\, d\theta = \frac{4b^3 a}{3}\left(\frac{3}{4}\cdot\frac{1}{2}\cdot\frac{\pi}{2}\right) = \frac{ab^3\pi}{4}$$

19. *Evaluate* $\iint\limits_R dx\,dy$ *where R is the region bounded by the lines* $y = x$, $x + y = 4$, $y = 1$ *and* $y = 0$

➡ Let $I = \iint\limits_R dx\,dy$

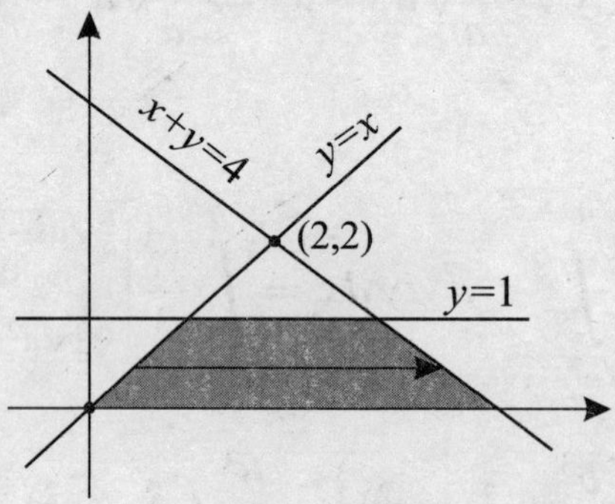

Figure 4.8

Here y varies from 0 to 1 and x varies from the line $y = x$ to the line $x + y = 4$ as shown in Fig. 3.8.

$$\text{i.e.,}\quad y : 0 \to 1, \quad x : y \to 4 - y$$

Therefore,

$$I = \int_0^1 \int_y^{4-y} dx\,dy = \int_0^1 x\,|_y^{4-y} dy = \int_0^1 (4 - y - y)\,dy$$

$$= \int_0^1 (4 - 2y)\,dy = 4y - \frac{2y^2}{2}\bigg|_0^1$$

$$= 4\,(1 - 0) - (1 - 0) = 4 - 1 = 3$$

20. *Evaluate* $\iint\limits_R dx\,dy$ *where R is the region bounded between the parabola* $y = x^2$ *and the line* $x + y = 2$

➡ Let $I = \iint\limits_R dx\,dy$

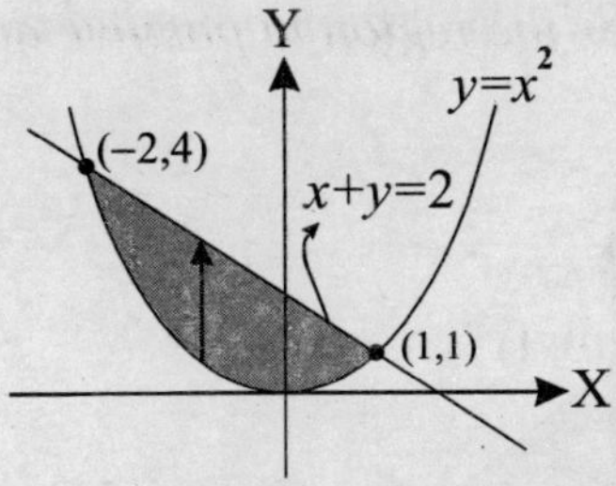

Figure 4.9

$$y = x^2 \tag{1}$$

$$x + y = 2 \tag{2}$$

Substituting (1) in (2), we get

$$x + x^2 = 2$$
$$x^2 + x - 2 = 0$$
$$x^2 + 2x - x - 2 = 0$$
$$x(x+2) - 1(x+2) = 0$$
$$(x-1)(x+2)$$
$$x = 1, \ -2$$

If $x = 1 \Rightarrow y = 1$, if $x = -2 \Rightarrow y = 4$
Here $x : -2 \to 1$, $y : x^2 \to 2 - x$
Therefore,

$$I = \int_{-2}^{1} \int_{x^2}^{2-x} dy\, dx = \int_{-2}^{1} y]_{x^2}^{2-x} dx = \int_{-2}^{1} \left[(2-x) - x^2\right] dx$$

$$= 2x - \frac{x^2}{2} - \frac{x^3}{3}\Big|_{-2}^{1}$$

$$= 2(1-(-2)) - \frac{1}{2}\left(1-(-2)^2\right) - \frac{1}{3}\left(1-(-2)^3\right)$$

$$= 2(3) - \frac{1}{2}(-3) - \frac{1}{3}(9) = 6 + 3/2 - 3- = 3 + 3/2 = 9/2$$

21. *Evaluate* $\iint xy\, dx\, dy$ *over the region in positive quadrant for which* $x + y \leq 1$

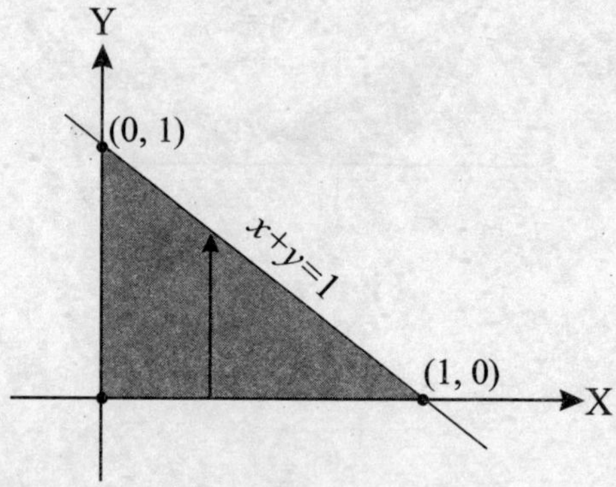

Figure 4.10

➡

$x : 0 \to 1, \quad y : 0 \to (1 - x)$

$$I = \iint xy\, dx\, dy = \int_0^1 \int_0^{(1-x)} xy\, dy\, dx$$

$$= \int_0^1 x \left[\frac{y^2}{2}\right]_0^{(1-x)} dx = \int_0^1 \left[x \frac{(1-x)^2}{2}\right] dx$$

$$= \frac{1}{2} \int_0^1 \left[x\left(1 - 2x + x^2\right)\right] dx = \frac{1}{2} \int_0^1 \left(x - 2x^2 + x^3\right) dx$$

$$= \frac{1}{2}\left[\frac{x^2}{2} - \frac{2x^3}{3} + \frac{x^4}{4}\right]_0^1$$

$$= \frac{1}{2}\left(\frac{1}{2} - \frac{2}{3} + \frac{1}{4}\right)$$

$$= \frac{1}{24}$$

Exercises

I. *Evaluate the following integrals*

1) $\int_0^1 \int_{x^2}^{x} dy\, dx$

2) $\int_1^2 \int_y^{3y} (x + y)\, dx\, dy$

3) $\int_0^\infty \int_y^\infty x e^{-\frac{x^2}{y}}\, dx\, dy$

4) $\int_0^\pi \int_0^{\cos\theta} r \sin\theta\, dr\, d\theta$

5) $\int_0^1 \int_0^{1-x} xy\, dy\, dx$

6) $\int_1^2 \int_0^x \frac{dy dx}{x^2 + y^2}$

7) $\int_0^1 \int_0^{x^2} x e^y\, dy\, dx$

8) $\int_0^1 \int_0^{\sqrt{x}} \left(x^2 + y^2\right) dy dx$

9) $\int_0^\pi \int_0^{2a\cos\theta} r^3 dr d\theta$

10) $\int_0^\pi \int_0^{\sin y} dx dy$

11) $\int_0^a \int_0^{\sqrt{a^2 - x^2}} x^2 y dx dy$

12) $\int_0^1 \int_0^{x^2} e^{\frac{y}{x}}\, dy\, dx$

13) $\int_0^a \int_0^{\sqrt{a^2 - y^2}} \sqrt{a^2 - x^2 - y^2}\, dx\, dy$

14) $\int_0^{4a} \int_{y^2/4a}^{2\sqrt{ay}} dx dy$

15) $\int_0^{\pi/2} \int_0^\infty \frac{r\, dr\, d\theta}{\left(r^2 + a^2\right)^2}$

16) $\int_0^1 \int_0^{\sqrt{(1+x^2)}} \frac{dy\, dx}{1 + x^2 + y^2}$

II 1) *Evaluate* $\iint_A x^2 y^2 dx\, dy$, *where A is the region bounded by* $x = 0,\ y = 0$ *and* $x^2 + y^2 = 1$

2) Evaluate $\int_A xy(x+y)\, dA,$ where A is the area bounded between the parabola $y = x^2$ and the line $y = x$

3) Evaluate $\iint_A y\, dx\, dy$, where A is the region enclosed between the parabolas $y^2 = 4x$ and $x^2 = 4y$

4) If A is the triangular area with vertices (0,0), (10,1) and (1,1), evaluate $\iint_A \sqrt{xy - y^2}\, dx\, dy$

5) If A is the area bounded by the lines $y = 0$ and $x = 1$ and the parabola $y = x^2$, then evaluate $\iint_A xy^2\, dx\, dy$

6) Evaluate $\iint_A e^{2x+3y}\, dx\, dy$ over the region A bounded by $x = 0$, $y = 0$ and $x + y = 1$

7) Evaluate $\iint_R \left\{1 - \frac{x^2}{a^2} - \frac{y^2}{b^2}\right\}^{1/2} dx\, dy$ where R is the region bounded by the ellipse $\frac{x^2}{a^2} + \frac{y^2}{b^2} = 1$

8) Evaluate $\iint_A y\, dx\, dy$, where A is the region in the first quadrant bounded by the ellipse $\frac{x^2}{a^2} + \frac{y^2}{b^2} = 1$

9) If R is the region bounded by the lines $x = 2$, $y = 1$ and the parabola $y = x^2$, show that $\iint_R (x^2 + y^2)\, dx\, dy = \frac{1006}{105}$

10) If R is the triangular bounded by the x-axis, y-axis and the line $\frac{x}{a} + \frac{y}{b} = 1$, show that $\iint_R xy\, dx\, dy = \frac{a^2b^2}{24}$

11) *If R is the region bounded by the circle $x^2 + y^2 = 1$ in the first quadrant, evaluate* $\iint_R \frac{xy}{\sqrt{1-y^2}}\, dx\, dy$

Answers

I. 1) $\frac{1}{6}$ 2) 14 3) $\frac{1}{2}$

4) $\frac{1}{3}$ 5) $\frac{1}{24}$ 6) $\frac{\pi}{4}\log 2$

7) $\frac{1}{2}(e-2)$ 8) $\frac{3}{35}$ 9) $3\pi\,\frac{a^4}{4}$

10) 2 11) $\frac{a^5}{15}$ 12) $\frac{1}{2}$

13) $\frac{\pi\, a^3}{6}$ 14) $\frac{16}{3}a^2$ 15) $\frac{\pi}{4a^2}$

16) $\frac{\pi}{4}\log(1+\sqrt{2})$

II. 1) $\frac{\pi}{96}$ 2) $\frac{3}{56}$ 3) $\frac{48}{5}$

4) 6 5) $\frac{1}{24}$ 6) $\frac{1}{6}(e-1)^2(2e+1)$

7) $\frac{2\pi ab}{3}$ 8) $\frac{ab^2}{3}$ 11) $\frac{1}{6}$

4.4 Triple Integrals

Triple integral can be evaluated by expressing it in terms of three integrals in the form

$$I = \iiint_v f(x,y,z)\, dx\, dy\, dz = \int_{x_1}^{x_2}\int_{y_1}^{y_2}\int_{z_1}^{z_2} f(x,y,z)\, dz\, dy\, dx$$

If x_1, x_2 are constants; y_1, y_2 are constants or functions of x; z_1, z_2 are constants or functions of x and y then the above integral is evaluated as follows:

First $f(x, y, z)$ is integrated with respect to z between z_1 and z_2 keeping x and y fixed. The resulting expression is then integrated with respect to y treating x as constant between y_1 and y_2. The result thus obtained is finally integrated with respect to x from x_1 to x_2

$$\text{i.e.,} \int_{x_1}^{x_2}\left[\int_{y_1(x)}^{y_2(x)}\left\{\int_{z_1(x,y)}^{z_2(x,y)} f(x,y,z)\,dz\right\}dy\right]dx$$

where the integration is carried out from the innermost bracket to the outermost bracket.

Note Evaluation of the integral may be performed in any order if all the limits are constants.

Worked Examples

1. *Evaluate* $\int_0^1\int_0^1\int_0^1 (x+y+z)\,dx\,dy\,dz$

➡ Let

$$I = \int_0^1\int_0^1\int_0^1 (x+y+z)\,dx\,dy\,dz = \int_0^1\int_0^1 \frac{x^2}{2} + (y+z)\,x|_0^1\,dy\,dz$$

$$= \int_0^1\int_0^1 \left(\frac{1}{2} + (y+z)\right)dy\,dz = \int_0^1 \left(\frac{1}{2}y + \frac{y^2}{2} + zy\right)_0^1 dz$$

$$= \int_0^1 \left(\frac{1}{2} + \frac{1}{2} + z.1\right)dz = \int_0^1 (1+z)\,dz = z + \frac{z^2}{2}\Big|_0^1 = 1 + \frac{1}{2} = \frac{3}{2}$$

2. *Evaluate* $\int_0^3 \int_0^2 \int_0^1 (x + y + z)\, dz\, dx\, dy$

➡ Let

$$I = \int_0^3 \int_0^2 \int_0^1 (x + y + z)\, dz\, dx\, dy = \int_0^3 \int_0^1 (x + y)\, z + \frac{z^2}{2}\Big|_0^1 dx\, dy$$

$$= \int_0^3 \int_0^2 \left[(x + y)\,(1 - 0) + \frac{1}{2}(1 - 0)\right] dx\, dy$$

$$= \int_0^3 \int_0^2 \left(x + y + \frac{1}{2}\right) dx\, dy = \int_0^3 \left[\frac{x^2}{2} + \left(y + \frac{1}{2}\right) x\right]_0^2 dy$$

$$= \int_0^3 \left[\frac{1}{2}(4 - 0) + \left(y + \frac{1}{2}\right)(2 - 0)\right] dy = \int_0^3 (2 + 2y + 1)\, dy$$

$$= \int_0^3 (2y + 3)\, dy = \frac{2y^2}{2} + 3y\Big|_0^3 = (9 - 0) + 3\,(3 - 0) = 18$$

3. *Evaluate* $\int_0^1 \int_0^1 \int_0^y xyz\, dx\, dy\, dz$

➡ Let

$$I = \int_0^1 \int_0^1 \int_0^y xyz\, dx\, dy\, dz = \int_0^1 \int_0^1 \frac{x^2}{2}\Big|_0^y yzdydz$$

$$= \int_0^1 \int_0^1 yz\frac{1}{2}\,(y^2 - 0)\, dy\, dz$$

$$= \frac{1}{2} \int_0^1 \int_0^1 zy^3\, dy\, dz = \frac{1}{2} \int_0^1 z\, \frac{y^4}{4}\Big|_0^1 dz$$

$$= \frac{1}{8} \int_0^1 z\,(1 - 0)\, dz = \frac{1}{8}\, \frac{z^2}{2}\Big|_0^1 = \frac{1}{16}$$

4. *Evaluate* $\int_0^1 \int_0^2 \int_1^2 x^2 yz \, dx \, dy \, dz$

➠ Let

$$I = \int_0^1 \int_0^2 \int_1^2 x^2 yz \, dx \, dy \, dz = \int_0^1 \int_0^2 \left[\frac{x^3}{3} yz\right]_1^2 dy \, dz$$

$$= \frac{1}{3} \int_0^1 \int_0^2 yz \, (8 - 1) \, dy \, dz = \frac{7}{3} \int_0^1 \left[z \frac{y^2}{2}\right]_0^2 dz$$

$$= \frac{7}{6} \int_0^1 z(4 - 0) \, dz = \frac{4 \times 7}{6} \left[\frac{z^2}{2}\right]_0^1 = \frac{7}{3}[1 - 0] = \frac{7}{3}$$

5. *Evaluate* $\int_0^1 \int_0^1 \int_0^1 e^{x+y+z} \, dx \, dy \, dz$

➠ Let

$$I = \int_0^1 \int_0^1 \int_0^1 e^{x+y+z} \, dx \, dy \, dz = \int_0^1 \int_0^1 \int_0^1 e^x e^y e^z \, dx \, dy \, dz$$

$$= \int_0^1 \int_0^1 e^y e^z [e^x]_0^1 \, dy \, dz = \int_0^1 \int_0^1 e^y e^z [e^1 - e^0] \, dy \, dz$$

$$= (e - 1) \int_0^1 e^z [e^y]_0^1 \, dz = (e - 1) \int_0^1 e^z (e^1 - e^0) \, dz$$

$$= (e - 1)^2 e^z]_0^1 = (e - 1)^2 (e^1 - e^0) = (e - 1)^3$$

6. *Evaluate* $\int_0^a \int_0^x \int_0^{x+y} e^{x+y+z} \, dx \, dy \, dz$

➡ Let

$$I = \int_0^a \int_0^x \int_0^{x+y} e^{x+y+z}\, dx\, dy\, dz = \int_0^a \int_0^x \int_0^{x+y} e^x e^y e^z\, dz\, dy\, dx$$

$$= \int_0^a \int_0^x e^x e^y [e^z]_0^{x+y}\, dy\, dx = \int_0^a \int_0^x e^x e^y [e^{x+y} - e^0]\, dy\, dx$$

$$= \int_0^a \int_0^x (e^{2x} e^{2y} - e^x e^y)\, dy\, dx = \int_0^a \left[e^{2x} \frac{e^{2y}}{2} - e^x e^y \right]_0^x dx$$

$$= \int_0^a \left[\frac{e^{2x}}{2}(e^{2x} - e^0) - e^x(e^x - e^0) \right] dx = \int_0^a \left[\frac{1}{2} e^{4x} - \frac{1}{2} e^{2x} - e^{2x} + e^x \right] dx$$

$$= \int_0^a \left[\frac{1}{2} e^{4x} - \frac{3}{2} e^{2x} + e^x \right] dx = \frac{1}{2}\left(\frac{e^{4x}}{4} \right) - \frac{3}{2}\left(\frac{e^{2x}}{2} \right) + e^x \Bigg]_0^a$$

$$= \frac{1}{8}(e^{4a} - e^0) - \frac{3}{4}(e^{2a} - e^0) + (e^a - e^0) = \frac{1}{8} e^{4a} - \frac{3}{4} e^{2a} + e^a - \frac{1}{8} + \frac{3}{4} - 1$$

$$= \frac{e^{4a} - 6e^{2a} + 8e^a - 1 + 6 - 8}{8} = \frac{1}{8}(e^{4a} - 6e^{2a} + 8e^a - 3)$$

7. *Evaluate* $\displaystyle\int_0^1 \int_0^{1-x} \int_0^{1-x-y} xyz\, dz\, dy\, dx$

➡ Let

$$I = \int_0^1 \int_0^{1-x} \int_0^{1-x-y} xyz\, dz\, dy\, dx = \int_0^1 \int_0^{1-x} xy \left(\frac{z^2}{2} \right)_0^{1-x-y} dy\, dx$$

$$= \frac{1}{2} \int_0^1 \int_0^{1-x} xy \left\{ [(1-x) - y]^2 - 0 \right\} dy\, dx$$

$$= \frac{1}{2}\int_0^1 \int_0^{1-x} xy\left[(1-x)^2 + y^2 - 2y(1-x)\right] dy\, dx$$

$$= \frac{1}{2}\int_0^1 \int_0^{1-x} \left[x(1-x)^2 y + xy^3 - 2x(1-x)y^2\right] dy\, dx$$

$$= \frac{1}{2}\int_0^1 \left[x(1-x)^2 \frac{y^2}{2} + x\frac{y^4}{4} - 2x(1-x)\frac{y^3}{3}\right]_0^{1-x} dx$$

$$= \frac{1}{2}\int_0^1 \left[\frac{x(1-x)}{2}((1-x)^2 - 0) + \frac{x}{4}((1-x)^4 - 0) - \frac{2x(1-x)}{3}((1-x)^3 - 0)\right] dx$$

$$= \frac{1}{2}\int_0^1 \left[\frac{x(1-x)^4}{2} + \frac{x(1-x)^4}{4} - \frac{2x(1-x)^4}{3}\right] dx$$

$$= \frac{1}{2}\int_0^1 x(1-x)^4\left(\frac{1}{2} + \frac{1}{4} - \frac{2}{3}\right) dx$$

$$= \frac{1}{2}\int_0^1 x(1-x)^4\left(\frac{6+3-8}{12}\right) dx = \frac{1}{24}\int_0^1 x(1-x)^4\, dx$$

$$= \frac{1}{24}\left[\left[x\frac{(1-x)^5}{5(-1)}\right]_0^1 - \int_0^1 1\,\frac{(1-x)^5}{5(-1)}\, dx\right]$$

$$= \frac{1}{24}\left[-\frac{1}{5}(0-0) + \frac{1}{5}\frac{(1-x)^6}{6(-1)}\right]_0^1$$

$$= \frac{1}{24}\left[-\frac{1}{30}(0-1)\right] = \frac{1}{720}$$

8. *Evaluate* $\int_{-1}^{1}\int_{0}^{z}\int_{x-z}^{x+z}(x+y+z)\,dy\,dx\,dz$

➡ Let

$$I=\int_{-1}^{1}\int_{0}^{z}\int_{x-z}^{x+z}(x+y+z)\,dy\,dx\,dz=\int_{-1}^{1}\int_{0}^{z}\left[(x+z)\,y+\frac{y^2}{2}\right]_{x-z}^{x+z}dx\,dz$$

$$=\int_{-1}^{1}\int_{0}^{z}\left\{(x+z)\,[x+z-(x-z)]+\frac{1}{2}\left[(x+z)^2-(x-z)^2\right]\right\}dx\,dz$$

$$=\int_{-1}^{1}\int_{0}^{z}(x+z)\,2z+\frac{1}{2}\,(4xz)\,dx\,dz$$

$$=\int_{-1}^{1}\int_{0}^{z}\left(2xz+2z^2+2xz\right)\,dxdz=\int_{-1}^{1}\int_{0}^{z}\left(2z^2+4xz\right)dx\,dz$$

$$=\int_{-1}^{1}2z^2x+4z\left.\frac{x^2}{2}\right]_0^z dz=\int_{-1}^{1}(2z^3+2z^3)dz=\int_{-1}^{1}4z^3dz$$

$$=4\left.\frac{z^4}{4}\right]_{-1}^{1}=\left(1^4-(-1)^4\right)=0$$

9. *Evaluate* $\int_{0}^{a}\int_{0}^{\sqrt{a^2-x^2}}\int_{0}^{\sqrt{a^2-x^2-y^2}}\frac{dz\,dy\,dx}{\sqrt{a^2-x^2-y^2-z^2}}$

➡ Let

$$I=\int_{0}^{a}\int_{0}^{\sqrt{a^2-x^2}}\int_{0}^{\sqrt{a^2-x^2-y^2}}\frac{dz\,dy\,dx}{\sqrt{a^2-x^2-y^2-z^2}}=\int_{0}^{a}\int_{0}^{\sqrt{a^2-x^2}}\int_{0}^{k}\frac{dz\,dy\,dx}{\sqrt{k^2-z^2}}$$

Where $k^2 = a^2 - x^2 - y^2$

$$= \int_0^a \int_0^{\sqrt{a^2-x^2}} \sin^{-1}\left(\frac{z}{k}\right)\Big|_0^k dy\,dx$$

$$= \int_0^a \int_0^{\sqrt{a^2-x^2}} \left[\sin^{-1}\left(\frac{k}{k}\right) - \sin^{-1}(0)\right] dy\,dx$$

$$= \int_0^a \int_0^{\sqrt{a^2-x^2}} \left[\frac{\pi}{2} - 0\right] dy\,dx = \frac{\pi}{2}\int_0^a y]_0^{\sqrt{a^2-x^2}}\,dx$$

$$= \frac{\pi}{2}\int_0^a \left[\sqrt{a^2-x^2}\right] dx$$

$$= \frac{\pi}{2}\left[\frac{a^2}{2}\sin^{-1}\left(\frac{x}{a}\right) + \frac{x}{2}\sqrt{a^2-x^2}\right]_0^a$$

$$= \frac{\pi}{2}\left[\frac{a^2}{2}\left(\frac{\pi}{2} - 0\right) + (0-0)\right] = \frac{\pi^2 a^2}{8}$$

10. *Evaluate* $\int_0^{\pi/2}\int_0^{\pi/4}\int_0^{\sec\theta} r^3 \sin\theta\, dr d\theta d\phi$

➡ Let

$$I = \int_0^{\pi/2}\int_0^{\pi/4}\int_0^{\sec\theta} r^3 \sin\theta\, dr d\theta d\phi = \int_0^{\pi/2}\int_0^{\pi/4} \frac{r^4}{4}\Big|_0^{\sec\theta} \sin\theta\, d\theta\, d\phi$$

$$= \frac{1}{4}\int_0^{\pi/2}\int_0^{\pi/4} (\sec^4\theta - 0)\sin\theta\, d\theta\, d\phi$$

$$= \frac{1}{4}\int_0^{\pi/2}\int_0^{\pi/4} \sec^4\theta \sin\theta\, d\theta\, d\phi = \frac{1}{4}\int_0^{\pi/2}\int_0^{\pi/4} \frac{\sin\theta}{\cos^4\theta} d\theta d\phi$$

Put $\cos\theta = t \Rightarrow \sin\theta\, d\theta = -dt$

If $\theta = 0 \Rightarrow t = 1$, if $\theta = \dfrac{\pi}{4} \Rightarrow t = \dfrac{1}{\sqrt{2}}$

$$I = \frac{1}{4}\int_0^{\pi/2}\int_1^{1/\sqrt{2}} \frac{1}{t^4}(-dt)\, d\phi$$

$$= -\frac{1}{4}\int_0^{\pi/2}\int_1^{1/\sqrt{2}} t^{-4} dt\, d\phi = -\frac{1}{4}\int_0^{\pi/2} \left.\frac{t^{-3}}{-3}\right|_1^{1/\sqrt{2}} d\phi$$

$$= \frac{1}{12}\int_0^{\pi/2}\left[\left(\frac{1}{\sqrt{2}}\right)^{-3} - 1\right] d\phi = \frac{1}{12}\left(2\sqrt{2}-1\right)\phi\Big]_0^{\pi/2}$$

$$= \frac{1}{12}\left(2\sqrt{2}-1\right)\left(\frac{\pi}{2}-0\right) = \frac{\pi}{24}\left(2\sqrt{2}-1\right)$$

11. *If R is the region bounded by the co-ordinate planes and the planes $x = a, y = a, z = a$, in the first quadrant then show that* $\iiint_R \left(x^2+y^2+z^2\right) dx\, dy\, dz = a^5$

➡ Let $I = \iiint_R \left(x^2+y^2+z^2\right) dx\, dy\, dz$

Here $x : 0 \to a,\ y : 0 \to a$ and $z : 0 \to a$

$$\therefore\ I = \int_0^a\int_0^a\int_0^a \left(x^2+y^2+z^2\right) dx\, dy\, dz = \int_0^a\int_0^a \left(\frac{x^3}{3} + \left(y^2+z^2\right)x\right)_0^a dy\, dz$$

$$= \int_0^a\int_0^a \left[\frac{a^3}{3} + \left(y^2+z^2\right)a\right] dy\, dz = \int_0^a \left(\frac{a^3}{3}y + a\frac{y^3}{3} + az^2y\right)_0^a dz$$

$$= \int_0^a \left(\frac{a^4}{3} + \frac{a^4}{3} + a^2z^2\right) dz = \int_0^a \left(\frac{2a^4}{3} + a^2z^2\right) dz$$

$$= \frac{2a^4}{3}z + a^2\frac{z^3}{3}\Big]_0^a = \frac{2a^5}{3} + \frac{a^5}{3} = \frac{3a^5}{3} = a^5$$

Exercises

I. *Evaluate the following triple integrals.*

1) $\int_0^2 \int_1^3 \int_1^2 xy^2 z \, dz \, dy \, dx$

2) $\int_{-3}^3 \int_0^1 \int_1^2 (x+y+z) \; dx \, dy \, dz$

3) $\int_0^1 \int_{y^2}^1 \int_0^{1-x} x dz dx dy$

4) $\int_0^1 \int_0^x \int_0^{x+y} e^{x+y+z} \, dz \, dy \, dx$

5) $\int_0^4 \int_0^{2\sqrt{z}} \int_0^{\sqrt{4z-x^2}} \; dy \, dx \, dz$

6) $\int_0^1 \int_0^{\sqrt{1-x^2}} \int_0^{\sqrt{1-x^2-y^2}} xyz \; dz \, dy \, dx$

7) $\int_0^1 \int_0^1 \int_{\sqrt{x^2+y^2}}^2 xyz \, dz \, dy \, dx$

8) $\int_0^e \int_1^{\log y} \int_0^{e^x} \log \; z dz dx dy$

9) $\int_0^{\frac{\pi}{2}} \int_0^{a \sin\theta} \int_0^{\frac{(a^2-r^2)}{a}} r dr d\theta dz$

10) $\int_0^1 \int_0^{\sqrt{1-x^2}} \int_0^{\sqrt{1-x^2-y^2}} \frac{dz \, dy \, dx}{\sqrt{1-x^2-y^2-z^2}}$

11) $\int_0^a \int_0^{a-x} \int_o^{a-x-y} \left(x^2+y^2+z^2\right) \; dz \, dy \, dx$

12) $\int\limits_0^a \int\limits_0^{\sqrt{a^2-z^2}} \int\limits_0^{\sqrt{a^2-y^2-z^2}} \left(x^2+y^2+z^2\right)\, dx\, dy\, dz$

13) $\int\limits_0^1 \int\limits_0^{1-x} \int\limits_0^{1-x-y} \frac{dx\, dy\, dz}{(1+x+y+z)^3}$

14) $\int\limits_0^a \int\limits_0^{\sqrt{a^2-x^2}} \int\limits_0^{\sqrt{a^2-x^2-y^2}} \frac{dz\, dy\, dx}{\sqrt{a^2-x^2-y^2-z^2}}$

15) $\int\limits_0^\infty \int\limits_0^\infty \int\limits_0^\infty e^{-(x+y+z)}\, dx\, dy\, dz$

16) $\int\limits_0^1 \int\limits_0^{1-x} \int\limits_0^{1-x-y} \frac{dz\, dy\, dx}{(1+x+y+z)^3}$

17) $\int\limits_0^{\frac{\pi}{2}} \int\limits_0^{a \sin\theta} \int\limits_0^{\frac{a^2-R^2}{a}} R\, dz\, dR\, d\theta$

18) $\int\limits_{r=0}^{a} \int\limits_{\theta=0}^{\frac{\pi}{2}} \int\limits_{\phi=0}^{\frac{\pi}{2}} r^2 \sin\theta\, d\phi\, d\theta\, dr$

II. *If R is the region bounded by the planes $x = 0$, $y = 0$, $z = 0$ and $x + y + z = 1$, show that*

(i) $\iiint\limits_R z\, dx\, dy\, dz = \frac{1}{24}$ (ii) $\iiint\limits_R (x+y+z)^9\, dx\, dy\, dz = \frac{1}{24}$

III. *If R is the region $-a \le x \le x \le a$, $-b \le y \le b$, $-c \le z \le c$, show that*

$$\iiint\limits_R \left(x^2+y^2+z^2\right)\, dx\, dy\, dz = \frac{8}{3}abc\left(a^2+b^2+c^2\right)$$

Answers

I. 1) 26 2) 12

3) $\frac{4}{35}$ 4) $\frac{1}{8}e^4 - \frac{3}{4}e^2 + e - \frac{3}{8}$

5) 8π

6) $\dfrac{1}{48}$

7) $\dfrac{3}{8}$

8) $\dfrac{1}{2}\left(e^2 - 8e + 13\right)$

9) $\pi\ a^3$

10) $\dfrac{\pi^2}{8}$

11) $\dfrac{a^5}{20}$

12) $\pi\dfrac{a^5}{10}$

13) $\dfrac{1}{2}\log\left(2 - \dfrac{5}{8}\right)$

14) $\left(\dfrac{\pi^2}{8}\right)a^2$

15) 1

16) $\dfrac{\pi\ a^3\ \left(2 - \sqrt{2}\right)}{3}$

17) $\dfrac{5\pi}{64}a^3$

18) $\dfrac{\pi}{6}a^3$

CHAPTER 5

Ordinary Differential Equations

5.1 Introduction

A large number of basic laws of nature in engineering mathematics, applied sciences etc., appear mathematically in the form of differential equations. The differential equations is the general goal of differential and integral calculus and the theory of differential equations has a very important role in mathematics for understanding physical sciences.

In the study of differential equations, we generally come across two types of problems. They are

(i) *Formation of differential equations.*

(ii) *Solution of differential equations.*

In this chapter we discuss the solutions of first order, first-degree differential equations.

Definition

An equation containing one dependent variable and its derivatives with respect to one or more independent variables is called a differential equation.

There are two types of differential equations namely,

(i) Ordinary differential equations (ODEs)

(ii) Partial differential equations (PDEs)

If the dependent variable depends on one independent variable, the differential equation is called an ordinary differential equation. If it depends on two or more variables, the differential equation is called partial differential equation (PDEs). Here we discuss only ordinary differential equations (ODEs).

Examples

(i) $\dfrac{dy}{dx} + x = 0$

(ii) $\dfrac{dy}{dx} = a + bx + cy$

(iii) $\dfrac{d^2y}{dx^2} + y = e^{-x}$

(iv) $x^2\dfrac{d^2y}{dx^2} - 2x\left(\dfrac{dy}{dx}\right)^2 + 2y = 0$

(v) $\dfrac{\partial^2 u}{\partial x^2} + \dfrac{\partial^2 u}{\partial y^2} = 0$

(vi) $\dfrac{\partial^2 u}{\partial t^2} = c^2\dfrac{\partial^2 u}{\partial x^2}$

Examples (i)–(iv) are ODEs and (v) and (vi) are PDEs.

Order and Degree of an Ordinary Differential Equation

The order of an ODE is the order of the highest derivative present in that equation. The degree is the power to the highest order derivative appearing in an ODE when the differential coefficients are free from radicals and fractions.

In the above examples (i) and (ii) are of first order and first degree, (iii) and (iv) are of second order and first degree.

Now we consider the following ODEs

(vii) $\left(\dfrac{d^2y}{dx^2}\right)^{\frac{2}{3}} = x + y$

Cubing on both sides, we get

$$\left(\frac{d^2y}{dx^2}\right)^2 = (x + y)^3$$

This is an ODE of order 2 and degree 2.

(viii) $y - \frac{dy}{dx} = \sqrt{1 + \left(\frac{dy}{dx}\right)^3}$

Squaring both sides, we get

$$\left(y - \frac{dy}{dx}\right)^2 = 1 + \left(\frac{dy}{dx}\right)^3$$

This is an ODE of order 1 and degree 3.

Equations of First Order and of First Degree

In this section we discuss some methods for finding the general solution of an ODE of first order and first degree. These methods depend on the form of the ODE.

Some of the types of ODEs we are going discuss here are:

1. Equations in which variables are separable
2. Homogeneous equations
3. Reducible to homogeneous equations
4. Linear equations
5. Bernoulli's equations (Reducible to linear equations)
6. Exact equations
7. Reducible to exact equations.

General Solution

Given an nth order linear ordinary differential equation, the general solution contains all n linearly independent solutions, with a constant multiplying each one. For example, the differential equation $y'' + y = 1$ has the general solution.

$y(x) = 1 + c_1 \sin x + c_2 \cos x$, where c_1 and c_2 are arbitrary constants.

Particular Solution

Given a linear differential equation, $F(y, y', y'', \cdots) = f(x)$, the general solution can be written as $y(x) = y_p(x) + \sum_i c_i y_i(x)$, where $y_p(x)$, the particular solution, is any solution that satisfies $F(y, y', y'', \cdots) = f(x)$. For example, the differential equation $y'' + y = 0$ has the general solution

$$y(x) = c_1 \sin x + c_2 \cos x$$

If we impose the boundary conditions $y\,(0) = 1,\ \ y\,(\pi/2) = 1$, then $c_1 = c_2 = 1$.

Hence, $y(x) = \sin x + \cos x$ is the particular solution. *That is, in the general solution if we know the values for arbitrary constants, then it becomes the particular solution for the given differential equation.*

Singular Solutions

A singular solution of a differential equation is one, which is not derivable from the general solution by any choice of the arbitrary constants appearing in the general solution. Only nonlinear equations have singular solutions.

Trivial Solution

The trivial solution is the identically zero solution. For example, in the differential equation $y'' + y = 2,\ \ y(x) = 2$ is the trivial solution.

5.2 Separation of Variables

If the differential equation can be put in the form

$$\frac{dy}{dx} = \frac{f(x)}{g(y)}, \quad g(y) \neq 0$$

then the equation is said to be of variable separable form.

In this case the solution of the given differential equation can be obtained as follows.

$$g(y)dy = f(x)dx$$

On integration, we get

$$\int g(y)dy = \int f(x)x + c,$$

where c is constant of integration.

Illustrative Examples

1. *Solve* $\dfrac{dy}{dx} = \dfrac{1+\cos 2y}{1+\cos 2x}$

➡ $\dfrac{dy}{dx} = \dfrac{1+\cos 2y}{1+\cos 2x}$

$$\frac{dy}{1+\cos 2y} = \frac{dx}{1+\cos 2x}$$

$$\int \frac{dy}{1+\cos 2y} = \int \frac{dx}{1+\cos 2x} + c$$

$$\int \frac{dy}{2\cos^2 y} = \int \frac{dx}{2\cos^2 x} + c \qquad [\because\ 1+\cos 2A = 2\cos^2 A]$$

$$\frac{1}{2}\int \sec^2 y dy = \frac{1}{2}\int \sec^2 x dx + c$$

$$\frac{1}{2}\tan y = \frac{1}{2}\tan x + c$$

$\tan y = \tan x + c_1$, where $c_1 = 2c$

2. *Solve* $\sec^2 x\ \tan y\, dx + \sec^2 y \tan x\, dy = 0$

➡ $\sec^2 x\ \tan y\, dx + \sec^2 y \tan x\, dy = 0$

$$\sec^2 x \tan y dx = -\sec^2 y \tan x dy$$

$$\frac{\sec^2 x}{\tan x} dx = -\frac{\sec^2 y}{\tan y} dy$$

$$\int \frac{\sec^2 x}{\tan x} dx = -\int \frac{\sec^2 y}{\tan y} dy + c$$

Put $\tan x = t$ and $\tan y = z$

$$\sec^2 x dx = dt \qquad \sec^2 y dy = dz$$

$$\int \frac{dt}{t} = -\int \frac{dz}{z} + c$$

$\log t = -\log z + \log c_1,$ where $c = \log c_1$

$\log t + \log z = \log c_1$

$$\log(tz) = \log c_1$$
$$tz = c_1$$
$$\tan x \tan y = c_1$$

5.3 Linear Differential Equations

The differential equation of the form

$$\frac{dy}{dx} + P(x)y = Q(x), \tag{1}$$

where $P(x)$ and $Q(x)$ are functions of x only is called linear differential equation in y

$$\text{OR} \qquad \frac{dx}{dy} + P(y)x = Q(y) \tag{2}$$

where, $P(y)$ and $Q(y)$ are functions of y only is called linear differential equation in x.

If the differential equation can be put in the form $\frac{dy}{dx} + P(x)y = Q(x)$, then multiply the given equation by $e^{\int p(x)dx}$, we get

$$e^{\int Pdx}\frac{dy}{dx} + Pye^{\int Pdx} = Qe^{\int Pdx}$$
$$e^{\int Pdx}\frac{dy}{dx} + y\frac{d}{dx}\left(e^{\int Pdx}\right) = Qe^{\int Pdx}$$

i.e., $\frac{d}{dx}\left(ye^{\int Pdx}\right) = Qe^{\int Pdx}$

Integrating, we get

$$ye^{\int Pdx} = \int Qe^{\int Pdx}\,dx + c$$

i.e., $y\,(I.F.) = \int Q\,(I.F.)\;dx + c$, where I.F $= e^{\int Pdx}$

which is the required general solution.

Working Rule

Case (i) If the differential equation is linear in y i.e., equation (1), then

Step (1) Find the integration factor (I.F.)

$$\text{I.F.} = e^{\int P(x)dx}$$

Step (2) Substitute IF in the equation

$$y\,(\text{I.F.}) = \int Q\,(\text{I.F.})\,dx + c$$

On integrating the RHS of the above equation, we get the solution of the given differential equation.

Case (ii) If the differential equation is linear in x i.e., equation (2)

Step (1) Find the integration factor (I.F.)

$$\text{I.F.} = e^{\int P(y)dy}$$

Step (2) Substitute IF in the equation

$$x\,(I.F.) = \int Q(y)\ \ (I.F.)\,dy + c$$

On integrating the RHS of the above equation, we get the solution of the given differential equation.

Worked Examples

1. *Solve* $\dfrac{dy}{dx} + y\cot x = \sin x$

➡ $\dfrac{dy}{dx} + y\cot x = \sin x$, this is linear in y

$$P = \cot x \qquad Q = \sin x$$

$$\text{I.F.} = e^{\int Pdx} = e^{\int \cot x dx} = e^{\log \sin x} = \sin x$$

Therefore, the solution of the given equation is

$$y\,(I.F.) = \int Q\,(I.F.)\,dx + c$$

$$y\,(\sin x) = \int (\sin x)\,(\sin x)\,dx + c = \int \sin^2 x dx + c$$

$$= \int \frac{1-\cos 2x}{2} dx + c \quad \sin^2 A = \frac{1-\cos 2A}{2}$$

$$= \int \left(\frac{1}{2} - \frac{1}{2}\cos 2x\right) dx + c = \frac{1}{2}x - \frac{1}{2}\frac{\sin 2x}{2} + c$$

$$y \sin x = \frac{1}{2}x - \frac{1}{4}\sin 2x + c$$

2. *Solve* $x \log x \dfrac{dy}{dx} + y = 2\log x$

➡ $x \log x \dfrac{dy}{dx} + y = 2\log x$

Divide on both sides by$x \log x$, we get

$$\frac{dy}{dx} + \frac{1}{x\log x}y = \frac{2}{x}, \text{ this is linear in } y$$

$$P = \frac{1}{x\log x} \quad Q = \frac{2}{x}$$

$$\text{I.F.} = e^{\int P dx} = e^{\int \frac{1}{x\log x}dx}$$

Put $\log x = t \Rightarrow (1/x)\,dx = dt$

$$\therefore\ I.F. = e^{\int (1/t)dt} = e^{\log t} = t = \log x$$

Therefore, the solution of the given equation is

$$y\,(I.F) = \int Q\,(I.F)\,dx + c$$

$$y \log x = \int \frac{2}{x}\log x dx + c$$

Put $\log x = t \Rightarrow (1/x)\,dx = dt$

$$\therefore y \log x = 2\int t\,dt + c = t^2 + c$$

$$y\,(\log x) = (\log x)^2 + c$$

3. *Solve* $x^2\dfrac{dy}{dx} = 3x^2 - 2xy + 1$

➡ $x^2\dfrac{dy}{dx} = 3x^2 - 2xy + 1$

$$x^2\frac{dy}{dx} + 2xy = 3x^2 + 1,$$

Dividing both the sides by x^2, we get

$\dfrac{dy}{x} + \dfrac{2}{x}y = \dfrac{3x^2+1}{x^2}$, this is linear in y

$$P = \frac{2}{x} \qquad Q = \frac{3x^2+1}{x^2}$$

$$\text{I.F.} = e^{\int P\,dx} = e^{\int (2/x)dx} = e^{2\log x} = e^{\log x^2} = x^2$$

Therefore, the solution of the given equation is,

$$y\,(\text{I.F}) = \int Q\,(I.F)\,dx + c$$

$$yx^2 = \int \left(\frac{3x^2+1}{x^2}\right) x^2 dx + c = x^3 + x + c$$

$$yx^2 = x^3 + x + c$$

4. *Solve* $x\left(1 - x^2\right)\dfrac{dy}{dx} + \left(2x^2 - 1\right)\,y = x^3$

➡ $x\left(1 - x^2\right)\dfrac{dy}{dx} + \left(2x^2 - 1\right)\,y = x^3,$

Dividing both sides by $x\left(1 - x^2\right)$, we get

$$\frac{dy}{dx} + \frac{2x^2 - 1}{x(1 - x^2)}y = \frac{x^2}{(1 - x^2)}$$

$$P = \frac{2x^2 - 1}{x\left(1 - x^2\right)} \quad Q = \frac{x^2}{1 - x^2}$$

$$P = \frac{2x^2 - 1}{x\left(1 - x^2\right)} = \frac{2x^2 - 1}{x\,(1 - x)\,(1 + x)} = \frac{A}{x} + \frac{B}{1 - x} + \frac{C}{1 + x}$$

$$\Rightarrow 2x^2 - 1 = A\,(1 - x)\,(1 + x) + Bx(1 + x) + Cx\,(1 - x)$$

Put $x = 0 \Rightarrow -1 = A$
Put $x = 1 \Rightarrow 1 = 2B \Rightarrow B = 1/2$
Put $x = -1 \Rightarrow 1 = -2C \Rightarrow C = -1/2$

$$\therefore\ P = \frac{-1}{x} + \frac{1/2}{1 - x} - \frac{1/2}{1 + x}$$

$$\int P dx = \int \left(-\frac{1}{x} + \frac{1}{2}\frac{1}{(1 - x)} - \frac{1}{2}\frac{1}{(1 + x)}\right) dx$$

$$= -\log x + \frac{1}{2}\frac{\log\,(1 - x)}{-1} - \frac{1}{2}\log(1 + x)$$

$$= -\frac{1}{2}\left[2\log x + \log\,(1 - x) + \log(1 + x)\right]$$

$$= -\frac{1}{2}\log\left[x^2\,(1 - x)\,(1 + x)\right]$$

$$= -\frac{1}{2}\log\left[x^2\left(1 - x^2\right)\right]$$

$$\int P dx = \log\left[x^2\left(1 - x^2\right)\right]^{-\frac{1}{2}}$$

$$\text{I.F.} = e^{\int P dx} = e^{\log\left[x^2\left(1 - x^2\right)\right]^{-\frac{1}{2}}}$$

$$\text{I.F.} = \left[x^2\left(1 - x^2\right)\right]^{-\frac{1}{2}} = \frac{1}{x\sqrt{1 - x^2}}$$

Therefore, the solution of the given equation is

$$y\,(I.F) = \int Q\,(I.F)\,dx + c$$

$$y\left(\frac{1}{x\sqrt{1 - x^2}}\right) = \int \frac{x^2}{1 - x^2}\frac{1}{x\sqrt{1 - x^2}}dx + c$$

$$= \int \frac{x}{(1-x^2)^{\frac{3}{2}}} dx + c$$

Put $1 - x^2 = t \Rightarrow -2xdx = dt \Rightarrow xdx = -\frac{dt}{2}$

$$\frac{y}{x\sqrt{1-x^2}} = \int \frac{-dt/2}{t^{3/2}} + c$$

$$= -\frac{1}{2}\int t^{-\frac{3}{2}} dt + c = -\frac{1}{2}\frac{t^{-\frac{1}{2}}}{(-1/2)} + c = \frac{1}{\sqrt{t}} + c$$

$$\frac{y}{x\sqrt{1-x^2}} = \frac{1}{\sqrt{1-x^2}} + c$$

$$\therefore\ y = x + cx\sqrt{1-x^2}$$

5. *Solve* $dx + xdy = e^{-y} \sec ydy$

➡ $dx + xdy = e^{-y} \sec ydy$

$$\frac{dx}{dy} + x = e^{-y} \sec y, \text{ this is linear in } x$$

$P = 1\ Q = e^{-y} \sec y$

$$\text{I.F.} = e^{\int Pdy} = e^{\int 1dy} = e^y$$

Therefore, the solution of the given equation is

$$x\,(I.F.) = \int Q\,(I.F.)\ dy + c$$

$$xe^y = \int e^{-y} \sec ye^y dy + c = \int \sec ydy + c$$

$$xe^y = \log(\sec y + \tan y) + c$$

6. *Solve* $ye^y dx = \left(y^3 + 2xe^y\right) dy$

➡ $ye^y dx = \left(y^3 + 2xe^y\right) dy$, this equation can be written as

$$\frac{dx}{dy} = \frac{y^3 + 2xe^y}{ye^y}$$

$$\frac{dx}{dy} = \frac{y^2}{e^y} + \frac{2x}{y}$$

$$\frac{dx}{dy} - \frac{2}{y}x = y^2e^{-y}, \text{ this is linear in } x$$

$$P = \frac{-2}{y}, \quad Q = y^2e^{-y}$$

$$\therefore \text{ I.F.} = e^{\int P\,dy} = e^{\int -\frac{2}{y}dy} = e^{-2\log y} = e^{\log y^{-2}} = y^{-2}$$

Therefore, the solution of the given equation is

$$x\,(I.F) = \int Q\,(I.F)\,dy + c$$

$$xy^{-2} = \int y^2e^{-y}y^{-2}dy + c = \frac{e^{-y}}{-1} + c$$

$$\frac{x}{y^2} = -e^{-y} + c$$

$$\frac{x}{y^2} + e^{-y} = c$$

7. *Solve* $\frac{dy}{dx} + x\sin 2y = x^3\cos^2 y$

➡ $\frac{dy}{dx} + x\sin 2y = x^3\cos^2 y$

$$\frac{dy}{dx} + 2x\sin y.\cos y = x^3\cos^2 y,$$

Dividing on both the sides by $\cos^2 y$, we get

$$\sec^2 y\frac{dy}{dx} + 2x\tan y = x^3$$

Put $\tan y = t \Rightarrow \sec^2 y\frac{dy}{dx} = \frac{dt}{dx}$

$$\therefore\ \frac{dt}{dx} + 2xt = x^3, \text{ this is linear in } t$$

$$P = 2x, \quad Q = x^3$$

$$\text{I.F.} = e^{\int 2x dx} = e^{x^2}$$

Therefore, the solution of the given equation is

$$t\,(I.F) = \int Q\,(I.F)\,dx + c$$

$$\tan y \left(e^{x^2}\right) = \int x^3 e^{x^2}\,dx + c$$

Put $x^2 = z \Rightarrow 2xdx = dz \Rightarrow xdx = dz/2$

$$e^{x^2} \tan y = \int x^2 e^{x^2} x dx + c = \int z e^z \frac{dz}{2} + c$$

$$= \frac{1}{2}\left(z e^z - \int 1.e^z dz\right) + c$$

$$= \frac{1}{2}\left(z e^z - e^z\right) + c$$

$$e^{x^2} \tan y = \frac{1}{2}(x^2 e^{x^2} - e^{x^2}) + c$$

8. *Solve* $\dfrac{dy}{dx} = e^{x-y}\left(e^x - e^y\right)$

➡ $\dfrac{dy}{dx} = e^{x-y}\left(e^x - e^y\right) = e^x e^{-y}\left(e^x - e^y\right)$

$$\frac{dy}{dx} = e^{2x} e^{-y} - e^x$$

$$e^y \frac{dy}{dx} = e^{2x} - e^x \cdot e^y$$

$$e^y \frac{dy}{dx} + e^x e^y = e^{2x}$$

Put $e^y = z \Rightarrow e^y \dfrac{dy}{dx} = \dfrac{dz}{dx}$

$$\frac{dz}{dx} + e^x z = e^{2x}, \text{ this is linear in } z$$

$$P = e^x \qquad Q = e^{2x}$$
$$\text{I.F.} = e^{\int p dx} = e^{\int e^x dx} = e^{e^x}$$

Therefore, the solution of the given differential equation is,

$$z\,(I.F) = \int Q\,(I.F)dx + c$$
$$e^y e^{e^x} = \int e^{2x} e^{e^x} dx + c = \int e^x e^{e^x} e^x dx + c$$

Put $e^x = t \Rightarrow e^x dx + dt$

$$e^y e^{e^x} = \int te^t dt + c = te^t - \int 1 \cdot e^t dt + c = te^t - e^t + c = (t-1)\,e^t + c$$
$$e^y e^{e^x} = \left(e^x - 1\right) e^{e^x} + c$$

9. *Solve* $\dfrac{dy}{dx} - \dfrac{\tan y}{1+x} = (1+x)\,e^x \sec y$

➡ $\dfrac{dy}{dx} - \dfrac{\tan y}{1+x} = (1+x)\,e^x \sec y$

Dividing sec y on both sides, we get

$$\frac{1}{\sec y}\frac{dy}{dx} - \frac{\tan y}{1+x}.\frac{1}{\sec y} = (1+x)\,e^x$$
$$\cos y\frac{dy}{dx} - \frac{1}{1+x}\frac{\sin y}{\cos y}.\cos y = (1+x)\,e^x$$
$$\cos y\frac{dy}{dx} - \frac{1}{1+x}\sin y = (1+x)\,e^x \qquad (1)$$

Put $\sin y = t \Rightarrow \cos y\dfrac{dy}{dx} = \dfrac{dt}{dx}$

$\therefore$ (1) becomes, $\dfrac{dt}{dx} - \dfrac{1}{1+x}t = (1+x)\,e^x$, this is linear in t

Here $P = -\dfrac{1}{1+x}$, $\quad Q = (1+x)\,e^x$

$$\text{I.F.} = e^{\int p dx} = e^{\int -\frac{1}{1+x}dx} = e^{-\log(1+x)} = e^{\log(1+x)^{-1}} = (1+x)^{-1} = \frac{1}{(1+x)}$$

Therefore, the solution of the given equation is

$$t\,(I.F) = \int Q\,(I.F)dx + c$$

$$\sin y\left(\frac{1}{1+x}\right) = \int (1+x)e^x\left(\frac{1}{1+x}\right)dx + c = \int e^x dx + c$$

$$\frac{\sin y}{1+x} = e^x + c$$

10. *Solve* $dy + \left(2x\tan^{-1}y - x^3\right)\left(1+y^2\right)dx = 0$

➠ $dy + \left(2x\tan^{-1}y - x^3\right)\left(1+y^2\right)dx = 0$

$$dy = -\left(2x\tan^{-1}y - x^3\right)\left(1+y^2\right)dx$$

$$\frac{1}{1+y^2}\frac{dy}{dx} = -2x\tan^{-1}y + x^3$$

$$\frac{1}{1+y^2}\frac{dy}{dx} + 2x\tan^{-1}y = x^3$$

Put $\tan^{-1}y = t \Rightarrow \frac{1}{1+y^2}\frac{dy}{dx} = \frac{dt}{dx}$

$$\therefore\ \frac{dt}{dx} + 2xt = x^3,\ \text{this is linear in } t$$

$P = 2x,\ Q = x^3$

I.F. $= e^{\int 2x dx} = e^{x^2}$

Therefore, the solution of the given equation is

$$t\,(I.F) = \int Q\,(I.F)\,dx + c$$

$$\tan^{-1}y\left(e^{x^2}\right) = \int x^3 e^{x^2}dx + c$$

Put $x^2 = z \Rightarrow 2xdx = dz \Rightarrow xdx = \frac{dz}{2}$

$$e^{x^2}\tan^{-1}y = \int x^2 e^{x^2}xdx + c = \int ze^z\frac{dz}{2} + c = \frac{1}{2}(ze^z - \int 1.e^z dz) + c$$

$$= \frac{1}{2}(ze^z - e^z) + c$$

$$e^{x^2} \tan^{-1} y = \frac{1}{2}(x^2 e^{x^2} - e^{x^2}) + c$$

11. *Solve* $(\sin^3 x)\, y' + y \sin x = \cos x$

➡ $(\sin^3 x)\, y' + y \sin x = \cos x$

Dividing both sides by $\sin^3 x$, we get

$$\frac{dy}{dx} + y\frac{\sin x}{\sin^3 x} = \frac{\cos x}{\sin^3 x}$$

$$\frac{dy}{dx} + y\text{cosec}^2 x = \cot x\,\text{cosec}^2 x,\ \text{this is linear in } y$$

$$P = \text{cosec}^2 x,\ Q = \cot x\,\text{cosec}^2 x$$

$\text{I.F.} = e^{\int p\,dx} = e^{\int \text{cosec}^2 x\,dx} = e^{-\cot x}$

Therefore, the solution of the given differential equation is

$$y\,(I.F.) = \int Q\,(I.F)\,dx + c$$

$$ye^{-\cot x} = \int \cot x\,\text{cosec}^2 x\, e^{-\cot x} dx + c$$

Put $\cot x = t \Rightarrow -\text{cosec}^2 x\,dx = dt \Rightarrow \text{cosec}^2 x\,dx = -dt$

$$ye^{-\cot x} = \int te^{-t}\,(-dt) + c$$

$$= -\left[t\frac{e^{-t}}{-1} - \int 1.\frac{e^{-t}}{-1}dt\right] + c$$

$$= te^{-t} - \frac{e^{-t}}{-1} + c = te^{-t} + e^{-t} + c$$

$$= (t+1)\,e^{-t} + c$$

$$ye^{-\cot x} = (\cot x + 1)\,e^{-\cot x} + c$$

12. *Solve* $\frac{dy}{dx} = \frac{1}{e^{-y}\sec^2 y - x}$

$$\Rightarrow \frac{dy}{dx} = \frac{1}{e^{-y}\sec^2 y - x}$$

$$\Rightarrow \frac{dx}{dy} = e^{-y}\sec^2 y - x$$

$$\frac{dx}{dy} + x = e^{-y}\sec^2 y, \text{ This is linear in } x$$

$$P = 1, \quad Q = e^{-y}\sec^2 y$$

$$\text{I.F.} = e^{\int P dy} = e^{\int 1 dy} = e^y$$

Therefore, the solution of the given equation is

$$x\,(I.F) = \int Q\,(I.F)\,dy + c$$

$$xe^y = \int e^{-y}\sec^2 y\, e^y dy + c$$

$$xe^y = \tan y + c$$

13. *Solve* $\left(1+x^2\right)\dfrac{dy}{dx} + 2xy - 6x^2 = 0$

$$\Rightarrow (1+x^2)\frac{dy}{dx} + 2xy - 6x^2 = 0$$

$$(1+x^2)\frac{dy}{dx} + 2xy = 6x^2,$$

Dividing both the sides by $1 + x^2$, we get

$$\frac{dy}{dx} + \frac{2x}{1+x^2}y = \frac{6x^2}{1+x^2}, \text{ this is linear in } y$$

$$P = \frac{2x}{1+x^2} \qquad Q = \frac{6x^2}{1+x^2}$$

$$\text{I.F.} = e^{\int P dx} = e^{\int \frac{2x}{1+x^2}dx} = e^{\log(1+x^2)} = \left(1+x^2\right)$$

Therefore, the solution of the given equation is

$$y\,(I.F) = \int Q\,(I.F)\,dx + c$$

$$y(1+x^2) = \int \frac{6x^2}{1+x^2}(1+x^2)\,dx + c = 6\frac{x^3}{3} + c$$
$$y(1+x^2) = 2x^3 + c$$

14. *Solve* $\dfrac{dy}{dx} = (\sin x - \sin y)\dfrac{\cos x}{\cos y}$

➡ $\dfrac{dy}{dx} = (\sin x - \sin y)\dfrac{\cos x}{\cos y}$

$$\cos y\frac{dy}{dx} = (\sin x - \sin y)\cos x$$
$$\cos y\frac{dy}{dx} + \sin y\cos x = \sin x\cos x$$

Put $\sin y = z \Rightarrow \cos y \;\dfrac{dy}{dx} = \dfrac{dz}{dx}$

$$\frac{dz}{dx} + z\cos x = \sin x\cos x,\text{ this is linear in } z$$
$$P = \cos x \qquad Q = \sin x\cos x$$
$$\text{I.F.} = e^{\int p dx} = e^{\int \cos x dx} = e^{\sin x}$$

Therefore, the solution of the given equation is

$$y\,(I.F) = \int Q\,(I.F)dx + c$$
$$ze^{\sin x} = \int \sin x\cos x e^{\sin x}dx + c$$

Put $\sin x = t \Rightarrow \cos x dx = dt$

$$ze^{\sin x} = \int te^t dt + c$$
$$\sin y e^{\sin x} = te^t - \int 1\cdot e^t dt + c = te^t - e^t + c$$
$$= (t-1)\,e^t + c$$
$$\sin y e^{\sin x} = (\sin x - 1)\,e^{\sin x} + c$$
$$\sin y = \sin x - 1 + ce^{-\sin x}$$

Exercise

Solve the following equations

1. $(x+\tan y)\,dy = \sin 2y dx$
2. $\dfrac{dy}{dx} + y\cot x = 4x\text{cosec}x$
3. $\dfrac{dy}{dx} + y\tan x = \sec x$
4. $\left(x^2-1\right)\dfrac{dy}{dx} + 2xy = 1$
5. $\dfrac{dy}{dx} - y\cot x = 2x\sin x$
6. $\dfrac{dy}{dx} - \dfrac{2y}{x} = x^2\sin 3x$
7. $\left(\cos^3 x\right)y' + y\cos x = \sin x$
8. $y' + y\cos x = \sin 2x$
9. $\sqrt{1-y^2}dx = \left(\sin^{-1} y - x\right)dy$
10. $e^y\left(\dfrac{dy}{dx}+1\right) = e^x$
11. $y' + y\sec x = \tan x$
12. $y' + y\cot x = \cos x$
13. $\tan y\dfrac{dy}{dx} + \tan x = \cos y\cos^3 x$
14. $x\dfrac{dy}{dx} + y\log y = xye^x$
15. $\dfrac{dy}{dx} = \dfrac{e^{-2\sqrt{x}} - y}{\sqrt{x}}$
16. $\dfrac{dy}{dx} + 3x^2y = x^5e^{x^3}$
17. $\cos^2 x\dfrac{dy}{dx} + y = \tan x$
18. $y' - y\tan x = e^x\sec x$
19. $xy' - y = x^5\log x$
20. $(1-x^2)y' + 2xy = x\sqrt{1-x^2}$ given that $y=0$ when $x=0$

Answers

1. $x = \tan y + c\sqrt{\tan y}$
2. $y\sin x = 2x^2 + c$
3. $y = (\tan x + c)\cos x$
4. $y\left(1-x^2\right) = c - x$
5. $y\text{cosec}x = x^2 + c$
6. $x^2\cos 3x + 3y = cx^2$
7. $1 + y = \tan c - ce^{-\tan x}$
8. $y + 2 = 2\sin x + ce^{-\sin x}$
9. $x = \sin^{-1} y - 1 + ce^{-\sin^{-1} y}$
10. $e^y = \dfrac{1}{2}e^x + ce^x$
11. $(y-1)(1+\sin x) = (c-x)\cos x$
12. $2y\sin x - \sin^2 x = c$
13. $\sec y\sec x = \dfrac{1}{2}x + \dfrac{1}{4}\sin 2x + c$
14. $x\log y = (x-1)\,e^x + c$
15. $ye^{2\sqrt{x}} = 2\sqrt{x} + c$
16. $12y = e^{x^3}\left(2x^3-1\right) + ce^{-x^3}$

17. $y + 1 = \tan x + ce^{-\tan x}$

18. $y \cos x = e^x + c$

19. $16y = x^4 (4 \log x - 1) + cx$

20. $y\left(1 - x^2\right)^{-1} = \left(2 - x^2\right)^{-1/2} - 1$

5.4 Bernoulli's Equation

An equation of the form

$$\frac{dy}{dx} + P(x)y = y^n Q(x) \tag{1}$$

is called Bernoulli's equation and the other form is

$$\frac{dx}{dy} + P(y)x = Q(y)x^n \tag{2}$$

If $n = 0$, then (1) and (2) are linear D.E, for other values of n, (1) and (2) not linear D.E, but they can be transformed to linear D E by small transformation.

Dividing y^n on both sides of equation (1), we get

$$y^{-n}\frac{dy}{dx} + P(x)y^{1-n} = Q(x)$$

Put $z = y^{1-n}$ i.e., $\frac{dz}{dx} = \frac{dz}{dy}.\frac{dy}{dx} = (1-n)\, y^{-n}.\frac{dy}{dx}$,

Therefore, (1) becomes, $\frac{dz}{dx} + (1-n)\, P(x)z = (1-n)\, Q(x)$ which is a linear D.E. Similarly, we can reduce equation (2) to linear D.E by dividing x^n on both sides.

Worked Examples

1. *Solve* $\frac{dy}{dx} + \frac{y}{x} = y^2 x$

➡ $\frac{dy}{dx} + \frac{y}{x} = y^2 x$

This is a Bernoulli's equation, dividing by y^2 on both sides, we get

$$y^{-2}\frac{dy}{dx} + \frac{1}{x}y^{-1} = x \tag{1}$$

Put $y^{-1} = t \Rightarrow -1y^{-2}\frac{dy}{dx} = \frac{dt}{dx} \Rightarrow y^{-2}\frac{dy}{dx} = -\frac{dt}{dx}$

$\therefore$ (1) becomes, $-\frac{dt}{dx} + \frac{1}{x}t = x$

i.e., $\frac{dt}{dx} - \frac{1}{x}t = -x$, this is linear in t.

Here $P = -\frac{1}{x}$ $\quad Q = -x$

I.F. $= e^{\int P\,dx} = e^{-\int \frac{1}{x}dx} = e^{-\log x} = e^{\log x^{-1}} = x^{-1} = \frac{1}{x}$

Therefore, the solution of the given equation is

$$t\,(I.F.) = \int Q\,(I.F.)\,dx + c$$

$$y^{-1}\left(\frac{1}{x}\right) = \int (-x)\,\frac{1}{x}dx + c$$

$$\frac{1}{xy} = -x + c$$

$$\frac{1}{xy} + x = c$$

2. *Solve* $x\frac{dy}{dx} + y = x^3y^6$

➡ $x\frac{dy}{dx} + y = x^3y^6$, dividing by xy^6 on both sides, we get

$$y^{-6}\frac{dy}{dx} + \frac{1}{x}y^{-5} = x^2 \tag{1}$$

Put $y^{-5} = t \Rightarrow -5y^{-6}\frac{dy}{dx} = \frac{dt}{dx}$

$$y^{-6}\frac{dy}{dx} = -\frac{1}{5}\frac{dt}{dx}$$

$\therefore$ (1) becomes, $-\frac{1}{5}\frac{dt}{dx} + \frac{1}{x}t = x^2$

i.e., $\frac{dt}{dx} - \frac{5}{x}t = -5x^2$, this is linear in t,

Here $P = -\frac{5}{x}$, $\quad Q = -5x^2$

$$\therefore \text{ I.F.} = e^{\int P dx} = e^{\int -\frac{5}{x} dx} = e^{-5 \log x} = e^{\log x^{-5}} = x^{-5} = \frac{1}{x^5}$$

Therefore, the solution of the given equation is

$$t\,(I.F.) = \int Q\,(I.F.)\, dx + c$$

$$y^{-5}\left(\frac{1}{x^5}\right) = \int -5x^2\left(\frac{1}{x^5}\right) dx + c$$

$$\frac{1}{x^5 y^5} = -5\int x^{-3} dx + c = -5\frac{x^{-2}}{-2} + c$$

$$\frac{1}{x^5 y^5} = \frac{5}{2x^2} + c$$

3. *Solve* $x^3 \dfrac{dy}{dx} - x^2 y = -y^4 \cos x$

➡ $x^3 \dfrac{dy}{dx} - x^2 y = -y^4 \cos x$, dividing by $y^4 x^3$ on both sides, we get

$$y^{-4}\frac{dy}{dx} - \frac{1}{x} y^{-3} = -\frac{\cos x}{x^3} \qquad (1)$$

Put $y^{-3} = t \Rightarrow -3y^{-4}\dfrac{dy}{dx} = \dfrac{dt}{dx}$

$$y^{-4}\frac{dy}{dx} = -\frac{1}{3}\frac{dt}{dx}$$

$\therefore$ (1) becomes, $-\dfrac{1}{3}\dfrac{dt}{dx} - \dfrac{1}{x}t = -\dfrac{\cos x}{x^3}$

i.e., $\dfrac{dt}{dx} + \dfrac{3}{x}t = \dfrac{3\cos x}{x^3}$, this is linear in t,

Here $P = \dfrac{3}{x}$, $Q = \dfrac{3\cos x}{x^3}$

$$\text{I.F.} = e^{\int \frac{3}{x} dx} = e^{3 \log x} = e^{\log x^3} = x^3$$

Therefore, the solution of the given equation is

$$t\,(I.F.) = \int Q\,(I.F.)\,dx + c$$

$$y^{-3}\left(x^3\right) = \int \left(\frac{3\cos x}{x^3}\right) x^3 dx + c$$

$$\frac{x^3}{y^3} = 3\sin x + c$$

4. *Solve* $\left(x^2y^3 + xy\right)\dfrac{dy}{dx} = 1$

➡ $\left(x^2y^3 + xy\right)\dfrac{dy}{dx} = 1$

This equation can be written as

$$x^2y^3 + xy = \frac{dx}{dy}$$

$\dfrac{dx}{dy} - xy = x^2y^3$, dividing by x^2 on both sides, we get

$$x^{-2}\frac{dx}{dy} - yx^{-1} = y^3 \qquad (1)$$

Put $x^{-1} = t \Rightarrow -1x^{-2}\dfrac{dx}{dy} = \dfrac{dt}{dy}$

$$x^{-2}\frac{dx}{dy} = -\frac{dt}{dy}$$

$\therefore$ (1) becomes , $-\dfrac{dt}{dx} - yt = y^3$

i.e., $\dfrac{dt}{dx} + yt = -y^3$, this is linear in t.

Here $P = y$, $Q = -y^3$

$$\text{I.F.} = e^{\int P dy} = e^{\int y dy} = e^{\frac{y^2}{2}}$$

Therefore, the solution of the given equation is

$$t\,(I.F.) = \int Q\,(I.F.)\,dy + c$$

$$x^{-1}e^{\frac{y^2}{2}} = \int -y^3 e^{\frac{y^2}{2}}\,dy + c$$

$$\frac{e^{\frac{y^2}{2}}}{x} = -\int y^3 e^{\frac{y^2}{2}}\,dy + c$$

Put $\frac{y^2}{2} = t \Rightarrow ydy = dt$

$$\therefore\ \frac{e^{\frac{y^2}{2}}}{x} = -\int y^2 e^{\frac{y^2}{2}}.ydy + c$$

$$= -\int 2te^t dt + c = -2\left[te^t - \int 1.e^t\right] + c$$

$$= -2te^t + 2e^t + c$$

$$\frac{e^{\frac{y^2}{2}}}{x} = -y^2 e^{\frac{y^2}{2}} + 2e^{\frac{y^2}{2}} + c$$

or $1 = -xy^2 + 2x + cxe^{-\frac{y^2}{2}}$

5. *Solve* $y(x^2y + e^x)\,dx = e^x dy$

➡ $y(x^2y + e^x)\,dx = e^x dy$

$$y\,(x^2y + e^x) = e^x \frac{dy}{dx}$$

$$\frac{dy}{dx} = \frac{y\,(x^2y + e^x)}{e^x}$$

$$\frac{dy}{dx} = x^2y^2e^{-x} + y$$

$\frac{dy}{dx} - y = x^2y^2e^{-x}$, dividing by y^2 on both sides, we get

$$y^{-2}\frac{dy}{dx} - y^{-1} = x^2e^{-x} \tag{1}$$

Put $y^{-1} = t \Rightarrow -y^{-2}\frac{dy}{dx} = \frac{dt}{dx} \Rightarrow y^{-2}\frac{dy}{dx} = \frac{-dt}{dx}$

$\therefore$ The equation (1) gives, $\frac{-dt}{dx} - t = x^2e^{-x}$

$$\frac{dt}{dx} + t = -x^2e^{-x}, \text{ this is linear in } t.$$

Here $P = 1$,$Q = -x^2e^{-x}$

$$I.F = e^{\int Pdx} = e^{\int 1.dx} = e^x$$

$\therefore$ The solution of the given equation is,

$$t\,(I.F.) = \int Q\,(I.F.)\,dx + c$$

$$y^{-1}\left(e^x\right) = \int -x^2e^{-x}.e^x dx + c$$

$$\frac{e^x}{y} = -\frac{x^3}{3} + c$$

$$\frac{e^x}{y} + \frac{x^3}{3} = c$$

6. *Solve* $\frac{dy}{dx} = \frac{x^2 + y^2 + 1}{2xy}$

➡ $\frac{dy}{dx} = \frac{x^2 + y^2 + 1}{2xy}$

$$\frac{dy}{dx} = \frac{x^2 + 1}{2xy} + \frac{y}{2x}$$

i.e., $\dfrac{dy}{dx} - \dfrac{y}{2x} = \dfrac{x^2+1}{2xy}$

i.e., $\dfrac{dy}{dx} - \dfrac{y}{2x} = \dfrac{x^2+1}{2x} y^{-1}$, dividing by y^{-1} on both sides, we get

$$y\frac{dy}{dx} - \frac{y^2}{2x} = \frac{x^2+1}{2x} \tag{1}$$

Put $y^2 = t \Rightarrow 2y\dfrac{dy}{dx} = \dfrac{dt}{dx}$

$$y\frac{dy}{dx} = \frac{1}{2}\frac{dt}{dx}$$

$\therefore$ (1) becomes, $\dfrac{1}{2}\dfrac{dt}{dx} - \dfrac{t}{2x} = \dfrac{x^2+1}{2x}$

i.e., $\dfrac{dt}{dx} - \dfrac{t}{x} = \dfrac{x^2+1}{x}$, this is linear in t,

Here $P = -\dfrac{1}{x}$, $Q = \dfrac{x^2+1}{x}$

I.F. $= e^{\int P dx} = e^{\int -\frac{1}{x} dx} = e^{-\log x} = e^{\log x^{-1}} = x^{-1} = \dfrac{1}{x}$

$\therefore$ The solution of the given equation is

$$t\,(I.F.) = \int Q\,(I.F.)\,dx + c$$

$$y^2\left(\frac{1}{x}\right) = \int \frac{x^2+1}{x}\left(\frac{1}{x}\right) dx + c$$

$$\frac{y^2}{x} = \int \frac{x^2+1}{x^2} dx + c$$

$$\frac{y^2}{x} = \int \left(1 + x^{-2}\right) dx + c = x + \frac{x^{-1}}{-1} + c$$

$$\frac{y^2}{x} = x - \frac{1}{x} + c$$

$$\therefore \quad y^2 = x^2 - 1 + cx$$

7. *Solve* $(y\log x - 2)\, ydx = xdy$

➡ $(y\log x - 2)\; ydx = xdy$

$$\frac{dy}{dx} = \frac{y^2\log x - 2y}{x} = \frac{y^2\log x}{x} - \frac{2y}{x}$$

$$\frac{dy}{dx} + \frac{2}{x}y = \frac{\log x}{x}y^2, \text{ dividing by } y^2 \text{ on both sides, we get}$$

$$y^{-2}\frac{dy}{dx} + \frac{2}{x}y^{-1} = \frac{\log x}{x}$$

Put $y^{-1} = t \Rightarrow -y^{-2}\dfrac{dy}{dx} = \dfrac{dt}{dx}$

$$\Rightarrow y^{-2}\frac{dy}{dx} = -\frac{dt}{dx}$$

$$\therefore\; -\frac{dt}{dx} + \frac{2}{x}t = \frac{\log x}{x}$$

$$\text{or } \frac{dt}{dx} - \frac{2}{x}t = -\frac{\log x}{x}, \text{ this is linear in } t.$$

Here $P = \dfrac{-2}{x}, \quad Q = \dfrac{-\log x}{x}$

$$\text{I.F.} = e^{\int pdx} = e^{-2\int \frac{1}{x}dx} = e^{-2\log x} = e^{\log x^{-2}} = x^{-2}$$

Therefore, solution of the given equation is

$$t\,(I.F.) = \int Q\,(I.F.)\;dx + c$$

$$y^{-1}x^{-2} = \int \left(\frac{-\log x}{x}\right)\left(x^{-2}\right)\,dx + c$$

$$\frac{1}{x^2y} = -\int \frac{\log x}{x^3}dx + c$$

$$= -\int \log x.\frac{1}{x^3}dx + c$$

$$= -\left[\log x.\frac{x^{-2}}{-2} - \int \frac{1}{x}\,\frac{x^{-2}}{-2}dx\right] + c$$

$$= \frac{\log x}{2x^2} - \frac{1}{2}\int x^{-3}dx + c$$

$$= \frac{\log x}{2x^2} - \frac{1}{2}\left(\frac{x^{-2}}{-2}\right) + c$$

$$\frac{1}{x^2 y} = \frac{\log x}{2x^2} + \frac{1}{4x^2} + c$$

or $4 = 2y \log x + y + c4x^2 y$

8. *Solve* $\frac{dy}{dx} - y \tan x = y^2 \sec x$

➡ $\frac{dy}{dx} - y \tan x = y^2 \sec x$, dividing y^2 on both sides, we get

$$y^{-2}\frac{dy}{dx} - y^{-1} \tan x = \sec x$$

Put $y^{-1} = t \Rightarrow -y^{-2}\frac{dy}{dx} = \frac{dt}{dx} \Rightarrow y^{-2}\frac{dy}{dx} = -\frac{dt}{dx}$

$$-\frac{dt}{dx} - t \tan x = \sec x$$

$$\frac{dt}{dx} + t \tan x = -\sec x, \text{ this is linear in } t.$$

Here $P = \tan x,\ Q = -\sec x$

$$\text{I.F.} = e^{\int P dx} = e^{\int \tan x dx} = e^{\log(\sec x)} = \sec x$$

Therefore, the solution of the given equation is

$$t\,(I.F) = \int Q\,(I.F)\,dx + c$$

$$y^{-1}\,(\sec x) = \int (-\sec x).\sec x dx + c$$

$$\frac{\sec x}{y} = -\tan x + c$$

9. *Solve* $\frac{dz}{dx} + \frac{z}{x}(\log z) = \frac{z}{x^2}(\log z)^2$

➡ $\frac{dz}{dx} + \frac{z}{x}(\log z) = \frac{z}{x^2}(\log z)^2$

Dividing z on both sides, we get

$$\frac{1}{z}\frac{dz}{dx} + \frac{\log z}{x} = \frac{(\log z)^2}{x^2}$$

Put $\log z = y \Rightarrow \frac{1.dz}{z\,dx} = \frac{dy}{dx}$

Therefore, $\frac{dy}{dx} + \frac{1}{x}y = \frac{y^2}{x^2}$

Dividing y^2 on both sides, we get

$$y^{-2}\frac{dy}{dx} + \frac{1}{x}y^{-1} = \frac{1}{x^2} \tag{1}$$

Put $y^{-1} = t \Rightarrow -1y^{-2}\frac{dy}{dx} = \frac{dt}{dx}$

$$y^{-2}\frac{dy}{dx} = -\frac{dt}{dx}$$

(1) becomes, $-\frac{dt}{dx} + \frac{1}{x}t = \frac{1}{x^2}$

$\frac{dt}{dx} - \frac{1}{x}t = -\frac{1}{x^2}$, this is linear in t

$P = -\frac{1}{x}, \qquad Q = -\frac{1}{x^2}$

$I.F = e^{\int p dx} = e^{\int -\frac{1}{x}dx} = e^{-\log x} = e^{\log x^{-1}} = x^{-1} = \frac{1}{x}$

Therefore, the solution of the given equation is

$$t\,(I.F) = \int Q\,(I.F)dx + c$$

$$t\left(\frac{1}{x}\right) = \int -\frac{1}{x^2}\left(\frac{1}{x}\right)dx + c$$

$$y^{-1}\left(\frac{1}{x}\right) = -\int x^{-3}dx + c$$

$$\frac{1}{xy} = -\frac{x^{-2}}{-2} + c$$

$$\frac{1}{xy} = \frac{1}{2x^2} + c$$

$$\frac{1}{x \log z} = \frac{1}{2x^2} + c$$

Exercise

Solve the following equations

1. $x\dfrac{dy}{dx} - 2y = xy^4$
2. $\dfrac{dy}{dx} + xy = xy^3$
3. $\dfrac{dy}{dx} - \dfrac{y}{x} = \dfrac{1}{2y}$
4. $\dfrac{dy}{dx} - 2y \tan x = y^2 \tan^2 x$
5. $\dfrac{dy}{dx} - \dfrac{2y}{x} = \left(\dfrac{y}{x}\right)^3$
6. $xy - \dfrac{dy}{dx} = y^3 e^{-x^2}$
7. $\dfrac{dy}{dx} + y \cos x = y^n \sin 2x$
8. $\dfrac{dz}{dx} + \dfrac{z}{x} \log z = \dfrac{z}{x^2} (\log z)^2$
9. $x (x - y)\, dy + y^2 dx = 0$
10. $\dfrac{dy}{dx} - y \tan x = \dfrac{\sin x}{y^2 \sec^2 x}$
11. $\dfrac{dy}{dx} = x^3 y^2 + xy$
12. $\dfrac{dy}{dx} + xy = x^3 y^3$
13. $x\dfrac{dy}{dx} + y = y^2 \log x$
14. $\dfrac{dy}{dx} + x (x + y) = x^3 (x + y)^3 - 1$
15. $\dfrac{dy}{dx} + xy = y^2 e^{\frac{x^2}{2}} \log x$

Answers

1. $-y^{-3} x^6 = \dfrac{3}{7} x^7 + c$
2. $\dfrac{1}{y^2} = 1 + c x^{x^2}$

3. $y^2 = -x + cx^2$

4. $\dfrac{\sec^2 x}{y} = \dfrac{\tan^3 x}{3} + c$

5. $\left(x^2 + y^2\right) x^2 = cy^2$

6. $-\dfrac{e^{x^2}}{y^2} = c - 2x$

7. $y^{1-n} = 2\left[\sin x + \dfrac{1}{n-1}\right] + ce^{n-1} \sin x$

8. $\dfrac{1}{\log z} = \dfrac{1}{2x} + cx$

9. $\dfrac{y}{x} = \log y + c$

10. $y^3 \cos^3 x = c - \left(\dfrac{1}{2}\right) \cos^6 x$

11. $\dfrac{1}{y} = x^2 - 2 + ce^{-\frac{x^2}{2}}$

12. $\dfrac{1}{y^2} = \left(1 + x^2\right) + ce^{x^2}$

13. $y\,(1 + cx + \log x) = 1$

14. $(x + y)^{-2} = \left(x^2 + 1\right) ce^{x^2}$

15. $y\,(x - x \log x + c) = e^{-\frac{x^2}{2}}$

5.5 Exact Differential Equations

A differential equation of the form

$$M(x, y)dx + N(x, y)dy = 0$$

Such that $\dfrac{\partial M}{\partial y} = \dfrac{\partial N}{\partial x}$ is called an exact differential equation.

To solve an exact differential equation we should remember the following steps

Step 1. Verify $\dfrac{\partial M}{\partial y} = \dfrac{\partial N}{\partial x}$

Step 2. Integrate M with respect to x keeping y as constant.

Step 3. Integrate the terms in N those are free from x, with respect to y.

Step 4. Add step (2) and step (3) and equate to an arbitrary constant, which is the required solution i.e.,

$$\underset{\text{treating } y \text{ as constant}}{\int M(x, y)dx} \quad + \quad \underset{\text{terms in } N \text{ which are free from } x}{\int N(x, y)dy} \quad = c$$

Worked Examples

1. *Solve* $\left(2x^3 - xy^2 - 2y + 3\right)\,dx - \left(x^2y + 2x\right)\,dy = 0$

➡ $\left(2x^3 - xy^2 - 2y + 3\right)\,dx - \left(x^2y + 2x\right)\,dy = 0$

$$M = \left(2x^3 - xy^2 - 2y + 3\right) \quad N = -\left(x^2y + 2x\right)$$

$$\frac{\partial M}{\partial y} = -2xy - 2 \qquad \frac{\partial N}{\partial x} = -2xy - 2$$

$$\therefore \frac{\partial M}{\partial y} = \frac{\partial N}{\partial x}$$

Hence, the given equation is an exact equation.

$\therefore$ The general solution of the given equation is

$$\underbrace{\int \left(2x^3 - xy^2 - 2y + 3\right)dx}_{\text{treating } y \text{ as a constant}} \; - \; \underbrace{\int \left(x^2y + 2x\right)dy}_{\text{the terms do not contain } x} = c$$

$$2\frac{x^4}{4} - \frac{x^2}{2}y^2 - 2xy + 3x = c$$

$$\frac{1}{2}x^4 - \frac{1}{2}x^2y^2 - 2xy + 3x = c$$

2. *Solve* $\dfrac{dy}{dx} = \dfrac{x^2 - 2xy}{x^2 - \sin y}$

➡ $\dfrac{dy}{dx} = \dfrac{x^2 - 2xy}{x^2 - \sin y}$

This equation can be written as

$$\left(x^2 - \sin y\right)\,dy = \left(x^2 - 2xy\right)\,dx$$

$$\left(x^2 - 2xy\right)\,dx - \left(x^2 - \sin y\right)\,dy = 0$$

$$M = x^2 - 2xy \quad N = -\left(x^2 - \sin y\right)$$

$$\frac{\partial M}{\partial y} = -2x \quad \frac{\partial N}{\partial x} = -2x$$

$$\therefore \frac{\partial M}{\partial y} = \frac{\partial N}{\partial x}$$

Therefore, the given equation is exact, and the solution is

$$\int \left(x^2 - 2xy\right)\, dx \quad - \quad \int \left(x^2 - \sin y\right)\, dy = c$$

treating y as constant the terms do no contain x

$$\frac{x^3}{3} - 2\frac{x^2}{2}y - (0 - (-\cos y)) = c$$

$$\frac{x^3}{3} - x^2 y - \cos y = c$$

3. Solve $\left(x^2 + y\right) dx + \left(y^3 + x\right) dy = 0$

➡ $\left(x^2 + y\right) dx + \left(y^3 + x\right) dy = 0$

$$M = x^2 + y \qquad N = y^3 + x$$

$$\frac{\partial M}{\partial y} = 1 \qquad \frac{\partial N}{\partial x} = 1$$

$$\therefore \frac{\partial M}{\partial y} = \frac{\partial N}{\partial x}$$

Therefore, the given equation is exact and the solution is

$$\int \left(x^2 + y\right) dx + \int \left(y^3 + x\right) dy = c$$

$$\frac{x^3}{3} + xy + \frac{y^3}{3} = c$$

$$x^3 + y^3 + 3xy = 3c$$

$$x^3 + y^3 + 3xy = c_1$$

4. *Solve* $(e^y + y\cos xy)\, dx + (xe^y + x\cos xy)\, dy = 0$

➡ $(e^y + y\cos xy)\, dx + (xe^y + x\cos xy)\, dy = 0$

$$M = e^y + y\cos xy \quad N = xe^y + x\cos xy$$

$$\frac{\partial M}{\partial y} = e^y + y\,(-\sin xy.\ x) + 1.\cos xy = e^y - xy\sin xy + \cos xy$$

$$\frac{\partial N}{\partial x} = e^y + x\,(-\sin xy.\ y) + 1.\cos xy = e^y - xy\sin xy + \cos xy$$

$$\therefore \frac{\partial M}{\partial y} = \frac{\partial N}{\partial x}$$

Therefore, the given equation is exact and the solution is

$$\int \left(e^y + y \cos xy\right) dx + \int \left(xe^y + x \cos xy\right) dy = c$$

$$xe^y + y\frac{\sin(xy)}{y} = c$$

$$xe^y + \sin xy = c$$

5. *Solve* $(2xy + y - \tan y)\, dx + \left(x^2 - x\tan^2 y + \sec^2 y\right) dy = 0$

➡ $(2xy + y - \tan y)\, dx + \left(x^2 - x\tan^2 y + \sec^2 y\right) dy = 0$

$$M = (2xy + y - \tan y) \qquad N = x^2 - x\tan^2 y + \sec^2 y$$

$$\frac{\partial M}{\partial y} = 2x + 1 - \sec^2 y \qquad \frac{\partial N}{\partial x} = 2x - \tan^2 y$$

$$= 2x - \left(\sec^2 y - 1\right)$$

$$= 2x - \sec^2 y + 1$$

$$\therefore \frac{\partial M}{\partial y} = \frac{\partial N}{\partial x}$$

Therefore, the given equation is exact and the solution is given by,

$$\underbrace{\int (2xy + y - \tan y)\, dx}_{\text{Treating } y \text{ as constant}} + \underbrace{\int \left(x^2 - x\tan^2 y + \sec^2 y\right) dx}_{\text{The terms do no contain } x} = c$$

$$2\frac{x^2}{2}y + yx - x\tan y + \tan y = c$$

$$x^2 y + xy - x\tan y + \tan y = c$$

6. *Solve* $y \sin 2x dx - \left(1 + y + \cos^2 x\right) dy = 0$

➡ $y \sin 2x dx - \left(1 + y + \cos^2 x\right) dy = 0$

$$M = y \sin 2x \qquad N = -\left(1 + y + \cos^2 x\right)$$

$$\frac{\partial M}{\partial y} = \sin 2x \qquad \frac{\partial N}{\partial x} = -[2\cos x\,(-\sin x)]$$

$$\frac{\partial N}{\partial x} = 2\sin x.\cos x$$

$$\frac{\partial N}{\partial x} = \sin 2x$$

$$\therefore\ \frac{\partial M}{\partial y} = \frac{\partial N}{\partial x}$$

Therefore, the given equation is exact and the solution is,

$$\int y \sin 2x\ dx - \int \left(1 + y + \cos^2 x\right) dy = c$$

$$y\left(-\frac{\cos 2x}{2}\right) - \left(y + \frac{y^2}{2}\right) = c$$

$y\cos 2x + 2y + y^2 = c_1$, where $c_1 = -2c$

7. *Solve* $(y\cos x + \sin y + y)\ dx + (\sin x + x\cos y + x)\ dy = 0$

➡ $(y\cos x + \sin y + y)\ dx + (\sin x + x\cos y + x)\ dy = 0$

$$M = y\cos x + \sin y + y \qquad N = \sin x + x\cos y + x$$

$$\frac{\partial M}{\partial y} = \cos x + \cos y + 1 \qquad \frac{\partial N}{\partial x} = \cos x + \cos y + 1$$

$$\therefore\ \frac{\partial M}{\partial y} = \frac{\partial N}{\partial x}$$

Hence, the given differential equation is exact and the solution is

$$\int (y\cos x + \sin y + y)\,dx + \int (\sin x + x\cos y + x)dy = c$$

$$y\sin x + x\sin y + xy = c$$

8. *Solve* $\left(5x^4 + 3x^2y^2 - 2xy^3\right)\ dx + \left(2x^3y - 3x^2y^2 - 5y^4\right)\ dy = 0$

➡ $\left(5x^4 + 3x^2y^2 - 2xy^3\right)\ dx + \left(2x^3y - 3x^2y^2 - 5y^4\right)\ dy = 0$

$$M = 5x^4 + 3x^2y^2 - 2xy^3 \qquad N = 2x^3y - 3x^2y^2 - 5y^4$$

$$\frac{\partial M}{\partial y} = 6x^2y - 6xy^2 \qquad \frac{\partial N}{\partial x} = 6x^2y - 6xy^2$$

$$\therefore \frac{\partial M}{\partial y} = \frac{\partial N}{\partial x}$$

Hence, the given equation is exact and the solution is

$$\int (5x^4 + 3x^2y^2 - 2xy^3)\, dx + \int (-5y^4)\, dy = 0$$

$$x^5 + x^3y^2 - x^2y^3 - y^5 = c$$

9. *Solve* $\left[y\left(1 + \frac{1}{x}\right) + \cos y\right] dx + \left[x + \log x - x \sin y\right] dy = 0$

➡ $$\left[y\left(1 + \frac{1}{x}\right) + \cos y\right] dx + \left[x + \log x - x \sin y\right] dy = 0$$

$$M = y\left(1 + \frac{1}{x}\right) + \cos y \qquad N = x + \log x - x \sin y$$

$$\frac{\partial M}{\partial y} = \left(1 + \frac{1}{x}\right) - \sin y \qquad \frac{\partial N}{\partial x} = 1 + \frac{1}{x} - \sin y$$

$$\therefore \frac{\partial M}{\partial y} = \frac{\partial N}{\partial x}$$

Hence, the given differential equation is exact and the solution is

$$\int \left[y\left(1 + \frac{1}{x}\right) + \cos y\right] dx + \int \left[x + \log x - x \sin y\right] dy = c$$

$$yx + y \log x + x \cos y = c$$

10. *Solve* $[\cos x \tan y + \cos(x + y)]\, dx + \left[\sin x . \sec^2 y + \cos(x + y)\right] dy = 0$

➡ $$[\cos x \tan y + \cos(x + y)]\, dx + \left[\sin x . \sec^2 y + \cos(x + y)\right] dy = 0$$

$$M = \cos x \tan y + \cos(x + y), \; N = \sin x \sec^2 y + \cos(x + y)$$

$$\frac{\partial M}{\partial y} = \cos x . \sec^2 y - \sin(x + y)$$

$$\frac{\partial N}{\partial x} = \cos x . \sec^2 y - \sin(x + y)$$

$$\therefore \frac{\partial M}{\partial y} = \frac{\partial N}{\partial x}$$

Hence, the given differential equation is exact and the solution is

$$\int [\cos x.\tan y + \cos (x + y)]\, dx + \int \left[\sin x \sec^2 y + \cos(x + y)\right] dy = c$$

$$\sin x.\tan y + \sin (x + y) = c$$

11. *Solve* $\left(6x^2 + 2xy - 2xy\, e^{-x^2}\right) dx + \left(e^{-x^2} + x^2 + 3y^2\right) dy = 0$

➡ $\left(6x^2 + 2xy - 2xy\, e^{-x^2}\right) dx + \left(e^{-x^2} + x^2 + 3y^2\right) dy = 0$

$$M = 6x^2 + 2xy - 2xye^{-x^2} \qquad N = e^{-x^2} + x^2 + 3y^2$$

$$\frac{\partial M}{\partial y} = 2x - 2xe^{-x^2} \qquad \frac{\partial N}{\partial x} = -2xe^{-x^2} + 2x$$

$$\therefore \frac{\partial M}{\partial y} = \frac{\partial N}{\partial x}$$

Hence, the given differential equation is exact and the solution is

$$\int \left(6x^2 + 2xy - 2xye^{-x^2}\right) dx + \int \left(e^{-x^2} + x^2 + 3y^2\right) dy = c$$

$$2x^3 + x^2y - y\int 2xe^{-x^2} dx + y^3 = c$$

$$2x^3 + x^2y + ye^{-x^2} + y^3 = c$$

12. *Solve* $(x^2 - y^2)\, dx = 2xydy$

➡ $(x^2 - y^2)\, dx = 2xydy$

$$(x^2 - y^2)\, dx - 2xydy = 0$$

$$M = x^2 - y^2 \qquad N = -2xy$$

$$\frac{\partial M}{\partial y} = -2y \qquad \frac{\partial N}{\partial x} = -2y$$

$$\therefore \frac{\partial M}{\partial y} = \frac{\partial N}{\partial x}$$

Therefore, the given equation is exact and the solution is

$$\int \left(x^2 - y^2\right) dx - \int 2xydy = c$$

$$\frac{x^3}{3} - xy^2 = c$$

Exercise

Solve the following equations

1. $\left(x^2 - 4xy - 2y^2\right) dx + \left(y^2 - 4xy - 2x^2\right) dy = 0$
2. $\left(x^2 - ay\right) dx + \left(y^2 - ax\right) dy = 0$
3. $(ax + hy + g)\, dx + (hx + by + f)\, dy = 0$
4. $(x - 2e^y)\, dy + (y + x \sin x)\, dx = 0$
5. $3x\,(xy - 2)\, dx + \left(x^3 + 2y\right) dy = 0$
6. $(e^y + 1) \cos x dx + e^y \sin x dy = 0$
7. $\left(\frac{2x}{y^3}\right) dx + \left\{\frac{\left(y^2 - 3x^2\right)}{y^4}\right\} dy = 0$
8. $\left(3x^2y^2 + x^2\right) dx + \left(2x^3y + y^2\right) dy = 0$
9. $2xydy + \left(a + y^2\right) dx = 0$
10. $(3 - x + 2xy)\, dy + \left(3x^2 - y + y^2\right) dx = 0$
11. $\left(x^3 + 2y - y^2\right) dy + 3x^2ydx = 0$
12. $[x \sin xy + \cos (x + y) - \sin y]\, dy + [y \sin xy + \cos (x + y) + \cos x]\, dx = 0$
13. $(e^x + xe^y)\, dy + (ye^x + e^y)\, dx = 0$
14. $\left(2 - 6xy + x^2 \sec^2 y\right) dy + \left(2x \tan y - 3y^2\right) dx = 0$
15. $xdy + \left(y - x^3\right) dx = 0.$

Answers

1. $x^3 + y^3 - 6xy\,(x + y) = c$
2. $x^3 + y^3 - 3axy = c$
3. $ax^2 + 2hxy + by^2 + 2gx + 2fy + c = 0$
4. $xy - x\cos x + \sin x - 2e^y = c$
5. $x^3y - 3x^2 + y^2 = c$
6. $(e^y + 1)\sin x = c$
7. $x^2 - y^2 = cy^3$
8. $x^3 + y^3 + 3x^3y^2 = c$
9. $x\left(a + y^2\right) = c$
10. $x^3 + xy^2 - xy + 3y = c$
11. $y\left(3x^3 + 3y - y^2\right) = c$
12. $\cos xy - \sin(x + y) - \sin x - \cos y = c$
13. $xe^y + ye^x = c$
14. $x^2 \tan y + 2y = c + 3xy^2$
15. $4xy = x^4 + c.$

5.6 Equations Reducible to Exact Equations

If $Mdx + Ndy = 0$ is not exact i.e., $\dfrac{\partial M}{\partial y} \neq \dfrac{\partial N}{\partial x}$, then it can be made exact by multiplying with an integrating factor (I.F). The following methods are followed for finding the I.F.

1. If $\dfrac{1}{N}\left(\dfrac{\partial M}{\partial y} - \dfrac{\partial N}{\partial x}\right)$ is a function of x only, say $f(x)$, then $e^{\int f(x)dx}$ is an integrating factor.
2. If $\dfrac{1}{M}\left(\dfrac{\partial N}{\partial x} - \dfrac{\partial M}{\partial y}\right)$ is a function of y only, say $g(y)$, then $e^{\int g(y)dy}$ is an integrating factor.
3. If an equation is of the form $f_1(x, y)ydx + f_2(x, y)xdy = 0$ i.e., $M = yf_1, N = xf_2$ and if $Mx - Ny \neq 0$, then $\dfrac{1}{Mx - Ny}$ is an integrating factor.

Worked Examples

1. *Solve* $3x\left(x+y^2\right)dy+\left(x^3-3xy-2y^3\right)dx=0$

➡ $3x\left(x+y^2\right)dy+\left(x^3-3xy-2y^3\right)dx=0$

i.e., $(x^3-3xy-2y^3)\,dx+\left(3x^2+3xy^2\right)dy=0$

$$M=x^3-3xy-2y^3 \qquad N=3x^2+3xy^2$$

$$\frac{\partial M}{\partial y}=-3x-6y^2 \qquad \frac{\partial N}{\partial x}=6x+3y^2$$

$$\frac{\partial M}{\partial y}-\frac{\partial N}{\partial x}=-9x-9y^2$$

$$\therefore\ \frac{1}{N}\left(\frac{\partial M}{\partial y}-\frac{\partial N}{\partial x}\right)=\frac{-9\left(x+y^2\right)}{3x\left(x+y^2\right)}=-\frac{3}{x}=f(x)\ \text{[say]}$$

Therefore I.F. $=e^{\int f(x)dx}=e^{\int-\frac{3}{x}dx}=e^{\log x^{-3}}=x^{-3}=\dfrac{1}{x^3}$

Multiplying this I.F to the given equation, we get

$$\left(1-3x^{-2}y-2x^{-3}y^3\right)dx+\left(3\frac{1}{x}+x^{-2}y^2\right)dy=0$$

This is an exact differential equation, and the solution of the given equation is

$$\underbrace{\int\left(1-3x^{-2}y-2x^{-3}y^3\right)dx}_{\text{treating } y \text{ as constant}}+\underbrace{\int\left(\frac{3}{x}+x^{-2}y^2\right)dy}_{\text{the terms do no contain } x}=c$$

$$x-3\frac{x^{-1}}{-1}y-2\frac{x^{-2}}{-2}y^3=c$$

$$x+\frac{3y}{x}+\frac{y^3}{x^2}=c$$

$$x^3+3xy+y^3=cx^2$$

2. *Solve* $[1+(x+y)\tan y]\dfrac{dy}{dx}+1=0$

➡ $[1+(x+y)\tan y]\dfrac{dy}{dx}+1=0$

i.e., $[1 + (x + y)\tan y]\, dy + dx = 0$
or $dx + [1 + (x + y)\tan y]\, dy = 0$

$$M = 1 \qquad\qquad N = 1 + (x + y)\tan y$$

$$\frac{\partial M}{\partial y} = 0 \qquad\qquad \frac{\partial N}{\partial x} = \tan y$$

$$\frac{1}{M}\left(\frac{\partial N}{\partial x} - \frac{\partial M}{\partial y}\right) = \tan y = g(y) \text{ [say]}$$

$$\therefore \text{ I.F.} = e^{\int g(y)dy} = e^{\int \tan y dy} = e^{\log(\sec y)} = \sec y$$

Multiplying the I.F to the given equation we get,

$$\sec y dx + [\sec y + (x + y)\sec y \tan y]\, dy = 0$$

This is an exact equation and the solution of the given equation is

$$\int \sec y dx \qquad + \int (\sec y + x \sec y + y \sec y \tan y)\, dy = c$$

Treating y as a constant   The terms do not contain x

$$x \sec y + \log(\sec y + \tan y) + \int y (\sec y \tan y)\; dy = c$$

$$x \sec y + \log(\sec y + \tan y) + y \sec y - \int 1. \sec y dy = c$$

$$x \sec y + \log(\sec y + \tan y) + y \sec y - \log(\sec y + \tan y) = c$$

$$x \sec y + y \sec y = c$$

$$(x + y)\sec y = c$$

3. *Solve* $(1 + xy)\, ydx + (1 - xy)\, xdy = 0$

➡ $(1 + xy)\, ydx + (1 - xy)\, xdy = 0$

$$M = (1 + xy)\, y = yf_1(x, y)$$

$$N = (1 - xy)\, x = xf_2(x, y)$$

$$\therefore\; Mx - Ny = xy(1 + xy) - xy(1 - xy)$$

$$= xy + x^2y^2 - xy + x^2y^2$$

$$= 2x^2y^2 \neq 0$$

$$\therefore\ I.F = \frac{1}{Mx - Ny} = \frac{1}{2x^2y^2} \text{ or } \frac{1}{x^2y^2}$$

Multiplying I.F to the given equation, we get

$$\frac{(1+xy)\,y}{x^2y^2}dx + \frac{(1-xy)\,x}{x^2y^2}dy = 0$$

$$\left(\frac{x^{-2}}{y} + \frac{1}{x}\right)dx + \left(x^{-1}y^{-2} - \frac{1}{y}\right)dy = 0$$

This is an exact equation and the solution of the given equation is,

$$\underbrace{\int\left(\frac{1}{y}x^{-2} + \frac{1}{x}\right)dx}_{\text{Treating } y \text{ as constant}} + \underbrace{\int\left(x^{-1}y^{-2} - \frac{1}{y}\right)dy}_{\text{The terms do not contain } x} = c$$

$$\frac{1}{y}\frac{x^{-1}}{-1} + \log x - \log y = c$$

$$-\frac{1}{xy} + \log x - \log y = c$$

Note:

1. $xdy + ydx = d\,(xy)$
2. $d\left(\frac{y}{x}\right) = \frac{xdy - ydx}{x^2}$
3. $\frac{ydx - xdy}{y^2} = d\left(\frac{x}{y}\right)$
4. $g(y)f'(x)\,dx + g'(y)f(x)\,dy = d\,[f(x)g(y)]$

4. *Solve* $xdy - ydx + a\left(x^2 + y^2\right)dx = 0$

➡ $xdy - ydx + a\left(x^2 + y^2\right)dx = 0$

$$\Rightarrow \frac{xdy - ydx}{x^2} + \frac{a\left(x^2 + y^2\right)}{x^2}dx = 0$$

i.e., $d\left(\frac{y}{x}\right) + a\left[1 + \left(\frac{y}{x}\right)^2\right]dx = 0$

put $\frac{y}{x} = v$

$$dv + a\left(1 + v^2\right) dx = 0$$

which is variable separable form,

$$dv = -a\left(1 + v^2\right) dx$$
$$\frac{dv}{1+v^2} - adx$$
$$\int \frac{dv}{1+v^2} = -a \int dx + c$$
$$\tan^{-1} v = -ax + c$$

5. *Solve* $(x^4 + y^2)dy = 4x^3 ydx$
➡ $(x^4 + y^2)\, dy = 4x^3 ydx$

$$x^4 dy + y^2 dy = 4x^3 ydx$$
$$y^2 dy = 4x^3 ydx - x^4 dy$$
$$dy = \frac{y(4x^3 dx) - x^4 dy}{y^2} = \frac{yd(x^4) - x^4 dy}{y^2}$$
$$dy = d\left(\frac{x^4}{y}\right)$$
$$\int dy = \int d\left(\frac{x^4}{y}\right) + c$$
$$y = \frac{x^4}{y} + c$$

6. *Solve* $ydx - xdy - 3x^2y^2e^{x^3}dx = 0$
➡ $ydx - xdy - 3x^2y^2e^{x^3}dx = 0$
Dividing by y^2on both sides, we get

$$\frac{ydx - xdy}{y^2} - 3x^2e^{x^3}dx = 0$$

$$d\left(\frac{x}{y}\right) - 3x^2 e^{x^3} dx = 0$$

$$\int d\left(\frac{x}{y}\right) - \int 3x^2 e^{x^3} dx = c$$

$$\frac{x}{y} - \int e^t dt = c \qquad x^3 = t \Rightarrow 3x^2 dx = dt$$

$$\frac{x}{y} - e^t = c$$

$$\frac{x}{y} - e^{x^3} = c$$

7. *Solve* $(x+y)^2\left[x\frac{dy}{dx} + y\right] = xy\left[1 + \frac{dy}{dx}\right]$

➡

$$(x+y)^2\left[x\frac{dy}{dx} + y\right] = xy\left[1 + \frac{dy}{dx}\right] \tag{1}$$

Put $x + y = t$ and $xy = z$

$$1 + \frac{dy}{dx} = \frac{dt}{dx} \qquad y + x\frac{dy}{dx} = \frac{dz}{dx}$$

(1) becomes,

$$t^2\frac{dz}{dx} = z\frac{dt}{dx}$$

$$\frac{dt}{t^2} = \frac{dz}{z}$$

Integrating the above equation, we get

$$\int \frac{dt}{t^2} = \int \frac{dz}{z}$$

$$-\frac{1}{t} = \log z + c \Rightarrow -\frac{1}{(x+y)} = \log(xy) + c$$

8. *Solve* $(x-y)^2\left(1+\frac{dy}{dx}\right)=(x+y)^2\left(1-\frac{dy}{dx}\right)$

➡ $(x-y)^2\left(1+\frac{dy}{dx}\right)=(x+y)^2\left(1-\frac{dy}{dx}\right)$

Put $x-y=t$ and $x+y=z$

$$1-\frac{dy}{dx}=\frac{dt}{dx} \qquad 1+\frac{dy}{dx}=\frac{dz}{dx}$$

Substituting the above equations in the given equation, we get

$$t^2\frac{dz}{dx}=z^2\frac{dt}{dx}$$

$$\frac{dt}{t^2}=\frac{dz}{z^2}$$

Integrating the above equation, we get

$$\int\frac{dt}{t^2}=\int\frac{dz}{z^2}+c$$

$$\int t^{-2}dt=\int z^{-2}dz+c$$

$$\frac{t^{-1}}{-1}=\frac{z^{-1}}{-1}+c$$

$$-\frac{1}{t}+\frac{1}{z}=c$$

$$-\frac{1}{(x-y)}+\frac{1}{(x+y)}=c$$

9. *Solve* $x^2y^2\,(xdy+ydx)=e^{xy}\sec^2(x+y)\,(dx+dy)$

➡

$$x^2y^2\,(xdy+ydx)=e^{xy}\sec^2(x+y)\,(dx+dy)$$

$$(xy)^2\,d\,(xy)=e^{xy}\sec^2(x+y)\,d\,(x+y)$$

Put $xy = t \quad x + y = z$

$$t^2 dt = e^t \sec^2 z dz$$

$$\int \frac{t^2}{e^t} dt = \int \sec^2 z dz + c$$

$$\int t^2 e^{-t} dt = \tan z + c$$

$$t^2 \frac{e^{-t}}{-1} - \int 2t \frac{e^{-t}}{-1} dt = \tan(x + y) + c$$

$$-t^2 e^{-t} + 2t \frac{e^{-t}}{-1} - \int 2 \frac{e^{-t}}{-1} dt = \tan(x + y) + c$$

$$-t^2 e^{-t} - 2te^{-t} + 2 \frac{e^{-t}}{-1} = \tan(x + y) + c$$

$$-e^{-t}\left(t^2 + 2t + 2\right) = \tan(x + y)$$

$$e^{-t}\left(t^2 + 2t + 2\right) + \tan(x + y) = c_1$$

$$e^{-xy}\left(x^2 y^2 + 2xy + 2\right) + \tan(x + y) = c_1$$

10. *Solve* $(x + y)^2 (dx + dy) = \sec xy \tan xy (xdy + ydx)$

➡

$$(x + y)^2 (dx + dy) = \sec xy \tan xy (xdy + ydx)$$

$$\Rightarrow (x + y)^2 d(x + y) = \sec xy \tan xy d(xy)$$

Put $x + y = t \quad xy = z$

$$t^2 dt = \sec z \tan z dz$$

$$\int t^2 dt = \int \sec z \tan z dz + c$$

$$\frac{t^3}{3} = \sec z + c$$

$$\frac{1}{3}(x + y)^3 = \sec xy + c$$

11. *Solve* $[\cos x \tan y + \cos(x+y)]\, dx + \left[\sin x \sec^2 y + \cos(x+y)\right] dy = 0$

➡ $[\cos x \tan y + \cos(x+y)]\, dx + \left[\sin x \sec^2 y + \cos(x+y)\right] dy = 0$

$$\cos x \tan y dx + \cos(x+y)\, dx + \sin x \sec^2 y dy + \cos(x+y)\, dy = 0$$
$$\tan y \cos x dx + \sin x \sec^2 y dy + \cos(x+y)\, d(x+y) = 0$$
$$\tan y d(\sin x) + \sin x d(\tan y) + \cos(x+y)\, d(x+y) = 0$$
$$\Rightarrow d(\tan y \sin x) + \cos t dt = 0, \text{ where } t = x + y$$
$$\Rightarrow \int d(\tan y \sin x) + \int \cos t dt = c$$
$$\tan y \sin x + \sin t = c$$

i.e., $\tan y \sin x + \sin(x+y) = c$

12. *Solve* $xdx + ydy + \dfrac{xdy - ydx}{x^2 + y^2} = 0$

➡ $xdx + ydy + \dfrac{xdy - ydx}{x^2 + y^2} = 0$

$$xdx + ydy + \frac{xdy - ydx}{x^2\left[1 + \frac{y^2}{x^2}\right]} = 0$$
$$xdx + ydy + \frac{d(y/x)}{1 + (y/x)^2} = 0 \text{ where } d\left(\frac{y}{x}\right) = \frac{xdy - ydx}{x^2}$$
$$\int xdx + \int ydy + \int \frac{dt}{1+t^2} = c$$
$$\frac{x^2}{2} + \frac{y^2}{2} + \tan^{-1} t = c$$
$$\frac{x^2 + y^2}{2} + \tan^{-1}\left(\frac{y}{x}\right) = c$$

Exercise

Solve the following equations

1. $\left(x^2 + y^2 + x\right) dx + xdy = 0$
2. $\left(2xy^4e^y + 2xy^3 + y\right) dx + \left(x^2y^4e^y - x^2y^2 - 3x\right) dy = 0$

3. $x^2ydx - (x^3 + y^3)\ dy = 0$
4. $(x^4 + y^4)\ dx - xy^3dy = 0$
5. $y\,(x + y)\ dx - x^2dy = 0$
6. $(x^3 - 3xy^2)\ dx - (y^3 - 3x^2y)\ dy = 0$
7. $(8ydx + 8xdy) + x^2y^3\,(4ydx + 5xdy) = 0$
8. $(5x^3 + 3xy + 2y^2)\ dx + (x^2 + 2xy)\ dy = 0$
9. $(y^4 + 2y)\ dx + (xy^3 + 2y^4 - 4x)\ dy = 0$
10. $(xy\sin xy + \cos xy)\ ydx + (xy\sin xy - \cos xy)\ xdy = 0$
11. $ydx - xdy + \log x dx = 0$
12. $(1 + xy)\ ydx + (1 - xy)\ xdy = 0$
13. $y\,(xy + 2x^2y^2)\ dx + x\,(xy - x^2y^2)\ dy = 0$
14. $\left(y - 3x^2y^2e^{x^3}\right) dx - xdy = 0$
15. $ydx + x\log x dy = 0$

Answers

1. $\dfrac{x^4}{4} + \dfrac{x^3}{3} + \dfrac{x^2y^2}{2} = c$
2. $x^2e^y + \left(\dfrac{x^2}{y}\right) + \left(\dfrac{x}{y^3}\right) = c$
3. $\sin^{-1}(y/x) = \log x + c$
4. $y^4 = 4x^4 \log x + cx^4$
5. $\dfrac{x}{y} + \log x = c$
6. $(x^2 + y^2)^4 = c\,(x^2 - y^2)^2$
7. $4x^2y^2 + x^4y^5 = c$
8. $x^2y^2\,(y^2 - x^2) = c$
9. $\left(y + \dfrac{2}{y^2}\right) x + y^2 = c$
10. $x\sec xy = cy$
11. $y + cx + \log x + 1 = 0$
12. $\log\left(\dfrac{x}{y}\right) - \left(\dfrac{1}{xy}\right) = c$
13. $\left(\dfrac{1}{xy}\right) = c + \log\left(\dfrac{x^2}{y}\right)$
14. $(x/y) - e^{x^3} = c$
15. $y = \dfrac{c}{\log x}$

Index